George

A Mexicotexan Novel

Américo Paredes

Arte Publico Press
Houston
Texas
1990

This volume is made possible through a grant from the National Endowment for the Arts, a federal agency.

Recovering the past, creating the future

Arte Público Press
University of Houston
452 Cullen Performance Hall
Houston, Texas 77204-2174

Photo by Mark Piñón

Paredes, Américo
    George Washington Gómez / Américo Paredes.
    p. cm.
    ISBN 978-1-55885-012-5
    1. Mexican Americans—History—Fiction.   I. Title.
PS 3531.A525G4   1990
813'.54—dc20   94-6919
                                                               CIP

∞ The paper used in this publication meets the requirements of the American National Standard for Information Sciences for Permanence of Paper for Printed Library Materials Z39.48-1984.

7 8 9 0 1 2 3 4 5 6   14 13 12 11 10 9 8 7 6 5

My thanks to Ramón Saldívar and Ricardo Romo for their encouragement, and to Rolando Hinojosa for taking the time to write the Introduction. And a special word of appreciation to my co-worker of more than twenty years, Frances Terry, whose knowledge of the ways of word processors (still a mystery to me) transformed an archeological piece into a presentable manuscript.

Introduction

Some thirty years ago, around 1958, on the corner of Eleventh and Elizabeth, Brownsville, Texas's main drag, stood Daddy Hargrove's bookstore. It was the only store of its kind then, and my sister Clarissa and I walked downtown to buy (each) a copy of Américo Paredes's *With His Pistol In His Hand*. Hargrove's had dedicated its front display window to the book, a work by a hometown boy who had made good, so to speak.

Paredes, however, was not an unknown quantity in his hometown: he'd been born and raised there, he'd graduated from Brownsville High and from the local community college once known as Brownsville Junior College. Added to this, the Paredeses on both sides of the river had lived and worked in the area, el Río Abajo, since the 18th century. And, as many Lower Rio Grande Valley families, we were and are blood-related. So, we had to buy the book, although it wasn't an *obligación* where we bought *Pistol* because of friendship or blood kin, however. We knew him, and we knew of his work.

As a youngster, Américo had published poetry in *Los lunes literarios* in the San Antonio, Texas *La Prensa*, in *The Brownsville Herald*, and elsewhere, but his latest effort had come when its author was a man, *un hombre hecho y derecho*: a World War II veteran, a former reporter for the *Stars and Stripes* in Japan, an administrator for the international Red Cross in China and Manchuria, and the holder of a baccalaureate, a master's, and a doctorate from The University of Texas.

The degrees, by the way, were earned in quick order while at the same time he and his wife, Amelia, were raising a family.

Pistol, of course, is a scholarly work which has stood the many tests of time. It is also a work which very early influenced many Texas Mexicans and others who followed his example as teacher-scholar-writer. As musician, too, but I'll touch on that in a minute. *Pistol* remains also as one of the most enduring of U.T. Press publications.

The present work, *George Washington Gómez*, was started in 1936 and finished in 1940. It's a first draft, and it should be seen and appreciated as an historical work, not as an artifact. Between times, from '36 to '40, Paredes continued his work on the *Herald* and would stop writing to devote time to his other love: music. The manuscript would be set aside from time to time while he practiced 8 to 10 hours on the piano. The guitar study continued too, as did his singing. Aside from working on both the English and the Spanish versions of the *Herald*, he also drove a delivery van and held other jobs until he could attend Brownsville Junior College.

A picture of feverish activity, then, but *George Washington Gómez*, *sin prisa pero sin pausa*, without haste but without rest, was being worked on. It is a dated work, but not in the pejorative sense: it is dated authentically, a first draft of a work set against the Great Depression, the onset of World War II in Europe, and set also against the over 100-year-old conflict of cultures in the Lower Rio Grande Valley of Texas, not far from where the Rio Grande empties into the Gulf.

Obviously, the manuscript could have been rewritten for these times; to have done so, however, would have damaged its integrity. Américo Paredes is too honest a writer to force history into some rigid mold or point of view, and so *George Washington Gómez* is published as written, and we are the better for it: the '30s are not seen through the prism of nostalgia, that half-sister of debased romanticism, but rather through the eyes of a young writer, true to the times, to his family and himself, and, ultimately, to us, the readers.

Rolando Hinojosa
Austin, Texas

George Washington Gómez

Part I

"LOS SEDICIOSOS"
THE SEDITIONISTS

1

It was a morning late in June. The flat, salty *llano* spread as far as the eye could see ahead and to the right. To the left it was bordered by the chaparral, which encroached upon the flats in an irregular, wavering line. Along the edge of the chaparral wound the road, and down the road four Texas Rangers were riding. Their horses' hooves stirred the flour-fine dust, and it rose and covered their beards, penetrated down their shirt collars despite the blue bandanas around their necks, lay in a thin film on their rifle-stocks and the big handles of their revolvers. One was a middle-aged man with a John Brown beard; two were sour-looking hardcases in their thirties; the fourth was a boy in his teens, with more dust than beard upon his face. At first sight one might have taken them for cutthroats. And one might have not been wrong.

On the road ahead a cloud of dust came into view. In the middle of it there was a buggy drawn by a pair of smart-stepping mules. Two men were in the buggy, and one of them had a rifle cradled in the crook of his arm. The driver was sitting on the right, and even at that distance the Rangers could see that his face was a very dark brown. They spurred their horses into a lope and strung out to surround the buggy, but the driver edged his vehicle against the chaparral until his side was scraping the thorny huisache bushes. The middle-aged Ranger cursed under his breath as all four of them came up on the rifleman's side of the buggy.

9

The rifleman, a sallow, skinny runt of a man, had shifted ever so slightly so that his gun barrel was pointing directly toward the Rangers. The driver was a much bigger man, with Negroid features; he was holding the reins in his left hand. His right hand was out of sight. "Hello, MacDougal," the rifleman said, his sharp little nose twitching in what might have been a smile. "Old man Keene, he paying you extra these days?"

"Well, if it ain't Lupe," said the middle-aged Ranger. "Whose money are *you* taking lately?"

"Nobody's."

"Whatcha got there?"

"Groceries," replied Lupe. Then in Spanish to the driver, "Show him, Negro."

"*Sí, cómo no,*" said El Negro. He reached back with his left hand and lifted a corner of the tarp covering the back of the buggy. There were some parcels underneath, and several boxes of soap.

"Whatcha gonna do?" asked MacDougal, pointing at the soap boxes with his quirt. "Take a bath every day?"

Lupe laughed shortly and after his laugh there was a silence. El Negro dropped the corner of the tarp and put his left hand back on the reins. The three younger Rangers played with their saddle pommels. Their light-colored eyes shifted from MacDougal to Lupe and back to MacDougal. MacDougal was looking into Lupe's face; Lupe was looking at MacDougal but he was also seeing the other three. Finally MacDougal said, "Okay, Lupe, see you some other time." He spurred his horse and the other three did likewise. The buggy continued on its way until it was hidden from view by a bend in the road.

The four Rangers settled down to an easy trot, but the youngest one was very much disturbed. He kept turning in his saddle to stare at the buggy as long as it was visible. After he had done so several times MacDougal asked him, "Anything wrong, son?"

"They might of had ammunition," said the youngest Ranger.

MacDougal clucked his tongue sympathetically. "That was Lupe García," he said. The youngest Ranger thought hard, trying to remember if he knew Lupe García. "They also call him 'Lupe the Little Doll,' " MacDougal added. "About as cuddly as a coral snake. But Lupe is a business man. He steals money. Or cattle. He wouldn't join up with a crazy bunch like De la Peña's and their Republic of the Southwest. There's no money in it."

"Lupe was one of them that held up the Isabel train," continued MacDougal. "Took eighty thousand in silver off of it." The youngest Ranger looked back again at the now empty distance, and his look was so full of indignation that MacDougal laughed.

"Let me tell you about that time," he said. "They trailed him down into the brush near Alamo Creek. About a dozen men led by Sheriff Critto, who was killed during a dance by Red Hercules. But that was later. Red Hercules was guiding them that time, since he knew the country. He was riding down the trail when he stopped and said, 'There's Lupe García.' "

The other two Rangers, who were riding ahead, slowed their horses to a walk and squinted into the distance. "A nigger," one of them said, "a nigger-greaser. What do you think of that?"

"Sure enough," MacDougal went on, "there was little Lupe walking acrost a clearing about a hundred yards away. Had this 30-30 in the crook of his left arm, just like you saw him back there. Red Hercules told the Sheriff, 'There he is, Sheriff, but he'll get three or four of us before we can get our rifles out. At this distance I've seen him get a deer jumping over a barb-wire fence.' Then Red Hercules laughed and said, 'And you'll be the first one, Sheriff.' "

The Rangers ahead had stopped and were drawing their rifles from their boots. MacDougal and the young Ranger slowed down to a walk and came up to them.

"Sheriff Critto wa'nt no fool," said MacDougal. " 'Let him go,' he said. 'We'll catch him napping some other time.' " MacDougal reined in and took out his rifle.

The young Ranger laughed without mirth. "And for all these years nobody's caught Lupe García napping, is that it?"

MacDougal chuckled. "He's gotta sleep sometime," he said. "Better take out your rifle."

The cloud of dust came nearer. It was an automobile, a Model T Ford of the latest make. "That's Doc Berry," said MacDougal. "Put them away." The others hesitated briefly and then slid their rifles back into their boots.

Driving the automobile was an old man in a white goatee and a wide-brimmed panama. Beside him, hatless, sat a stocky, red-haired man of about thirty, blue work-shirt open at the neck and sleeves rolled-up. The Model T drew abreast of the Rangers and stopped.

"Morning, gents," said the old gentleman in the goatee.

"Morning, Doc," MacDougal answered. "Seen anything of De la Peña hereabouts?"

"Who, me?" said the old man. "You look for him, I'm tired."

MacDougal laughed and the other Rangers grinned. "Keeping you busy?" asked MacDougal.

"Obstetrical case," said the Doc. "This fellow's wife," he added, jerking a thumb at the man sitting beside him.

"That so," said MacDougal. "A serious case, eh?"

Doc Berry smiled. "Oh, I think she'll be all right," he said.

The two sour-faced Rangers were staring at the red-haired man, as though trying to place him. The man fidgeted in his seat and avoided their eyes. Finally one of the Rangers spoke, "What's your name, feller?"

"He doesn't speak much English," Doc Berry said.

"Mexican, eh?" said MacDougal. "For a minute there I thought he was a white man." He looked steadily at the man, who began to show signs of nervousness.

"He's a good Mexican," Doc said. "I can vouch for him."

"He's okay if you say so, Doc," MacDougal answered. "But it's getting kinda hard these days to tell the good ones from the bad ones. Can't take any chances these days. But he's all right if you say so."

"Thanks," said Doc Berry. He stepped on the clutch, and the Model T began to move away. "So long, gents," he said. He waved and Mac-Dougal and the youngest Ranger waved back. The Ford continued on its way.

The man with Doc Berry rubbed at the reddish stubble on his chin. "Quicker, doctor," he said in Spanish. "Please!"

The doctor laughed. "No hurry, Gumersindo. They won't hurt you now."

Gumersindo clasped and unclasped his hands. "It's not that; it's my wife. Can't you go any faster?"

"Fast as she can go. Don't worry."

They rode in silence until the shacks on the outskirts of San Pedrito appeared in the distance. "We're almost there," said the doctor brightly. Gumersindo wet his lips.

About a half mile from town the Ford turned off the road, puttered up a rutted lane and stopped before a one-room shack made of mud, sticks, and pieces of lumber, and roofed with flattened-out tin cans. Flanking it some distance back were a pigsty and an outhouse, while beside its only doorway grew a flowering rose bush, and on the other side was a papaya plant, fruitful and slender, like a many-breasted girl. Farther back and to one side was a small corral built around a shady mesquite, and in the corral a well-fed horse and a pair of skinny mules stood sleeping.

As the men climbed out of the car a baby's wail came out of the shack, mingled with a woman's moaning. Gumersindo rushed inside, and immediately an old woman appeared at the threshold screaming angrily at the doctor, "*Viejo cabrón! Pendejo! Ándale!*"

"Shush, shush," said Doc Berry, handing her his bag. He entered, dropping the curtain of burlap bags which served as a door. Inside the woman was still moaning. From behind the house came a man, flat-chested but wide-shouldered, long and tough like a leather quirt. His drooping black mustache curved down the sides of his cheeks. Slowly and thoughtfully he took a cornhusk cigaret from his shirt pocket. He squatted down a few paces from the doorway and lighted the cigaret, his eyes on the burlap-covered doorway. Now the woman was screaming, and the doctor's voice spoke low and soothingly. The curtain was pushed aside, and Gumersindo came out, his face pale and sweaty.

"Feliciano," he said unsteadily. The other man rose from his haunches effortlessly. The woman in the shack screamed piercingly, and Gumersindo jerked around and stared at the burlap curtain. Then he turned and looked pleadingly at Feliciano. "He's sewing her up," he quavered. Feliciano's face tightened. Gumersindo stumbled over to the flivver and plumped down on the running board. Feliciano came and sat beside him.

"She's all bloody," complained Gumersindo weakly, "all bloody, all bloody."

"You should have got the midwife, like you did with the other two," said Feliciano harshly, "but you had to have a Gringo doctor." Then more softly, "It sometimes happens that they have to be sewed up."

The woman had stopped screaming. Gumersindo looked at Feliciano curiously. "How do you know?" he asked.

Feliciano shrugged. "What was it?"

"A boy this time!" Gumersindo went suddenly from grief to joy. "A boy, a boy. The doctor says he weighs nine pounds if he weighs an ounce."

Feliciano slapped Gumersindo on the back. "Fine!" he said, his face twisting into a smile. "It's like the Gringo game where you have strike one, then strike two, and the third time you hit the ball."

"Yes." Gumersindo was sad again. "A son, an orphan maybe."

"Don't be a fool. This is her third child. Did you bring any newspapers?"

"In the car."

Feliciano reached into the Model T and brought out a handful of papers. He shuffled them angrily. "You went and bought Gringo newspapers again!" he said. "Why didn't you bring some reading matter in a Christian language?"

Gumersindo smiled. "I've got to practice," he answered.

"Well then," said Feliciano, "practice now and tell me at least what the big letters say. Austria, Austria, it says there. What about Austria?"

Gumersindo pored over the headlines. "I can't make them all out," he confessed. "But it's something about the duke of Austria getting shot. Sara Jevo. No, that sounds like a woman's name."

"A duke?" said Feliciano. "That's fine. They ought to kill all those sons-of-bitches. Look farther down the page and see what it says about

Carranza."

2

There was frost in the Golden Delta, that heavy killing frost Mexicans call *hielo prieto*. It was a beautiful thing to see. Everything was encased in an icy sheath that scintillated in the evening sun. The grass was a carpet of little glass slivers, and one half-expected it to tinkle when the wind blew over it. The papaya plant stood incrusted in a coat of shimmering transparence. Tomorrow, when the ice melted, it would be a brown corpse, burned paradoxically by the cold. But tomorrow, well tomorrow is tomorrow.

The wind was clear and keen like a shining blade. It made sudden fitful rushes at the ungainly little shack, causing it to shake and clatter, seeking to pry its way through the cracks stopped up with rags and newspapers, through the paneless window frame into which an old pillow had been stuffed. Under the burlap covering the doorway it forced an occasional chilly breath into the shack's only room, even though the door faced south and the burlap was held down with heavy concrete blocks.

Though it was not yet twilight, the family was preparing for bed. On the side of the room farthest from the window and the door was a rusty iron bed raised from the dirt floor on wooden blocks, the bed where Gumersindo, his wife, and the new baby slept. A screen made of burlap bags stretched on poles separated it from a bigger wooden bed which belonged to the grandmother and the two little girls. Feliciano, who slept in the open when the weather was good, had laid his canvas folding cot at the drafty end of the room. He had pushed the table against the wall and put the cot close to the wood stove that sizzled away pleasantly, still warm and greasy from the supper cooked an hour before. In the middle of the room was a battered washtub half-filled with earth and ashes, and on this was a charcoal fire, around which the adults were sitting. The two little girls, blondish Maruca and dark Carmen, were already in bed shivering under the bedclothes, only their heads showing above the blue and red quilt that covered them. The grandmother, sitting by the fire, counted on her twisted fingers.

"He's almost seven months old," she said. "We must baptize him soon." Gumersindo snorted and the old woman turned on him angrily. "Son of a demon!"

Gumersindo laughed. "I didn't say a thing," he protested. The grandmother muttered to herself about the godlessness of some men and where they would go when they died.

The baby, meanwhile, was feeding greedily at his mother's breast. Born a foreigner in his native land, he was fated to a life controlled by others. At that very moment his life was being shaped, people were already running his affairs, but he did not know it. Nobody considered whether he might like being baptized or not. Nobody had asked him whether he, a Mexican, had wanted to be born in Texas, or whether he had wanted to be born at all. The baby left the breast and María, his mother, propped him up in a sitting position. She looked at him tenderly. "And what shall we name him?" she wondered aloud.

After a brief, surcharged silence, Gumersindo was the first to speak. "Crisósforo!" he said grandiosely.

"Virgin! What a name," cried the grandmother.

"Sounds like *fósforo* to me," said Feliciano. "Who wants to be named after a safety match?" He spat on the coals for emphasis.

"José Ángel," said the grandmother. "That's the name."

"Ángel!" protested Feliciano. "It would ruin him for life!"

"Well, you think of one," retorted his mother.

"Venustiano," said Feliciano promptly.

"Like that *cabrón* of a Carranza?" exclaimed the grandmother. "No grandson of mine—"

"Cleto, then," interrupted Feliciano, looking squarely at Gumersindo.

Gumersindo smiled absently and shook his head.

"He'll do fine if he's half as good as Anacleto de la Peña," said Feliciano stiffly.

"It isn't that," answered Gumersindo in a soft voice. "It isn't that."

"Gumersindo ought to be his name," said the grandmother. "That's the way you tell families apart. When he grows up people will say, 'Oh, you're Gumersindo Gómez, the son of Gumersindo Gómez and María García, and old Gumersindo Gómez, he was your grandfather.' That's the way to keep track of people and no need to put it down in writing."

"I said I didn't want him to have my name," said Gumersindo.

"How about María," said Feliciano, turning to his sister. "Maybe she has a name."

María had not joined in the argument. She had been busy holding the baby's squirming little body. She was a pale, pretty girl of twenty. Bearing three children had not slackened the hard, slender lines of her body. But she had been married only five years. A couple of decades and eight more children hence, she would be like her mother, who sat beside her, toothless and wrinkled, like a prophecy.

"I would like my son ... '' she began. She faltered and reddened. "I would like him to have a great man's name. Because he's going to grow up to be a great man who will help his people."

"My son," said Gumersindo playfully. "He is going to be a great man among the Gringos."

The baby gurgled and stretched out its arms to him. "See!" exclaimed María. "He understands." She passed the child to her husband. Gumersindo kissed it, pricking its tender skin with his bristly face. The baby squirmed and kicked and made little grunting noises of displeasure.

"A Gringo name he shall have!" cried Gumersindo in sudden inspiration. "Is he not as fair as any of them? Feliciano, what great men have the Gringos had?"

"They are all great," growled Feliciano, "Great thieves, great liars, great sons-of-bitches. Show me a man of them who isn't money-mad and one of their women who is not a harlot."

"Feliciano!" said María sharply.

"It's the truth," answered her brother, "and truth never sins, though it may cause discomfort."

"Oh, never is the lion as he is painted," said Gumersindo. "You are beginning to talk like one of Cleto de la Peña's men."

"And I wish I was," said Feliciano, almost shouting. "I wish I was out there with Lupe, shooting them the way they shoot us every chance they get. Lupe's out there! I could bet you my life Lupe's out there!"

"Hush!" said María. "Remember Mama!"

The old woman had begun to weep. Feliciano looked at his mother and then stared shamefacedly at the ground. There was a long, awkward pause during which the grandmother's quiet sobbing gradually died away.

After a while Gumersindo said, "About the name. I was thinking of the great North American, he who was a general and fought the soldiers of the king."

The grandmother brightened up and said, "That was Hidalgo, but he was a Mexican."

"I remember," said Gumersindo. "Wachinton. Jorge Wachinton."

"Guálinto," said the grandmother, "what a funny name."

"Like Hidalgo, eh?" said Feliciano.

"Yes. Once he crossed a river while it was freezing. He drove out the English and freed the slaves."

"I wish the English would have stayed," said Feliciano. "I met an Englishman once, and he was a good man. *Muy gente.*"

"Papa," said Carmen from the bed, "Maruca's pinching me."

"I didn't, I didn't, I didn't," said Maruca.

"Hush, both of you," said Gumersindo. "You should be asleep."

"Guálinto," said the grandmother. "What a funny name."

"I think you're a fool," Feliciano said to Gumersindo, "but he's your son. You can name him anything you like." Gumersindo laughed and shrugged his shoulders.

"Guálinto," repeated the grandmother, "Guálinto Gómez."

"Wachinton," corrected Feliciano. He got up and went outside, hunching his shoulders against the cold as he reached the doorway, all the while singing softly to himself: *En la cantina de Bekar, se agarraron a balazos.*

"Guálinto," said the grandmother, with the pride of one who finally succeeds at a difficult task.

"It's a good name," said Gumersindo. "How do you like it, *viejita*?"

María smiled at the term of endearment. "It is a very good name," she said.

3

Mormón, mormón. Mormón, mormón, mormón. Coffee watah! Coffee watah!

Feliciano cursed under his breath as he massaged his feet, still covered by a pair of tattered socks that once were white. Within reach of his hand were his boots, and just beyond sat El Negro, also engaged in massaging his stocking feet. They were in a bower within a stand of young mesquites in the dense chaparral, some distance from the road. They had walked that road a good part of the night, warily, watchfully. With the first gray of dawn they moved into the chaparral, stepping on little patches of sickly grass, on weeds and spots of hard ground, to leave no trail in the deep dust. Here they would rest for a good long while, out of concern for feet not much used to walking. Then they would thread their way through the chaparral, even more warily than before, to the place where Lupe the Little Doll and his band were waiting. But the distance now would be shorter, they would be there by nightfall.

Shortly after dark the day before, they had reached a shack some ten miles beyond San Pedrito, to meet with Anacleto de la Peña. That had been Feliciano's job as Anacleto's contact man with Lupe. But Lupe had insisted that El Negro go along. Feliciano objected, "I can do it better alone. I don't need a *padrino*."

Lupe didn't smile. "You need somebody to back you up. And nobody knows the chaparral like El Negro." He stared at Feliciano. "Except me," he added.

"And there's nobody you trust more than El Negro," Feliciano retorted. "What's the matter? Do you think I'll run away?"

This time Lupe smirked. "No," he said, "but you might do something foolish. Like sneaking into San Pedrito to see Mama and the rest."

"I'm not crazy," Feliciano replied. But he went with El Negro and found that Lupe had not lied. The black man knew trails in the chaparral Feliciano had not known about. But all for nothing, worse than nothing. They had waited in the dark outside the empty shack for more than an hour, until an old woman showed up, a bent and black form in the habitual mourning clothes old women wore, blacker than the night around them.

"Who are you?" she asked when they came up to her. "What do you want here?"

"Just strangers passing by," Feliciano replied. "Could we trouble you for some coffee?"

"There's no coffee here," the old woman said. "No fire, even. There's nobody here but me."

"Will anybody else be coming?"

"Not tonight. Nor any other night," the old woman said. Then in a firmer tone, edged with a kind of bitter amusement, "*Se rajó el cabrón.*" She spat on the ground. "He's halfway to Monterrey by now, with his tail between his legs."

So now he and El Negro were resting not too far from the road, getting ready to go back and tell Lupe. No more ammunition or horses, or food or money or men. No more Anacleto de la Peña. It was all over. Mormón, mormón; mormón, mormón, mormón. Coffee watah! He gave his head a sudden shake, as if there were flies buzzing around his eyes. The words would not get out of his head. Perhaps it was because San Pedrito was so very close by. María, his mother, the children. Gumersindo.

Yes, Gumersindo. That was why the words kept going through his mind. It was the last time they had been in town together, before it all started, before the boy was born. Mormón, mormón. Funny word, Feliciano had thought, like a bee inside a pumpkin flower. MorMON, morMON, the young man kept saying it again and again. Feliciano drained his coffee cup slowly. There was great activity in the little lunchroom that called itself a restaurant in big letters painted on its plate-glass front. The April night was cool and coffee falls well on the stomach on nights like that. All down the length of the lunchroom, men were sitting on the stools before the counter, men in dull-colored drill trousers and imitation-leather jackets, wearing stetson hats.

"Coffee watah!" bawled the waiter, a thin, pale-faced boy in a dirty apron and a paperbag cap.

"Coffee watah!" answered the voice of the kitchen boy. "*Ahi va!*"

Feliciano wondered why they didn't say it all in Spanish. Maybe because in English it was shorter, maybe not because of that. But he didn't like it, he wished they would say it all in Spanish. Mormón, mormón. He played with the word as a child plays with a strange toy, turning it over and over, looking at it from all angles. And the more he fooled with it, the stranger it sounded. Above the clatter of dishes and the murmur of conversation he could sometimes hear Gumersindo, one seat beyond his, answering the priest, who sat between the two. *Pastor*, the priest called himself. Feliciano smiled. A *pastor* herds sheep and goats, and when someone is ill-mannered or stupid you tell him, "Hey, *pastor*, go back to your sheep!"

But this *pastor* was no sheepherder. Feliciano leaned back and took another look at him. A pink-cheeked young man, almost a boy, in suit and tie and a look as if he was praying all the time beneath his breath. But he didn't fool anybody with that holy-holy face. Feliciano had seen plenty of priests before, and he didn't care much for them. Besides, this one was a Gringo even though he spoke understandable Spanish. But here he was, putting silly ideas into Gumersindo's head. It was all very well for him, who came from up north to talk about love between all men and everybody being brothers. And it was very well for Gumersindo, who came from the interior of Mexico to be taken in by such talk. But a Border Mexican knew there was no brotherhood of men.

Feliciano had exhausted his coffee and his patience, but Gumersindo and the preacher were still talking. Abandoning good manners he rose, wiping his mustache with the back of his hand. "Let's go," he said roughly, staring at the preacher, who looked back at him with his mild expression. The preacher went with them as far as the door and shook hands with both of them. As soon as he was gone, Feliciano wiped the palm of his hand on his trousers.

The night was clear. There was no moon, but the sky was full of sparkling stars. As they walked homeward through the dark, silent streets of San Pedrito both men glanced upward now and then. "Look at those stars," said Gumersindo, a vibrant ring in his voice that seemed to rise deep in his chunky frame. "You're taller than me, Feliciano. Reach up and pluck me one."

Feliciano shrugged. "Pluck it yourself," he said. Gumersindo did not answer and Feliciano went on, "Why do you listen to that queer bird?"

"Who? Oh, the preacher. He's all right."

"He's not. He's a Gringo."

"Not all Gringos are alike."

"*Mierda!* The preacher told you that." Gumersindo was silent. "Religion," said Feliciano, "is the opium of the people. Remember that."

They walked in silence for a while, then Gumersindo said, "After all, it's their country."

"Their country!" Feliciano half-shouted. "Their country! There you are. Their filthy lies are all over you already. I was born here. My father was born here and so was my grandfather and his father before him. And then they come, they come and take it, steal it and call it theirs." He dropped his voice. "But it won't be theirs much longer now, not much longer, I can tell you. We'll get it back, all of it."

Gumersindo's frightened eyes glistened in the half-light as he looked up into Feliciano's face. "Go on," he said in an anxious attempt at humor, "don't go around talking like that. Somebody's going to take you seriously."

Feliciano made a gesture of impatience. "I'm not joking."

"Not joking?" Gumersindo echoed querulously.

"No. This time we're going to taste blood."

"What about them?"

"Who?"

"The *americanos.*"

"The Gringos are cowards; they don't know how to fight. Any one of us is worth ten of them."

"If so, then they'll send twenty against you. You don't know how big their nation is. You don't know how many of them there are."

"We are not alone. We have friends."

"You can't win."

"We *will* win."

"It won't do any good," Gumersindo persisted. "A lot of our people will get killed and we'll be worse off than we are now. And most of the people killed will be peaceful, innocent people. You know how the *rinches* are."

"It has to be done. After it's over there won't be any *rinches.*"

They stopped at the corner as if by mutual consent. In the dim light of the street lamp Gumersindo's face had a dazed, wounded look. "Feliciano," he said, "in the name of your mother, stay out of it."

"You'd better move to Jonesville before it starts, Gumersindo. I can't tell you when but it will be soon. Here in this town even the dogs hate Mexicans."

"My boss is kind to me," Gumersindo mumbled.

"He's also kind to his mules."

Gumersindo took off his wide-brimmed hat as if to cool his head in the night air. "No," he said. "No, no, no! This is all wrong! You can't do it, you can't. What did I come here from Mexico for? Because I thought that here I could find work and peace. Why do we have to hate each other? It's a sin, I tell you!"

"Shut up," Feliciano said. "You're talking too loud."

Gumersindo bowed his head. "I'm staying in San Pedrito," he said.

And he had stayed, thought Feliciano as he sat beside El Negro wiggling his toes. Through all the shooting and killing, Gumersindo had kept the family together, protected by his Gringo boss no doubt. Perhaps he had been right, after all. And now that Anacleto de la Peña had sneaked away, the raiding and the killing would soon be over.

A couple of shots sounded not far up the road. Quickly Feliciano and El Negro slipped their boots on and crept closer to the edge of the road, rifles at ready. Soon they heard the chink of a bridle chain, then a horse sneezed. Now they could hear the rhythmic creak of saddle leather. They came around a bend in the road, a party of four Rangers, an old man and three younger ones, with pistols and knives all over their belts. They were joking and laughing. It would be so easy to get all four of them before they knew what was happening. El Negro seemed to guess Feliciano's thoughts, for he shook his head. The *rinches* passed. They disappeared around another bend in the road, and as their voices were fading, one of them began to sing a funny-sounding nasal song.

Now El Negro and Feliciano worked their way through the brush parallel to the road, toward the place where they had heard the shots. They found him soon enough. The short, chunky body was lying face down in a cringing attitude that made it look smaller and more pitiful. The uncombed red hair was full of dirt, and an ant was crawling over it. The squarish work shoes had a pathetic strangeness, their heels pointing skyward, their soles facing the empty air. There was something very funny in the sight of the dead man's shoes. Feliciano's lips twitched as he bent over the corpse. He felt his grief and rage settling deep inside him in a cold, dead lump. Very carefully he put out his hand to Gumersindo's shoulder and turned him over.

Gumersindo opened his eyes and looked at Feliciano with no hint of surprise. "Don't tell him," he mumbled through bruised lips.

"Who?" asked Feliciano, attempting to wipe the blood and dust off Gumersindo's swollen face.

"My son. Mustn't know. Ever. No hate, no hate."

Feliciano was shocked. "He must know. It is his right to know."

Gumersindo made an attempt to shake his head. "No," he said in a whisper that was more like a hiss. "Promise. Please promise."

"I promise," Feliciano said. Gumersindo smiled and closed his eyes.

He did not open them again, and after a few moments his face seemed to sag. Feliciano kept looking at him.

"He's dead now," El Negro said gently. "We must go."

"We can't leave him here like this. Like an animal."

"What else can we do? Take him into San Pedrito?"

"That's what we should do."

"It would be a very foolish thing," El Negro said, his voice no longer gentle.

Feliciano jerked his head up and stared at El Negro's impassive face. "Ah, I see now ... " he began.

"Shh," said El Negro, listening. Feliciano could hear it now, the creaking of a loaded wagon coming down the road. They were back in the brush when the wagon appeared. It came slowly down the road, pulled by a team of sleepy mules and loaded with bundles of corn stalks. Beside it walked old Don Hermenegildo Martínez and his two grown sons. The wagon halted before Gumersindo's body, and Don Hermenegildo came forward. He was gray-haired and his deep-brown skin was a mass of wrinkles, but he carried himself as straight as a young man.

"Mother of mine!" said the old man. "It's Gumersindo Gómez."

"Let's get away from here, Papa," one of the sons said.

"Don't tell me what to do," replied the old man sharply. "Quick! Pull down the bundles from the middle of the wagon!" His sons set frantically to work. Then, under the old man's direction they placed Gumersindo's body on a bed of stalks in the middle of the wagon and covered him with the bundles they had removed, all the while casting anxious glances up and down the road. Finally they kicked the dust around to cover up signs of the body. And then the wagon moved on toward San Pedrito at its same slow pace.

"Curse them!" Don Hermenegildo was saying as the wagon moved away. "Curse them both! It's the innocents who pay." Feliciano and El Negro watched the wagon until it was out of sight before resuming their journey toward Lupe's camp. They walked through the chaparral until the sun was low, El Negro leading, Feliciano following, without saying a word to each other. Then they stopped to rest in a little clearing, but this time neither of them took off his boots. Finally El Negro spoke.

"One of our people brought word he had been arrested for questioning. But it was the San Pedrito deputy who was holding him, and the Gringo he worked for had hired a lawyer to see that he was treated right. That was all we knew." Feliciano looked at El Negro but said nothing.

"The *rinches* had found out he was Lupe's brother-in-law (they don't know anything about you), and they wanted to make him say where Lupe was. Of course he didn't know." Feliciano nodded and El Negro went on, "The lawyer told the deputy he should not hand him over to the *rinches*, and the deputy went along with that. That much Lupe and I knew when you and I went looking for De la Peña. We were sure he was pretty safe. Lupe told you no lie. All he was worried about was that somebody—De la Peña maybe—would tell you and that you might get it into your head to go into San Pedrito."

"Pretty safe, he was," Feliciano said, "pretty safe."

"It was the city judge, without a doubt, you remember how it happened to Muñiz. The judge signs a paper authorizing the *rinches* to take the prisoner from San Pedrito to the Jonesville jail. Two miles is about as far as they go."

"We saw them ride by afterward. Did you know any of them?"

"Only the old one, and I've seen him only once. Lupe knows him well, though. Used to be a preacher, Lupe says. Perhaps he'll tell you his name."

"I don't intend to ask him anything," Feliciano replied.

"Well, let's get going," said El Negro, "we're almost there."

4

They were hiding in the brush, not far from the road, waiting. Twenty-three of them, led by Lupe the Little Doll. They were in a park-like space dotted with scrub mesquites, puny tortured little trees whose trunks and branches had been twisted into oddly human shapes. They lay almost motionless in the heat, under the scanty shade, in their faces a slow suffering.

Their clothes were soiled with blood, grass stains and manure. The dust had worn itself into the leather of their boots; their hats were misshapen and torn. Only their eyes looked new, their listening, waiting eyes.

They were waiting for the American patrol to pass. When the soldiers rode by they would shoot at them from the thorny brush, trying to kill as many as they could. Saying as they fired:

"For my father."

"For my cousin."

"For my brother."

"For my ranch, you thieving sons-of-bitches!"

Some of the soldiers would fall, an expression of pained surprise on their young, red faces. As if they were amazed at it all. As if to say, "What is this all about, anyway? What do we know about your fathers and brothers and the lands you say you lost?" Then, as other soldiers returned the fire, they would fall back through leaf-mold-covered trails to their horses. They would scatter and thread their way through the easier parts of the dense brush toward the river, trying to get to the Mexican side with as few casualties as possible.

That would be all. Except that next day the Rangers would come. To kill everyone they found close to the scene of the ambush, that is every-one who could not speak English. Until the dead reached a satisfying total, and then they would go back to Jonesville and wire headquar-ters in Austin, reporting a certain number of bandits killed. So thought Feliciano, who was one of the twenty-three bearded, dirty men in torn work clothes. He had a rifle and a revolver, and he carried two car-tridge belts, one around his middle and the other across his chest. But in both of them he had fifteen cartridges at the most. There were no more, Lupe had said. This was to be the last blow they would strike at the Gringos before giving up the fight.

Of the twenty-three only Lupe the Little Doll appeared relaxed and unconcerned. He moved among his men, his tiny booted feet making almost no sound, his rifle barrel cradled in the crook of his left arm, as was his custom. Except for his hard, sharp little face with its pointed nose, a face made old by sun, wind and the hard life of the chaparral, he looked like a half-grown boy playing *vaquero*. He walked over to Fe-liciano who was wiping his face with the sleeve of his jumper. Feliciano looked up into Lupe's mild, almost humorous eyes.

"Hot, isn't it, Brother Feliciano?" said Lupe in a voice scarcely above a whisper.

Feliciano smiled. "Yes, hot enough," he replied. Lupe moved on to the next man and put his hand on the man's shoulder.

Many years before, Lupe had killed a Gringo who had laughed at him because Lupe looked so puny. Lupe had been an outlaw ever since, wanted by the law, feared by many. But he still retained the old Border Mexican custom of calling his elder brother by the respectful title of *Hermano* rather than simply by his given name, and addressing him with the formal *usted* instead of the familiar *tú*. Feliciano was reminded of the time when Lupe was a boy. Now Lupe was the leader here, and Feliciano obeyed though he was the elder. Lupe was his leader, now that Anacleto de la Peña was gone. Gone across the river to the safety of his Carrancista friends. Anacleto de la Peña, the Liberator, the Bolívar of the Border, who loved to quote a poem that said, "I would rather be a corpse than be a worm."

When the American soldiers came, Anacleto de la Peña decided he would rather not be a corpse, and the movement for a Spanish-speaking Republic of the Southwest had collapsed. Who would have thought the Gringos had so many soldiers? Gumersindo, of course. He had known. When Feliciano left to join De la Peña, he had told his mother and his sister María that he was going to Monterrey, and he had it noised about that he was stealing a girl and taking her with him to Mexico. That was the only wise thing he had done, Feliciano thought as he lay in the chaparral waiting for the soldiers. Not so much for himself as for those he had left behind. Only Gumersindo had known where Feliciano was going. He said, "And nothing can stop you from going?"

"No," Feliciano answered.

"Then go," Gumersindo said, "and God have mercy on us all." Now Feliciano knew what Gumersindo had meant.

Lupe was coming toward him again. But on the way he stopped in front of a very young boy who looked out of place in his overalls, straw hat, and heavy work shoes. Lupe touched the boy's shoulder, and the boy looked up. Lupe smiled at him. The boy shut his eyes and turned his face away. Lupe came and squatted beside Feliciano. "I wish you would go with us to the other side, Brother," he said.

Feliciano did not answer. "It's a different war over there," Lupe continued. "Really good men like you and me can get rich, get to be generals maybe."

"Somebody's got to take care of Mother and María and her kids. You know Gumersindo is dead."

"Yes," Lupe said shortly. His face hardened momentarily and then relaxed into its usual expression of watchful unconcern. "But South Texas still is Gringo land."

"I don't care whose land it is anymore. Why don't you make that child go home now?"

"Who? Remigio? He's almost sixteen. And he wants revenge."

"Revenge? He can't ride, he can't shoot. The soldiers will get him for sure."

"His grief will soon be over, then. And it will make it easier for the rest of us to get away."

Feliciano twisted his face in disgust. He started to speak when he realized someone was standing over them. It was Remigio, the boy who was almost sixteen. His straw hat was in his hands. "Yes?" Lupe said.

Remigio cleared his throat, his long face pale and trembly. He tried to speak softly but his voice broke. He hesitated, then spoke in a high, rasping whisper. "I would like to go home," he said.

"Eh?" Lupe's yellow eyes opened wide. Remigio twisted his hat. Lupe said in a calm, friendly voice, "I didn't expect this of you, Remigio.

You haven't fired a shot yet."

Remigio shifted his weight from one foot to the other and toyed with his hat. "Well, sir, I—I was thinking last night. Now that they are—they are dead. Well, I guess my mother and the younger ones need me. Who will take care of them now?"

"And your father? And your brother?"

"I'll leave that to God. God will punish those men."

Lupe tilted his head to one side in a parody of reminiscence. "Just how do people scream when they're being burned to death? Come on, Remigio, tell me." Remigio's lips twitched, he blinked and twisted his straw hat. "I bet you would have liked to have a rifle then, hiding there in the brush, watching the *rinches* drinking whiskey and laughing."

Remigio began to cry. "Don't sir! Don't!" he said. "Please stop, please stop." He covered an ear with one hand, his hat still in the other.

"You saw and heard it all, remember? Your little brother screaming and your father yelling at them, 'Shoot! For the love of God shoot!'"

Remigio dropped his hat and put both hands over his face. Sobs shook his spindly frame. Instantly Lupe was on his feet, putting his arm around the boy's waist. "*Ya, ya,*" Lupe said in a soothing voice. "Don't cry. Don't cry or they'll hear us. They'll be coming up the road soon, and then you'll hear *them* scream. You want to shoot them, don't you?" Remigio wiped his eyes with his fist and nodded. Sobbing noiselessly he returned to the place where he had left his rifle.

"Agh!" Feliciano said savagely. "You are a vicious man."

"Revenge is good," Lupe said mildly. "Remigio is a better shot than you think. He'll get at least one. And after that, what if he dies? His soul will be at peace."

"Don't talk to me like a preacher," said Feliciano in a tense whisper. "You're a beast, a beast with fangs and claws. All you want is blood– Remigio's, mine, everybody's!"

Lupe leaned carelessly against the mesquite and looked down at Feliciano. "And you," he said, "are a hypocrite." For the first time he used the familiar *tú*. "It was all my idea; you and Anacleto de la Peña didn't call me in." Suddenly his face was contorted by an intense, almost fiendish hate. "You needed me then! You and De la Peña with his high starched collars and highclass way of talking. There was dirty work to be done, so you needed a bandit like me. For your lands and your liberty and your pure ideals. So you could all be presidents maybe, or ministers, or something. Remember?"

Feliciano drew back in spite of himself, but Lupe's outburst ended abruptly. "I've seen plenty of corpses in my time," Lupe continued in a matter-of-fact tone. "But they were *men*, men who had been shooting at me. These Gringo bastards butcher our people like sheep." His voice changed again to the reflective tone of one who ponders a deep philosophical question, "Tell me, Brother Feliciano, who burned Remigio's father alive? Who killed Gumersindo?" Feliciano looked up into Lupe's yellow eyes, but Lupe turned his head away.

A lazy little whistle came floating on the breeze. It began on one high but soft note and fell to a lower and softer one, which was repeated over and over. It was a very quiet sound, and one had to be listening for it to hear it at any great distance. Lupe straightened up, his carbine in his arms, listening. The whistle sounded again, nearer this time. A sentinel hidden in the brush outside the clearing whistled an answer. The men of the band rose hurriedly, their rifles ready. A few seconds passed in silence. Then came the soft crunch of dead leaves. The horizontal branch of a huisache shrub swayed back and forth, and El Negro stepped into the clearing. He came directly to Lupe.

"They're not coming," he said. "They took the other road."

"Better get out of here quick," somebody said.

"Quiet!" said Lupe. "Let El Negro talk. Is that all?"

"No," El Negro said, grinning broadly. "We caught something for you boys." He turned. "All right!"

The brush crackled and moved, and a couple of other scouts came into the clearing, pushing two bound men before them. "Spies," El Negro said.

One of the captives was a gangly middle-aged Anglo. His gold-rimmed glasses and blue suspenders made him a strange sight in the middle of Lupe's band. The other was young and Mexican, a stocky laborer dressed in blue denim, his brown face burned a glossy black by the sun. Both looked from one guerrilla to another with anxious eyes.

One of the band came up to the Mexican captive. "Here's one of ours," he said, "the Gringo-loving son ... '' he struck the captive across the face, " ... of a bitch." The bound man cringed and said, "Don't hit me, *señor*, don't hit me please." Others crowded forward, but Lupe said, "*Suave, suave*," and stepped to the front.

"What's your name?" he asked the Anglo.

"Sneed," said the man, "Jack Sneed." He had to try twice before he could speak distinctly.

"You know Spanish," Lupe said. "You were sent ahead to spy."

"No, *señor*," Sneed replied. "I'm a merchant, a poor merchant, that's all I am. I sell notions, you know ... '' His voice grew strained. "Notions, hair ribbons, perfume, things like that. You can have it all, the wagon and the horse too."

No one replied.

"I don't have much money," Sneed added, "but under the wagon seat ... ''

El Negro laughed. "We already got it."

"You're a spy," one of the men behind Lupe said.

"Oh, no, *señor!* I'm just a humble peddler. A how do you call it? A *varillero*, that's it. I sell perfume and hair ribbons and ... "

A big raw-faced man stepped up to Lupe's side. "Let's get it over with," he said, "and let's go."

"Kill him. Kill him," the others said. Lupe grinned.

"No, no," Sneed shook his head. "I am your friend. All Mexicans are my friends." Several of the men laughed.

"Just a moment," said Feliciano, pushing his way forward. He turned and faced the others. "We can't kill this man."

"Why not?" asked Lupe in mock surprise.

"This man is not a *rinche*, he's a peaceful man. Why kill somebody who has done you no harm?"

"I guess you're right," Lupe sounded convinced. "How would I feel if I was walking along the road, without a bad thought in my mind and suddenly somebody shows up and ... " He passed a forefinger across his throat.

Nobody laughed this time. Some glanced at Feliciano, others stared at the ground. Feliciano turned away.

Remigio, the farmer boy, had been edging closer and closer to Sneed. Now he stood directly in front of the *varillero*, his face twisted in hatred and fear. The others watched him as he shifted his rifle from one hand to the other. But Remigio did nothing except look at Sneed. The raw-faced *vaquero* who had been standing beside Lupe drew his revolver and stepped up to the peddler.

"Let's go!" he said. He pressed the gun against the back of Sneed's head at an upward angle and pulled the trigger. Sneed fell forward on his knees, blood gushing from his mouth and nostrils like vomit.

Remigio screamed and lunged at the *vaquero*, kicking his shins and pushing at him with the flat of his rifle. The man gave ground, half-laughing, half-angry. He raised his revolver as if to shoot, but Remigio turned and emptied his rifle into Sneed's back as he lay face down. Then he ran and got his horse and tried to make it trample the corpse, but the horse would not do it. So Remigio slid from the saddle and took a machete from his saddle scabbard. He hacked at the corpse until the machete hit bone and stuck. Then he tried to trample Sneed with his big, clumsy farm shoes, but two men took him by the armpits and dragged him away. When they let him go he sat beneath a tree and cried, high and loud like a girl.

Someone said, "We'd better get out of here!" In a moment men were rushing about, leading horses out of the brush, mounting and riding off in different directions. "Let's go, let's go," they all said. "Let's get out of here." Lupe the Little Doll sneered as he saw them go, but he did nothing to stop them.

The Mexican who had been captured remained bound and standing close to Sneed's body. Lupe seemed to notice him for the first time, and he walked toward him, his rifle resting in the crook of his left arm. The bound man did not see him. He was absorbed by the sight of his employer's mangled body. His eyes were opened to a painful wideness, as if the sight were too big for him and he were trying to make his eyes large enough to let it into his head. Lupe came up softly behind him and raised his bent arm so the rifle pointed at the man.

"You're not going to kill this one," Feliciano said. He had come up just as softly behind his brother. Lupe turned around slowly and stiffly, a look of annoyance on his face. Then he relaxed and smiled.

"*Tiene usted razón, Hermano,*" he said. "You are right, Brother; I will not kill him." Then after a pause he added, "It is you, Brother, who will kill him."

Feliciano had taken out his knife to cut the ropes around the man. He stopped and stared at Lupe. "You are mad," he said.

"Yes?" said Lupe. "But again, no." They stood facing each other, a few paces apart. Over on the far side of the clearing Remigio was stumbling toward his horse, his head in his hands. All the others were gone.

Lupe laughed and pointed the muzzle of his rifle toward the ground. He turned to the captive, who had been watching them with idiotic intentness. "This man is letting you go," he said. "Take a good look at him so you will remember him later. You don't want to forget the face of the man who saved your life." The captive looked at Feliciano.

Lupe went on, "His name is Feliciano García. Feliciano García, brother to Lupe García, the bandit. You can find him in San Pedrito, living at his sister's house." The bound man stared again at Feliciano. "You will need to remember that," Lupe continued, "because when the *rinches* come to visit you they will ask you questions. They will want to know who killed your *patrón*, and you'd better tell the truth. They have ways of making you tell the truth." The bound man began to tremble. As Lupe moved away toward the other end of the clearing he looked back and said, "Don't forget."

Feliciano stood motionless, his knife in one hand, his rifle in the other, as Lupe the Little Doll stepped into the chaparral. For some time, Feliciano kept staring at the spot where Lupe had disappeared.

Once in the brush, Lupe picked up his horse's reins and mounted slowly. He turned his horse's head into a trail leading down toward the river, traveling at a walk, listening. After a while he heard it. One report, then a second. He clucked his horse into a trot.

5

Again he was going down the same winding dusty road, this time toward Jonesville-on-the-Grande. He was walking now, clean-shaven and wearing the blue denim work clothes, heavy shoes and straw hat of a farmer. But his nerves were still taut, and he kept listening, half-expecting the familiar ping of a bullet. Feliciano switched the mule with a slender willow stick to hurry it along. He did not hit it too hard. It was the last animal the family had, and it was half-starved and weak. He did not dare push it too much, impatient though he was. If the cursed beast doesn't decide to walk faster, he thought, we won't reach Jonesville before dark.

On the two-wheeled cart were the few belongings remaining to the family—a bed, a canvas cot, bedding, dishes, pots and pans, and old clothes. In the midst of this sat the black-clad widow, holding her little boy in her arms. The two girls sat at the rear of the cart, dangling their legs and staring at the chaparral and the dusty *llano*, each one trying to spot birds and other interesting things before the other one did. The grandmother was not with them, she had died shortly after Gumersindo was killed. Feliciano had told nobody but Gumersindo where he was going, but as soon as he left—María told him—the old woman began to act strange. She talked little and barely touched her food. And soon after Gumersindo was buried she died. She must have worried about Lupe and Feliciano, but she never talked about it. Only when she was dying and out of her head had she asked for them.

She had known about him all along, thought Feliciano. The story about the girl and Monterrey never fooled her. But she had kept her troubles to herself. And now she was dead, the tough old woman. A hard old woman with more wrinkles than teeth, always smoking a corn-husk cigaret. Feliciano had loved her and he knew she had loved him, though she wasted no time in kind words or caresses. She had been pretty once, people used to say. And she knew kind words then. Feliciano, her first born, vaguely remembered being kissed and petted when he was very little. But that was before life had hardened her—working side by side with Feliciano's father in the fields, grinding corn on the *metate* and carrying water, and frequent childbirth.

She had seen most of them die, some at birth, others in their infancy, others of various ailments—this one of consumption, that one of snake-bite, another of a strange pain in the guts that no herbs could heal and for which there was no cure except in a Gringo hospital that was only for Gringos. Then her husband, killed by hard labor and mezcal, and little Lupe an outlaw, removed from the family. Through all this the old woman had endured with grim purpose, never letting either births or burials distract her from the daily struggle to dull the edge of hunger one more day. Only Feliciano, the eldest, and María, the youngest, had been left to her of the sixteen she had borne. And then Feliciano left, and only María had been with her when she died. At last the old rawhide had lost its toughness, frayed and split apart.

If only Gumersindo had moved to Jonesville when Feliciano told him to, the little old woman would not have died. Nor Gumersindo. Feliciano himself by this time would have been somewhere south of the river. He wondered how long he would be able to get away with living under their very noses. Especially . . . . He shrugged. Perhaps pity was a weakness too. Like religion. Anway, he had to take care of María and her chidren while he could. He would think about those other things later.

Jonesville was a friendly place, mostly Mexican. Even the Gringos spoke Spanish there. It would be easier to make a living and avoid dangerous questions. Besides, it was right at the edge of the river. So Feliciano was taking his sister and her children to Jonesville, as he had wanted Gumersindo to do. Gumersindo had not done it; he had stayed in San Pedrito, stubbornly insisting he had no reason to run away since he had done nothing wrong. He who is guilty of nothing fears nothing, Gumersindo had repeated the old saying. But it was just a saying. He had been a strange man. He had made Feliciano promise something he never should have promised. Never to tell his son how Gumersindo had died. Many times before, Gumersindo had said that he wanted his son to have no hatred in his heart. He must grow up to be a great man and help his people. And that was Gumersindo's last thought before he died.

Now Feliciano was sorry he had promised such a thing to a dying man. It would be very hard to keep such a terrible truth from this male child. Never to tell him how his father died, never to give him a chance at vengeance. That was a hard task, and it was not fair to the boy either. For after all, what were men for but to live and die like men. What would he give to have a son who would avenge him if some day he were at last killed by the *rinches*. He prodded the mule. In Jonesville, it was said the *rinches* were not allowed to enter.

Where the road dipped into a dry resaca bottom they ran into a bunch of men. Six or seven of them, blocking the road. *Rinches*. Feliciano's right arm tensed, then relaxed. He was unarmed, a peaceful farmer now. Grasping the mule by the bridle he brought the cart to a stop. They were all youngish men, unshaven and slouching in their saddles, grinning with a kind of fascinated anticipation. A strange thought came to Feliciano. Not too many years ago they must have been catching frogs alive to pull off their legs,or trying to ram a burning stick under the tail of somebody else's mare. With that same look on their lobster-red faces. From beneath half-lowered lids he watched them, the thin twisting lips, the squinting light-colored cat's eyes full of contempt. One of them rode up closer to the cart. There was a trace of a smile on his face as he leaned down to stare at Feliciano.

"Where you goin', greaser?" he inquired casually.

Feliciano shrugged. "Inglis," he said mildly, "no spik."

"Aw, that's what all you bastards say."

Feliciano kept his expression as pleasant and vacuous as he could. The *rinche* shifted his glance from Feliciano to the cart, and the sight of María made him open his eyes a little wider. María was good to look at, and her beauty was enhanced by her black clothing and her pale, frightened face. The baby in her arms stared curiously at the stranger, but the little girls behind her peeped over her shoulder in breathless terror. They were looking at a *rinche* for the first time. The *rinche* was staring at María, appraising her as he would a horse. Feliciano felt real fear for the first time that afternoon.

"Let me pass, please," he said in Spanish.

The *rinche* paid no attention. He was looking now at the child in María's arms. The light-brown hair, pink skin, blue eyes. Behind him the others had noticed the child and were talking among themselves. The *rinche* pointed at the baby with his quirt. "Where'd you get that white child?" Then he added, *"Chico americano."*

"Americano no," Feliciano said, *"mexicano."*

The *rinche* stared at him. "You're a goddamn liar," he said without much heat. Then a sudden fancy made him turn to the pale woman in black. "Saynyoreeta," he said with mock courtliness, "if you might pardon the introoshun, but I would like to know if you remember from what stump this here little chip come from." The other men guffawed and Feliciano prodded the mule.

"Let me pass," he said fiercely in Spanish. *"Déjame pasar, gringo sanavabiche!"*

Abruptly the *rinche* stopped laughing. His face took on a nasty, deliberate expression. "Well," he said thoughtfully, "well, well, well." His hand wandered to his thigh. Feliciano's eyes fixed on that freckled hand as it traveled slowly, slowly up the dirty leather chaps toward the pistol holster. María and the children were very far away. The world narrowed down to focus on that slow-moving hand. Naked, helpless he waited for the *rinche* to draw and fire. Finally the *rinche* drew and aimed at Feliciano, who stared at the end of the barrel. Must be a forty-four, he thought, but the muzzle looks huge.

Someone began to talk loudly and angrily behind Feliciano. He wondered whether another *rinche* had come behind him and was cursing him before they shot him. But the *rinche* in front of him was putting his gun away. Feliciano turned around very slowly. Behind him, close to the cart, was a massive Gringo sitting on a big and powerful horse. The big Gringo was dressed like a city man except for his stetson and boots, and in spite of his white beard he did not look old. Except for a few words like "law" and "jail," Feliciano could understand little of what the big Gringo was saying. But he did catch the curse words and there were a lot of them. The *rinches* looked sullen and uncomfortable.

"Awright, Jedge," their leader said in a conciliatory tone.

The big man flared out again as if he had been insulted. He stood up in his stirrups and yelled, "Vamoose!" The *rinches* vamoosed, wooden-faced.

After the *rinches* were gone, the old Gringo's anger disappeared. "And what is your name?" he asked Feliciano in clear Spanish.

Feliciano took off his hat. "Feliciano García, at your service."

"You are a rash man. It almost cost you your life."

"I am deeply grateful to you. I don't usually lose my head, but I feared for the family when they would not let me pass."

The old Gringo looked briefly at the cart. "Nice family," he said. "Pretty baby." Then, more gently, "Is he your nephew?"

"*Sí señor*. That is my sister María and her children."

The old Gringo did not ask where the children's father was. He looked down at Feliciano, studying him. Finally he said, "You are a brave man. Rash at times perhaps, but a brave man. I was watching when that roughneck threw down on you."

"You are the brave one, the way you talked to those *rinches* and sent them about their business. I thought only the governor of the state could do that."

The old Gringo smiled briefly. "Those were not real *rinches*. The governor has called them off and things are supposed to be peaceful now. These are just cowhands from ranches around here who got themselves deputized. They knew I could put them in jail."

"Just the same, I am deeply grateful."

"You are going to Jonesville?" He said it "Hon-esbil" the way Mexicans did.

"Yes sir. It still is not safe in San Pedrito for a Mexican, even if men like those are not real *rinches*."

"What are you going to do when you get to Jonesville?"

"Look for a job. And a place for us to stay."

"Can you read and write?"

"Only in Spanish."

"That's good enough."

Again the old Gringo looked Feliciano over. "On Polk Street," he said, "right close to Fort Jones, there is a *cantina* called El Danubio Azul. Have you ever worked in a *cantina*?"

"No sir, but it should not be too hard to learn."

"Go there and ask for the man who runs the place and tell him Judge Norris sent you. That's me. I own the *cantina* but Faustino runs it for me. Faustino Bello is his name. They also call him 'El Barrilito'; when you see him you'll know why. Tell him I said for him to find you some place to stay, and that I've hired you as a bartender."

"*Señor juez*, I don't know how to thank you."

"No need to." The judge picked up his reins and pulled his horse's head to one side. "By the way," he said, "were you born in San Pedrito?"

"Yes sir."

"Have you ever voted?"

Feliciano shook his head. "You'll learn," said the judge, and he trotted away ahead of them on his giant of a horse.

Feliciano trudged on beside the mule for a few moments before he realized he was still clutching his hat in his left hand.

Part II

"JONESVILLE-ON-THE-GRANDE"

1

Early in the eighteenth century, before there was a United States and when Philadelphia was a little colonial town, Morelos was founded on the south bank of the river. During the century that followed it grew into a large and prosperous city. Its outer limits extended north across the river into what was then part of the same province, a vast expanse of territory teeming with the half-wild cattle and horses that were a prime resource for the people of Morelos. Then came the Comanches and the *yanquis*. And so it came to pass that one day in 1846 an army of the United States was encamped on the north bank of the river which different Hispanic explorers had given different names: Río de las Palmas, Río Grande del Norte, Río Bravo. The army was preparing to push southward toward the heart of Mexico.

It was on that river bank, on top of a make-shift parapet, that one Captain Jimmy Jones was observing the main city of Morelos through a field glass when a fateful cannon ball from the southern bank carried off his head. That was, without a doubt, an extraordinary shot, for the Mexican army's artillery, made up of antique brass cannon firing equally antique brass cannon balls, was not distinguished for its range, let alone its accuracy. This remarkable cannon ball did exceed its reach, however, and it succeeded in immortalizing Captain Jones. The fortifications built around the spot became Fort Jones, and the Mexican *barrios* adjacent to it on the north side of the river in time came to be Jonesville, Texas, U.S.A.

For more than half a century Jonesville remained a Mexican town, though officially part of the United States. A few English-speaking adventurers moved in, married into Mexican landowning families, and became a ruling élite allied with their Mexican in-laws. But Spanish remained the language of culture and politics, and Mexican money was legal tender in local commerce. Then came the railroad early in the 20th century, and with it arrived the first real-estate men and the land-and-title companies, and a Chamber of Commerce, of course, which renamed the little town "Jonesville-on-the-Grande" and advertised it to suckers from up north as a paradise on earth: California and Florida rolled up into one. Mexicans labored with axe and spade to clear away the brush where the cattle of their ancestors once had roamed. To make room for truck farming and citrus groves. And the settlers poured in from the U.S. heartland, while Mexicans were pushed out of cattle raising into hard manual labor. It was then also that Jonesville-on-the-Grande came to have a Mexican section of town, and it was this section of Mexican *barrios* that Feliciano García sought once he reached the limits of "Hon-esbil."

Feliciano reached the outskirts of Jonesville-on-the-Grande when the sun was low in the west. The first person he met, a man who looked like a clerk or a lawyer perhaps, not only told him where Polk Street was but walked with him to the corner to point out the way. He asked no questions about the young woman in black and her children; he had no need to. The cart had just turned left into Polk Street in the direction of Fort Jones when a cannon was fired at the fort. The sound made the mule jump, tired and old though she was, and it alarmed María and the children.

"It is just the evening *cañonazo*," explained the man who had guided them to the corner. "It means that it is six o'clock." He said goodbye and went his own way.

Feliciano guided the mule down the street until he was a block from El Danubio Azul. He could tell exactly where it was, nestled close to the fence of the post, because soldiers were beginning to gather at the entrance for their first drink of the evening. He could hear music and laughter. A stoutish young woman in a striped dress and wearing her reddish hair loose as if she had just taken a bath was leaning on her front fence. She said, "*Buenas tardes*," as they came up. Feliciano decided to take a chance.

"*Señora*," he said, "could I ask you a favor? I have to go to that *cantina* to look for a job, but I don't want to take my family there. Could we stop the cart here in front of your house?"

"With great pleasure," the woman said. "You can hitch the mule to the post there. And you, *señora*, please get down with your children and have a cup of coffee while your ... relative goes to El Danubio Azul."

"He's my brother," María said softly, "But we don't want to give you any bother." Feliciano protested too, out of politeness, but the lady in the striped dress replied, "It's a very small thing to do for you."

The mule was hitched to a post at the edge of the dirt street, María and the children got down, and the lady called a young man from the house to bring a bucket of water for the mule. Feliciano hurried down the street toward the *cantina*. The sun was just setting, and there was still plenty of light. The saloon was a building with a false front, on which "El Danubio Azul" was painted in large black letters. Beneath the letters was a broad, wavy swath of blue paint, representing the billows of the Blue Danube. Soldiers were still crowding in as Feliciano came up to the entrance. One of them waved at him and shouted, "Hey buddy! Come and get it before it's all gone!"

"*Aló*," said Feliciano and waved. He decided to go around the back. It was enclosed by a high wooden fence, but there was a door on the side of the building just where the fence began. He knocked on the door several times before it was opened by a very dark, stocky young man. The young man took a step backward and Feliciano asked, "Are you Faustino Bello?"

"No," said the young man, "my name is Juan Rubio."

"I'm Feliciano García. I came to see *el señor* Bello about a job."

"Oh. Come in."

Feliciano stepped into a long back room filled with beer casks and cases of whiskey while the young man hurried through another door into the saloon. Juan Rubio, thought Feliciano, Blond John. What a name. Then Faustino Bello rolled in from the saloon, and Feliciano recalled the Judge's words, "When you see him you'll know why they call him El Barrilito." Bello was short and broad like a beer barrel and he looked just as solid as a wooden cask. Above the formidable body was a chubby babyface topped by a big skull covered with short-cropped black hair.

Bello shook hands. He was perspiring and obviously busy. "You're the man the Judge told me about. Good. We have a house for you. Juan will take you there now and help you in any way he can, and I'll see you about ten tomorrow morning." Sounds of English-speaking voices raised in anger came through the half-open door. "I have to go front now. Two *mochos* are getting ready to fight, and I'll have to make peace between them or toss them out." And he left for the saloon.

Feliciano and Juan Rubio looked at each other for a moment. Then Rubio said respectfully, "If I may ask, where is your family?"

"Up the street a block, at the corner. A good woman allowed us to hitch our mule and cart there."

"At the corner? Sorrel-colored hair?"

"Yes. Do you know her?"

"Her name is Tina. They call her La Alazana. She works here sometimes."

Feliciano shrugged. "There are different ways of being good."

Juan Rubio nodded. "Bring your cart to the corner opposite. I will meet you there."

Feliciano returned to Tina's house, and after many expressions of gratitude and other polite phrases for Doña Tina, María got back on the cart with her children. As he slowly led the mule down the street, Feliciano thought that sooner or later he would have to tell María who Doña Tina was. But that could wait.

When they got to the corner opposite El Danubio Azul, they saw Juan Rubio waiting for them on a light spring wagon pulled by a big work horse and loaded with firewood and other things. "What is all this for?" asked Feliciano.

"The house has a wood stove. Have you lanterns?"

"One."

"I brought a couple more. And some kerosene. A few groceries."

"Friend, I cannot accept all this from you."

"It is not from me," Juan Rubio said in his soft, respectful voice. "You and your family can ride on the wagon."

"I don't think I want to do that."

"Think of the lady and the children. With your permission I'll move some of your things to the wagon." He began to transfer some of their belongings from the cart to the wagon, and Feliciano helped him, too tired to argue.

Once things were arranged to Juan Rubio's satisfaction, he walked ahead, leading the cart. The mule, with a short rest and a lighter load, traveled somewhat faster than she had earlier that afternoon. Feliciano and his family followed on the wagon. East for three blocks, then a turn to the right and four blocks more. They were at the edge of town. The chaparral loomed in the gathering dusk some two hundred yards away, but the street was graveled, in contrast to the dirt streets they had traversed. The house stood almost alone on the right side of the street. Another house near the corner, a corral, then the house. And empty space to the next street.

"It has a big yard," said Juan Rubio as they went inside with a couple of lanterns. "There's running water. A privy."

It was a big, solid house, divided lengthwise into two long rooms, something like El Danubio Azul. The sturdy two-by-fours on the inside and the unpainted boards they held together looked almost new. Large and weatherproof. Feliciano marveled. He had never lived in a place like this before.

Juan Rubio helped Feliciano unload the cart and the wagon. When they finished, Feliciano asked, "How much do I owe you?"

"Don Faustino will tell you."

"Let me give you something. For your help." Juan Rubio shook his head. "I work for Don Faustino," he said mildly.

They exchanged "good nights" and as Juan Rubio started to leave, Feliciano asked, "Do you live in a house like this one?"

Juan Rubio half-smiled. "I live in a little room, behind El Danubio Azul. That's all I need, I have no family. Not anymore."

After Juan Rubio left, Feliciano unharnessed the mule and began to assemble María's bed while she made coffee. The children were asleep on a mattress laid on the floor. Rubio had left them a large sack of groceries and several loaves of bread. Feliciano felt he was dreaming all this, that perhaps the *rinche* had shot him before they entered Jonesville and he was out of his head.

2

Feliciano was at El Danubio Azul just before ten next morning. Juan Rubio had opened the saloon and was sweeping. It was not until some time later that Faustino Bello arrived, bouncy and bright-eyed. "*Buenos días,*" he said to both of them. Then to Feliciano, "Are you settled? How do you like the house?"

"It's a very good place. But I wonder if I'll be able to afford it."

"I think you will. Was Juan helpful?"

"He was very kind."

"That's his way. He hasn't been here long, but I already depend a lot on him. Doesn't say much, though."

"I would like to know about the house. Whether I can afford it."

"If you want to rent, it will be four dollars a month, you pay for the water. If you want to buy, it will cost you $230, $200 for the house and $30 for the lot. You pay two dollars a week. It's a big lot, 75 by 150 feet, and good land too."

"It is very much land, and a good house."

"It was a *cantina* for a very short while. That's why the street is graveled. Called Sobre Las Olas, the Judge likes waltzes. But it didn't make any money. Property will be going up in price because we soon will be at war. But the Judge does not want to wait. Some tenants can tear a place to pieces. And if it's vacant, people will carry off most of the house, bit by bit. If I were you I'd buy it."

"I'm not sure I could pay that much a week and feed my family."

"You don't think you could live on eight dollars a week?"

"Eight dollars a week?" echoed Feliciano. He had expected seven dollars at the most.

"That's after I take out the two dollars weekly for the house and lot," replied Faustino. "Your salary will be ten dollars. That's all we can pay you now. It may be more later on, if the Judge finds you useful in other ways. I think he expects to. But this way the house and lot will be yours in a little more than two years. I wouldn't miss the chance."

"I think I will buy," Feliciano said, "and perhaps, if I can go home at noon, I can give you a down payment."

"You will be working from noon till midnight, so you can go home now if you want. Eat your noon meal at home. Early, so you can be here at twelve. And bring a taco or two, *lonche* as people call it, to grab a bite as you work. No time off for supper; our busiest time is from six to eleven, when the soldiers come. You can keep what you bring for supper on ice with the beer. By the way, are you religious?"

"Truth is I am not."

"So much the better, because you will be working Sundays. But you can take Wednesdays off."

"It's all right with me."

Feliciano thanked him and left to tell María about their good fortune. Faustino Bello stared at his retreating form for a few moments. "Down payment?" he said to himself.

María was overjoyed at the news. "God is helping us! Because of little Guálinto, I just know! Gumersindo is begging Him to help us. And Mama too. So Guálinto can go to school and to college and become a leader of his people as Gumersindo wanted."

Feliciano did not believe God took an interest in their affairs. In fact, he was not sure God existed. But he too was happy about his good luck and aware of his promise to Gumersindo. He now had a chance to fulfill that promise. He ate hurriedly and got ready to go. Before he put on his hat he reached under María's bed and took out a worn saddlebag. "Now is the time to make use of what Mama left us," he told María.

"She must have foreseen this," María answered. "She had a gift, you know. And now she too is looking after us in Heaven."

"So be it." Feliciano chucked the baby under the chin and left for his new job. He got to El Danubio Azul well before noon. Faustino was behind the bar, polishing some glasses. He looked up and saw Feliciano with the saddlebag on his shoulder. Calling Juan Rubio to tend the bar, he followed Feliciano into the back where he had a desk, a table and some chairs in the corner farthest from the doors.

"What's that?" he asked as Feliciano laid the heavy leather bag on the table. "Did you find buried treasure?"

"It isn't much," replied Feliciano, "all quarters and half-dollars. See?" He poured out the contents. "Our mother left it to us when she died. She had been saving them since she and my father got married, I believe. She saved nickels and dimes and changed them for quarters and half-dollars."

Faustino arranged the coins in little piles. "Sixty-nine dollars and seventy-five cents. How long did your mother live after she married?"

"About forty-five years, I guess."

"She saved about a dollar fifty per year. She must have been a strong-willed woman."

"She was," said Feliciano, taking a quarter out of his pocket and laying it down on the table. "That makes seventy dollars even for the down payment on the house and lot."

Faustino shook his head. He reached down and opened a little safe on the floor beside his desk, swept the coins into a canvas moneybag and put the bag in the safe. From the safe he took five gold eagles and put them on the table. "Twenty dollars down is enough. You keep the other fifty, for things that might happen. Illness, let's say. And these five *onzas* are easier to carry and easier to hide than a hundred half-dollars. I'd tell you to put the money in the bank, but I'm sure you wouldn't want to do it." Feliciano shook his head. "Well, take them! The Judge's lawyer will be by this evening and we can draw up the papers. And now to work." Feliciano thanked him and put the coins in his pocket, thinking, "In less than two years."

The afternoon hours were fairly quiet and pleasant for Feliciano. He helped Juan Rubio bring some beer kegs from the back room, and he took lessons from Faustino on how to polish a glass, how to serve a drink of whiskey. Then Faustino sat down at one of the tables and had Feliciano bring a tray crowded with beer mugs full of water. Feliciano placed the mugs all around the table without spilling any of the water. *Barrio* men dropped in now and then and ordered shots of mezcal which Feliciano served them. During the hottest part of the afternoon two drummers walked in, carrying their heavy sample cases and sweating in their blue suits. They ordered beer and Faustino took Feliciano with him behind the bar.

"I'm going to show you how to draw a beer with a good head," Faustino said. He drew the beer and handed the mug to one of the drummers while Feliciano watched. "Now, you get the other one." The second drummer did not look too pleased being part of a practice session, but

Feliciano drew a mug much like the one Faustino had drawn. The second drummer looked happier when he took the mug.

It was cool and pleasant inside the *cantina*, and Feliciano thought about his good fortune. But for Judge Norris he might be dead or out in the hot sun, pulling stumps out of the ground for a dollar a day or less, and the prospect of earning nothing when it rained. It was the lot of the Mexicotexan that the Anglosaxon should use him as a tool for the Mexican's undoing. The chaparral had been the Mexicotexan's guarantee of freedom. While it existed, it served as a refuge to the *ranchero* fleeing from an alien law. The chaparral and the flats had made cattle-raising possible; and even the small farmers—their little parcels of land tucked deep in the brush—had been comparatively independent.

But the American had begun to "develop" the land. He had it cleared and made it into cotton fields, into citrus orchards and towns. And it was the Mexicotexan's brown muscular arms that felled the trees. He wielded the machete against the smaller brush and strained his back pulling tree stumps out of the ground. For this he got enough to eat for the day and the promise of more of the same tomorrow. As day laborer clearing more chaparral, as cotton and fruit picker for as few cents a day as he could subsist on. Every stroke of the ax, every swing of the mattock clinched his own misfortune. Feliciano had been spared all that. He had a quiet well-paying job in the shade.

Some time later a bugle at Fort Jones blew a lively little tune. Faustino pulled out his watch. "Five o'clock. On the dot." The clock on the wall said five ten. "The bugle is calling the soldiers to supper," Faustino explained. "They'll be here between five-thirty and six." Feliciano thought he was ready for them until he saw their sweaty red faces as they came pouring in, laughing and talking among themselves with a lot of back-slapping and friendly goddams. The muscles of his back tightened as he stared at them, not moving from the spot where he stood. Some of the soldiers crowded up to the bar, and Faustino and Juan Rubio began to draw beer for them. Others sat at tables and pounded on them, chanting, "Beer! Beer! Beer!"

Faustino came up to him and told him to draw for six of the "boys" at the corner table. "And get rid of that vinegar look on your face. Smile, man! Smile!" He went back to the beer kegs, joking and laughing loudly with the soldiers standing at the bar. Juan Rubio was also at the spigots. He did not joke or laugh the way Faustino did, but he did smile and answer in his quiet way when the soldiers talked to him. Swallowing hate and pride, Feliciano went to one of the barrels and drew six mugs of beer. He must not give himself away, he told himself. For his sister's sake, for Gumersindo's son. He kept his eyes on the spigots, though he was aware that the soldiers at the bar were trying to talk and joke with him. In silence he served the beer at the table. The soldiers stopped talking among themselves, and the biggest of them said something to Feliciano. The others laughed. Feliciano kept his eyes on the table as he finished putting down the mugs. "Hey!" the big soldier said. "I'm talking to you, man!" Feliciano looked at the soldier, his eyes full of hatred, and then turned away toward the bar. "Hey!" the big soldier shouted after him. "Hey, you! Can't you take a joke?"

Feliciano did not look back. He drew a round of beer for the table next to the one he had just waited on. As he was serving the beer the big soldier at the corner table kept staring at him. When Feliciano finished setting down the mugs and turned to leave, the big soldier got up and grabbed at his shoulder. "What's the matter with you?" he said. "Looking for a fight?"

Instantly Faustino the Little Barrel came bounding between them. "Hold everything, you two! Hold everything!" He was facing the big soldier, his hands palm outward.

"What's the matter with him, anyway?" the big soldier said. "Looks as if he hates the fellahs at this table or something."

"You don't understand," Faustino said soothingly. "You just don't understand." Then, lowering his voice a little, "He's just in from the country, doesn't speak much English. This is his first day on the job. He doesn't understand what you're saying, and he thinks *you* are insulting him and trying to pick a fight." Then, lowering his voice to a near whisper, "I think he's just a little bit scared of you."

"Ahah!" the soldier's face broke into a smile as big as himself. "Ah-meego!" he said to Feliciano over Faustino's head. "Me mucho like may-hee-can-oe! No worry. No com-bat-tee you and me. Shake!" He stretched out his hand.

Feliciano took it, forcing a grin. *"Amigo. Bueno,"* he said. The soldier's hand was big and strong but oddly soft at the same time.

"So everything's okay," said Faustino. "Enjoy your beer." The big soldier sat down and waved as Feliciano left with El Barrilito. Feliciano waved back.

Faustino took Feliciano aside. "Listen," he said. "I know how you feel, but don't ruin your chances at this job. You know it wasn't soldiers who killed your brother-in-law. Or all those other people. The only shooting they've done was at armed men who were shooting at them." Men like me, thought Feliciano. "They're just a bunch of kids, most of them. They'd just as soon be home far away from here if they could. They've been trying to joke with you, not laugh at you. And you know enough English to understand that, if you would just listen instead of flying into a rage. Smile when they talk to you, and if you don't understand what they say, just nod your head. But smile, godammit! Smile!

Smile!"

"I'll try," Feliciano replied. And he did try, though at first it was hard because he could not keep his mind off the very recent past. But as the evening wore on he found it easier, and he even began to exchange a few words with the soldiers in his halting English. They began to call him "Cowboy" instead of "Gloomy Gus." Soon it was nine o'clock and the bugle at Fort Jones blew a sad, lonely call.

"They call that 'Taps,'" Faustino told Feliciano. "It means all soldiers must go back to the barracks." But only a few of them did. Feliciano remarked on that and El Barrilito explained. "There's a second call at eleven. Then they shut the gates. Most of them wait for the second call before leaving, and they get in through a hole in the fence they know about."

"What if they get caught?"

"It's bad for them. But the fact that they stay until eleven is good for us. Here, I have another job for you." Faustino took a couple of cognac bottles, loosened the corks and put them on a tray along with a dozen small glasses. Go through the back door and take them to the *señores* who are sitting out there."

Feliciano had forgotten about the high board fence that enclosed the back of the saloon. There was another room there, behind the saloon's back room, hidden from public view by the fence and with its own entrance through a doorlike gate at the very back of the fence. Many chairs and two large tables were there, but only one table was occupied. Several men sat around it, all of whom appeared to be Mexicans, except for Judge Norris.

"*Buenas noches, señores*," Feliciano said and began to put the bottles and the glasses on the table.

"*Hola, García*," said the Judge, "*¿cómo van las cosas?*"

"Things are going very well, *señor juez*."

"I hear you bought yourself a house."

"I have begun to do so, *señor juez*. And again, I am deeply indebted to you."

"Has Faustino got you your papers and your poll tax yet?"

"Not yet, *señor*."

"He'll do it tomorrow," said the Judge. "He'd better. I'll be giving you some extra work pretty soon."

3

After the Civil War the Fifteenth Amendment gave the right to vote to all male citizens of the United States, but in some parts of the country, including most of Texas, Mexicans as well as Negroes were denied that right by being barred from voting in the primaries. Not so in Jonesville-on-the-Grande, which was more than 90 percent Mexican. In Jonesville everybody voted, including some gentlemen residing in the cemetery, not to mention a few of the living and breathing whose residence and place of birth was the sister city of Morelos across the river.

The same political party was always in power, but that did not preclude the free exercise of democracy. The party was divided into two factions, the Blues and the Reds, led by two influential men with pioneer roots. Privately they were the very best of friends, but publicly they attacked each other in print and in speeches when campaigning for city and county elections. These were hotly fought political contests, which always led to fistfights and occasionally a shooting or two. But whichever side won, and usually it was the Blues, life went on as before, except for a few of the voters who insisted on holding grudges from one election to the other. The successful side always was the one that was able to convince the most voters to allow their campaign workers to buy them their poll taxes and to school them in the voting process.

The leader of the Blues was Judge Robert (Bob) Norris. He was bilingual, with blood ties to his constituents. His grandmother, if you were speaking in English, had been Spanish. Pure Castilian, daughter of an *hidalgo* family. If you were speaking in Spanish, she had been Mexican. Even Judge Norris himself said so when he was making campaign speeches in Spanish. Some gossips whispered that Grandmother had worn her straight black hair in two long braids, and that she made her tortillas from corn she ground on her own *metate*. There were cynics, however, who believed Judge Norris encouraged such rumors to please his Mexican constituents. There were no flyspecks on him. It was he who had invented the knotted cord as a voting device.

The Blue party headquarters was—appropriately enough—at El Danubio Azul, the saloon run by one of the Judge's ward bosses, and quite profitably since most of its clientele was made up of soldiers from nearby Fort Jones. Political meetings were held in the back, where strategy for the Blue party was planned, and where political refugees from Mexico were allowed also to meet and plot the overthrow of whatever Mexican government happened to be in power. In the saloon up front Faustino Bello, alias El Barrilito, was king. He was a short man, not over five feet six, but he weighed close to two hundred pounds. This ball of belly, fat and muscle could move with incredible speed when the situation demanded, and he carried a devastating punch in each of his pudgy fists. He knew nothing about the finer points of boxing. When he had to fight, he let his opponent hit him until he got a chance to hit back. Once was usually enough.

Faustino was host, entertainer and bouncer at El Danubio Azul. The soldiers loved him in his first two capacities, and respected him in the third. He would sit on an empty beer barrel at the end of the bar now and then during the night, laughing uproariously in a great voice, telling dirty jokes in broken English, calling soldiers by name or nickname. Or he would go around from table to table patting them on the back. Every now and then he broke open a keg of low-priced beer, and drinks were on the house. El Barrilito was probably the only Mexican in Jonesville who could beat up a soldier and not get mobbed by the rest of the army. And he only did it when it was necesary to keep the peace in El Danubio Azul.

Here it was that Feliciano came to work as bartender on Judge Norris' recommendation. He did not get his poll tax the very next day after he started work, as the Judge had said he would. It took several days, but when he did get it, he also was given a copy of his newly issued birth certificate, prepared from information in the baptismal records of the Catholic church in San Pedrito. Judge Norris prided himself on his ability to judge the character of men, and he thought he had seen something in Feliciano that he could make use of, now that the Blue faction seemed to be losing ground against the Reds. In a few weeks Feliciano had a new job, assistant to Faustino Bello in Bello's capacity as boss of the Second and Third Wards of Jonesville where most of the Mexicans lived. Feliciano's new home was in the Second Ward, Twenty-second Precinct, or as its inhabitants called it, El Dos Veintidós. He still worked behind the bar when political business was slack, but that was not often. Elections were coming soon, and the Judge was worried about the chances of the Blues.

Feliciano was outfitted with a buggy drawn by a fine-looking sorrel gelding. His job was to visit every house in the Second and Third Wards and talk the men into letting the Blues buy their poll taxes. If they were willing, he took down their names, addresses and their ages. Feliciano discovered he was very good at this kind of work. He was an earnest and fluent speaker. Taller than most Mexicans, he cut a good figure in his boots, cowboy hat and full mustache, which he had grown again. The buggy had a folding top, and he drove with the top down. He had what some people called a manly presence. He talked to people in their homes, convincing them of the benefits of voting for the Blues. I have become a drummer, he thought at times, except that I buy votes from door to door instead of selling anything.

Once the canvassing for votes was over, it was time for the *carne asada* parties given the faithful, where barbecued beef and goat were abundant as were cold beer and mezcal. It was Feliciano's job, with Juan Rubio's help, to arrange for and supervise these feasts. Sheriff Emilio Apodaca named him a special deputy at this time, and he began to wear a forty-four in his belt, just as in other times. Sometimes they get drunk and disorderly, he had been told, and you may have to use your pistol barrel on a few heads. But try not to shoot anybody. He must have looked quite imposing to the celebrants, for he never had to use the gun on anyone. He also made use of the buggy to take gifts of food—mostly eggs and vegetables—and candy for the children to the homes of the main supporters of the Blues in each precinct, the ones who had many relatives and *compadres* and could deliver many votes. The candy he bought at the Rodríguez grocery store; vegetables and eggs he got from his neighbor Don José's farm, all with the Judge's money, of course. He also took it upon himself to make the same gifts to needy people in his precinct, including a widow named Vera, who of course could not vote but who was raising two little boys and having a hard time supporting them. They lived on the block behind his house, and his nephew often played with the boys, though they were a bit older than he.

It was a week before the election, and in spite of all the preparations, Judge Norris felt the voting would be close. That was when Feliciano came up with his *Arriba los azules* idea. Many years before, the Judge had thought up the use of the knotted cord. Since most of his constituents could not read, he took a cord and tied little knots on it, spaced so that the knots would coincide on the ballot sheet with the names of his candidates. The cord was the same length as the ballot sheet, so all the voter had to do was lay the cord on the ballot and mark every name that was opposite a knot. The knotted cords were prepared by precinct workers and given out to voters along with their poll tax receipts just before election time. The Blue party won big that year. The Reds, however, were quick to catch on, and they too had their precinct workers make little knotted cords for their supporters. So the Judge's idea no longer was a major factor in his election victories.

Furthermore, the device was not perfect. Some of the Blues had trouble deciding which end of the knotted cord was up, and they often placed it on the ballot sheet upside down. This produced some odd results on the ballots, and many of the Blue votes were invalidated. Since the Reds were stronger in the more prosperous and more literate precincts—which included more and more newly arrived Anglos—they were beginning to pose a serious challenge to Bob Norris' control of the city. Feliciano's solution was as simple as the Judge's original idea. He suggested that the top end of the cord, down to the first knot, be dyed blue; and that the Blue supporters use "Up With the Blues" as their battle cry. There were no knotted cords used upside down among the Blues that year, and the Reds were buried by an avalanche of Blue votes.

Judge Norris was delighted, both with the results of the election and with his own foresight in having hired Feliciano García. To Feliciano the Judge's success meant higher pay and better working hours. He now helped Juan Rubio open the saloon at ten in the morning and ran it on his own until two in the afternoon, when Faustino Bello arrived and took charge. From two until five, he ran political errands on the buggy that was now practically his own, and he took advantage of those hours downtown to take care of personal matters as well. At ten p.m. he went home, except that on two weekdays he worked from ten in the morning until two in the afternoon. Feliciano liked the new hours, even though it meant that he did not get a full day off each week. He was away from the drunken soldiers a good deal of the time. Although he had learned to tolerate them and they had come to be quite friendly toward him, he still felt uncomfortable in the presence of so many Gringos. And his new schedule gave him time to do things around the house.

The far back of the yard flooded whenever it rained, so he planted it with shoots from banana bushes and soon had a banana grove in the making. On one side of the house he planted a fig tree and a papaya plant like the one in their old home in San Pedrito. On the other side was a guayaba tree. He now had enough money to hire Blue partisans to help him fix up the house. The two long rooms became four, the board windows were replaced with glass window panes. The inside was finished with thin planking, and the two doors facing front were replaced by "store-bought" ones with locks and knobs. Inside and out, the house was painted a bright blue. He added another room a few yards back of the main house to serve as storeroom and bedroom for himself. In front he added a porch which soon was covered with honeysuckle, and on the porch—as the crownpiece of his efforts—there was a swing. Some day, when electric and sewage lines reached their *barrio*, they would have electric lights for Guálinto to study by, and a "patent" toilet with water and a chain. A phonograph, even. But for the present the porch swing was enough of a symbol of the family's prosperity. At the same time he was putting away as many of the little gold eagles as he could manage.

Life was good, but he was still unhappy. The guilt over Gumersindo's death hung over him, and some nights he dreamed that he and El Negro had just found Gumersindo dying in the dusty road outside San Pedrito. Except that Gumersindo would look up at him in the dream and ask accusingly, "Are you keeping your promise?"

And in his dream Feliciano would answer, "I am doing all I can. Your son will grow up to be a great man, a leader of his people."

The boy must grow up without hate in his heart, Gumersindo had always said. But how could Feliciano teach him not to hate Gringos when Feliciano could not stop hating them. There were a few good ones. And then there was Don Roberto, the Judge, but he was Mexican in Feliciano's eyes. He also hated himself. His sister would mourn for Gumersindo till the end of her days, he thought every time he saw her black-clad figure. There was Don José, next door, who obviously was interested in her, but she paid him no attention.

So Feliciano must make as much money as he could, at jobs he enjoyed but that sometimes made him doubt whether he was doing the right thing. All for his nephew's education. The little girls did not enter into his plans. They would grow up and marry like all girls did. But for the little boy Feliciano worked and hoped. Guálinto would have to be a learned man in order to help his people. How he would help them Feliciano had no idea, but he knew he must give the boy as much education as he could.

When the boy began to walk and say his first words, to ask questions and to explore, his uncle was always finding in him signs of precocity and future greatness. On his evenings off he would sit down in the kitchen and take the little boy between his knees, listening to his childish talk. "See, María!" he would say to his sister, who moved about preparing supper. "This boy is going to be somebody some day!"

And María's face, puckered up by the heat of the stove, would relax into a smile. Growing old before her time, irritable and moody, for a moment she was like the María that Gumersindo had loved.

One day Feliciano told María, "You must teach him his letters soon, just as we learned them at the *escuelita* in San Pedrito."

"In this town Mexicans can go to public school."

"I know. But he will learn his letters the Gringo way. It is not the same. How good it would be if he learned to read in Spanish before that."

"I will do so," María replied.

"I wish I had time to help you."

"Perhaps Doña Domitila will help me. She reads a lot."

Feliciano frowned and did not reply. Doña Domitila always made him feel uncomfortable. María turned back to her stove to hide a smile.

4

In later years George W. Gómez would remember his childhood home as an enchanted place. The porch of the blue frame house was covered with honeysuckle vines that screened a corner of it entirely from view, forming a fragrant, shady cave. The front yard was full of rose bushes with flowers of many colors, which he scrupulously avoided for fear not only of the thorns but of his mother's wrath as well. Then there were the figs, the papayas, the guayabas growing by the sides of the house.

But it was the vast jungle of banana trees choking the backyard that fascinated him. Here he loved to wander in the cool sunny mornings and the drowsy silent afternoons when everybody else who was not at work slept the siesta. The green stalks, waving ten or twelve feet above the ground, looked like forest giants to him, and he would swear when he was a man that they were at least twenty-five feet high. Here Guálinto hunted tigers and engaged pirates. Here he became a lone Indian tracking the wounded deer. Here he was first startled by beauty in the brilliant red of a cardinal bird against the wet-green leaves and saddened by the cool, gentle whisperings of the evening breeze.

But night changed the world. With darkness the banana grove and the trees beyond it became a haunted wood where lurked demons, skeletons and white-robed women with long long hair. The city's stormy politics had thrown up a vomit of murders and gun battles. Guálinto's immediate neighborhood, being at the edge of town, had seen more than its share of bloodshed. By that tree a man was killed by his best friend. Politics. Over there a woman was attacked and murdered. On a big hackberry beyond the backyard fence was a cross made of big nails driven into the trunk. Nobody knew exactly why the cross was there, but there were many stories explaining it. Here, there, everywhere were memories of the unhallowed dead. They haunted the night. They made the darkness terrible. So Guálinto's nights were filled with delicious thrills and wide-eyed terror. His mother tried to calm his fears with religion. Everybody believed, with the possible exception of his Uncle Feliciano, who seemed to believe in nothing. However, he did not interfere with his mother's teaching religion to her son. So the boy learned a whole rosary of paternosters, aves and credos to protect him from evil.

He wore a tin likeness of the Virgin hung around his neck on a string, and he was taken to church on Sundays, where he learned more about Hell than about Heaven. And when he went to bed every night he said a prayer along with his mother:

"I must die, I know not when,
I must die, I know not where,
I must die, I know not how.
But this I do know:
If I die without the grace of God
I shall burn in Hell forever."

Then his mother put him to bed, satisfied she had done her duty toward making him an upright, God-fearing man. But after the lamp was blown out he feared sleep, for it might bring death silently on its wings. He hated God for being so cruel. That gave him a terrible sinking feeling and he started to pray, fervently and with trembling lips, for God had heard his thoughts and even now He was frowning in rage.

But sleep would take hold of him unawares. When he woke, the blessed sun was shining, and the only feeling in his stomach was hunger. "Mama," he asked one morning after breakfast, "why can't I remember things when I was little like you do? You can tell the prettiest stories about the time you were little."

"Because you are still little, *hijito*," his mother replied.

"Oh," he said, not understanding at all. After a short silence he came back to the question. "But Mama, why can you remember so many things while I can't? You can remember back to ten years ago."

"Ten years ago you weren't born yet." His mother was silent for a while. Then, "Ten years ago you were in Heaven with the little angels."

"But I don't remember."

"Of course you can't, silly. Nobody can."

He was silent, thinking. Thinking, thinking. If I was up there I ought to remember, just like I remember I was in the banana grove yesterday because I was. I was born but I don't remember that either. And she says I was up there. Was it me? With wings? How can Mama know? If nobody can remember. Maybe it wasn't me at all. Maybe it was somebody else. Maybe I'm somebody else!

A cold emptiness settled into his stomach. Familiar objects suddenly looked strange to him, as though he were out of his body and looking at himself and all other things from a distance. Strange, terrible questions surged inside of him, questions for which he had no words, no concrete form, so that they floated around in his head like little clouds. Why am I, I? Why am I not somebody else? This was as close as he could come to expressing them. Why is my mother my mother? Why are things things and how do I know that they are? Will they be the same when I die like the prayer says, and how will I know they will be the same when I am dead and can't see them any more? A numbing loneliness seized him and he felt like crying out. Then, for a moment, he almost grasped and put into solid thought the vague and desolating questions which floated inside his head. But as his mind reached out to hold on to them they dissolved like spots before his eyes. His mother was his mother again, and she was asking him if he wasn't feeling well.

"No, Mama," he replied. "I'm all right."

Thinking, remembering.

5

There were years when spring came early to the Golden Delta of the Rio Grande, and this was one of those years. The morning sun, shining from a clear-blue sky, gave a warm, pleasant tang to the cool breeze that still smelled of winter. Already was the sour-orange tree by the fence putting out its delicate shoots that soon would become white perfume. This was the time of year when the chaparral for a brief time became a kind of fairyland. When the little dew-covered plots of grass that grew between each thorny tree were carpeted with pink primroses, and the patches of open field were purple with the wild violet that Mexicans call *alfombrilla*, little carpet. The thorny trees of the chaparral—the mesquite, the ebony, the huisache—were covered with their fluffy flowers, the first in pastel shades, the second an ivory white, the third an old-gold yellow, all three of a delicate, almost imperceptible fragrance that purified more than perfumed the air. The yucca shot out its wax-like blossoms like a white-robed sentinel of the woods, until Lent arrived and people would harvest the white leaves and boil them into a salad that tasted very much like the meat they abstained from during the Lenten period. Spiders spread out their webs from one branch to another, and in the early morning sun their dew-covered strands shone like jewels set on lace. The mocking bird sang in the thickets all through the sunny day and on into the moonlit night. It was such a morning in late February, and Doña Domitila walked into the yard back of the house, where María was washing. Doña Domitila was the spinster sister of Doña Teodora Gracia and lived with the Gracia family across the street. Two sisters never looked so unlike each other as Doña Teodora and Doña Domitila. When Doña Teodora walked into a house the floorboards creaked. She was big, fat and aggressive. Doña Domitila was spare and self-effacing, inquisitive and gossipy. But she also was a learned woman by community standards; she read a lot of novels. And she was helping María teach Guálinto to read in Spanish.

"*Ave María Purísima*," Doña Domitila said in the sing-songy manner the phrase required.

"*Buenos días de Dios*," María replied, turning from the soapy tub beneath the willow. "Doña Domitila!" she continued as she wiped her reddened hands on her apron. "The shots, did you hear them? What was it? Do you know?"

"Know! Goodness, yes! It was horrible! Oh, Doña María, it was horrible!"

"Who? What?"

"It was Filomeno Menchaca."

"Oh," María said shortly. Then with something of compassion, "Poor Filomeno. But he was bound to end that way, may God forgive him." She crossed herself.

"Hmph," said Domitila with a toss of her head. "He's probably roasting in the Fifth Hell by now. After all the men *he* killed. I'd swear the law themselves had him killed. He knew too much about a lot of things."

"You shouldn't talk about such things," María said. "It could be dangerous, you know."

"Perhaps you're right. But it was horrible."

"Did you see it?"

"Mercy no. Not the incident." Domitila mouthed the word with relish. It was a popular word these days in the papers: international incidents all over the world. "Not the incident, Doña María, but I saw the body. Then the law came and made us go away. Oh, but it was horrible. Have you ever seen a dead man all torn up by bullets, Doña María?"

María shuddered. "No," she said in a small voice. "No. Never."

"Don Feliciano must have." Domitila gave María a shrewd look. "Some people say he was in the Revolution."

"He may have been," said María with a frown.

"By the way, was he home during the shooting? Isn't today his day off?"

"He went to Morelos. On an errand."

"Still in politics. That man is going to be rich someday, Doña María." María frowned. "Sometimes I wish he wasn't in politics."

Domitila sighed. "Oh, he's a wonderful man, your brother Feliciano. He wasn't made to stay in the country pulling up stumps like so many

other men. I wonder why he's never married. Is it true that he's thinking
of running for sheriff?"

"Absolutely not," María said quickly. "On the contrary, he hopes to
rent some land and grow his own vegetables for the new store."

"A farm owner too! How wonderful! When is he starting, Doña
María?"

"It's just in his mind," replied María, sorry she had said anything
about it.

Guálinto's head appeared beside the trunk of the willow. He remained half-hidden as if reluctant to be seen. That was not peculiar in
itself, he was still somewhat shy before Doña Domitila. But there was
more than shyness in his appearance. His lips were pale and he was
shaking. His mother's casual glance became a sharp look.

"What's the matter with you?" she demanded. "Where have you
been?"

Guálinto tried to slow his heavy breathing. He swallowed hard.
"Nothing," he mumbled. "Nowhere."

"It was probably the shooting, poor little dear," said Doña Domitila.
Guálinto shot her a look of startled hostility.

"That was it," María agreed. "It must have frightened him. But it's
silly to get so worked up over the sound of a few shots. Why, he's almost
dead of fright."

Guálinto hung his head and lost some of his tenseness. "Look at
Doña Domitila," his mother said. "She *saw* the dead man. Is she scared
like you?"

Guálinto remained silent, his eyes on the ground. "Go into the
house, you coward," his mother ordered. "In a little while I'll go and
make you some tea."

He walked off docilely toward the house. As he moved away he
heard his mother say to Doña Domitila, "He scares so easily."

Doña Domitila said something he could not catch. But he breathed
a bit easier. It had come out all right, his mother did not suspect. But
he felt a hot lump in his throat. He was no coward. Someday he would
show them, his mother and all the rest. Someday he would grow up and
then he would go out and kill five or six Gringos like Gregorio Cortez
and Cheno Cortinas. But now he had to be a coward to all the world.
He climbed into bed and relaxed his tense little limbs. But though he
buried his face in the pillow, he could still see it, everything.

Doña Domitila, she *saw* the body. He snorted into the pillow in
spite of the hot throbbing at his temples. His mother had told him many
times not to play with the Vera boys at their house. If they wanted to
play with him they should come to Guálinto's yard and play there. It
wasn't because of Mrs. Vera, she said; she was a nice lady. She just

didn't like for Guálinto to play on that street. But the Vera boys were such wonderful guys. Chicho, who was seven, was a regular fellow. You could suggest any old game and Chicho would play it with you. And he would let you win too. He was always smiling with those big white teeth of his. And nine-year-old Poncho was Guálinto's hero. He walked with a self-confident swagger and laughed in a way that made you laugh too. Nothing was too difficult for Poncho. He could climb the highest trees, going out over the intertwining branches from one tree to another like Tarzan. He knew where the birds' nests were, and he could make the best slingshots and bows and arrows you ever saw. And though he never looked for a fight, there were few boys in the *barrio* Poncho couldn't lick.

So Guálinto liked to play with the Vera boys over at their house, and he did so whenever he had a chance, though his mother always scolded him if she found out. That morning Guálinto was playing with Chicho out on the sidewalk in front of the Veras. The sun shone on their unheeding heads as they bent over a captive red ant. The man next door had been splitting wood. He stopped now and came over to the fence to watch, his silk shirt wet with sweat. "That ant is going to sting you," he said.

"Oh, no," answered Guálinto. "We're good ant-catchers. We've caught hundreds and millions of them, haven't we, Chicho?"

Chicho giggled and nodded and the man chuckled. "You don't even know how much a million is," he said.

Chicho looked up admiringly. "You know how much a million is, Meno?"

Meno scratched his head. "Can't say that I do exactly. But it's more than a thousand."

"More than a hundred even?" persisted Chicho.

"Sure, sure. A thousand's more than a hundred." Meno looked up the street where two men were walking toward them. "Some friends of mine," he said and moved down along the fence to meet them at the gate. "*Qui'ubo, muchachos,*" he said with a grin.

One of the pair smiled a frank, engaging smile. "Nothing new, Filomeno. How's things with you?" Still smiling he pulled a gun from under his coat and fired.

Filomeno clutched at his shirt front. His mouth tightened and his eyes grew big with surprise. For a dull, heavy moment he swayed drunkenly, one hand shielding his breast and the other pawing at his empty belt. Then the other man shot him—once, twice. Filomeno gave two short grunts as the bullets thudded into him, blasting the fabric of his shirt into little bits that flew in all directions like paper from a firecracker. He stumbled backward and fell heavily over the wood he had been splitting.

The two opened the gate and walked in. Filomeno was twisting and thrashing in the dirt, making choking piglike noises. Once his fingers closed over a stick of wood. He turned over and managed to sit up against the wood-pile, his silk shirt sticky and dark with blood, his face distorted and set like the flattened face of a wax figure. The two men watched him in silence. Then the first one shot him in the face. The bullet made a splattering sound and Meno pitched forward and didn't move any more. The two men walked out, carefully shutting the gate behind them.

Guálinto had stood watching it all, his hands tightly clenched around the pickets of the fence, his face pressed against them. He wanted to run when he saw the men walking out but he could not, anymore than he could take his eyes off the stained carcass sprawled on the woodpile. After the killers closed the gate they came toward him. He clung to the fence, and as the men came closer he shut his eyes. A hand touched his head and a voice said, "Better go home, boy." And the killers' measured steps died away.

When Guálinto opened his eyes at last, the men were a half-block away in the direction of the brush and the river. They walked leisurely, without a seeming care in the world. People were beginning to gather, all kinds of people. They seemed to spring out of nowhere and everywhere with the suddenness of apparitions. A big boy on a bicycle carrying some packages. Another on foot, in overalls, with a bag of groceries. Pale-faced and frightened. Then a fat red-faced man in a dimity undershirt, a portly woman wearing a dirty apron. They were quickly engulfed by a sea of faces that heaved and moved about in confusion. Dark faces, red faces, white pasty ones. Bearded faces and faces clean-shaven, thin ones, round ones. Men, women, hair top-knots, mustaches, shawls, hats. Faces high on tall men, faces closer to the ground. Faces with open, breathless mouths. Faces with lips tight and twisted as if their owners were holding back the need to vomit. Grim-looking faces, morbid strained faces with hungry probing eyes. A little girl's eyes peering from behind a skirt. The serious, puzzled face of a baby in a man's arms.

They had no eyes for Guálinto, those hungry searching faces. But he shrank from them, along the fence to a clump of *quelite* weeds growing by the fence post where Filomeno's yard bordered on that of the Veras. Here he crouched, darting looks in every direction through the maze of thick purple stalks. There was no sign of Chicho. He had vanished with the first shot. Some people opened the gate and went in, where they milled and pushed around the body till Guálinto could no longer see it. Everybody was speaking at once, softly as if in church, creating with their combined voices a deep, buzzing sound. Now and then a louder voice rose sharp and discordant above the hum of the crowd. Then the voice of an old man, dry and shallow like the twang of a cheap guitar. But commanding. The murmur of voices stopped.

"Don't touch him," the old man said. "We must leave everything as it is for the law. You over there, don't kick up the dirt. The law won't like it if you rub out any signs."

The law! The words pulsed in Guálinto's head. Half-pronounced, they set his throat throbbing. The law. He pushed himself deeper into the clump of weeds. They would come. They would take him away, pushing him along in front of them and cursing him. Then they would beat him to make him tell all he knew. They would make him a witness. The horror of the word struck him like a blow. Witness, informer, pariah. He had to escape before the police came. If only his legs would carry him. But they were limp like wet rags. He pleaded with himself for just a little strength and courage. Now ... One effort only ...

The murmur of the crowd took on a new sound and out of it leaped the words, "*Ahi viene la ley!*" Guálinto sank back against the fence. The law had come.

The gray touring automobile creaked to a stop by the sloping sidewalk amid an eddy of dust, and out of it stepped some men in Sunday suits and big hats. They walked casually up to the gate. Two were soft-looking, middle-aged men, one red-faced and clean-shaven, the older one a bit grizzled. The third was a pale slender young man. He was not wearing boots or a hat. He carried a pencil and a pad in one hand. The young man looked all around him with quick, curious eyes. He stared for a moment at the clump of weeds, and Guálinto quaked. But no. He was not looking at Guálinto. He was looking down the road. Stealthily Guálinto turned his head to look also and his heart beat faster. The men who had killed Filomeno were still in plain sight.

The young man with the pad and pencil pointed at the two men in the distance. The policemen glanced idly in that direction and turned to enter the gate. Again the young one pointed, and he said something Guálinto did not understand. The older of the other two answered, and he sounded annoyed. By now the crowd had begun to gather around the policemen. Their faces were animated, expectant. Even professional killers can be likable, and Filomeno Menchaca had many friends in the *barrio*. With a kind of repressed excitement the crowd glanced now at the officers, now at the distant figures. Men began telling each other just loud enough so the law could hear, "*Esos son.* That's them. They can still catch them." The killers were growing smaller and smaller in the distance.

The elder of the two policemen was annoyed. It was more than apparent in his voice when he addressed the young man. The young man talked back and the policeman spoke sharply and with finality. Then he turned to the crowd, *"Vamoose,"* he shouted. *"Vamoose pa' la casa."*

The law opened the gate and walked in while the crowd dispersed slowly and with many backward looks. Little groups of three or four straggled off in different directions, muttering and glancing at the officers and at the empty distance into which the two killers had disappeared. Angry, accusing looks were directed at the men of the law, who either did not notice them or did not care. After the crowd was gone they just stood around. They did not look for signs or anything like the old man had said they would. They just looked at the body. The oldest stepped over and stirred the body with the toe of his boot. He gave it a little kick and said something which made the red-faced one laugh. The young one did not laugh. After a while they moved away from the body and started talking to each other. They passed cigarets around and smoked. Even the young one was laughing by this time.

"Now!" Guálinto said to himself, trembling. He crawled out of the weeds and stood up. To get home he would have to pass in front of the gate, but he would do it slowly as if he were just walking by. He started on shaky legs, his eyes studying the ground in front of him. When he reached the gate, one of the men inside turned toward him and yelled. Guálinto froze. Out of the car came a fourth man carrying a black bag. He staggered up the grassy slope to the sidewalk and stood before Guálinto, breathing heavily. There was a strong smell of liquor on his breath. Then he pushed the boy aside and went in through the gate. Guálinto ran all the way home.

6

On Sunday mornings Guálinto went to church with his mother and the girls. It was an irksome thing, this going to church, but this Sunday it was worse. His mother had bought them all new clothes so there they went, all dressed up. Mama wore black as usual, but Maruca and Carmen were resplendent in yellow organdie. And Guálinto? He was dressed in something his mother called a sailor suit, a striped sissy-looking outfit with a big white collar, stiffly starched so that it chafed his neck. Not to mention a pair of new shoes, white like the collar, that pinched his feet. But his hair, that was what really got to him. His hair! Normally it was unruly and full of cowlicks that tended to make it wave and curl in all the wrong places. On Sundays, however, his mother rubbed it with brilliantine and combed it straight. That wasn't bad at all, not only because it smelled good but because his plastered-down hair looked darker brown than usual and that pleased him. He disliked being called *güero* and *gringo* because his hair was not as dark as that of other people. This time, though, his mother had been so busy buying clothes that she forgot to see if there was enough brilliantine. When time came for him to be dressed, she found only a little bit in the bottle. So she mixed some shortening with it to make it do.

"I smell of shortening!" he complained.

"No, you don't," said his mother. "You smell fine."

And now they were at church and already Guálinto was wishing the whole thing was over. It was just plain torture having to sit there for one whole hour. You couldn't move, you couldn't talk, you couldn't scratch. And kneeling was worst of all. At home his mother punished him by making him kneel in a corner until his knees were sore. And that was just for a little while.

Then there was the priest with his raspy voice and his holy threats. Guálinto had to sit at the very front with the rest of the boys, right underneath the pulpit. Here you couldn't fool around or stare out the window as easily as you could in the back rows. The priest leaned out of the pulpit over the boys like a thunder cloud over a cornfield. His looks were dark and threatening, and he rumbled and flashed as he worked up to the full fury of his verbal storm. He pounded on the pulpit, he stretched out his fist over their heads. He screamed out a phrase of holy anger. Then he stopped abruptly while the echo went screaming on. He let all the awful meaning of his words sink in during the silence. Then he spoke again and his speech was soft, his speech was sweet. His words were a lazy little stream that wandered through cool green reeds.

Like stalks before a storm, so were the children before the priest. They flinched at his out-thrust fist, they cowered at his shout. They rustled and sighed when he softened. Their faces mimicked his face. And they shuddered, wide-eyed and silent, while he painted the agonies of Hell.

"Hold one finger, just one finger, over a candle flame and see what pain it will cause you. In less than one minute. Then try to imagine the agony of Hell, where the fire that shall burn your whole body forever and ever shall be as that candle is to the sun."

The children moved restlessly and rubbed at their fingers. The priest was droning now. " ... And even in communities that call themselves pious, so weak is our flesh that for every soul that is saved a thousand shall burn." Guálinto gave a fleeting moment of sympathy to the thousand souls that must burn so he might go directly to Heaven. He tried to think of all the bad people he knew and he wondered if they would number up to a thousand. He didn't know how much that was but he did know it must be an awful lot. There was Manuel the pickpocket and Concho who drowned little puppies. And Pedrito the homosexual. And Filomeno Menchaca. He was dead already but maybe God would be in a good mood when Guálinto came up and would count Filomeno among Guálinto's thousand. But gee! He hadn't thought about his uncle, his mother and his sisters. He counted them out on his fingers. Five including himself. Five thousand. The sum had an infinite ring to it. Whew! Were there that many people in the world? Oh, well. Maybe you could count bad people who had died long ago and bad people that hadn't been born yet.

The priest ended his sermon all of a sudden, and Guálinto's thoughts broke off. After mumbling a few words and making the sign of the cross the priest left the pulpit, walking down the steps with his hand on the handrail just like any other person. Every time the priest did that, his crabby old man's back toward the congregation, he lost most of his awesomeness. The boy expected the priest to fly off the pulpit or disappear in a puff of smoke.

There followed a tiresome stretch of time, hours it seemed, during which bells clanged and tinkled while the priest and his acolytes went through mysterious motions in front of the altar. You were supposed to kneel and keep your head bowed during this time, and the adults did. This gave the boys an opportunity to relieve their tedium by whispering to each other and playing minor, unobtrusive pranks on each other. The kid next to Guálinto began to pester him.

"Psst, you got shortening on your hair, haven't you?"

"Shut up!" hissed Guálinto.

"But you do have shortening on your hair, don't you?"

"It isn't so. It's brilliantine."

The other boy brought his pale feminine face close to Guálinto's hair and sniffed lightly several times. He moved away at a threatening gesture from Guálinto. "It's shortening," he said with a malicious smile. "Smells like a frying pan."

The boy one down had been listening and he stifled a grin behind his hand. Guálinto's face burned. He glared savagely at his tormentor. "As soon as we get outside," he said, "I'm going to kick the hell out of you."

The boys around them were watching with furtive glances, one eye on the pair and the other on the lookout for the Marist brothers who were supposed to keep them quiet. "Kick me?" whispered the sniffer. "You must be a mule then. People don't fight with their feet."

"They do in the Dos Veintidós."

"Where is that?"

The boy who had grinned was the one who answered. "A part of town . . . the river . . . don't you know? Bad people, rowdies, tough characters . . . ." His whisper was very low and he glanced at Guálinto as he spoke.

Guálinto bristled just a little at being called a rowdy; being tough was the Two Twenty-Twoer's greatest pride. Yet he did not like the way the two boys looked at him. His erstwhile derider gave him the once-over with an expression of mingled awe and condescension, as if he were looking at a rare beast. His eyes lingered on Guálinto's starched collar. Guálinto knew the other boy was comparing Guálinto's clothes to his own fine suit and shiny patent leather sandals. He felt an urge to trample the little "gentleman" into the dirt. Then his hate drained away, leaving him weak and crushed.

The inquisitive boy seemed impressed by his neighbor's description of the Dos Veintidós and its inhabitants, so much so that when he saw the hatred on Guálinto's face, he moved away, jostling the other boys to put three of them between himself and Guálinto. In his miserable mood, Guálinto barely took notice of his victory. And when one of the Marist brothers approached to stop the whispering and the moving about, all the boys had their heads bowed.

The mass ended and the church bells rang. Each stroke made the air vibrate and sing under the high vaulted ceiling. Clang-clang! Clang-clang! It's over, it's over, the bells were saying. Out into the sun to breathe again. No more mass for one whole week. But the bells could say other things as well. They were very wise, those bells of the old gray church, and they spoke a language all their own. When a funeral procession came in, with its black coffin and its red-eyed attendants, the beat of the bells was slow and heavy like the tread of the mourners' feet.

Then there were the special times when the bells went wild with joy. They frisked and gamboled. They shouted in deep ringing bass, they sang in clear rich tenor, they laughed in liquid soprano tones. Their mingled notes poured forth in sweet confusion like a cataract of scintillating stones of all colors and sizes. They filled the air and lingered on it. You could imagine beautiful things as you listened to them, and you wondered if Heaven was like that. And still the bells would ring on, inviting, inviting other people into church as those inside went out, telling of beautiful things inside. You went in almost expecting to find the church full of white angels with harps of gold, although you knew that inside there were only hard benches and monotonous prayers. But the bells lent illusion. They soothed, they compelled. They sang and wept. Bells, beautiful bells. They were the warm color in Guálinto's bleak church life. To him they were nearer to God than the sermons of the priests.

But today Guálinto had no ears for the bells. Everybody was leaving and he rose also, moving dully toward his mother and sisters. The finely dressed boy of a few minutes ago passed by, glancing furtively in Guálinto's direction. With obvious relief he joined a lady, his mother no doubt. Guálinto looked at her admiringly. She was a tall, broadly handsome woman dressed in shiny black. On her thick neck, her round arms and fat fingers glittered rings and bracelets and necklaces. What a woman! No wonder the sissy strutted proudly to her side.

The lady had stopped near the door. She seemed to be waiting for the crowd to pass out of the church. But no. She was looking for someone. Then her eyes lit up as that someone approached. It was a little girl about Guálinto's age. She must have been sitting in the girls' section. Guálinto stared at her from across the aisle. She was pretty, very pretty. The fine-looking lady gathered her two children and swept out of the church in a wave of perfume and a glitter of jewelry. Guálinto stood staring after them until Maruca came and nudged him.

"Come on," she whispered. "Mother is waiting."

Guálinto stared at her freckled sunburned face, at her taffy-colored braids. He was thinking of the fine lady's little girl, of her massive black curls and her white chubby face. He felt angry with Maruca because she was not pretty. Outside Carmen and their mother were waiting. "What kept you so long, *hijito*?" his mother asked.

Guálinto stuck out his lower lip and frowned. "The people," he answered curtly.

On the way home María and the girls walked very slowly. His mother now and then had to speak gently to Guálinto, who was possessed of an irritated impatience that made him want to walk faster and faster, to run and run until he was tired out. He hated his mother, he hated everybody, he was alone in the world. His mother's gentle words grated on his ears. It was as if she were throwing a blanket over him to hold him down and that he must shake his head and shoulders to get rid of it. Why wasn't his family rich, so sissies in fancy clothes would not laugh at him. He kept walking ahead of his mother and the girls, feeling so sorry for himself that his eyes watered. That infuriated him and he hissed at himself all the curses he had ever heard. He was glad he was walking ahead of them, so they would not see his tears. Again his mother annoyed him by calling to him to walk more slowly. Why didn't she leave him alone? After all she had done to make him miserable. Putting ... shortening ... on his hair!

He choked and walked faster, his lower lip trembling. He would go away. They would be sorry, all of them. He would go away and become a big bandit. Or a *rinche* maybe. And then he would come back and kill people. He would kill that sissy, but not his sister. And he would kill

the chief of police who kicked Meno Menchaca after he was dead. He'd
kill everybody and burn the houses down and his mother would come
out crying and asking him not to kill her too. Then he'd sneer coldly
and ride away on his big black horse all covered with shiny silver things.
Yes, the sissy's sister would notice him then, all dressed up like a *charro*
in black and gold and silver. And Uncle Feliciano . . .

No. He couldn't be a *rinche*, after all. Uncle Feliciano hated the
rinches and he'd have to kill him too. Guálinto did not want to do that,
so he couldn't be a *rinche*. But he could fight against the *rinches* and
get killed. That was it. Then they would bring his body home all covered with dirt and blood like Meno Menchaca's. Guálinto shuddered
deliciously. Then everybody would be sad and they would cry. And
his mother would be sorry she had put shortening in his hair. Self-pity
surged within him and broke out in a half-choked sob. That brought him
back to earth and he became aware that people they met were staring
at him. A few paces behind him his mother caught the faint sound.

"What's wrong?" she asked anxiously.

Guálinto swallowed hard. "Nothing," he said in a voice intended to
be matter-of-fact. And it was a pretty even voice. Just a slight quaver
in it. Then they turned from Fourteenth Street into the Dos Veintidós,
and he felt better.

7

An air of suspense hung over the house that Saturday morning. The
whole family walked more lightly than usual, talked more softly. María
would not go out into the yard to take down the clothes from the line
without a towel over her head, and Maruca and Carmen would not go
out at all. Guálinto lurked in the corners sulking. He watched how his
mother and sisters flitted about, taking furtive glances out the windows,
peeking at the house next door. He wondered why they were doing that,
so he went to the window to find out.

Maruca jerked him back. "Get away from that window, stupid!" she
said. "They'll see you."

"I won't!' he blurted indignantly. "I won't!" Maruca's little eyes
danced in her thin face, half angry, half amused.

"Hush, both of you," their mother said sharply and they hushed and
moved away from the window.

The house next door was the cause of all the commotion. For almost six years the Gómezes had lived with a vacant lot between them and the corner. Now they had neighbors next door. It was a neat little house, white with green trim, and with a well-to-do air about it. All Thursday afternoon mules had strained and tugged at the house that came inching its way down the street. All afternoon long men had shouted and moved about, lashing the curved backs of the mules, running here to close a door that had swung open, there to steady a wall, sweating, yelling, laughing, while dogs barked and people from the surrounding blocks came to see the show. At last the house had been brought to rest at its new site and there it passed the night, a strange unsteady visitor that tipped to one side like a drunken man.

All day Friday sun-blackened men in faded blue trousers and sleeveless undershirts worked in the hot July sun, setting the house straight on brick foundations. Fence posts were set up and a fence was nailed on three sides of the yard. The other side bordered on the fence around the yard of the Gómezes. It was a brand-new picket fence and the red kalsomine came off when you touched it. Guálinto had done so and got it all over his hand. These men, about a dozen of them, worked slowly, leisurely, without the bustle and the shouting of the previous day, but before dark they had finished their work. Meanwhile, plumbers had come and laid pipes for the bathroom, which somebody said included not only a toilet and washbowl but a bathtub as well. That night wagons brought furniture into the house. Again there was bustle and hurry, but no shouting and little noise. People flitted here, people flitted there in the light of many lamps and lanterns, as the furniture was moved in. Much furniture. Carmen said she saw four beds moved in, four full-sized beds. Maruca guessed it must have been two small beds since Carmen was always making things twice their size. But still, the beds that had been seen were made of wood instead of hollow metal, rich-looking wood.

The new people also moved in a queery shiny thing which Don Pancho the woodcutter said was a stove. A stove that burned oil instead of wood, just like lamps did. How they ever were going to cook food on a thing like that was a source of wonderment for María. Many other things were brought in when nobody was watching. What the Gómezes and other people living nearby did get to see was the man of the new house. They saw him many times directing the work. Everybody agreed that he was a smallish man with glasses, and that he was dressed in a dark suit with a white stiff collar, and that he was wearing a hat all the time. And everyone came to the same conclusion: he was a Protestant preacher.

So on Saturday morning the air felt different. Feliciano came in from

the country about seven o'clock, and he discussed things with María in
low tones while he ate breakfast. Guálinto, sitting at the kitchen doorway, listened to their conversation. "Protestants!" his mother said, raising her voice just a little. Then in anguish, "Good Heavens! What shall
we do?"

"Do?" echoed Feliciano. He chuckled. "Treat them nice, of course.
Protestants are good people. They won't eat you."

"You're making fun of me!" María complained. "Dealing with god-
less people that?"

"Don't get upset," Feliciano replied. "I am not joking, though. Protestants believe in the same God you do. But the people next door aren't
Protestants; they're as Catholic as the Pope."

"How do you know?"

"I know the man. I met him the day Filomeno Menchaca was killed,
to be exact."

"You know them? What's she like? Is she pretty? How was she
dressed?"

"You ask more questions than a little girl. I met the man only; he
came to see me at the grocery store. He told me then he was thinking
of moving next door to us. He likes this street because it's graveled and
he has an automobile."

"And you never told me!"

"Why get you excited about something that might or might not happen?"

"But why does he go about dressed up in a suit and hat if he isn't a
preacher?"

"He's a lawyer, *el Licenciado* Santiago López-Anguera. He's from
Mexico, him and his brother."

"A lawyer!" María was not sure what was more dismaying, having a
lawyer or a Protestant as next-door neighbor. "But why would a lawyer
move into this part of town?"

"To be close to his work," Feliciano said smiling. "He wants to help
poor Mexicans who have problems with the law. His brother's a musician, he lives on the other side of town."

"He's a lawyer and wants to help his people? That's it! That's what
Guálinto is going to be when he grows up."

"Perhaps. But that will be up to him. Anyway, I have to get going."

"God keep you."

"Bye, fella." Feliciano mussed up Guálinto's hair, stepped over him
and walked to the back, where his horse and buggy were waiting, while
Guálinto looked admiringly after him. Feliciano swayed just the slightest bit as he walked in his high-heeled boots, as if one of his legs were a
bit shorter than the other, or as though he carried a heavy gun buckled

across his waist. Guálinto loved to imitate his uncle's walk. He dreamed of a day when he would be able to wear cowboy boots and long pants and ride horses. By the time his uncle was leading the horse out of the back gate, though, Guálinto had turned toward the table. "Mama, I'm hungry," he said. The delicious smell of fried eggs and beans and flour tortillas had his stomach trying to gobble itself up.

"You can come now," said his mother, stopping her steady gliding from stove to table, from table to stove. Guálinto came to the table at once and dug in greedily. "Eat slowly," María said. He slowed things down a bit by taking a long drink from his coffee cup. "You'll be sick in your stomach if you eat like that," his mother scolded. "The trouble you give me. If you'd die right away and didn't bother anybody it would be all right. But you'll be there, 'Mama, it hurts, Mama it hurts.' And who has to worry over you? Who has to take care of you and stay up nights watching you?"

Guálinto grinned and rolled his eyes in a parody of dying. "That's enough," his mother said, a smile in her voice. "Finish your breakfast and quit clowning."

Guálinto kept on eating, very slowly now and chewing firmly and deliberately. He chewed the last morsel from his plate slower and slower until his chewing was the slowest of slow motion.

"And what's the matter now?" asked María.

Guálinto swallowed and took a drink of coffee. "Oh, I was just thinking," he said, his cup gravely held in midair.

"Thinking? And what would a little puppy like you think about?"

"Oh, about our new neighbors, you know." He set down the cup and passed the palm of his hand over his upper lip as his uncle did when he wiped the coffee from his mustache.

María gave him a sharp look. "You can think all you want about them. But be very carefull that you do not talk about them, especially what you hear around this house, you understand?"

"Aw, Mama, I won't say a thing, honest I won't. What's a Protestant, Mama?"

"Hush now. Finish your breakfast and go play."

"What's a lawyer?"

"I told you to finish your breakfast and go out and play."

"Oh, all right. I'm finished." He bounced out of his chair and hopped on one foot to the kitchen door.

"You are leaving the table," his mother said sternly.

"Oh, I forgot. Please-may-I-have-permission-to-leave-the-table." And he went out the door without waiting for an answer.

It was early and the sunlight was pleasantly warm, not yet hot enough to prickle the skin. Mornings like this one stirred a queer feeling in the pit of his stomach, at once sad and pleasant. In the backyard the banana plants glittered in the sun, their long leaves still damp with dew. They were gathered in clumps like little groups of girls whispering to one another and touching each other with their slender arms. Perhaps they were talking over what they had seen during the night. He felt a little chill run down his back. He looked back towards the fig tree near the house. No luck there. He had eaten all the ripe ones already. He was not allowed to touch the guayabas or the papayas. So he turned back to the banana grove. Lots of bunches but all green and pretty small. After all, it was only midsummer. Later, some of the bunches would ripen on the plants. But with the beginning of fall Uncle Feliciano would cut the green fruit that began to show streaks of black, for the days would not be warm enough to let them ripen on the bush. Uncle Feliciano would wrap these bunches up in old newspapers, rags, and old coats and sweaters. He would then put them away in the big trunk in the kitchen, where they would ripen quickly enough. When it began to look like frost, he would cut all the big ones down and hang them from the rafters in the kitchen, where they made a beautiful sight as they went from green to yellow, to orange and red.

But the banana grove gave Guálinto more than delicious fruit. It was his best friend. When he was to be whipped by his mother he ran into it, dodging among the shiny leaves and the mantle of blue-flower dotted vines that covered the plants. And he stayed there, half-enjoying his distress until darkness or hunger made him come out to take his punishment. The grove also was playground and playmate.

He paused at its edge as an actor pauses before coming on stage. Then, as he entered, his step became stealthy. His eyes darted this way and that. No. There was no hidden enemy. He proceeded a few steps, and from beneath his dotted calico shirt he drew a piece of knotted pine wood whittled into a fair imitation of a dagger. Suddenly he stopped in his tracks. "*Rinche!*" Dagger in hand he eyed the plant in front of him. The shiny-green stalk made no move toward him. Guálinto's eyes narrowed, his lip curled, his body tensed. For a moment there was a deep dangerous silence. Then he frowned.

"Where is Apolonio González?" His voice was a hiss. "Speak, you dog!" His fingers clasped and unclasped the dagger's haft. The banana trunk was silent, but it seemed to cringe with the passing of a gust of wind. Guálinto laughed a harsh laugh. "A coward," he said. "A coward like all your kind." The object of his hate took the insult meekly, offering no resistance.

"What have you done with Apolonio Rodríguez? If you have harmed him I will tear out your heart!" Perhaps the switching of last names confounded the banana trunk, perhaps it didn't know. One way or another, it refused to answer.

"So you won't tell, eh?" He advanced stiffly up to close quarters. "I know what you have done to him. You have killed him, you murderer! You have killed another Mexican who never hurt you." The cynical silence of the accused enraged Guálinto, and he slashed out face high. The sharpened wood furrowed the lustrous, paper-like skin of the trunk, and a thin trickle of clear fluid oozed out.

Guálinto sneered a self-satisfied sneer. "You mangy dog. Why don't you fight now? Why don't you try to kill me, eh? Because you shoot people in the back. Because you kill unarmed men and little children. Go back to your camp and tell old man Keene that Guálinto Gómez doesn't kill men who won't fight."

Half out of breath, the champion turned to leave and the treacherous *rinche* went for his forty-four. Guálinto spun around and buried his dagger into the wretch's side before the gun was half-drawn. Crackslish! The blade sank deep into his pulpy flesh. But the *rinche* was not dead yet. He fought back with all the strength of his mighty frame, and it became a struggle to the death that rocked the whole grove. Again and again Guálinto's knife found the *rinche's* side. He held the killer's gun arm powerless with his left hand as he stabbed sharply, viciously, while his adversary spent his strength in the most titanic but unavailing struggles. At last a particularly savage thrust found the *rinche's* heart. Guálinto pressed against him, driving the buried dagger deeper and deeper, working it around in the wound to make it more surely fatal.

The light breeze brought the sound of his mother's voice. Calling him? No, calling Maruca. He was still embracing the trunk and all of a sudden he disengaged himself as if it were burning hot. The once-smooth stalk was a pulpy oozing mess, scratched, stabbed and cut, with patches of the skin-like bark hanging loose. Guálinto withdrew his terrible dagger from the last wound he had inflicted, and the plant's mushy stalk sucked at it as if to hold it back. He looked at the damage he had done and he was frightened. He had almost killed the plant.

He tried to make things right, to close up the wounds, putting the loose patches back into place, all the while with a numb feeling of impending disaster. What if his mother were to call for him just now? Why, even the roots were loosened in his mad rushes at the plant. Though he tried, he could not hide everything. Absently, he was going to put the dripping dagger back under his shirt but stopped abruptly, hurling it away as far as he could.

He sat down on a little patch of grass because his knees would not hold him up. Now he was thoroughly scared. His shirt was damp from the banana stalk sap. Already wet spots were beginning to dry and to take on a brownish color. When the shirt was washed, he knew, it would show brown spots that no amount of scrubbing could take off. Tears came to his eyes. Why did he have to be such a fool? Why in the name of anything couldn't he keep out of trouble? If only he hadn't hugged the trunk so closely. If he hadn't bumped it so hard that he had mashed it. And mashed his shoulder too. Or if he had just stabbed lightly. That's what he had intended to do in the first place. Why did he ever make that dagger, anyway? He searched for it with his eyes, not moving his head. Couldn't find ... good riddance! Oh, he'd look for it some other time. It was a pretty nice dagger, too nice to throw away.

Perhaps something would come up. Maybe there would be company when his mother discovered the ruined shirt and he wouldn't be punished. Maybe his mother wouldn't notice it at all. The shirt had black dots on it anyway. Maybe Uncle Feliciano wouldn't notice the torn banana plant either. And if his uncle was home, he wouldn't be whipped too hard. After all, even if he was switched, it had happened before and it didn't kill him. He stretched out on the little grassy patch, the numb feeling fading away until it was only a lurking shadow in the background of his mind.

It was quiet in the grove. The sun was hot enough now to make it pleasant lying in the shade. A breeze from the sea came in at intervals, rustling the leaves as it passed. Then he heard a steady sleepy buzz and looked for the bee. There it was, maneuvering around a purple bract that was swaying like a pendulum. The bract looked like a great egg, sharp at the small end and attached to a knotty stem at the other. The petal-like leaves that formed it were shut tight, so after some zooming about and one or two brief, nervous landings, the bee hummed off to the next bush. There the topmost leaf had curled upward like a curtain, revealing a row of tiny flowers, like a line of girls in purplish-pink dresses and yellow caps. In a few days the purple leaf would turn black and fall, and the little row of flowers would become a row of tiny pale-green fruit.

Now the bee entered the base of the leaf and hummed intermittently, exploring among the flowers. Its buzzing was like a faint snore. It was out of sight now and Guálinto felt too lazy to move and see where it was. The buzzing made him sleepy. Suddenly the buzzing stopped. There was a querulous hum. Another. Then a desperate buzz that rose and rose till there was a miniature tornado under the purple leaf. The whole bract moved and a pinkish flower floated down to the grass below. With a final abrupt buzz the bee freed itself from the place where it had been wedged. It flew out and circled the bract, silent and wobbly. Then, getting its bearings, it floated upward, disappearing into a patch of blue sky that was surrounded by green leaves. As it disappeared it resumed its soft sleepy murmur.

Guálinto laughed out loud. The laugh brought him to life again and he got up from the grass, dusting off the seat of his pants. That reminded him of his shirt and his heart went cold again. Slowly, soberly, he walked a short distance parallel to the house and near the fringe of the grove. Before he knew it he was out of the grove, and before him was the new neighbors' yard. He gave a silent whoop. Why hadn't he thought of that before? Boy-oh-boy! They had neighbors and his mother wouldn't whip him because he'd yell his head off. He was saved, saved.

He danced up and down. Saved. Rescued. To the rescue we go, boys! On your horses! Five miles down and a battle. No! Attacked from behind and torn off his horse. He fell to the ground and rolled over and over furiously, choking, choking. Got to get those fingers ... almost ... al—most. Free! How do you like that! And that! And *that*! He struggled to his feet, but the cursed *rinche* clung to him like a leech. They broke apart and slugged at each other. Give ... take, give ... take. The big fellow clinched again. He shoved his fist against Guálinto's chin. Back, back went his head. His spine curved and tightened. Back still further, still further. His eyes popped and his breath came hard. Everything was turning misty ... no. He must keep his head. The gun! He slipped his free hand around the *rinche's* body. The cartridge belt. A little, a ... little ... more. The handle ... ah!

"Ah-ha-ha-ha!"

Guálinto froze. The thin laughter came from the fence and his back was to the fence. He was looking skywards, his left hand at his chin pushing his head far back, while his right hand encircled his body and clawed at his hip. For one long foolish moment he held this pose. Then he disentangled himself and turned around, his ears burning. Squatting on the fence was a dark skinny boy behind a pair of big horn-rimmed glasses.

"Hee-hee-hee!" said the thin boy. "Fighting himself." He put a bony fist to his chin in mocking imitation. Guálinto took a look at the knobby knees and the long legs. "Fighting himself," repeated the thin boy. "Fighting himself."

Guálinto rushed up to the fence. "Shut up, Four-Eyes!" He reached up and grabbed at an ankle.

"Don't do that," said Four-Eyes. "I'll fall." Guálinto tried again but he was too short to reach the boy's ankle.

"I'm gonna knock you down. I'm gonna punch your nose."

"You can't do that," said the boy. "I'm wearing glasses, can't you see? If you hit me they'll arrest you."

"What?" Guálinto stopped and looked at Four-Eyes carefully

"Just what you heard," replied the boy, easing himself into a less precarious position on the fence. "If you hit somebody wearing glasses, you'll be arrested and sent to jail."

Guálinto was impressed. "For how long?"

"Twenty years and a day."

Guálinto thought this over. "Say," he said, "come down from off the fence." Four-Eyes hesitated. "Aw, we won't fight. Come on over and let's play."

The other boy slipped gingerly down into Guálinto's side of the fence. Once on the ground he brushed off his brown corduroy suit and looked warily at Guálinto, who was looking him over too.

"What's your name?"

"Francisco López-Lebré, your humble servant."

"Your humble servant, what does that mean?"

"I don't know. That's what my father told me to say."

"Is that your father, the man who's a lawyer?"

"Oh, no. It's my aunt and uncle who live here. They don't have a family."

"Then your father is the musician who lives on the other side of town."

"How did you know that?"

"Oh, I just heard. Are you a musician too?"

"I'm learning to play the violin. What's your name?"

"Guálinto Gómez. How old are you?"

"Seven. I'm almost eight."

"I'm almost seven," lied Guálinto. He had just turned six a couple of weeks before. "How much did your glasses cost?"

"Oh, maybe a hundred dollars."

"Gee! You must have a lot of money."

"My father has lots of it."

Guálinto looked at Francisco with something like respect. "Let's be friends," he said. "When you come visit your aunt and uncle we can play."

"All right," Francisco answered, a bit loftily. "But I must go now. My uncle will be taking me home in his automobile."

8

After his talk with María over breakfast that July morning, Feliciano drove his buggy to El Danubio Azul, for twenty years a *cantina*, now for the past six months a grocery store, Feliciano García proprietor. So

Santiago López-Anguera, *el Licenciado* López-Anguera, was now his neighbor in the Dos Veintidós. He had not lied to María, but he had not told her all the truth either. He had met López-Anguera the day somebody in Jonesville had decided that Filomeno Menchaca was more of a liability than an asset to changing times. But he had also seen López-Anguera several times during the past five months. Don Roberto the Judge was still powerful in the city; however, he had been losing political ground for some time. The Reds were taking over the county. Sheriff Apodaca had lost the last election to a Gringo; consequently, Feliciano no longer was a special deputy, though he still was active in getting out the vote for the Blues and in supervising the *carne asada* fiestas just before elections.

Politically, though, the new law against liquor had done the Judge no good. He kept El Danubio Azul open until early in January of the year, just before the law went into effect. Then Feliciano, Faustino and Juan Rubio had carted all remaining cases of liquor to the Judge's basement, as his private property. There followed a wild farewell party to El Danubio Azul by its ex-customers and the Judge's supporters. The party went on until the last keg of beer in the *cantina* had been consumed, all free, compliments of Bob Norris. In a couple of weeks El Danubio Azul reopened, this time as a grocery store owned by Feliciano.

The Judge had done his best to take care of his own. The year before, when it became certain the law would pass, he had talked to Feliciano at El Danubio Azul. "After we have to close the *cantina*," he said, "I will need you and Juan *en la política*. You will be getting something for that work. But I can't give either of you a steady paying job. It's all I'll be able to do to keep Faustino on my payroll."

"I understand," Feliciano said. "*Así son las cosas*. I am grateful for all you've done for me these past years."

"But I will help you find another job. I have many friends."

Feliciano said, "What are you going to do with this building?"

"I haven't thought about it yet. Move it, rent it, tear it up."

Feliciano came out with what he had been thinking for the past few days. "Would you consider renting it to me?"

"To you? What for?"

"To open a grocery store. It would still be called El Danubio Azul. The Blues would come buy from me. And when we have *carne asadas* I could furnish you the meat at the lowest price I could. The baskets of groceries we give away could also be filled here. It would be cheaper for you, and I could build up a business."

The Judge looked at him as if he were seeing him for the first time. "I think you can do it. In fact, I'm sure you can. But it will take some preparation, and you will have to change some of your ways of doing things."

"How?"

"You will have to learn to borrow money, from the bank, of course, in order to lease the building, make changes inside, and stock it with groceries. I'm sure you have a number of gold coins put away somewhere, but they will not be enough. And to borrow money from the bank you will have to open an account there. You can do that with some of your savings. That will establish you as a business man. I know you mistrust banks, but they have their uses."

Feliciano swallowed hard. "I suppose I can do it," he said.

He did it and things worked out well. He had put almost half of his store of gold eagles into the bank (Judge Norris' bank, of course) and secured a loan large enough to lease El Danubio Azul for two years, modify the exterior to make it a grocery store instead of a *cantina*, and stock it with all kinds of meats and groceries. The outside remained as it had always been, except that the word "Groceries" in big black letters was added under the wavy blue paint. Juan Rubio had readily agreed to stay on for his meals, the little room he was living in behind El Danubio Azul, and a weekly salary of two dollars more than he had been making at the *cantina*. At first, profits were almost nonexistent after Feliciano had paid Juan Rubio his ten dollars a week and had paid the installment on what he owed the bank. But things had gotten better recently as word spread among the adherents of the Blue party. They came in larger numbers to buy groceries and meat for their families from the man who served these things to them for free during the Judge's *carne asada* fiestas. Everybody was happy: Feliciano, Juan Rubio, the Judge and the Blues. The only people in the *barrio* who were unhappy about Feliciano's success as a merchant were Don Crispín Rodríguez and his sons, who lost a great many of their customers to El Danubio Azul, Groceries. They also lost Feliciano as a customer. He had been buying groceries from Don Crispín to distribute to key people in the Blue party in Judge Norris' name.

That February day when Filomeno Menchaca died, the grocery store had been open for just two of weeks. It had not taken too much work to transform the *cantina*. The bar became a counter, the ice-case for the beer became a container for meats, shelves were built to hold cans of different sorts. The mirror and the portraits of naked ladies came down, but the copy of "Custer's Last Stand" and a still life depicting fruit and a glass of beer remained as reminders of the past and as objects to enliven the present establishment.

Feliciano had made a quick trip early that morning to his neighbor Don José's farm to talk about buying most of his crop of vegetables whenever it was ready to harvest. He returned to find a man waiting for him at the store, a small man in a dark suit, felt hat and tie. He looked very Indian in spite of his eyeglasses, something like pictures Feliciano had seen of Benito Juárez.

"This gentleman has been waiting for you," Juan Rubio said.

"Good morning, Señor García," the man said. "May I have a little of your time? I must speak to you about an important matter. My name is Santiago López-Anguera, I am a lawyer."

They shook hands. "I am pleased to make your acquaintance," Feliciano said. "I see you know my name. Please come to the back where we can talk."

They went into the back room of the building, now a storehouse for sacks of grain and boxes of canned and packaged goods instead of beer kegs and cases of whiskey. Feliciano had his "office" in the same corner where he had first met Faustino Bello the day he had arrived in Jonesville with his family. The desk was still there, the tables and the safe. After they had sat down, López-Anguera said, "I thought I would drop by and make your acquaintance. We should be next-door neighbors very soon. I have bought the lot on the corner and will be moving a house into it."

Feliciano lifted his eyebrows. "Pardon the question," he said, "but why would you, a man of culture, move into the Dos Veintidós?"

López-Anguera smiled. "I am something of an idealist, you might say. I want to represent our people in any way I can. Their rights are very often ignored, they often get in trouble through ignorance of the law. I want to live in the *barrios* where they will feel more at ease coming to me."

"I see. That is very good of you."

López-Anguera smiled again. "Finding a lot for sale on your street was a stroke of luck for me. It is the only graveled street in the area, and I have an automobile."

"The streets do get muddy when it rains," Feliciano said.

"The Ford is a good car in the mud, but I will enjoy driving out to Fourteenth Street without having to worry about getting stuck. You are lucky in the United States. A brother of mine and I moved our families to Texas just recently from Mexico. Over there some towns are nothing but mud in rainy weather, even in front of the municipal palace."

"I know," Feliciano said without much interest.

"I am also in the import-export business."

Feliciano merely nodded. There was a pause and then Feliciano said, "Well, it was good to meet you," and half-rose from his chair.

"Just a moment, if you please," said López-Anguera. "I have a message of some importance to impart." Feliciano sat down again. "It is from an old friend and comrade of yours, Don Santos de la Vega. He was named Chief of Customs at Morelos recently and he would like to meet with you as soon as possible."

"I have never known any Santos de la Vega."

"Surely you have heard of Don Agustín de la Vega."

"Of course, everybody has. The big *hacendado* in Coahuila and Chihuahua. But I never met him or any of his family. Anyway, the *villistas* killed them all some years ago."

López-Anguera seemed reluctant to come to the point. "All except one son. He was ... ah ... ah ... elsewhere at the time. Your friend, Don Santos."

"I tell you, I never knew a Santos de la Vega."

López-Anguera dropped his voice. "You knew him ... ah ... .as El Negro."

"El Negro?"

"He was ... ah ... his mother was ... was not married to Don Agustín."

"El Negro?"

"He would like very much to see you, as soon as possible."

Feliciano was perturbed. Was it news about his brother Lupe? Was he, Feliciano, in danger of being reported to the law as a former *sedicioso*? He looked at the lawyer intently. Perhaps the man was lying. But he could not take a chance. "How soon can I see Don Santos?"

"As soon as you wish. This morning, let us say."

Feliciano took out his watch. "It's nine-thirty. Tell him I'll be in Morelos by eleven-thirty."

"Very well," said López-Anguera. "He will want to meet you at home. Here is his address." He scribbled it on a card and gave it to Feliciano.

9

And so it happened that about the time Filomeno Menchaca was being executed a block from his home, Feliciano was driving his buggy across the international bridge to Morelos. He did not have to use the card with De la Vega's address. When he stopped for customs on the Mexican side, one of the officers on duty asked him his name. When Feliciano replied, the customs man said, "I have orders to direct you to the house of our Chief." Without waiting for an answer the man got into the buggy beside Feliciano and told him which streets to take. Finally he said, "*Aquí*," and Feliciano stopped. He gave his guide a half-dollar. The man thanked him and walked back toward the bridge.

The house was like many others in Morelos and elsewhere in Mexico constructed for the well-to-do before the Revolution. A fortress-like brick structure built right up to the narrow sidewalk, solid brick walls except for a few barred and curtained windows. And set into the brick wall at the end was the *zaguán*, a huge double-doored entrance leading into the patio, for vehicles and horses, with its *portillo*, a smaller door for ordinary use, set into the right-hand leaf. Feliciano was about to get down to knock at the *portillo* when the doors of the *zaguán* creaked open and a man wearing the light-brown uniform of a customs agent beckoned him in. Like visiting royalty, Feliciano thought as he drove his buggy into the patio. The man in brown took the horse's bridle and led the buggy away once Feliciano had alighted to be clasped in a massive *abrazo* by Santos de la Vega.

De la Vega led him into an office facing the patio and closed the door behind him. "Don Santos," Feliciano began, "it is very good to see you."

"Leave out the 'Don Santos' nonsense, Feliciano," De la Vega answered. "You're my comrade, my *compañero*." He was a bit stouter than before and resplendent in his Mexican army uniform with its colonel's star. Except for that, he had not changed much. He motioned Feliciano to a chair beside a little table on which were a bottle of cognac and a couple of glasses. He sat down on the opposite side. As he poured the brandy he said, "You have done pretty well by yourself, Feliciano, from all I hear."

Feliciano sipped at the cognac. "You have done even better," he said. "But what about this 'Santos' business? I thought your name was Santiago."

"That's the name I used when I was in Texas, though most people knew me simply as El Negro. That was all right with me."

They sipped their cognac in silence for a moment and then De la Vega said, "I'm sure you're wondering why I wanted to get in touch with you, and in such a hurry. But first let me thank you with all my heart for what you have done for my family these past four years."

"Your family?"

"I guess you never knew my full name, the one I used while I was in Texas. It was Santiago Vera."

"Vera? You don't mean that widow and her two boys that live close to my house? At least, everybody thought she was a widow."

"She's not a widow, at least not yet. She's a *tejana* and I married her as Santiago Vera. When things fell apart for us in Texas, I had to leave her and the boys. I sent them what I could, but when I became a *carrancista* officer I had to leave the border. If you hadn't helped them, out of the goodness of your heart, I wonder what would have become of them."

"I had no idea who they really were. They were just a family who needed help, more than the families with husbands who voted for the Blues."

"In any case I owe you much and I am grateful."

"It is nothing. But I am glad that it happened to be your family."

"I will be bringing them over to Morelos soon, and in a couple of years we'll be going away from the border, to my share of the lands my father once had."

"El Negro," Feliciano said, more to himself than to De la Vega. "Son of old Don Agustín de la Vega."

De la Vega drained his glass and poured himself another drink. Feliciano had barely tasted his. "I'm going to tell you the story of my life, in as few words as possible," De la Vega said, smiling his broad smile. "My father, Don Agustín de la Vera, was born in 1846, the year the Gringos invaded Mexico. He didn't marry until 1886, to a lady of *criollo* ancestry like himself and almost as old as he was. That's the way people of quality did things in those days." He smiled a twisted, tight-lipped smile. "She bore him two sons, Luis in 1888 and Joaquín in 1890. The lady died just after giving birth to Joaquín. A couple of years later Don Agustín took as his mistress and housekeeper a nineteen-year-old girl from Guerrero. As you know, there are a lot of black people on the coast. I don't remember my mother's parents, but I have been told they both were black, with some Indian mixed in. They had come north looking for work and found it at Don Agustín's *hacienda*. I have also been told that at nineteen my mother was very beautiful. She still was beautiful in her thirties, when she was killed. I took after her."

De la Vega laughed. "I'm not saying I inherited her good looks, but I did get from her my black skin and African features. People on the *hacienda* used to say that the African blood had been distilled in my veins. Nothing of *criollo* or Indian in me. My half-brothers didn't like me, of course. As far back as I can remember, they did all they could to make me miserable. They were the ones who first called me El Negro when we were kids. Even the servants made fun of me. They called me *negrito*, as if they were being affectionate, but I could tell that they were laughing at me and really calling me 'little black boy.'"

"But my mother loved me, and Don Agustín was kind to me and let me have all I wanted. By the time I was eight or nine I started spending more time with the *vaqueros* than at the house. I became a real *hombre de campo*: horseman, tracker, hunter. Life was good and so it remained until I was well past my fifteenth year."

Santos de la Vega drank from his glass and looked away from Feliciano toward the wall on the other side of the room. "I hope I'm not boring you with this tale," he said.

"Oh, no. No." Feliciano said quickly.

"Don Agustín was getting along, in his sixties already, and perhaps he was thinking of making his peace with Heaven. Or perhaps he loved my mother and me more than I had thought.

"One day he called us all into his study, Luis, Joaquín, my mother and me. It was a place full of books and smelled of leather, but a different kind of leather, not the leather of saddles and chaps and things of that sort. He came directly to the point: he had decided to marry my mother and to recognize me before the law as his legitimate son. Were there any objections? Nobody said a word, but I could see the rage and hatred on the faces of Luis and Joaquín.

"That night, soon after dark, there was a commotion in the corral behind the kitchen, where an Arabian stud just brought in from the Capital was being kept. Neighs, stamping, thuds crashing against the logs of the corral. We all came out—my father, my half-brothers, the help from the kitchen. Some *vaqueros* came and managed to calm the stallion. By the light of lanterns they found my mother's body, trampled to death. As I bent over her, crying, I noticed a puma hide near her body. I also knew that my mother was afraid of horses and would not have walked into that corral.

"Next day, after my mother had been buried with due ceremony, Don Agustín shut himself in his study with Luis and Joaquín. The rest of us in the house could hear their voices: Luis and Joaquín arguing loudly, Don Agustín shouting, almost screaming, '*¡Bandidos! ¡Bandidos!*' The two finally came out and I was called in to talk to the man who had recognized me as his son. '*Hijo*,' he said to me, 'you must go, you must go as soon as possible. Your brothers, my servants, all have turned against me. I am no longer master in my own house.'"

Santos breathed heavily and kept looking at the farther wall. "My father gave me what money he had in his desk drawer. I went to my room and got my rifle, my revolver, ammunition and cartridge belts. Nobody tried to stop me or said a word to me. I went to the stables and saddled my favorite horse and left. I would never see the three of them again."

Santos de la Vega took another swallow of cognac. "The rest does not take long to tell. I rode north until I crossed into Texas and drifted along until I got to the Delta. Soon after, I met Lupe and joined his band. I was sixteen or seventeen then. I married a girl whose father had his little ranch deep in the chaparral. I had already changed my name to Santiago Vera. The second of my boys was born about the time they killed Madero. Soon after I heard that my two half-brothers had been shot by the *villistas*. I would have been glad of that, but they killed my father too."

He turned and looked across the little table at Feliciano. His eyes were moist. "The rest of my stay in Texas is well known to you."

"You mean you were little more than twenty when we were *sediciosos* together?"

"As a boy I was big for my age. And I began doing a man's work pretty early. I'm twenty-seven right now. But I didn't bring you over here just to tell you my life story. After that strange little incident, the botched ambush, Lupe and I got together again on the Mexican side, and we joined the *carrancistas*. Lupe wanted to become a *villista*, but I would not join up with people who had killed my father. Lupe saw it that way too, once I told him."

"Did Lupe ever become a general?" There was a tinge of sarcasm in Feliciano's voice.

"No, we went too late into the Big Brawl. But he should have, he stood out of the crowd. As it was, he did make colonel as I did. I got a good deal more out of the fighting, though, a big chunk of what had been my father's lands."

"How did you manage that?"

"Who would have thought it, but the old man left a will naming me as one of his heirs. After we took over that part of the state, it was discovered by a *carrancista* friend of mine who also is a lawyer."

"Santiago López-Anguera?"

"The same. Carranza legitimized my claim, really it was Obregón. We are more *obregonistas* than *carrancistas*. Not all that Don Agustín had once held, but a good chunk of it."

"Who's holding it for you?"

"I did the right thing, for my *compañeros* and for me. I parceled out half of what I got among my closest comrades, including Lupe. He immediately sold his part, he wasn't made to be a farmer."

"Where's Lupe?"

"He's around here somewhere. I'll get you in touch with him if you like. And if he wants to."

"And the land you kept? Who's taking care of it while you are gone?"

"I have an administrator, one of López-Anguera's brothers who also is a lawyer. Santiago makes trips down there once a month to see how things are going. I will be going once every three months or so. It's a good arrangement. It's safer in the hands of a civilian lawyer than in the hands of one of my former brothers-in-arms. It's good land, well watered, good for farming and stock raising. But I need a lot of good, hard money to develop it and make it yield big profits. That's why I asked you here."

"Me? Why me?"

"Two years on this job, three at most, and I'll have enough capital— real money, gold—to make that land into a paradise. I kept my eyes open while I was in Texas, and I learned a few things about the way the Gringos do their farming and stockraising."

"How do I enter into this?"

Santos leaned over across the little table between them and said in a confidential tone, "I want you to join me in a little venture. In the import-export business."

"I have no experience in that line of work."

"You won't need any. All you'll have to do is sign your name to some papers now and then."

"You'd better tell me more than that."

Santos laughed and for an instant he was again El Negro of the old days. Then he was Don Santos de la Vega once more: Mexican army colonel, chief of customs and wealthy landowner. "It's very simple," he said. "Things are settling down in Mexico, and a lot of real money—not paper shinplasters—is beginning to surface. Except that it now belongs to different people than before the Revolution. These new people want a lot of things that Mexico doesn't have right now, and they are willing to pay for them. Elegant furniture, expensive textiles, cameras, victrolas and such goods. The import duties are very high. On top of that, importers have to pay heavy *mordidas*. So I'm going into the import business, duty-free let's say."

"Smuggling, you mean."

"Of course not. After all, I'm Chief of Customs at this port of entry. Everything will be perfectly legal. The goods will be exported with the proper permits from the other side. I'll be here to receive them at customs on this side, and that will be that."

"But I can't run my grocery business and go into all of that, as well."

"You won't have to. López-Anguera will do all the buying in your name. He'll prepare the papers by which you sell the goods to him. At a profit to you, of course. What he does after that is nothing you have to worry about."

Feliciano looked at the floor. "I see no risk for myself," he said quietly. "It's the moral side that bothers me. Isn't it, in a way, a betrayal of what you and thousands of others fought for? Of the Revolution itself?"

Santos laughed again, softly this time. "Ah, Feliciano, you really are an idealist. This *is* the Revolution, all the rest was just fine words. They all are robbers, from Old Whiskers on down. Why shouldn't I get my share? For me and those who were with me when things were hot? That is why I have come to you. I won't try to deceive you. You are in the right position for the job, you are competent, and I can trust you. But I also owe you a lot for what you did for my family. I could find somebody else to do this business for me. But I would very much like for you to be the man." He smiled. "You see, I too am something of an idealist."

Feliciano smiled back and was silent. Santos continued, "It will mean more than a little money for you, in American gold. And you may need it later on. Things are changing on the other side, from what I hear, and they may change even more."

"All right," Feliciano said, "I'm your man."

"Fine! *Salud!*" They clinked glasses and Santos leaned back in his chair. "And how do you like life as a merchant? Are you making any money?"

"It's better than being a bartender, though I still do political work for Judge Norris. As for money, very little in clear profits yet, but I have plenty of business."

"Whatever you make, change it into gold coins and put them away. Gold and land, they're the only things that stay with you, the only real wealth in the world."

"That also is my thinking, but I had to put money in the bank, open an account as they call it, so I could borrow money to lease El Danubio Azul and stock the store. I'm sunk in debt up to my ears right now, but I'm paying it back."

"Did you put all your money in the bank?"

"No, I kept out what I could."

"I didn't think you would risk it all in a Gringo bank."

"I've been thinking of renting some land, next to that worked by my neighbor José Alcaraz. There's money to be made in vegetables right now. They have these *priculas*, where they put the tomatoes and green peppers and all kinds of things on ice to ship them far up north."

"Why don't you buy the land? If you don't have enough, I'll help you."

"The old Gringo who owns the land won't sell. He thinks all the land downriver from Jonesville to the sea will soon become like California. That's where he lives. José Alcaraz works some forty acres of the old man's land on shares. Along the river. I hope I can rent the forty acres next to Alcaraz, and he could work all eighty acres."

They talked about Lupe and their days as *sediciosos* while they had their midday meal at Santos' house. Broiled meat, beans and rice, tortillas and aguacates. A norteño meal. Santos' tastes in drink might have changed, but he still ate the same kind of food he had eaten before he became Don Santos.

Then Feliciano took his leave. As he drove his buggy back to Jonesville, he thought somewhat sadly about the paths his life had taken in the past few years. From cowhand to seditionist and raider, from there to bartender for Gringo soldiers he had been shooting at a few months earlier. Soon after, a ward heeler whose job was to herd his own people into voting booths for the benefit of Gringo political bosses. And now, party to a smuggling operation. Nothing to be proud of. But his nephew was getting close to school age, and Feliciano would need money, much money.

10

When the weather was clear, the family gathered on the porch after supper. The lights were put out to keep away mosquitoes. Everyone enjoyed sitting in the cool night breeze. On the Delta there were no sun-painted hills, but clear nights were always beautiful. On this particular night the moon had not yet risen. But the darkness was restful for people to whom the day was a constant battle. The glaring blue sky of day had changed into a velvet cloth full of white stones, as if the light of day had broken up into pieces and shrunk into little bits of brilliance. And all the while the invisible fingers of the breeze groped over arms, legs and faces like a caress.

Tonight Don Pancho the woodcutter had come to visit. With him was his younger brother, Don José, who farmed a piece of land downriver from town. Visitors and family were transformed by the night. In the dark, María's silhouette was like that of an adolescent girl. Don José's raw-red face went unseen, the ungainly angles of his body assumed athletic lines, and the darkness gave him courage to speak in María's presence without stammering.

"It was hot today," said Don Pancho.

"Terribly hot," said María.

"Very hot," said Feliciano.

Don José could think of no other way of saying the same thing, so his shadow just nodded its head. The conversation had languished a bit after having browsed through various subjects of small importance. Don Pancho and Don José were sitting on the porch swing because they were guests. It was a very new swing, and the whole family was proud of it. It set them apart from the whole neighborhood. Not even the new neighbors, the López-Angueras, who had a motor car, had a porch swing. Feliciano had been very happy recently, and he had told the family that he didn't promise them a motor car yet, but a victrola maybe one of these days, if business kept getting better. But for the present a swing was enough to be proud of.

Don Pancho and Don José sat gingerly on the edge of the swing, afraid to lean back. They would have preferred a couple of good strong chairs with four stout legs, such as the ones Doña María and Don Feliciano's sat. Sitting on a swing was a ticklish job. If you made a sudden move, it bucked and swayed under you like a mean mustang. You had to sit very stiff and very still and very uncomfortable. But Don Pancho and Don José bore their ordeal stoically and tried to appear nonchalant and at their ease. They did not want to give the impression that they were crude yokels. They knew how to act in front of other people.

Guálinto and his sisters were sitting on the porch steps. Carmen, she of the dark serious face and the big eyes, was staring at the sky. Blondish Maruca spent her eternal restlessness on a rose that had fallen from one of the bushes nearby. She pinched and tore nervously at the petals while Carmen counted the stars. "Sixty-seven, sixty-eight, sixty-nine . . . ." Maruca ground those rose petals between her fingers rhythmically, keeping time with Carmen's counting. "Seventy-two, seventy-four—oh, I lost count again! There are so, so many that I get mixed up. If I could only mark up the sky into parts, little parts, then I could count them all."

Maruca rolled the ball of crushed petals back and forth between her hands. "You'd count only the stars in our sky," she answered brusquely. "You couldn't count the stars of other places."

Carmen said eagerly, "I once heard of a man who did a great sin. And God condemned him to count all the stars in the sky, in all places. He goes through the world, always traveling, always at night, looking up at the sky and counting, counting. He can't die and he can't stop. He must keep on traveling and counting." Carmen paused for an instant, breathless. "And all the time . . . "

"Hush," said Maruca, throwing the mashed rose at the darkness. "Hush. You just made that up. This minute."

"I did not," said Carmen hotly. "I heard it."

"You didn't," Maruca said with curt finality. Carmen did not reply. "Who did you hear it from?" Carmen turned her head away. "Who from?" insisted Maruca. "Who from?"

"Anyway," said Carmen in a small voice, "it's a pretty story."

"Humph!" said Maruca.

Guálinto was but half-listening to his sisters. Usually he liked to hear Carmen talk. She was very smart. She was only nine and was already in third grade, while Maruca, who was eleven, was in fourth. Carmen could make the nicest stories out of any little thing. She also read stories and little verses from her school books to Guálinto, who was not yet in school. Guálinto liked the verses that Carmen was always chanting, though they were in English and he didn't understand everything they said. He caught lines here and there and could say them himself, and that pleased Carmen. But when grownups were around, he had no ears for Carmen or Maruca. He loved to hear grownups talk. Their most random words had a pithy juiciness for him. Their slightest gestures were things to be imitated. Just now they were talking about somebody.

"And that's how it happened," said Don José.

"How strange!" exclaimed María.

Extrañ-ñ-ño. What a pretty word. It felt like a piece of candy rolling back and forth in your mouth. That kind of rock candy that has many colors and tastes and that crumbles slowly in your mouth as you move it around with your tongue. It was a nice-tasting word—*extraño*.

"Mama," asked Maruca, "can we go to Dora's house?"

"Don't interrupt," her mother answered. "Don't you see Don José is talking?"

"But can we go, Mama?"

"All right, but take your brother along."

Maruca hopped down the brick walk toward the gate and Carmen followed. At the gate they stopped for Guálinto, who came after them with less enthusiasm. Neither were the girls very happy about taking him along. But each took one of his hands, and with him between them they ventured into the blackness of the street. Over the smooth grassy sidewalk, across the rough foot-bridge that spanned the ditch between the walk and the street. As they crunched over the gravel Guálinto complained. "Go slower. The stones are hurting my feet." Then he stumbled and stubbed his toe, and the girls had to wait while he rubbed his foot. The street was awfully wide in the darkness. It seemed as if they would never reach the other side, where a light burned at the Gracias.

Guálinto pushed at the girls with his elbows. "Don't get so close. Are you afraid?" And he pushed himself forward.

"You're the one who's afraid," taunted Maruca. "You. Old woman, *vieja, vieja*. Pushing up front so girls will protect your back." She grabbed suddenly at the small of his back, making him jump.

Both his sisters laughed and Guálinto said, "Don't do that!"

"*Vieja, vieja*," repeated Maruca. "Needs girls to take care of him."

"Oh, leave him alone," said Carmen. "Are we going across or not." Guálinto did not budge.

"Let's go," said Maruca.

"I'm not going," he said.

Maruca moved closer. "Don't be like that, Guálinto."

"I'm not going."

Maruca groped for his arm but he shook her off. "I'm going back," he said.

There was a short silence. "See what you've done," Carmen told Maruca.

"All *right*," said Maruca, emphasizing the "right" with a tug at Guálinto's arm.

He tugged back. "Don't pull me around. Don't pinch me either. I'll yell for Mama."

Maruca let go of his arm. "All right," she repeated with repressed venom. They turned back home, Maruca ahead and Carmen holding Guálinto's hand. Quietly they came in through the gate and up the walk, so quietly that the adults did not notice them. Uncle Feliciano was talking to Don Pancho and Don José, pounding his fist on his other hand like an angry man. Guálinto perked up his ears. Uncle Feliciano talked very little most of the time. When he talked a lot it usually was about one of two things: Gringos or priests. When he talked about Gringos he talked low and bitter. When he got excited he was talking about priests.

Maruca gave Guálinto a vindictive shove, and the girls groped their way around the house toward the kitchen. Guálinto remained to one side of the steps. Dimly he could see his mother's empty chair. She had gone into the house. He eased himself down on the edge of the porch close to the vines.

"They talk about sanctity, they talk about holiness! Thieves, robbers. Why even the pope is a lusty old stud." He lowered his voice. "Who says the priests don't like women? Have they been gelded, eh?" He leaned aggressively forward, close to Don Pancho and Don José. Their shadowy forms leaned back as if fearing a blow.

There was a long awkward silence. Finally Don José, or maybe it was Don Pancho, stretched out a hand to Feliciano, "Smoke?"

The tobacco went round in silence except for the crackling of corn husk leaf as the men rolled their cigarets. Guálinto began to feel the chill of the night and he snuggled against the tangle of honeysuckle vines. Feliciano raised his head. "What was that?"

"Maybe the wind," said Don Pancho striking a match. The match flared as he held it up to the cigaret in his mouth, and for a moment his beard-bristled face stood out in the darkness like a picture pasted to a piece of black paper. Matches scratched again and there were momentary glimpses of screwed-up faces half-hidden behind cupped hands. Then three red eyes blinked and winked and widened in the blackness.

"Dark night."

"Moon will rise pretty soon," Feliciano said.

"What a night for spirits."

At this turn in the conversation Guálinto wished he were inside, that there were a big cheery fire, that it were daylight or even moonlight. Yet, he was afraid of being discovered. He would be sent inside and wouldn't hear the stories that were sure to follow.

"Fearsome things can happen at any time of day," his uncle said.

"You're right," said Don Pancho. "Dark or twilight, moonlight or daylight. The strangest ghost story I ever heard happened at dusk."

"At dusk?"

Guálinto could have moved then. He could have stood up and attracted attention. But he stayed where he was and heard Don Pancho tell the story of how God avenged a dead girl. Don Pancho told it slowly, with great awe and wonder. He spoke not only with words but with changes in his voice, which rose and fell, became soft and harsh as the story required it, which mimicked the speech of the people it told about. He also talked with his hands, his arms and his shoulders. And hidden by the darkness, Guálinto knew, Don Pancho's face was also speaking.

It had happened in West Texas, one winter many years past. Don Pancho had heard the story when he was still a young man. There was a little village of Mexicans up there and like most villages it had its drunkard, a handsome young man who had gone bad. The village's prettiest girl fell in love with the drunkard and married him in spite of all advice to the contrary. When people told her she had done a foolish thing, she would say, "I'm not afraid. God will be good to me."

The couple went to live in a little shack just outside the village, a hovel somebody else had made and then abandoned. The drunkard beat his wife on their wedding night and every day and night thereafter. This went on for several months. Everyone knew but nobody could or would do anything about it. Woodchoppers passing by at dusk could hear the blows, the husband's curses and the girl's moans. But the girl complained to no one. Autumn came and the days were cold and blustery when it became evident that the girl was with child. When her husband found out about it, he got drunker than usual but didn't beat her anymore. Passerby could not even hear curses coming from the drunkard's hovel now. The girl, when she came to the village, looked proud and happy. It was as if God had heard her and was being good to her because of her faith.

The days grew colder and in the mornings there was frost on the ground. The girl did not come to the village anymore. But one afternoon the husband showed up in the village with a lot of money he got, nobody knew where. He got into a card game and lost most of his money. In a rage he left the card game and went to the *cantina*, where he drank until late at night. Then he went home and beat his wife to death. Some of the village women found her next morning lying across her doorway, as if at the last moment she had tried to run away. The husband was asleep inside.

The villagers took the girl's body and buried it in their little cemetery. During the services it began to snow. The village had a priest, but it did not have any representative of civil law anywhere within walking distance. People did not know what to do with the husband of the girl they had just buried. Her father was dead and she had no brothers or near relatives to avenge her. The husband came to the funeral, drunk as usual. When the snow began to fall faster, the crowd at the graveyard broke up and went home. The husband was left alone, so he went back to his hut.

It was now about five o'clock of a winter evening, and the snow kept falling in big, silent flakes. As he neared the door of the shack, an idea came to his drunken mind. He stopped and, raising his voice, he called his wife by name. "Lucía! Is supper ready, goddamn you?"

Before he could laugh at this little joke, he heard his wife's voice from inside the shack. "I'm in bed," said the voice very weakly. "I have just borne you a little boy. Come in and see him."

The man was half-shaken out of his drunkenness. But he was a big strong man and he was not a coward. He did not believe in spirits either. "Some boy from the village," he thought. "I'll teach him a lesson." He raised his voice again. "I'm coming, Lucía. And I'm going to beat the hell out of you again."

He stepped to the doorway. It was darker inside, so he stood there for a moment getting used to the half-light. Then he looked at the bed and he saw it there. At first it was a round hairy ball lying on the bed, about the size of a bundle of laundry. Then it unrolled itself and stood up on its hind legs. It had a body something like a bear's and a devil-face that looked like a wolf. The face turned toward him, baring white sharp fangs in a demon's grin. Its perfectly round eyes, red and glowing, fixed upon him. Its long claws beckoned him toward the bed. The man stood rooted to the spot, his mouth open in a silent shout of horror. The beast's short furry legs flexed and it jumped soundlessly to the dirt floor. And then, with a low gurgle, it went after the man. Its fangs bit at his face, its paws tore at his breast, and its lower legs drew up to disembowel him.

The drunkard found his voice and screamed. He tried to tear away from the thing that hung to his throat, chest and belly. He managed to stagger out of the hut, fell and rolled in the snow. His screams brought the woodcutters who passed by every day at dusk. They found him slashed and holding his entrails, praying and cursing and screaming all at the same time. He told them what had happened before he died.

Don Pancho stopped and breathed deeply as if to let some of the compressed horror out of his chest. "But that," he continued, "was not the strangest thing of all. The woodcutters started looking for the beast. It had stopped snowing before they heard the man's screams, and anyone can follow a trail in the snow. But they found no tracks of any beast, either coming or going from the hut. There were only their own tracks and those of the man himself when he came up to the door of the hut and also where he ran out, and the bloody snow where he had thrashed about. But no tracks of any beast. That was not all. All around the hut, in a big circle without beginning or end, there were two pairs of tracks in the snow. There was no sign where the tracks had come into the circle and where they had gone out. The tracks, *señores*? They were made by the bare feet of a young woman and of a very small baby."

There was a long silence broken at last by Feliciano. "It might have been a bear. There are bears in those parts."

"But a bear would have left tracks."

"It might have snowed again by the time the woodcutters got there," persisted Feliciano.

"And the tracks of the girl and the baby?"

Feliciano did not answer. The red eye of his cigaret expanded and glowed as he drew on it. Guálinto meanwhile was almost under the porch swing. In the eastern sky a brightness was growing against the irregular black line of the chaparral. "There comes the moon," Feliciano said.

"Yes," said Don José, "a full moon. A shepherd's moon, as some people call it."

"Speaking of full moons ... " Feliciano dropped his cigaret and scraped it out with his heel. "Speaking of full moons and fearsome things, I have never been as scared as I was once under a full moon."

"Tell us about it," urged Don Pancho, and Feliciano told his story. He was not as vivid a speaker as Don Pancho. He did not use his hands so much and he spoke in a low conversational tone, as though confiding important information.

It had happened when Feliciano was a boy. He was riding through cattle country with a group of cowboys. Plains, plains and more plains. Here and there a clump of mesquite or huisache, a *mogote* in the distance that looked like a bunch of grass in a level field. Far off to the left the great chaparral, like a dark wall in the night. When the full moon came out you could see pretty far away. In a blurry sort of way, but you could distinguish cattle and horses under clumps of trees that were not too far away.

On a night like this Feliciano was riding across the plains with a dozen other cowboys. The eldest was his own father, an old *vaquero* who knew the plains and the chaparral. There were also three other middle-aged men and the rest were young, the youngest being Feliciano himself. The party had ridden long and hard, through sundown and into the night. As the moon rose, full and brilliant, the leader decided that they would rest a few hours and continue their journey before dawn. They were in open country about three miles from the chaparral, and they stopped and dismounted where they were.

Feliciano's father, being the oldest, offered some advice. "Don't unsaddle. Just take the bridle off your horse so he can graze and stake him out. And keep your hand close to the stake rope while you sleep. This is bad country."

The leader was a young man and he laughed. "Indian times are over," he said. "Besides, we are armed. Let's be comfortable while we sleep."

"Each man's head is a world of its own," Feliciano's father replied. He followed his own advice and so did Feliciano and two of the older men. The rest used their saddles as pillows. They hobbled their horses and turned them loose to graze. They were tired and soon were fast asleep. All but Feliciano. Wrapped in his blanket, he lay between sleeping and waking, listening to the cries of the night birds and the faint howls of the coyotes in the distance.

"It must have been a half-hour after we settled down," Feliciano related, "when I noticed something different in the night sounds. The coyotes gave a few short barks and were silent. A moment later a bird whirred above my head and woke me up completely. I turned over and saw that my horse was standing with his head raised high, facing toward the chaparral with his ears pointed forward. I took a firm hold on the stake rope and sat up. My father was already sitting up, holding on to his stake rope also. The horses were all facing the chaparral, listening. My father put on his hat and whispered, 'Do you hear anything?' I shook my head. 'Listen,' he said.

"I listened and at first I could hear nothing. I let my jaw hang down a little and held my breath, and then I heard it. It came from the chaparral and every breath of the wind brought it a little nearer. It was like a wailing, very faint and very far away. I had never heard anything like it before. It went loud and then soft, loud and soft, and every time it was nearer and clearer. The horses snorted and the hobbled ones scattered as fast as they could. Everybody was awake now, talking in whispers and listening. The wailing became clearer and now we were sure it was coming toward us. It was like nothing I had ever heard before, or have heard since. High like a woman's voice, then hoarse like a man's, wild like an animal's. It went on and on in screams and howls that sounded full of—I don't know—something like a crazy loneliness or desperation."

Feliciano lit another cigaret. "Now we could hear faint crashing sounds as if something was passing through the underbrush, and right on top of that the fainter cries of men, shouting like cowboys rounding up cattle. But stronger than these other noises was the wailing, sounding nearer every moment. At times we were sure it was a man who was making the noise. Then we thought it was a woman screaming. Or a puma, or a wolf even.

"I was glad I had taken my father's advice. Quick as I could I drew in my rope and used it to put a hackamore on my horse. By the time I had finished, my father and the two men who had followed his advice were already mounted. I did the same, and I tell you I felt much better with a horse under me. The others were running around trying to catch their horses, so we helped round them up. The hobbles were cut and the men mounted bareback."

Feliciano paused and took several puffs at his cigaret. No one spoke in the interval.

"And all the time we were catching the horses, the wailing went on and on. It grew louder, frightening the horses, so we had trouble holding them in. By now we could hear crashing in the underbrush and the shouts of men who seemed to be chasing the thing. The last of us had barely mounted when it broke out of the chaparral and came directly toward us. It was running on two legs. It looked like a man, a tall heavy man with long hairy arms. He waved them aimlessly about as he ran with his legs half-bent at the knees. He had no clothes on except for pieces of rags that hung like ribbons from his shirt collar and his belt. One of ours tried to draw his pistol, but another one stopped him. Another man started to pray. The thing passed a few yards in front of us and I don't think it ever saw us. It was looking up toward the sky. A man, no doubt of it. In the moonlight we saw his face for just a moment. I will never forget it. He had a long bushy beard like St. Peter in the church books. But his face was another thing. His eyes were popped out of his head and they shone in the light of the moon. His face was twisted, his mouth open and panting like a dog's. We could hear him champing and gnashing his teeth as he passed. And from his mouth, down his St. Peter's beard all the way to his chest, he was drooling a mess of foaming spittle that also gleamed in the moonlight. His naked body was torn and bleeding from the thorns in the chaparral, and I remember he reminded me of Christ in a strange and crazy way.

"As he ran past us he screamed again, a scream like a soul that cannot find peace. The horses reared and when we quieted them down, the thing was gone. Only the screaming, which grew fainter and fainter, made us sure that we had seen it. Next came the sound of galloping horses. We scattered out a bit, just as a precaution, and we waited. Soon a group of men came riding up. 'Friends,' said one of them in Spanish. 'Good evening, friends,' we answered.

" 'A bad one,' said one of them. 'Did you see our man pass by?'

" 'Was he a man?' asked my father.

" 'Yes, but with the curse of the beast. A bitten man. It happened some time ago and now that the moon is full he got his first attack. That was the night before last and he was going to drink the poison this morning at dawn. But he must have lost his nerve during the night. He broke out from where we had him and started running. We are his relatives and friends.' "

Feliciano threw his second cigaret on the floor and stepped on it. "They rode away," he continued. "We didn't sleep anymore that night."

Don José cleared his throat. "Rabies is a dangerous thing," he said.

"Yes," agreed Don Pancho. "Most people today have no idea what it was to be bitten in the old days. Then there were no injections, as they say they have now. Nothing except a hot iron and garlic, which almost never worked."

"But it's a natural thing," said Feliciano, "a disease. That man was not a ghost."

"Ghosts do exist," said Don Pancho. "Even here we have our own ghosts."

"Yes," agreed Don José.

"So they say," Feliciano answered.

"They say a small creature like a donkey runs around through the hackberries in this block at midnight," said Don Pancho.

"And a woman dressed in white," added Don José.

"She walks from the largest tree just outside your backyard to the end of the block where there's a tree with a cross of nails on it," said Don Pancho.

"Men who see her face die, though she usually keeps it covered with her white shawl," added Don José.

"Donaciano the milkman," said Don Pancho, "he died that way, of fright. If there ever was an old man as blasphemous and unbelieving as Donaciano, I haven't heard of him. Well, before there were any houses on this block, Donaciano used to drive his cows through here every evening. One night he was driving four or five of them along a trail that ran where your back fence is now. It was very dark and the air was still. Well, sir, he was driving his cows along when the animals stopped and wouldn't budge. The old man came cursing up to them and beat them with his stick. But no, they would not go an inch farther along the trail. Then Donaciano saw the woman in white. She was crossing the trail in front of the cows. The cows turned and bolted the way they had come and old Donaciano was left alone on the trail, stiff with fright and staring at the woman who by that time was moving out of sight between the trees.

"But he wasn't frightened for long. He got angry instead and cried, 'Stop, you slut. Scaring my cows. You'll pay for this.' He ran after her and the woman just kept on walking slowly. Old Donaciano caught up with her and was going to hit her with his stick when she turned. She raised the side of her shawl and let him see her face. Her face ...

"No! No!" screamed Guálinto. Sobbing violently, he lay face down on the porch steps. Feliciano bounded out of his chair and gathered him in his arms. Guálinto burrowed against his uncle's chest. The smell of Feliciano's sweaty denim was comforting.

"Don't let them," he cried, "don't let them talk any more!"

"*Ya, ya,*" said Feliciano softly. "Nobody is going to talk anymore."

The door flew open and María came out in a rustle of skirts. "What —what?" she said in a choked voice.

"It's all right," Feliciano told her. "He was on the porch and we scared him with our talk. We didn't know he was there."

"Oh, thank God!" Then María's relief gave way to anger. "Trouble-maker! What were you doing with the men? Just wait!"

"Hush," Feliciano said. "Can't you see he's badly frightened?"

"In truth," said Don Pancho. He stretched out a hand and touched the boy. "He's trembling like a little rabbit."

Suddenly the moon hit the porch like a floodlight. The little group was silent for a moment. Don José and Don Pancho took off their hats. José could now see María's face, and he stole furtive glances while María looked at the moon and pretended not to notice. "It's late," said Don Pancho.

"It is," said Don José.

"Late?" said María, sounding surprised at the idea.

"Eight-thirty at least," said Don Pancho.

"You needn't go so early," said Feliciano.

"We'd like to stay a while longer, but we must get up early."

"We must," repeated Don José.

Formalities over, the brothers made a self-conscious little bow to-ward María, shook hands with Feliciano and walked down the porch steps, hats in hand. At the gate they again said "*Buenas noches,*" put on their hats and left. Guálinto was still in his uncle's arms and wanted to stay there. He was sure his mother was still angry and shrank from her touch when María reached out to take him. His uncle understood.

"Let him sleep with me tonight," he said. "Why, he's six already, almost a grown man. Want to sleep with me in the room in the back, Guálinto?"

Guálinto nodded, rubbing his head against Feliciano's shirt. María had lighted a lamp so Feliciano could pass through the bedroom without stumbling over the girls, who were already in their folding beds but still wide-awake. Carmen's grave eyes looked at Guálinto with mild concern. Maruca could scarcely contain herself. She squirmed and edged around in her bed, and her little eyes almost danced right off her face. Guálinto gave her an injured look. He twisted his head to keep looking at her as they went into the kitchen. Maruca's lips were silently saying, "*Vieja, vieja*" as plain as could be.

There was a light in the kitchen, where María had been working before she had been startled by Guálinto's screams. Beyond the kitchen door, his uncle carried him over the wooden platform that connected the house with "the room in the back," as the family called it. Feliciano's huge cross-legged canvas cot was already laid out, and María added Guálinto's pillow under the tent-like mosquito netting that covered it. The netting was like a little playhouse to Guálinto and being under it was an adventure in itself. The cot was by the open window.

"I want to sleep by the window," Guálinto said.

"Said and done," answered Feliciano, lifting the netting and depositing him on the far side of the cot. In a few moments the cot creaked as Feliciano got into it, turned his back on Guálinto and went to sleep. But Guálinto remained wide awake. He was thankful for the bright moonlight, until he remembered his uncle telling of the madman and he shut his eyes tightly. He wondered whether his uncle was really asleep and he thought of punching him accidentally, but thought better of it. His moving about woke Feliciano, who mumbled, "Something bothering you?"

"No," he answered, with feigned drowsiness. He dozed off and the next time he looked at the sky it was the color of dirty milk. Everything was very still. Then came a long cool breath of air through the window. It began to rain, a steady downpour. Some of it hit the window sill and bounced off the mosquito net, splattering Guálinto's face. It felt cool and pleasant. Then it thundered, and his uncle got up and closed the window.

As he crawled back under the mosquito net he asked, "Did you get wet?"

"No sir," said Guálinto, though his face and neck were damp. He stretched out like a contented cat. Then he cuddled up against his uncle's back and went to sleep to the music of the rain.

11

Guálinto woke with the sun shining on his face. He was in his mother's bed, by the window where he usually slept, and it was late in the morning. Almost noon, perhaps. That was strange. He had gone to sleep on Uncle Feliciano's cot last night. He tried to sit up and fell back on his pillow. Dizzy, m-m-m. It was hot and stuffy in the room. But the window was wide open. Then, why ... he put the heel of his hand against his temples and rubbed with a jerky motion. Maybe stretching .... Why was it so hot? On the fig tree outside the window a bird was singing. The sound came as if from miles away.

Now he heard voices in the kitchen. Dead, disconnected sounds. "Kitchen" made him think of food. His stomach did a somersault and backed up against his spine. He burrowed under the sheet. Why didn't somebody close the window? It was so cold. Quick pattering steps came toward him and Guálinto, his eyes shut, knew Maruca was in the room.

"Mama-a-a!" Maruca's voice came from a great distance. "He's got the shivers again."

"Coming," said his mother from far away. "Close the window."

Maruca climbed on the bed and crawled over Guálinto to shut the window with a resounding bang. He protested feebly when her knees dug into his legs.

"Be careful." That was Carmen's voice. "You'll hurt him."

"Oh, I'm sorry, Guálinto," said Maruca. "I'm sorry, I really am."

Guálinto didn't answer. He kept his eyes shut.

Maruca touched his shoulder, then shook it gently. "I said I was sorry, Guálinto. I said I was sorry." Getting no answer she shook harder.

"Here, here." It was his mother. "Quit bothering him."

A heavy quilt descended on his shivering body. Then something heavier and smaller on top. But it was still very cold. His mother went, returned. A warm vapor breathed against his cheek and he opened his eyes to see his mother's serious face behind a steaming cup. "Drink this," she said.

"No, I don't want to," he mumbled. "I'll throw it up."

"Drink," said his mother. "Don't you want to get well?"

"I'll get well by myself. Honest, I will."

"Drink it. You're sick enough as it is."

He sat up and put out his hand to touch the cup, then drew it back. "It's too hot. I'll throw it up, I know I will."

"It doesn't taste bad," his mother said in a gentler tone. "Look." She tasted the tea and gave it to him. "Go on, or I'll have to hold your nose."

With a resigned air he took the cup. Ugh! A moment of panic when his gullet refused to swallow. There! He gulped the rest of it down. It didn't taste so bad, after all. The tea gave him a pleasant warmth in his stomach. His mother took the cup and went back to the kitchen. He leaned back and pulled the covers over himself and was beginning to doze off when he heard his uncle's voice in the kitchen.

"That's pure superstition," his uncle said. "He has a cold, that's all. The bedewing he got last night caused it, I'm sure. Give him some aspirin and rub him down with mentholatum, and he'll be all right by tomorrow."

"You just won't see what you don't want to see!" Guálinto had never heard his mother talk to his uncle like that. "It's fright, I tell you. Are you going to let him waste away because of your ideas?"

"All right, all right. I'll go get the woman."

"The sooner the better," his mother said. "We mustn't let it take root."

Guálinto wasn't sure whether he was frightened or just excited by what he had heard. His uncle had gone to get Doña Simonita la Ciega to cure him of fright sickness. Guálinto had heard about her many times, but he had never seen her. It was said she could talk with spirits and foretell the future. She was blind but she could see many things other people could not.

His mother glided into the room. She kissed his cheek. "How's my little one feeling? You've had a good sleep this time. It's almost noon."

"Why do you say I had a good sleep now?"

"Because you didn't sleep well last night. You cried and thrashed around in your uncle's cot, don't you remember? That's when I brought you to my bed."

Now he remembered, vaguely. His mother, his uncle and his sisters around him in the lamplight while he screamed and held on tightly to his mother's nightgown. Shadowy images came trooping back. He had been pursued. By a wolf. No. It had been a dog, or maybe … Eyes, red staring eyes, glimpses of frightful faces. And through it all a sense of being chased that even now sent chills caterpillaring up his back.

There were steps in the kitchen. Guálinto heard his uncle's deep voice saying, "Careful now; you climb a step here." Shuffling little steps with the squishy sound of rubber soles. They were drowned in Feliciano's "This way. Sit down here, please." More shuffling and a creak from the old wicker chair that was always by the dining table.

His mother patted Guálinto on the cheek. "I'll come back in a little while." She went through the doorway into the kitchen.

"Well, here she is," said Feliciano with obvious relief.

"Fine." There was a smile in María's voice. "How are you Doña Simonita?"

"Oh, more or less well," said a high shaky voice. "Can't feel much better, but that's the way the Lord wishes it. I won't complain."

"So be it," said María, "His will be done. The child is in the next room."

"Is everything ready?" Doña Simonita's voice brightened a bit.

"The water for the tea is beginning to boil and I'll take the ashes out of the stove when you want them."

"Let's start then." The chair creaked and Guálinto stared at the doorway.

"Here, don't go fall," said his uncle. He appeared at the doorway, his arm clutched by a brown wrinkled hand. Then the old woman came shuffling in. She was short and slight, all dressed in black with a black shawl over her head that hid her face. All black except for her feet. She was wearing a pair of white canvas shoes. Guálinto stared fixedly at her as she shuffled forward, trying to get a glimpse of her face. Did she have one? Finally he saw it. A square, brown, honest-to-goodness face. But it looked as if it had been scratched and clawed to pieces and then patched up again. Guálinto sat up in bed.

"What happened to your face?" he asked.

"Guálinto!" exclaimed his mother.

But Doña Simonita was not angry. She smiled the thoughtful detached smile of the blind, which makes you think that only part of them is here while the greater, inner part is absent, far above and beyond those around them who can see. "It was the smallpox, child," she answered. "It made holes in my face and put my eyes out when I was about the size of your older sister."

Guálinto wondered how she knew how big Maruca was if she couldn't see, but he decided not to ask any more questions after his mother shot a direful glance at him. "Sit down, Doña Simonita," his mother said solicitously. "Right here."

Doña Simonita felt her way into the chair and breathed gustily as she relaxed into it. She sat there for a long while, her head slightly bowed and nodding just very slightly. "God is very wise," said María softly. "He took away your sight but he gave you gifts that few people have."

"Since very young I have had them," replied Doña Simonita. "Once I was playing with my older brothers and sisters at a neighbor's house.

Suddenly I said, 'Let's go home. Our aunt is there.' We went home and there was our aunt we hadn't seen for years."

"Did you ever?" said María, clasping her hands.

"Another time I dreamed one of my sisters was dead and she died the next week. And since then, when I get it into my head that something is going to happen it happens. I'm afraid to even think about people because I might think of them as dead or hurt. If I do, they're bound to die or have an accident."

"How dreadful to know about dreadful things even before they happen," said María softly. Trepidation bounced up and down inside Guálinto. He prayed that Doña Simonita would never think about him at all.

"It comes of itself," continued Doña Simonita. "I can't do anything to stop it." She slipped once more into a meditative silence. Guálinto, scarcely breathing, could hear the sputtering crackle of firewood in the kitchen stove and the steady murmur of boiling water. These sounds must have pierced at last through Doña Simonita's thoughts. She straightened up.

"Let's tend to this child," she said. She edged her chair closer to the bed and reached out to touch Guálinto. He stared at her face, not so sure whether he wanted to be cured by her. When she touched his arm he shrank back a bit, not very much but enough for her to notice it. "Don't be afraid," she said. Then to his mother, "Will you take out the ashes from the stove so they'll cool a bit? And close the shutters, please." A fleeting thought crossed his mind: did she know or just guess the shutters were open.

He heard his mother leave the room, his eyes were fixed on Doña Simonita's scarred face, and he didn't like being alone with her in a half-darkened room. The old woman made the sign of the cross and started to pray. His mother's voice cut through the buzzing mumble of the prayer, "Maruca, close the shutters." Buzz-mumble, buzz-mumble went the old woman. Pattering feet outside and the wooden shutters close to the bed screeched and slammed shut. The running feet around the corner of the house, a creak and a slam. The room was in shadow now. His mother came in with a plate and Doña Simonita stopped praying. Doña Simonita took the plate, which was heaped with ashes. He felt their warmth on his cheek as the plate changed hands. Then his mother threw aside the covers and picked Guálinto up in her arms.

Doña Simonita felt over the bed to be sure the covers were not in the way. Assured, she made the sign of the cross once more with her free right hand. Then she dipped into the plate and sowed a crude cross of ashes on the bed. She talked while she did so, "Some people who heal like to do this part out in the yard at noon. They use a cross of quicklime and then add a little dirt from each arm of the cross to the tea. For me this is a better way." His mother lowered Guálinto onto the bed. The ashes grated against his back and their warmth penetrated his nightshirt. There was an air of mystery and danger in the room, a mixture of church and doctor's office. His mother left the room again and Guálinto was left face to face with Doña Simonita. Her eyeless, leathery face was but faintly visible against the black of her clothes. Another sign of the cross and she slipped out of her chair and dropped to her knees by the side of the bed.

"Pray with me," she said. "The Lord's Prayer first; don't be afraid."

His mother reappeared with a steaming cup in her hand. "Pray, *hijito*," she urged. "Pray with her."

Guálinto started to pray with the old woman, haltingly at first, then with more fluency. They repeated the prayer and this time, instead of following, he murmured in unison with her. Again. Then after that the Hail Mary three times. A special bond grew between him and Doña Simonita as they prayed together, she kneeling by the bed, he lying on his side. As if they were singing together in harmony. He was no longer afraid of her.

"Now the tea," she said. Guálinto sat up to take the tea, anxiety no longer gnawing at his breastbone. Doña Simonita took the cup and, reaching into the plateful of ashes, took a pinch and dropped it into the cup. In the cup also were a red ribbon tied to a gold ring. Guálinto took the tea readily. The spicy smell told him it was aniseed tea, and everybody knew the saying, *Para el susto el yerbanís*. But there were other things in it. He tasted it cautiously.

"Drink it," his mother said. "It's good."

He took a swallow. Not bad. He drained the cup except for the sediment of ashes and the ribbon and the ring at the bottom. He sank back into bed, the inside of his cheeks contracted against his gums in delicious reaction to the tang of the tea. A feeling of quiet comfort in his stomach soaked into his chest and limbs. Doña Simonita was kneeling beside the bed again, praying. She stopped praying now and raised her face. "Guálinto, Guálinto, Guálinto," she called. Then she said, "Where are you? Don't go away. Come closer. *¿Dónde estás? No te vayas. Acércate.* Where are you? Don't go away. Come closer." She murmured some prayers indistinctly. Then again she called his name and repeated the same words calling him to her, always in groups of three.

Guálinto felt that he was floating toward Doña Simonita through limitless space. He felt very sleepy and deliciously tired. His body became lighter and lighter except for his eyes. They were heavy, heavy, heavy. With some effort he opened them the tiniest bit. In the ever deepening gloom Doña Simonita's face was barely visible, floating around in the blackness of her clothes. It floated nearer and nearer. It was changing. He closed his eyes again, but he could still see her face. Deep down, way below, he could hear her voice, praying, calling and repeating his name. In the blackness behind his eyelids, strange forms went sailing by, like huge indistinct clouds. Women, all covered up to their heads, plunging horses, a man running wildly and never getting out of the same place. A shaggy bearish figure took form. A snarling face with red flaming eyes.

He opened his eyes with a start. Doña Simonita was still mumbling in the gloom. He closed his eyes again and saw her face behind his eyelids this time, instead of the scary images.

The pillow was wonderfully soft and airy. The bed began to push up and down gently, rising a bit from the floor at every push. Far, far away Doña Simonita was praying. Her voice became a murmur like that of a bee. Now the bed had become a cloud that moved slowly like a tall sailing ship just getting under way. Little by little it gathered speed. It circled the room—once, twice. The third time it floated out of the window.

12

He slept most of the next day. Toward evening he woke to the sound of children's voices. Laughing. Maruca and Carmen playing with the Gracia girls. But he felt no desire to be out with them. He felt lazy and contented where he was. The smell of frying beef in the kitchen made him hungry just as his mother appeared at the doorway.

"You're awake," she said. "I have some hot broth for you, with a tortilla shredded in it. Are you hungry?" Guálinto nodded vigorously and his mother returned to the kitchen. The laughter of the children had stopped.

"Good evening," a child's voice in the kitchen.

"*Buenas tardes.*"

"*Buenas.*" His mother's and his uncle's voices blended in response.

"That if you have any of that soda with the hammer, says my mother. She has a pain in her stomach."

"I'll take it over myself," his mother replied. "Just a moment, let me put something over my head. Will you give him the broth, Feliciano?"

Guálinto eagerly awaited the double pleasure of food and conversation with his uncle. A chair in the kitchen creaked, there were some tentative steps, and Uncle Feliciano came in, awkwardly holding a tray with a bowl and spoon upon it. Guálinto sat up in bed. "That sure smells nice, Uncle."

Feliciano's mustache rippled in a half smile. "It does," he said. He gave the tray to Guálinto, who started spooning away at once, while he eased himself into a chair beside the bed. "You're hungry now."

"You bet." Guálinto chewed on a piece of tortilla soaked in the meaty broth.

"That's good."

Guálinto finished off the pieces of tortilla and drank the rest of the broth directly from the bowl. He leaned back while his uncle put the tray on the floor beside his chair.

"It's strange," Guálinto said after a while. "Here it's almost Christmas and we haven't had a frost."

Feliciano chuckled. "We're at the end of August. Four full months before Christmas. No chance of a frost, and it's just as well. I have some fine vegetables coming in the land Don José is working for me."

"What vegetables, Uncle?"

"Tomatoes, cabbage, green beans, bell peppers."

"Gee, that's nice! It was sure a good idea growing the vegetables you sell, wasn't it?"

"Don José does all the growing, I just pay the rent for the land. I'm pretty busy at the grocery store and other things. I have *two* boys working for me now at the store, not counting Juan. Added the other one just yesterday."

"When will you take me again to the store, Uncle? And I'd like to go even more to the country to see your vegetables."

Feliciano laughed. "As soon as you're well, I'll take you to the store and also to the country. How do you feel now?"

"Oh, I feel fine. That old curing woman knows her stuff."

"Uh-huh."

"You think it was the prayers that did it?"

"We-e-ell, maybe it was the tea."

"Why don't you like prayers and priests, Uncle? Why?"

Feliciano laughed deep down in his chest. "You've seen the priest when he's saying the mass?"

"Yes."

"You've seen him when he swigs that wine. Mind you, now that a decent man can't keep a bottle of spirits in his house for medicine they can have their wine. You've seen how the priest bows and leans about.

Then he turns and waves the cup at the bunch of people in there. Know what he's saying?"

Guálinto shook his head.

"He isn't praying or mumbling dominus obispo. He turns around and raises the cup and says, 'To the health of all you jackasses.' That's what he's saying." Feliciano chuckled, then stopped suddenly. "Don't you be telling your mother or the girls what I told you."

Guálinto was delighted. "Go ahead, Uncle Feliciano. I won't let them in on a thing." But his uncle was lost in thought. Finally Guálinto said, "Uncle, do you believe in Santa Claus?"

Feliciano was startled out of his reverie. "Of course I believe in Santo Kloss. Who's been telling you different?"

"Oh, nobody. Then there's a God too?"

Feliciano looked at his nephew curiously. When he answered at last, there was a mixture of pride and wonder in his voice. "Yes," he said, "there is a God. But mind you, God is not in this world. The priests are only men."

Guálinto thought a moment. "Uncle Feliciano, how about ... how about my father?"

"What about him?"

"What was he like? What did he die of? Maruca was telling Carmen and me the other day he had been killed in a gunfight with the *rinches*."

"That Maruca! She's imagining things. Your father was a peaceful man."

"But what was he like?"

"Your father was a fine man. He looked a lot like you, except that his hair was red-like. He was honest and good."

That pleased Guálinto, but he persisted. "Yes, but what did he die of?"

There was a moment of quiet during which his uncle stroked his fingertips with his thumbs, his eyes fixed on the floor. "Your father died of his heart, Guálinto. His heart was too big and it killed him."

Guálinto was silent. He had heard of people whose hearts had burst. Horses too, if they were made to run for a long time.

"What you ought to know is that your father was a gentleman."

"A *caballero*?" echoed Guálinto. "He always rode horses?"

Feliciano almost smiled. "No, boy. That means he was educated and had fine manners. He was gentry, at least his family was."

"Were they rich?"

"Yes."

"Then, why aren't we rich, Uncle Feliciano?"

"Oh, the Revolution."

"Oh," echoed Guálinto. He did not question further. The Revolution was a household word, but half-understood by Guálinto. He had a confused picture of it as a tremendous tumult rolling along like a hurricane. A whirlwind of fire and smoke and shouting punctuated by shots and galloping horses and studded with scenes of firing squads. A storm without purpose or direction. No one could do anything about the Revolution. A strange boy moved into the Dos Veintidós. He had a well-to-do air, though his family was poor. His accent was sing-songy and he had come from Guadalajara or Querétaro or some other distant place with a strange name. A Mexican of the interior, a *pues*, so called because of his constant insertion of that word in his conversation. Why did he come here? He would shrug, "The Revolution, *pues*." Another boy lives with relatives because he is an orphan. The Revolution. We had. There was. They were. Then came the Revolution, the great changer of things.

"Weren't you ever rich, Uncle Feliciano?"

"No," answered Feliciano bitterly, "but I should have been. Damn these Gringos!"

"The Gringos?" Guálinto sat up. "They took your money away?"

In the half-darkness Feliciano's mustache was slowly melting into his face. He fondled the ends of it as he spoke. "They didn't exactly take it from me, and it wasn't counting, clinking money. It was a big cattle ranch that belonged to my grandfather, thousands of acres. It would have belonged to María and me now. And to you and the girls."

"What happened to it?"

"The Gringos got it. It's part of the Keene ranch now."

"The Keene ranch? Where the *rinches* come from?"

"That one."

"The *rinches* took it, then. Aw, Uncle. Why didn't your father and his father kill them?"

"There were too many of them. And they had the law on their side. Gringo law."

"But we could've gone inside the house," persisted Guálinto. "And we could have shot them down as they came riding up, just like this: Ping! Ping! Ping, ping, ping!"

Feliciano waited patiently until Guálinto got all the pings out of his system. Then he said, "That's the way it happens in the movies. But it just didn't happen like that. Let's not talk about it anymore." He rose and moved toward the table. A clink of glass, the scratching of a match, and the room was illuminated in the pale-yellow glow of lamplight. He sat down again. "They tell you, these Gringos, 'If you don't like it here, don't want to be American, get out. Go back to your own country.' Get out? Why? Let *them* get out, they came here last. And go where? *This* is our country. *This* is our home. They made it Gringo land by force, we cannot change that. But no force of theirs can make us, the land's rightful people, Gringo people."

"Just wait till I grow up!" Guálinto blurted out. He clutched tightly at the edge of the bed. "Just wait till I'm a man! I'll get our land back. I'll be like Gregorio Cortez and Cheno Cortinas and all of them." He pulled out an imaginary gun. "Shoot them down like dogs. Ping, ping ... '' Feliciano watched the boy thoughtfully. "I'll kill all the Gringos and the *rinches* too, and drive them away from here."

Feliciano tried to make a joke of it. "You can't kill them all and drive them out at the same time."

"Well, I'll drive out the Gringo women and children and also the *rinche* families." He paused, perplexed. "Are there women *rinches* and little *rinche* children too?"

"No, just men."

"Then where do they come from? If there are no little ones and no mothers."

Feliciano's smile became a low chuckle. "They are Gringos, Guálinto." The chuckle died. "Just Gringos whose job is to kill and frighten Mexicans. Then the rest of them can steal everything."

"Oh." Guálinto lay still, digesting Feliciano's words, chewing them in a mental cud, so to speak. He could not in an instant change his previous picture of the Texas Ranger, a particular kind of monster allied to no existing human race.

"But you shouldn't think of such things, much less talk about them," his uncle said softly. "It will only get you in bad. They are too many and too strong. You might as well try to stop the river with your fingers." He stopped and swallowed hard. "Other men have tried it," he continued in the monotonous voice of one reciting a written speech. "Many others have tried and they have all failed. All they did was make the Gringos hate us more and treat us worse, and it's better to live in peace and forget the past." He finished his last words in a hurry and wiped his brow at the effort the declaration had cost him.

But the speech had been lost on Guálinto. His mind was already on another track. "Uncle," he said, "why are the American women bad?"

"Bad?" echoed Feliciano. "What do you mean?"

"Well, I heard Doña Domitila talking to Mama the other day and she said that American women are bad and shameless. But when I asked Mama why, she wouldn't tell me. You'll tell me, won't you?"

His uncle scratched his head. "Oh, she meant bad in the way women are bad. Shameless, that's it, shameless."

"But how is that?"

"Well, they're plain bad. You'll have to grow up to understand."

"But I'm grown up enough. I'm going to be seven in June."

"That's still a long ways off. Ten months."

"Yes," Guálinto agreed. "Christmas has to come and then New Years. Gee, Uncle Feliciano, know what?"

"What," said Feliciano warily.

"Let's talk about Santa Claus."

"Sure, sure." Feliciano was much relieved. "Let's talk about Santo Kloss."

"Go on, Uncle. Go ahead and talk about Santa Claus."

Feliciano feigned ignorance. "But what can I talk about?"

"What he looks like. Where he lives."

"But you've heard all of that before."

"I know, but I want to hear about it again."

"All right. Santo Kloss is a fat old man with white whiskers ... "

"Uncle."

"Yes?"

"He must be a very old man, no?"

"Very, very old."

"And he has been bringing gifts to children for many years?"

"For hundreds of years."

"When you were little too?"

"Yes."

"Did he bring you a lot of toys and candy?"

Feliciano studied his fingertips. "We lived in a god-forsaken little place in the chaparral. I guess he never found it."

"That's awful. Why didn't you write him?"

"I guess I never thought of that."

"And Mama never got any toys either?"

"No."

"And my father?"

The smile came back to Feliciano's face. "He did. He got everything he wanted when he was little. Toys, candy, nuts, fruit you've never heard of. But Santo Kloss didn't bring them."

Guálinto was startled. "He didn't? Then his ... Then who did it?"

"The Three Wise Kings. The ones who brought gifts to the Child Jesus."

"Why?"

"Because your father lived in Mexico when he was a boy, and Santo Kloss doesn't go to Mexico. He gives away toys just in the United States. In Mexico the Three Kings come on their camels from the Orient. They come on the Sixth of January instead of Christmas Eve. And the children put their shoes out for them instead of their stockings."

"They ought to come over to this side too. Then I'd get gifts twice, in my stocking and in my shoes!"

"They have to stay on their side of the river."

"Why?"

"I don't know. Perhaps they don't have passports."

"Why do people have to have a passport to cross the river?"

"I don't know," answered Feliciano. "It's the law." And he sank into thoughts of the indignities heaped on Mexicans by immigration officials.

But Guálinto wanted to talk about Santa Claus. "Then Santa Claus is an American saint?"

Feliciano looked up. "I guess so. He is a Gringo saint, come to think of it. He speaks English only and he gives away gifts only on this side of the river."

Guálinto was silent. He leaned back in bed and thought. Feliciano took advantage of the lull to make himself a cigarrete. He was bending over it, licking the corn husk to make the roll stick, when he was surprised by Guálinto's exclamation.

"But Uncle!"

Feliciano raised his head. "But what?"

"Santa Claus is good, isn't he?"

"Yes."

"He's very kind to children and he wouldn't hurt anyone, would he?"

"No."

"He wouldn't kill anybody."

"Of course not. Why do you ask?"

"Because, if Santa Claus is so good, how can he be a Gringo too?"

Feliciano took a deep breath and walked over to the table. He lighted his cigarrete over the lamp chimney. After puffing at it several times he looked at his nephew. "Perhaps he's a different kind of Gringo." He peered out the window. "Sounds like your mother's coming back."

Part III
"DEAR OLD GRINGO SCHOOL DAYS"

1

When Maruca and then Carmen entered grammar school, Feliciano had driven María and each of her daughters to have them registered late in August. Each time he waited outside the building while María went to the office for registration and then talked to the teacher. In both cases the teacher's name had been Miss Josephine. But Guálinto was a boy and Feliciano decided he should be registered by a man. So Feliciano took his nephew to registration himself.

María was more nervous than usual as she prepared her son for his long-awaited first step on the road to an education, which would make him a great man some day. Kneeling in front of him she gave his face one last hectic wiping and threw the wet towel over her shoulder to give his starched blue-striped blouse another straightening.

"Remember to act nice," she said. "Be a gentleman. Stay away from those hoodlums you like to play with. Obey. Be sure to do what you are told. I don't want any complaints from the *profesora* about a son of mine. And above all, don't fight."

Guálinto stood before her with his arms at his sides, allowing himself to be handled like a clothing-store dummy. Only his face was alive, animated by anxious anticipation. "And always be careful crossing Fourteenth Street," his mother continued. "Oh, Feliciano, how afraid I'll be every time school is out."

Feliciano, who stood by watching, pushed his black Sunday hat away from his forehead. "Calm down," he said. "He's not being taken away as a soldier or anything like that. You're getting him all scared and fluttery like yourself."

"But he's still such a little boy."

"Nothing's going to happen to him. The girls will take care of him, if you want him to grow up that way."

"Oh," said María disgustedly, "you have no heart."

Feliciano's big mustache rippled in a grin. "Come on, Guálinto. Let's get going."

Guálinto took his uncle's hand and María, seizing a rag, took a few extra swipes at the boy's shiny patent leather sandals. "Remember," she said, following them to the door. "Remember what I told you." She planted a kiss on his forehead.

"*Hasta luego*," said Feliciano.

"'*Sta luego*," mumbled Guálinto.

"God keep you."

Once on the buggy Guálinto wiped his forehead. He wished his mother would stop kissing him like a baby. They rode in style. The buggy had been painted just the week before, and it was now pulled by a new gelding, a *bayo coyote*. They rode with the top raised because the sun was pretty hot and Guálinto was bareheaded. Two blocks from the school house they left the buggy at a stable and walked the rest of the way. Guálinto didn't take his uncle's hand again but walked beside him, swinging his arms the way Feliciano did. They met many people on the street and several were Mexican men. They all seemed to know Guálinto's uncle. It was mostly, "*Buenos días*, Don Feliciano." "*Buenos días*, Sóstenes." "Don Feliciano, how are you." "Well, Pedro, and how are you." Guálinto noticed that all the men they met called his uncle "Don Feliciano," while his uncle gave the "Don" to only some of them. It made him proud to be the nephew of an important man. Then they turned the corner and there was the grammar school, all two stories of it. And it was long, longer than any building Guálinto had ever seen.

His stomach began to feel funny and he took his uncle's hand again as they walked on the concrete sidewalk, along the iron fence, for an interminable block until they got to the gate that led into the front door of the building. Up the steps and along a short hall that went crosswise to another hall that ran the length of the building. They turned into the long hall, almost as long as the church. What impressed Guálinto most were the silence and the smells. The oiled-wood smell of the floor that was being swept by a man in blue denim at the far end of the hall. Smells of ground pencil lead and new books.

Nephew and uncle stared about them in silence. Tacked to the wall just above their heads was a big American flag, its red and blue bright against the grayish-green of the plastered wall. Feliciano took a couple of steps sideways so he would not be directly under it. On the wall opposite hung the picture of a man with some words printed under it. Feliciano walked carefully across the hall, followed by Guálinto. He peered at the words for a moment. Then he stretched out his hand to Guálinto, who was looking down the hall at the man who was sweeping.

"Psst," he said, touching Guálinto's shoulder. "Look. That's Guáchinton."

Guálinto looked up eagerly at the portrait of his namesake. What a terrible disappointment! He had expected a fierce-looking warrior in a medal-covered uniform. Riding a horse maybe, and holding a sword in his hand. He stared at the picture with disillusionment that was almost contempt. A face like an angry old woman. Long white hair. And that coat! What a man to be named after.

"Uncle—" he began and his voice boomed unexpectedly in the empty hall.

"Sh-h-h!" said Feliciano, much louder than he expected. They stood in embarrassed silence for a moment. The man at the end of the hall continued sweeping. Feliciano squared his shoulders and walked over to him.

"Pardon," he said, "but I would like to know where the office is."

Before looking up the old man pushed the oily dirt he was brushing against the baseboard. When he saw a man in a suit with shiny boots and a stetson hat, he stood up a little straighter. "Yessir," he said, wiping his ugly gum-doll face with a large red bandana. "What do you wish?"

"I would like to know where the school office is," Feliciano replied, a bit more confidently.

"Yessir. I will show you. Just follow me." He waddled down the hall, the bandana hanging out of his hip pocket like a signal flag. He led them back to the corner where the two hallways met. They followed him through a door beside George Washington's picture. The office was divided in half by a counter, as in a grocery store. Outside the counter were some small tables and chairs. Inside were green metal boxes with drawers and more tables, piled with books and papers. Beyond was a closed door with the words "PRINCIPAL" painted on it. A nice-looking young woman was behind the counter. "*Un niño nuevo*," the janitor said and left.

"*Buenos días*," said the young woman. "Do you wish to register your little boy?"

"*Sí señorita*," Feliciano said, taking off his hat.

"This is his first year?"

"It is."

The young woman looked at some papers on a table behind the counter. "We're pretty full in first grade already, but perhaps Miss Cornelia can find room for him in her class."

A middle-aged lady who had been sitting at one of the outside tables rose and came toward them. "Another little one?" she said sweetly. "I think I can fit the young man in my class." She smiled at Feliciano and patted Guálinto's head. "I'll fill out the form myself, Olivia," she told the girl behind the counter. You are very busy right now, I know." Miss Cornelia took a big white card from the counter and led them to the table where she had been sitting. She was a tall thin woman dressed in some kind of shiny gray material. She put the white card on the table. It was full of lines and printed words. She and Feliciano sat down while Guálinto stood holding on to one of his uncle's knees.

"Name?" asked Miss Cornelia, oozing honey from every pore.

Feliciano struggled with himself for a moment. Then he said firmly, "Guálinto. Guálinto Gómez."

It was Miss Cornelia's turn to hesitate. She paused, stroking her receding chin with a red and blue pencil. "With a G or with an H?"

"With a G."

She wrote. "Strange name, isn't it? Is it an Indian name?"

"Yes," said Feliciano. "It's an Indian name." He looked at Guálinto and then looked away.

Miss Cornelia wrote, asked, wrote. Address? Place birth? Date of birth? Vaccinated? Parents?

"His father is not living, ma'am. His mother is my sister."

"Then you're his guardian."

"No. I'm his uncle."

"But you're his guardian too." The honey in Miss Cornelia's voice thickened just a bit.

"What is that?" asked Feliciano warily. "Is there a Spanish word for it?"

"The person who is responsible for him," answered Miss Cornelia primly. "Your name, please?"

Feliciano had a fleeting vision of his name in some government file. "Better put his mother's name down there," he said. "María García de Gómez."

Registration was finished at last and Miss Cornelia smiled at Feliciano coyly. "I hope you will visit us again," she told him. Then to Guálinto. "I'll expect you tomorrow morning, dear. Bring a pencil and a tablet."

Guálinto smiled abashedly. He was still uneasy but Miss Cornelia's kind words were a comfort to him. It wouldn't be so hard tomorrow, when classes began.

As they went down the walk again toward the street, his uncle told Guálinto, "Just do what she says and everything will be all right. She looks like a good old lady."

Guálinto nodded absently. His mind was already forming scenes in the unknown setting of Miss Cornelia's classroom, scenes where Guálinto was the central figure while Miss Cornelia looked on approvingly. He was so pleased with himself that he forgot to ask his uncle why he had said Guálinto was an Indian name.

2

In September the days were still warm, but the mornings were cool enough to make one shiver. This particular morning at least made Guálinto feel cold under his new shirt and overalls. He was on his way to school for the first time with Maruca and Carmen. With Carmen really, because Maruca went skipping ahead of them, stopping now and then to look for wild flowers that were not there, to tease a toad with a stick, or to whirl round and round on the ball of one foot, arms stretched out like a dancer. Each time she would fall behind Carmen and Guálinto, but she would catch up with them and pass them again.

Carmen walked gravely along with Guálinto at her side. Pressed tightly under his arm he carried a brand-new Red Indian pencil tablet. A pencil still unsharpened was clutched in his other hand. He moved closer to Carmen when they reached Fourteenth Street, crossing it with elaborate care, looking this way and that many times until they were sure no speeding cars were within range. When they got to school Maruca saw some of her friends and ran off without a word. Carmen stayed with Guálinto until they were well inside the gate. "Maruca and I go to this side of the yard," she told him. "This is the girls' side. You go over there to the boys' side."

Guálinto looked idly toward the girls' side, where swings and see-saws were sprinkled with little girls in dresses of many colors. He stepped off the walk and over a line of plants to the hard, pebble-sprinkled yard of the boys' side. There were boys everywhere. Some were playing tops and marbles. Others were galloping over the far end of the yard playing cowboys and Indians. Another group close by were playing scissors-rock-paper. The boys all looked alike. Then among the sameness of the strange crowd he saw a flash of color, a red head. He looked again and his heart turned a somersault. El Colorado! Guálinto had seen El Colorado close up only once, before the Vera boys moved away, but he had never forgotten the big boy's face. Scowling, menacing, with fierce light-brown eyes. He had shown up one day when Guálinto was playing with the Vera boys in front of Meno Menchaca's house. He came up with some smaller boys who lived near the *masa* mill, looking for a fight with Poncho Vera. Poncho did not want to fight, but then El Colorado pushed Chicho and Guálinto and knocked them down. Then Poncho went after him. What a fight! They kept hittin—.

El Colorado was in front of him, and Guálinto didn't know which way to run. But the big redhead passed him by. Nothing happened. He just looked at Guálinto in an absent-minded sort of way and walked on. There was no menace in the tawny eyes. They looked watery and soft. Guálinto marveled at his escape, but just in case El Colorado changed his mind and came back he looked for a better haven on the steps leading to one of the doors into the school building. The concrete steps were built between two short brick walls, a faded red like the rest of the building, as high as the top step and stretching all the way to the bottom one. This gave the lower steps a fortress-like air, flanked as they were by the height of the walls, while the top step was a turret where the side walls became two parallel arms stretching from the top step outward. Sitting on the third step Guálinto had his flanks protected and a clear retreat into the school building.

No sooner had he sat down when he heard someone calling above him, "Psst! Psst!" He looked up. Perched above Guálinto's head was a round-faced boy with his legs dangling from the wall.

"How did you get up there?" asked Guálinto, craning his neck for a better look.

The other boy grinned. "That way," he said, pointing to the top of the steps. "Come on up." Guálinto ran up the steps and out on the cement top of the wall, easing himself down beside the boy with the round face.

"What's your name?" asked the boy, shifting away a little in a gesture of welcome.

"Guálinto. Guálinto Gómez. What's yours?"

"Orestes Sierra."

"Orestes?" Guálinto laughed. "That's a funny name."

"Yours is funny too," said Orestes.

"Uh-huh. I guess you're right."

They sat silently for a while and then Orestes asked, "Where do you live?"

"In the Dos Veintidós," answered Guálinto with a touch of pride.

"El Dos Veintidós? I live there too!"

"How come I've never seen you? You mustn't live near where I do. I live in the Hackberries."

"You saw me once, now I remember. I live up close to Fourteenth Street, near the *masa* mill."

"No kidding!" Guálinto looked at Orestes with new interest. "You live near El Colorado then."

"That's right."

"He sure is a tough guy."

"He sure is," agreed Orestes.

"They say he likes to beat up on little guys all the time."

"Nah. You leave him alone and he leaves you alone. He just fights guys his own size, or bigger even. But you make him mad he can be mean."

"I know he can be mean. One time he pushed me so hard he knocked me down. Chicho Vera too."

"I know. I was there with some other kids from around the *masa* mill. But all he wanted was to make the big one, Poncho, fight him and Poncho wouldn't."

"But Poncho did fight when El Colorado pushed Chicho and me. What a fight! Who do you think won?"

"Neither. Filomeno Menchaca came home and stopped the fight. Remember?"

"They both were pretty tired and neither one of them would give. I think they were glad Meno stopped the fight."

"I don't know," said Orestes. "I think El Colorado would've won if they had kept on fighting. He's really tough."

"That's what everybody says. But I met him in the yard just a little while ago, and he didn't look tough. He seemed sort of sad. Did somebody die?"

"No," said Orestes softly, his face taking on a conspiratorial look. "It's the way his folks carry on, his old man and the old lady. Last night they tore into each other prettier than ever. Boy! You should've seen it!"

"They were fighting?"

Orestes nodded. "They do it often but nothing like last night. The old man came home drunk just before dark and he finds all the doors and windows in the house locked. The old lady had shut herself inside with all the kids. The old man roars around, trying to peek through the windows. One of El Colorado's sisters sticks her head out a window and the old man yells at her, 'Go tell your mother to wash her head and see if she don't grow horns.' Then he starts pushing on a door till it works open and he gets inside."

Orestes stopped as if that were a suitable ending to his story. "Look at that bird," he said, pointing to a little sparrow peeping in and out of the eaves.

"Leave off on the bird," said Guálinto impatiently. "What happened then?" Orestes grinned. "Oh, about El Colorado's old man, you mean. Well, he gets in and the old lady and him start fighting. And what a scrap! You could hear chairs slamming around and swearing like you never heard before. Pretty soon the old lady comes running out into the yard with a kitchen knife in her hand and the old man right behind her. 'Gimme that knife,' he says. 'I won't,' she says and makes a pass at him. The old man whams her on the side of the head and down she goes. She gets up and he knocks her down again. One of the girls picks up a stick and hits her papa but he pays her no mind. Then El Colorado comes out of the house, crying, and with a piece of wood as big as a baseball bat. He cracks his papa on the shins and the old man yells, '*Huerco cabrón!*' and starts after him. El Colorado drops the stick and runs and the old man falls down and goes to sleep right there in the yard." Orestes' eyes were dancing. "Boy! You should've seen it. But don't you go tell anybody I told you."

"I won't. And that was all of it?"

"All the fun. By the time the law came the old man'd been pulled into the house and everything was still."

"He cried? You say he cried?"

"Who? Oh, El Colorado you mean? Sure he cried. Whatcha got there?"

"Pencil and tablet." Guálinto held them out.

Orestes took the tablet and looked at the feathered Indian head on the red cover. "Mine has an Indian on a horse," he said. He showed his tablet to Guálinto. "What book will you be in?"

"I don't have a book yet. We're just starting this morning."

"I meant what *grade*. You'll be in low first, I bet. Who's your teacher?"

"A tall old lady, Miss Something. Sort of homely looking."

"Miss Cornelia?" Orestes was delighted. "You'll be in my room." He bent the edge of his tablet between finger and thumb. The sheets ran through his fingers like a magician's playing cards. "It would be pretty nice in that room if it wasn't for Miss Cornelia. She sure is a son-of-a-bitch."

"Wha—why," Guálinto stuttered. "Isn't she nice?"

"Ha-ha. Wait till you get inside. She likes to rap you over the head with her ruler all the time. Sometimes on your knuckles, and only the boys. She almost never hits the girls."

Guálinto couldn't believe it. "And if she doesn't like your name she'll give you a silly nickname," Orestes went on. "She said Orestes wasn't a name so she started calling me 'Arrestas'. That's what the *palomilla* call me now, Arrestas. And they kid me that I'm going to grow up and be a cop."

Guálinto didn't want to think what she might do with his name so he changed the subject. "I wonder what the book will be like that we'll be reading," he said.

"I can tell you that," said Orestes. "It's the *Thisiswill*."

"Is that what it's called?"

"Sure," said Orestes. "And I can even tell you how it begins." He rattled it off in English: "This - is - Will - how - do - you - do - Will - this - is - May - how - do - you - do - May - this - is - Tom - how - do - you - do - Tom - this - is - Jane - how - do - you - do - Jane - Will - is - May's - brother - May - is - Will's - sister - Tom - is - Jane's - brother - Jane - is - Tom's - sister." He finished, out of breath and proud.

"*Chin-nn-gao!*" exclaimed Guálinto. "How do you know all that and we haven't even started school?"

"I started school last year," said Orestes. "I should be in low second with El Colorado this year. But I got sick."

"What did you get sick of?"

"September, October, just two months. And then bang! It happened. I got sick and now I have to repeat all of low first."

"But what was it?"

"*Dolor de costado*. I got it very bad. As my father says, 'When God gives he gives with both hands full.'"

Guálinto had heard about *dolor de costado*. Many people died of it. Your mouth and throat got full of bloody, sticky stuff and you would choke to death. "Gee!" he said. "You must have been very sick. Did they take you to the doctor?"

"The doctor came to see me at the house, many times. I don't know how many because I was out of my head most of the time."

"It must have cost a lot of money."

"Sure it did. But my father can pay. He's still paying the doctor off, though."

"Your father must make good money. What does he do?"

"He's a mechanic. He has his own shop where he works on cars. And he also sells used cars he fixes up himself."

"That sounds like a good job. I think I'll be a mechanic when I grow up."

"Not me," said Orestes. "It's very hard work and you're dirty all the time, with grease under your fingernails. I'd like to be a musician but my father says musicians are always poor. I think I'll be a druggist instead."

The bell behind the building began to clang. "We go in now," said Orestes, standing up on the concrete ledge. "I'll show you the way." Guálinto followed more slowly as the other boy disappeared into the school building.

3

In the 1920s racial segregation was the rule in the educational system of Texas. There were some significant variations, however, in the schooling offered to Mexican children, especially in the southern part of the state, where Mexicans were greatly in the majority. In some small towns and villages there was only one school, for whites only. Those ambitious Mexican parents who wanted their children to learn reading, writing and 'rithmetic sent their children for a couple of years or so to *escuelitas*, literally "little schools," where they learned the rudiments of the three Rs from the better educated women in the Mexican *colonia*. What they learned was taught to them in Spanish, of course. In larger communities Mexican children were offered an English-language education in elementary schools built especially for them—separate but unequal.

Not so in Jonesville-on-the-Grande, where schools were fully integrated from first grade up through high school, a fact always pointed to with pride by local politicians whenever they ran for re-election. There were three public school buildings in town—a grammar school, a junior high, and a high school—and they were open to Mexican as well as Angloamerican children. The grammar school was an old two-story brick building surrounded by an iron fence set on a concrete base. It stood more or less in the middle of town. The junior high was a much smaller building, while the high school was smaller still. These last were built close together far to the northwest of the grammar school.

There was a particularly interesting feature about the Jonesville grammar school, the classification of the first and second grades into "high" and "low" sections. Low first and low second served the great majority of entering pupils, who were of Mexican origin and knew little or no English when they came to school. They were taught bilingually by teachers who knew both English and Spanish and who had the job of teaching the English language to their charges, along with all the other skills first and second graders were supposed to know. High first and high second accepted those children fortunate enough to know the English language before they entered school, and who for religious or economic reasons were not sent to the private schools run by the Catholic church. The highs and the lows became fully integrated in the third grade, taught entirely in English. The idea seemed an excellent one, giving the Mexican children the chance to learn English during their first two years in school as they were worked into the Angloamerican school system.

High first was taught by a young woman named Miss Butler who was new to the Delta and whose classes usually totaled less than 20 pupils. High second was taught by a similar young woman named Miss Huff and had approximately the same number of pupils as did Miss Butler's high first. Low first and low second were taught by Miss Josephine and Miss Cornelia, a pair of middle-aged maiden ladies of Mexican descent who were native to Jonesville and had been with the Jonesville school system for many years. They taught both grades simultaneously, in the manner of the little red school houses of yore. Thirty-five first and fifteen second graders were assigned to each of them in the two largest classrooms in the school. There were good reasons for this old-fashioned arrangement. Had the low first and low second pupils been assigned to separate rooms, there would have been about 70 low first graders in one room and 30 low second graders in the other. For one thing, there was no classroom in the school big enough to hold 70 desks. For another, even if there had been such a room the disparity in class load would have raised a vexing problem. Which of the two bilingual teachers would be assigned which class? Where to assign the better-qualified teacher? Which of the two was better qualified? Miss Josephine was a high school graduate and had taken some advanced summer courses in Education. Her English was good and she always managed to get some of her low second pupils into the third grade. Miss Cornelia had a grammar school education. Her pupils rarely made it through the second grade, she spoke English with an accent, and her family had political connections.

So the double-class arrangement seemed the only alternative. At all events, more than half of the low-firsters dropped out after their first year of school, and considerably less than half of the second graders made it into the third grade. It was a process of not-quite-so-natural selection, and it did wonders for the school budget, while the few Mexicans who made it through high school did so by clawing their way to the top. Carmen and Maruca had the good luck of getting Miss Josephine as their teacher, and both had made it into the third grade and beyond under her persistent but gentle prodding.

Miss Cornelia was made of different stuff, a stern disciplinarian school officials said. Among her pupils and among many of their families she was called other names: Vieja Tarasca, Zopilota, Bruja and Guajolota were some of them. But she had the full confidence of her employers, who were convinced she knew how to handle the little Latin

Americans in her charge. Latin American (or simply Latin) was a polite term Anglotexans used when they meant Greaser. Or Mexican, for
that matter. The word Mexican had for so long been a symbol of hatred and loathing that to most Anglotexans it had become a hateful and
loathsome word. A kindly Anglo hesitated to call a friendly Mexican
a Mexican for fear of offending him. Even the Mexicotexan stumbled
on the word when he said it in English. In Spanish *mexicano* has a full
and prideful sound. The mouth opens on the full vowels and the voice
acquires a certain dignity in saying *mexicano*. But in English it is much
different. The lower lip pushes up and the upper lip curls contemptu-
ously. The pursed lips go "m-m-m." Then they part with a smacking,
barking sound, "M-m-mex-sican!" Who doesn't understand will think
he's being cursed at. It is also a word that can be pronounced without
opening your mouth at all, through clenched teeth. So the kindly Angloamerican uses Latin American to avoid giving offense.

Miss Cornelia was good at dealing with the children of these Latin
Americans. She was tall, angular, desiccated. Her long thin body was
topped by a head like a jellybean, the convex side being her face. Her
hairdo, built up something like a haystack and inclined slightly backward, together with her receding chin emphasized the convex appearance of her face. Her skin was grayish from the several coats of powder
with which she covered its naturally dark color. When she spoke to her
pupils, especially the boys, she opened her eyes wide and then squinted,
in alternate expressions of impatient disapproval and calculating anger.
To really appreciate her you had to see her fly at one of her charges like
an angry turkey hen attacking a little ugly duckling. It was La Guajolota,
the Turkey Hen, to whose care Guálinto Gómez was entrusted when he
entered the Jonesville grammar school.

4

Guálinto followed Orestes into the side door and was walking with
him down the long hall when he almost bumped into a girl who had
come in through the front door.

"I—I—," he stammered. There was no mistaking the pretty dimpled
face and the dark curls. It was the little girl he saw almost every Sunday
in church, La Nena Osuna, the sister of that big sissy who once had told
him he had shortening in his hair.

She smiled at him and said pleasantly, "It wasn't your fault. I was in a hurry."

"I—I'm sorry," Guálinto said at last. She smiled at him again and went into one of the classrooms. He stood there for a moment in happy befuddlement. She had smiled at him! She had talked to him!

"Psst! Come on!" Orestes was standing before a room a couple of doors away. As soon as Guálinto started toward him Orestes bolted into the room. By the time Guálinto reached the door Orestes was sitting at the far end of the room, close to the window among all the other boys. The beautiful feeling of a moment before left Guálinto. He stood by the doorway, nervously clutching his pencil and tablet and trying to keep out of the way of other boys and girls who were rushing in. There was much talking, laughing and scraping of feet on the wooden floor. The teacher was not in the room.

Guálinto's know-thirsty eyes noticed the pink rose in its dark-blue glass vase on top of the teacher's desk, a greenish apple beside it, and on both sides of them piles of books. Behind the teacher's desk a few words were printed on the board, and on the ledge—he was jostled heavily from behind. It was El Colorado, who went past him and sat down about the middle of the third row. Gradually the room settled into a semblance of order, though the loud talking continued. Only Guálinto remained at the door. Far away, at the other end of the room sat his new friend, Orestes. He and El Colorado were the only people he could recognize. The rest were not people but pairs of eyes staring at him. He looked again toward Orestes' row by the window. It was full like all the others. That row and the next one were occupied by boys mostly Guálinto's size. The front part of the third row was taken up by older boys, including El Colorado. The rest of the third row and the two rows closest to the door were filled with girls. Except for—.

Suddenly there was a loud handclap behind him that made him jump sideways. Miss Cornelia had arrived. "Here! Here!" she shouted. "Stop this, all this noise. What do you think this is? A *cantina*?"

Her pupils roared with laughter at Guálinto's frightened jump. Miss Cornelia stepped furiously into the room. She snatched a ruler from her desk and dealt a few random blows on the shoulders of the pupils nearest her, the low second boys sitting directly in front of her desk. When she reached El Colorado she struck him three or four times more than the others, about the head and shoulders. The redhead did not laugh like the others, and he didn't try to duck under the desk the way the other boys did. He parried the blows with his arms and glared at Miss Cornelia. She stopped hitting him and came back to Guálinto.

"And you?" she screeched. "What are you doing standing there like a chunk of mud? Go to your seat, you donkey!"

The class stifled a collective giggle and Guálinto wished the floor would give way and swallow him. He stood looking at Miss Cornelia, not knowing what to say and without the voice to say anything. "Speak up, animal!" screamed Miss Cornelia. Guálinto lowered his head. "Speak up!" she repeated, raising her hand to slap his face.

"There's no place for him to sit," said El Colorado. His voice was loud enough but colorless, monotonous, as if he were talking to himself.

Miss Cornelia paused, her hand in midair. "Oh," she said, "you're the boy who registered late. Why didn't you say so? Don't you have a tongue? Answer me!"

"Yes, Miss," he answered, and the effort caused his voice to break. He looked straight ahead and breathed hard to keep from crying. Miss Cornelia meanwhile was looking over the class in search of an empty seat. There was only one, the second seat in the row nearest the door, where the low second girls sat. Miss Cornelia pointed. "Right here. Sit down and behave yourself."

Guálinto plopped down miserably into the seat, his hands clenched tightly on his lap. Miss Cornelia paid no more attention to him. As she walked back to her desk she said, "Alicia?"

"Yes ma'am," answered the girl sitting behind Guálinto.

"Please come help me hand out the books, dear."

Alicia came promptly to the teacher's desk. "Here," said Miss Cornelia. "First take the books for your row. Nine, and one low first book for the boy sitting there." Alicia took the books and made a great show of giving Guálinto his, making a face at him when her back was turned away from Miss Cornelia.

Guálinto took the book with trembling hands. His first school book. A thin little book with stiff cardboard and cloth covers. It shone in the light as Alicia handed it to him, the white line of the leaf edges in immaculate contrast to the brightly painted green and gold covers. Guálinto took it as if it were made of fine glass. Carefully he opened it, the covers crackled as he did. It gave off a pleasant odor of glue, paint and cloth. He looked at the first page. He had never seen such brilliant colors in a book or a newspaper. In one corner was a picture of a boy in blue overalls and a yellow straw hat. In the opposite corner was a girl in a blue and white dress holding a sunbonnet of the same colors. She had golden hair. Between the two pictures were four lines of printed letters. Guálinto guessed that the first line said, "This is Will." He turned the page. On the second were another pair of children, boy and girl, and on the page opposite he saw all four. The boys were flying kites on a green hill against a blue sky. The girls were sitting on very green grass. Beside them was a yellow basket full of red apples. It was all so beautiful that for the moment he forgot where he was.

The rest of the class was affected in various ways by the scene they had witnessed just before the books were handed out. The low first girls seemed the most impressed. As Miss Cornelia bent over some papers on her desk, they stared in Guálinto's direction, trying to see him by leaning out of their seats. Pity, or perhaps fear made some of them bite their lips. The low first boys were less interested in Guálinto than in Miss Cornelia. They stole awed glances at her over the top of their new books. The low second boys, veterans of such skirmishes, stared at the blackboard with sullen faces.

Nothing like this among the low second girls, some of whom were repeating the grade. They tittered softly and whispered among themselves. Guálinto looked up from his book at the muffled sounds. Miss Cornelia also raised her head, and the tittering and whispers stopped. When Miss Cornelia looked down again they smiled maliciously. Some stuck out their tongues at him. Others made gestures at him that were but slightly expurgated versions of the obscene gestures boys used among themselves.

In front of Guálinto sat La India. She was an overgrown girl of ten. Her nickname was due to her close resemblance to the Indian pictured on the Red Indian pencil tablets, down to the long black braids. All she lacked was the Indian's feather bonnet, Guálinto thought. Once Miss Cornelia was absorbed in her papers, La India looked back at him.

"Poor baby," she whispered, "he wants his mother." Guálinto scowled at her. La India leaned to one side so she could see behind him. "Who sits on this row, Alicia?"

"Girls," whispered Alicia, leaning her dead-white face over Guálinto's shoulder, her thin lips twisted into a disdainful smile. Guálinto looked back at La India.

"What's your name?" she asked.

"I won't tell you."

La India gave him a calculating glance. She nodded thoughtfully, chewing on a piece of gum. Suddenly she pushed the gum against her cheek and turned front just as Miss Cornelia rose.

"I'm going out for a moment," said Miss Cornelia. "The first one of you I catch misbehaving will be sorry." She walked out of the room with a few sidewise looks at the class.

"I bet I know where she's going," said La India loudly as soon as Miss Cornelia's steps had died away.

Two rows away a boy about her size looked at La India and snickered. "She's gone to the toilet, I betcha," he said.

La India giggled and gave the boy a warm, morbid stare. Their eyes met and held for a moment before she dropped hers and giggled again. The other low second girls were laughing and acting shocked and saying, "How dirty!" Guálinto, no longer the center of attention, watched abstractedly. His hand strayed under the bib of his overalls and he scratched at his navel. La India's narrow eyes widened as she turned around and looked at him.

"Ahhh!" she said. "Look at what he's doing. Look what he's doing at me!" The low second girls left their seats and crowded around him. La India looked at him accusingly. "He had his hand in his pants and he was making dirty signs at me," she said loud enough for everyone to hear.

"The dirty little *pelado*," said Alicia.

"He ought to be ashamed," said another girl.

"Let's tell Miss Cornelia." There was a menacing babel around him. He cowered in their midst, completely unaware of the tinge of amusement in their voices.

"And you know what?" said La India, shouting above the hubbub. "He said he was sitting with the girls because he wanted to do bad things to us."

The girls chorused their indignation.

"That's not true!" exclaimed Guálinto.

"You did," countered La India. "And that isn't all. He said Alicia was his girl and that he did things with her once."

"I didn't!" Guálinto shouted. "I didn't."

La India glared at him. "You did. I swear you did."

"Why, you dirty good-for-nothing!" cried Alicia, her anger sounding very real. "I'll tell Miss Cornelia as soon as she steps into this room."

"It's a lie!' Guálinto shouted, tears gathering in his eyes. "It's a lie!" He buried his face in his arms and sobbed violently.

"Don't pay any attention to them," said a boy's voice close to him. "They're just trying—." Guálinto barely noticed the voice and its abrupt stop in the silence that followed. Miss Cornelia had entered the room. She took the scene at a glance, Guálinto crying at his desk, his head hidden in his arms and El Colorado standing over him, the two surrounded by girls. She strode over to them and the girls silently opened a way for her.

"Who made this boy cry?" demanded Miss Cornelia. Nobody answered. El Colorado looked at the floor and the girls glanced at each other nervously. Miss Cornelia prodded at Guálinto with the ruler in her hand. "You," she said. "What's the matter?"

Guálinto buried his head deeper in his arms. "Nothing," he said in a muffled voice. How could he tell her? Miss Cornelia took his arm and shook it roughly. "You are going to tell me what's going on," she said. She grabbed his hair and tried to make him look up. Guálinto rolled his head away. Miss Cornelia glanced sharply at El Colorado. She shook Guálinto again. "Look at me," she said. "Did this boy hurt you?"

Guálinto raised his wet face and barely recognized El Colorado. In his state of desperation he was almost convinced that what Miss Cornelia said was true. Before he knew what he was doing he nodded.

"Ah!" said Miss Cornelia, grabbing El Colorado by the shoulder. "I'll show you to disturb my class. Hitting boys half your size, you big elephant." She turned him around and the ruler in her hand whacked against the seat of El Colorado's pants with a terrifying sound. El Colorado endured the paddling in silence. Then he went back to his seat. The girls were subdued now.

Now Guálinto realized what he had done, and he felt alternately hot and cold. He wished the bell would ring so he could go outside, meet El Colorado and get his beating over with. But classwork began at last. Along the top of the blackboard there was a border on which the letters of the alphabet were painted in different styles. The low firsters were ordered to copy the block-letter capitals while Miss Cornelia went over the first reading lesson with the second graders. It was no great task for Guálinto since he had learned the Spanish alphabet from Doña Domitila more than a year before. He wondered why the CH, the LL, and the Ñ were missing from the list above the blackboard, but he did not dare ask. He included them in his list anyway. He was through long before the other first graders had finished.

Having nothing more to do, he listened to what Miss Cornelia was reading to the second graders in her fractured English. She looked up from her book and saw him looking at her. "Stop gawking and get busy with your work," she commanded.

"But I've finished, Miss." She came over and looked at his job of copying, neat and correct. "Now she is going to say something nice to me," he thought.

"What is this?" demanded Miss Cornelia. "Why did you write down these letters?" She red-penciled the CH, the LL, and the Ñ. "This is not a Mexican school. These letters do not belong in the American alphabet. Do it all over again, and this time do it the way you were told!"

He did it all over again on a new sheet of paper, finishing as the other first graders were getting through their first attempt. Then Miss Cornelia left the second graders to memorize their reading assignment while she led the first graders in a recitation of the alphabet. Finally the bell rang for recess.

Guálinto rose stiffly, looking neither to right nor left. He walked outside and stopped at the bottom of the steps to wait for El Colorado. The redhead frowned when he saw Guálinto and would have gone by, but the younger boy said softly, "Colorado." El Colorado stopped.

"You can give me a licking, now or after school on the way home."

El Colorado looked at him in a funny way. "Nah," he said, "that was nothing. I've taken lots of whippings before, worse than that." They walked a few steps in silence. Orestes was looking at them but he kept his distance. So did some other boys from the Dos Veintidós. "Besides," added El Colorado, "it was La India's fault, the dirty bitch."

Guálinto nodded. "I didn't know what I was doing because of her. But still, I did something very cheap and lowdown to you."

"Forget it. That India, she's the one that needs a beating."

"You're a really good guy, Colorado."

"Come along," said the redhead, "and I'll show you where you can wash your face." He led the way towards the boys' washrooms. "Girls are the dirtiest sonsabitches," he said.

"Uhuh," said Guálinto. But he made one silent exception.

5

"Eckles! Eckles!" Guálinto pretended not to hear. "Eckles! Oh, Mrs. García, how are you today? Are your pants dry?" Guálinto kept looking at his book, pretending to read. It was María Elena Osuna's brother, Miguel, who was taunting him. The same boy who more than a year before had told Guálinto in church that Guálinto had shortening in his hair. But he no longer was Miguelito, the skinny pale-faced boy Guálinto had scared so much that the sissy had moved several places away. He had grown during the past year and filled out, more than a match for Guálinto. After all, Miguel was ten years old and in the fourth grade. Besides, Miguel no longer thought Guálinto was a tough guy just because he came from El Dos Veintidós. The whole school knew by now about the way Guálinto was bullied and humiliated by Miss Cornelia and how the girls in low second had made him cry on the first day of school. This morning El Colorado had not shown up yet, and Miguel took the chance to get even. "Eckles! Eckles! Are your pants dry, Mrs. García?"

Life in Miss Cornelia's classroom had become a kind of hell for Guálinto. After the first school day Miss Cornelia had moved the girls one seat forward so that Alicia sat directly behind La India, and Guálinto took the seat that was vacated right behind the high second boys. The girls now left him alone, but Miss Cornelia continued to torment him in very much the same fashion La India had done on that first day. His misadventures were known throughout the school. But though he was humiliated a great deal and often had tears in his eyes when he left the classroom, he always washed his face and went home without complaint. Maruca and Carmen knew about his troubles, but they didn't tell on him when they got home. Their mother had established an inflexible rule. If they were punished at school for any reason, they would be punished again when they got home.

In a way it was his family's fault that Guálinto had so much trouble with Miss Cornelia. His mother, his uncle, and even Carmen had come to take it for granted that he would grow up to be a great man as his dead father had wished. A great man who would help and lead his people to a better kind of life. How this would be accomplished they did not know. Sometimes they thought he would be a great lawyer who would get back the lands they had lost. At other times they were certain he would become a great orator who would convince even the greatest of their enemies of the rightness of his cause. Or perhaps he would be a great doctor who would go around healing the poor and thus create an immense following. They had these and many other dreams about him and sometimes disagreed as to which would be the right one. But they agreed that he was not just another boy. He was greatly intelligent, gifted, and destined for wonderful things. His family's mission in life was to give him every opportunity possible to their limited means.

By the time Guálinto went to school he could read in Spanish, he could do simple arithmetic, and he knew some English that he had learned from Carmen, who was in the fourth grade. He was used to speaking out and being heard, to being right about many things. In class he always knew the answers to questions, or thought he did, and always wanted to answer them. This made Miss Cornelia furious, to the point that when he raised his hand she was apt to say, "Shut up and put that hand down." Miss Cornelia wanted an orderly class that would learn what she taught them and no more.

There was the time when she was teaching arithmetic to her first graders. She wrote on the blackboard, "1 + 1 = 2" and asked if anyone knew what that meant.

"I know, Miss Cornelia, I know," said Guálinto as soon as she had written it down.

"All right, genius," said Miss Cornelia, "what is it?"

"One plus one eckles two," he said.

"Eckles?" cried Miss Cornelia derisively. "ECKLES?" Though she knew that he meant "equals." "Sit down, Eckles, and don't think you know everything. One plus one *is* two, Mr. Eckles."

The class laughed loudly and echoed Miss Cornelia, "Eckles! Eckles!" Guálinto slumped down in his seat. From then on his name was Eckles and he hated Miss Cornelia just a bit more.

Then there was the time he signed his name Guálinto Gómez García on an exercise, as Uncle Feliciano had taught him his name should be written the Spanish way, Gómez for his father and García for his mother. When she got his paper Miss Cornelia called the class to attention and informed them that Guálinto had married a gentleman named García and that now he was Mrs. Guálinto G. García. The class really appreciated that one. It was slightly tinged with sex and those jokes are the best.

Miss Cornelia seemed to get a special pleasure from tormenting Guálinto. She did not whack him with her ruler the way she did El Colorado, but her tongue made him hurt just as much. And when she wasn't being cruelly funny she was simply cruel. Just yesterday something had happened that even now made Guálinto's face burn. The first graders were reading aloud. They stood in a semicircle beside Miss Cornelia's desk, books in hand, each reading the same sentence in turn. Almost since he had come in that morning Guálinto had been feeling more and more full of water. It hadn't been so bad sitting down but standing up for so long began to make things unbearable. He shifted from one foot to the other till Miss Cornelia noticed him.

"You," she said sharply. "Be quiet and stand up straight."

He endured the torture of standing still for a few seconds. Then he began to squirm and to rub one knee against the other. Finally he raised a forefinger. Miss Cornelia did not notice; a little girl was reading. But Guálinto was desperate. He snapped his fingers and called, "Miss Cornelia, Miss Cornelia."

Miss Cornelia looked up angrily. "Don't interrupt," she said.

"But I've got to go out. I just have to."

"You don't. You wait till recess and keep quiet."

By now everybody was watching Guálinto, especially the second graders, who could do so from their seats. For what seemed hours to him, Guálinto battled against nature, visibly and with a snickering class as an audience, while Miss Cornelia pretended not to see or hear. An instant before the recess bell rang, nature had its way, and Guálinto dribbled down his leg. He bolted out of the room ahead of everyone else, holding himself. Crying in shame he ran to the washroom, where he cleaned his leg with wet toilet paper. He spent the rest of the recess period leaning against a wash basin while El Colorado alternately comforted him and threatened other boys who came in to laugh.

That was a real friend, El Colorado. Because of him school life was bearable for Guálinto. If he had endured on the playground what he suffered in class he probably would have run away from school. But recess time was the bright spot in his school day. Once out of the classroom he was no longer Miss Cornelia's captive. He was the friend and protégé of El Colorado, the tough undisputed king of their corner of the playground. The redhead sympathized with the younger boy because they shared one thing in common, being prime targets for Miss Cornelia's vindictiveness. Guálinto, in turn, sometimes helped El Colorado with his lessons. On the playground they were inseparable, and nobody dared make fun of Guálinto when El Colorado was around. Guálinto enjoyed hanging around with El Colorado and the older boys, who had begun to accept him because of his feud with Miss Cornelia. The redhead himself had a rough sort of admiration for Guálinto because Guálinto could read in Spanish and figure better than most third graders. He held Guálinto up as a brainy guy, which made Guálinto feel right in his element. So instead of playing with other first graders, he played with El Colorado and his gang, with boys like Arty Cord, El Capitán, La Flaica, La Calavera, La Víbora, Sleeping Jesus, and El Coco. The only other first grader admitted into the circle was Orestes, El Arrestas, who was repeating first grade and who lived close to El Colorado. Arty Cord was so called because he was supposed to look like the movie cowboy Art Acord. El Capitán earned his name the first day he came to school, when he was wearing a soldier's cap and a double-breasted military jacket. He was one of the quietest of the bunch and certainly the most neatly dressed. La Víbora was called the snake for no particular reason as far as one could see, but La Calavera had a sickly-white bony face that looked very much like a skull. La Flaica was a tall, skinny boy with a long good-natured face. Sleeping Jesus, like Arty Cord, boasted a nickname in English, borrowed from a pious painting so entitled that hung on the wall behind Miss Cornelia's desk. It was done in different shades of brown and showed a baby sleeping in the hay. Sleeping Jesus walked about in a state of chronic exhaustion. The gang said that as soon as he was born he looked around wearily, wiping his baby brow with a chubby hand and said, "Chee, I'm tired!" Sleeping Jesus just smiled wanly at this story about his precocity. But when he wanted to he could move fast enough. El Coco had the jaw of a prize fighter, the forehead of a gorilla and almost no nose at all. He richly deserved the name of Bogeyman, and only El Colorado could make him back out of a fight.

These were the boys that were Guálinto's playground companions. They accepted him into their group with reservations due his age and strength. Guálinto was proud, nevertheless, and he felt very big and manly being a member of such a gang. That was on the playground. In class it was all different.

"Hey, Eckles! Are you asleep or afraid?" It was Miguel Osuna still. Guálinto was sitting on a piece of discarded sewer pipe by the slim shade of the school wall. In a few minutes the janitor would pull the bell rope and they would go inside for the morning's classes. He did not want to fight La Nena Osuna's brother. She would stop smiling at him when they met in the hall. In fact, he already thought of her as his girl. But Miguel persisted and when Guálinto continued to ignore him Miguel kicked gravel at him.

Guálinto raised his head. "Look who you're kicking pebbles at," he said. A crowd of boys had collected behind Miguel. Guálinto closed his book and got up. Miguel smirked and kicked more gravel at him. "You better leave me alone," said Guálinto.

"Leave me alone," mimicked Miguel. Guálinto was at a loss for words so he just glared at Miguel. Miguel glared back.

"Come on," said one of the bigger boys in the crowd. "Make the fart stink."

"Come on! Come on!" chorused the rest. But they just stood and glared at each other until El Coco stepped out of the crowd. He pushed Miguel against Guálinto, making Guálinto stumble back. This made Miguel a little bolder; he clenched his fists and strutted a bit. Somebody brought a stick and two lines were drawn on the ground, one in front of each of them. Guálinto put out his foot and rubbed out his line.

"See what he did," Arty Cord said to Miguel. "He rubbed his line out. It's the same as calling you by your mother." Miguel stuck out a foot very ceremoniously and wiped out his line. Guálinto looked up and saw they were too near the building, almost under a window of Miss Rathers' room. Miss Rathers taught high first. And La Nena Osuna was in her class.

"Look," he said to Miguel, "let's not fight here." The boys jeered at Guálinto.

"Go on, Miguel," they shouted, "he's afraid of you. Wet his ears."

Miguel stuck the forefingers of both hands into his mouth, as he had seen other boys do, and he stretched out his arms to wet the lobes of Guálinto's ears. This was the greatest insult of all, far greater than calling a fellow by his mother. But Guálinto had not lived all his life in the Dos Veintidós for nothing. As Miguel stretched out both his hands to Guálinto's ears, he dropped his book and swung at Miguel's belly. "Oof!" went Miguel and shut his eyes. Before he could recover Guálinto kicked his shins a couple of times and then tripped him. Miguel landed on his back and Guálinto was on top of him, gouging his body with his knees and jabbing viciously at his face. The other boys were raising a tremendous racket, whistling and cheering him on.

The noise stopped all of a sudden and someone was pulling at Guálinto's arm. "Here, here," said Miss Rathers. "Stop that, both of you. Get up, now. Get up and dust off your clothes." They got up and Guálinto looked at Miguel. His face was red but not really bruised at all. "Come on, now," Miss Rathers said. "I'm afraid I'll have to take you to Mr. Baggley's office."

Mr. Baggley, the principal. Even the boys in fifth grade were afraid of going to his office. They said he made you bend over and hold on to your ankles so the seat of your pants was stretched tight against your butt. And then he used a paddle on you, swinging it like a baseball bat. Guálinto had seen Mr. Baggley up close only once, the day all pupils were assembled on the platform behind the building to have their height and weight recorded. Mr. Baggley was operating the scales. He was a tall, fleshy man with a head like an egg. His face was the color of a white egg, and it went all the way to the top of his head, with hair growing only on the sides and back.

They were lined up to be weighed by Mr. Baggley, the first graders first. Ahead of Guálinto was Antonio Prieto, also a low firster with Miss Cornelia. Antonio was a dark and very thin little boy who came to school barefoot and in mended clothes. His lank black hair was always in need of a barber's shears. When his turn came, Mr. Baggley estimated his weight and set the scales accordingly. Antonio stepped on the scales and the arm did not rise. "*Más frijoles*," Mr. Baggley said in quite understandable Spanish. Everyone within earshot laughed. He nudged the counterweight just a little and again the arm did not move. "*Más frijoles, más frijoles, más frijoles*," Mr. Baggley kept saying as he nudged the counterweight back until the arm rose into balance. Antonio got off the scales looking more serious than usual, and Guálinto had never liked Mr. Baggley after that.

And now Guálinto and Miguel were being conducted to the holy of holies, the principal's office. When Mr. Baggley answered Miss Rathers' knock she told the principal, "These boys were fighting outside my window."

"Thank you, Miss Rathers," Mr. Baggley said. "I'll handle it from here. Come in, boys." Miss Rathers left and Mr. Baggley closed the door. He sat down and looked thoughtfully at the two boys standing before him. Problems, he thought, always problems. Why were there so many problems working in this god-forsaken town? Here was a first grader, not very large for his age, pale and frightened. Beside him was a boy from Miss Webb's fourth grade class, a head taller and obviously much stronger, though from the looks of him he seemed to have got the worst of it in the scuffle. It should be simple enough. Lecture the first grader about not getting into fights and paddle the big one for picking on little boys. But there was a catch. The big boy was named Miguel

Osuna, and you just didn't paddle Mr. Osuna's boy. Paddle the Gómez boy and lecture Miguel Osuna? He gagged on the thought. Lecture the Gómez boy and accuse him of having started the fight? He turned to Guálinto. "Why did you start a fight with this boy? Don't you know that you deserve to be punished for fighting?"

"But Mr. Baggley," said Miguel, "I started the fight." Both Mr. Baggley and Guálinto looked at Miguel with surprise. "I picked on him and picked on him. I called him all sorts of names until he finally fought back. If anybody deserves to be punished it is me."

"That is very generous of you," said Mr. Baggley. "It is a very gentlemanly thing to do." He smiled indulgently on both of them. "If you two will shake hands we will consider the matter closed." They shook hands. "All right," said Mr. Baggley, "you may go. I have a lot of things to do."

When they were again in the hall Guálinto said, "Chee! That was a brave thing you did, Miguel. You're a real man."

"It was nothing," Miguel replied, somewhat primly. "Nothing but the truth."

"Anyway, I appreciate it. He would have whacked me good."

"We better wash up and get to class," said Miguel. "We're late already." He smiled and shook hands with Guálinto again.

It was late enough when Guálinto got to Miss Cornelia's classroom, but classes had not begun there. Pupils were talking to each other in low voices as if they were at a wake, while Miss Cornelia stood by a window at the far side of the room, arms folded over her flat chest and staring at the door when Guálinto opened it. Miss Cornelia came and met him right in front of her desk.

"Ah!" she exclaimed. "Here is our famous pugilist now, and about time. Where have you been, you hoodlum?"

Guálinto hung his head. "In Mr. Baggley's office," he said.

"I know all about it. Attacking decent boys who don't know how to defend themselves from back-alley people like yourself! Did Mr. Baggley give you the whipping you deserved?"

Guálinto kept his head bowed. "No, Miss," he mumbled.

"Look at me when I talk to you!" screamed Miss Cornelia. Guálinto tried to look at her while keeping his head bowed as a sign of penitence. To Miss Cornelia it seemed that he was scowling at her. "Don't look at me like that, you bandit!" she said and gave him a resounding slap on the cheek. "I'll teach you to get into fights and to be late to my class." She grabbed him by the shoulder, turned him around and whipped him with her ruler. "Now go sit down and behave yourself."

Guálinto walked down the third row, past El Colorado to his seat behind the last of the second grade boys. He sat down carefully because of the sting of the ruler on his backside. His cheek burned where he had been slapped. But he felt a sense of pride, of victory. He had not cried.

That afternoon Guálinto walked home with El Colorado, Orestes and Francisco Four-Eyes, who was in low second with Miss Josephine. Francisco lived just a few blocks south of the school, but he liked to tag along with the others. After all, his uncle lived next door to Guálinto in El Dos Veintidós, so El Colorado tolerated him. Guálinto was telling the other three about the fight and his visit to the principal's office. Orestes and El Colorado had been late to school that morning and had missed the fight.

"He took the blame?" said Orestes of Miguel Osuna. "He's more of a man than I thought."

"He saved me from a real flogging," said Guálinto, "and he risked getting one himself."

"He did you a favor," said El Colorado, "but he was in no danger of getting his hide tanned. His father is an important man among the Reds."

"Perhaps he doesn't know it," Guálinto answered. "Anyway, he did me a favor."

"Did you cry very much when Miss Cornelia beat you?" asked Francisco.

"He didn't cry at all," said El Colorado. "He may be little but he shows all man in the very very."

Guálinto smiled and he felt a bit sore in the cheek Miss Cornelia had slapped. He touched it and asked the others, "Does it show? Are you sure it doesn't show?" The other three inspected his cheek carefully and agreed that the swelling had disappeared. His backside still ached a little, but he was sure he could get by without having his mother find out what had happened in school. His sisters, he knew, would also keep the matter quiet.

"It is truly incredible how much Miss Cornelia persecutes you, Guálinto," said Francisco.

"There you go again," complained El Colorado. "Why can't you talk plain *castellano* like everybody else?"

Francisco smiled. "I'm talking Castilian, Colorado."

"Aw," said El Colorado, "you'll never learn."

"He was born in Mexico," Guálinto said in Francisco's defense. "That's the way they talk down there."

"By the way," said Francisco, "what's your name? Your real name, I mean. I don't like to call people by their nicknames."

"It's José, but what the hell difference does it make? I'd rather you called me Colorado. And if any bastard calls me Pepe I'll push his face in. We call queers Pepes around here."

"All right, Colorado."

"I'm still thinking about Miss Cornelia," said Guálinto. "She sure has it in for me."

"Sometimes I feel like knocking her down," said El Colorado.

"Oh, no," exclaimed Francisco. "You mustn't do anything like that, Guálinto. Tell your parents and they will talk to her."

El Colorado snorted at such stupidity and Guálinto answered sadly, "She would just whip me again, Francisco."

"She shouldn't do it," persisted Francisco.

"But she does," said El Colorado.

"Yes," added Guálinto. "There's nothing to do but take it."

6

On November first Guálinto had been in Miss Cornelia's class for two months. He was learning fast, now that he had matched English sounds to the letters he had learned in Spanish. That morning Miss Huff, who taught high second, visited Miss Cornelia's room. She brought with her a box of chalk of different colors and began to draw a picture on one of the front blackboards, a tree with green leaves and a lot of little red fruit and a boy wearing a funny-looking hat and knickers, with an axe raised above his head and about to hit the tree.

As Miss Huff worked Miss Cornelia told the class, "A week from this coming Friday we will celebrate Armistice Day. It is the day the Great War ended just three years ago. There will be a PTA meeting where a boy or girl from each classroom will give a recitation about the history of this country." The class was barely listening. They were admiring Miss Huff's artistry. Miss Huff finished the picture and began to print something on the blackboard beside it.

"Miss Huff is now writing down the recitation assigned to our room. It is about George Washington. He was the father of our country. After Miss Huff finishes we will all read it together. Then you will copy it in your notebooks and learn it by heart. The first one that learns it can recite it next week at the PTA meeting."

Guálinto's ears tingled. George Washington! Nobody at school knew it, but that was his name too. He felt as if Miss Cornelia was talking about him. Immediately he started copying what Miss Huff was writing, and he finished almost as soon as she did. Miss Huff read the passage first, slowly and very distinctly. Then both classes read it with her. Miss Cornelia clapped her hands. "All right! Now get to work!" Everyone except Guálinto began to copy from the blackboard. He was looking at the board and repeating to himself, "George Washington was a little boy. His father and mother loved him—." Guálinto had been memorizing poems and words to songs since he had learned to talk. And this was so personal that he just could not fail. " ... I did it with my little hatchet. I cannot tell a lie." He went over it once, twice, three times. Then he closed his eyes and tried to repeat it. His stomach was trembling and he faltered for just an instant; then he repeated it all. He opened his eyes and kept reading it over and over.

Miss Huff had gathered up her colored chalks and was moving toward the door when Miss Cornelia noticed that Guálinto was not writing. "You!" she said, pointing her ruler at him. "Stop daydreaming and start writing."

"But Miss Cornelia, I copied it while Miss Huff was writing it down, and I already memorized it."

"You what?"

"I know the poem by heart."

"Don't lie!" said Miss Cornelia.

"Perhaps he does know it," said Miss Huff gently.

"All right," said Miss Cornelia. "Come here and recite it. And if you are lying I'll see that you regret it. Give me your paper and face the class, face the class. Do you want to read it off the blackboard?"

Guálinto marched up to the front with great assurance. He put his hands behind his back and began, "George Washington was a little boy ... " His ears reddened when he said the name. The whole room was watching him. " ... His father and mother loved him ... " He rattled off the piece without faltering. The class applauded and he returned to his seat, flushed and victorious.

"Hush! Hush!" said Miss Cornelia and the hand-clapping stopped, but the room did not quiet down immediately. "Ah! Ah!" said La India from the other side of the room. "How smart," she added sarcastically. El Colorado raised his clasped hands above his head and shook them at Guálinto. Alicia was frowning. As teacher's pet, she had expected to be the one chosen by Miss Cornelia to perform for the PTA.

"I don't know," Miss Cornelia said to Miss Huff. "He didn't do it so very well, don't you think?"

"He did exceptionally well," said Miss Huff enthusiastically. "And I'm surprised that his English pronunciation is so good." She colored a bit at her misstep. Among themselves the Anglo teachers made fun of Miss Cornelia's English. "I mean, for a little Latin boy his age he did an excellent job."

"Very well," said Miss Cornelia. And to Guálinto, "I suppose you will represent our room at the PTA. But you must stay after school every day from now until Armistice Day so Miss Huff can coach you on how to speak in public."

"I don't think that long a time will be necessary," said Miss Huff as mildly as she could. "Next Monday will be soon enough." Then to Guálinto, "Go over the recitation by yourself for the rest of the week. Then next week, from Monday through Thursday, we will work on it together after school." She patted Guálinto's head. "Only for a half-hour a day, dear." She smiled at Miss Cornelia and left.

The great day finally arrived and Guálinto lost a front tooth that morning. It chose to fall off this day of all days, and it left a gaping hole in his face when he smiled. He grimaced into the mirror as he tried to comb down his unruly taffy-colored hair. It would never stay down. The rectangular mirror in his mother's dresser pivoted at the middle. He pushed at the lower half so he could see all of himself. He was dressed in new clothes his uncle had bought him for the occasion. A double-breasted jacket complete with matching pants of a crisp light material with thin blue and white stripes. The coat was held together at the waist by a wide belt of the same cloth. His feet shone with new black shoes of patent leather tied with shiny buckles. He was all dressed up. If it wasn't for that tooth!

The day had another great adventure in store, and as Guálinto was at the mirror it heralded its arrival. An automobile horn croaked out in the street. It was Miss Cornelia, who was coming for Guálinto. María was bursting with pride. "Hurry," she called. "The lady is here." She opened the door and called to Miss Cornelia, "Would you care to come in to this poor house, *señorita*?"

"No, thank you," Miss Cornelia said a trifle disdainfully. "Tell him to hurry."

Guálinto came rushing to the door, still pressing down his unruly hair with one hand. María landed a kiss on his cheek as he went by. "God keep you," she told him. "I'll be there to see you."

His eyes were fixed on Miss Cornelia's Oldsmobile. He rushed up and tried to climb in on Miss Cornelia's side. "Go around," she commanded. Guálinto started around in front of the car. Halfway he stopped, remembering that he must never get in front of a car. He changed course and ran all the way around the rear. Miss Cornelia opened the door for him. He climbed in cautiously and sat down beside her on the black oilcloth-covered seat, very carefully lest he do it damage. Miss Cornelia shifted handles and things and the car sputtered and coughed. Then it shivered into action. It moved slowly down the street, while Guálinto leaned back and luxuriated in his first automobile ride.

The car was a touring model and as they rolled along at a good fifteen miles an hour Guálinto looked around at the empty streets. How he wished the whole Dos Veintidós could see him now. Ah, there was Don Pancho coming down the street. He nodded at him, afraid to wave because of what Miss Cornelia might think. Don Pancho did not see him. Guálinto stole a look at Miss Cornelia. She was sitting very straight and rigid, her hands tense on the steering wheel, her eyes squinting dead ahead. Guálinto looked ahead too. Driving a car must be a terrible responsibility. And so they reached the grammar school.

At last the big moment arrived. Guálinto was standing in the hall by the door leading into a big room where the PTA and other visitors were being entertained. With him were a number of other pupils, all dressed in costumes except for him. Almost all of them had already performed. A big boy dressed as a soldier with a helmet on his head, who had recited a poem about some fields where poppies grow. A girl dressed as a Red Cross Nurse who had sung about a rose in no-man's-land. Another girl dressed as the Statue of Liberty. President Lincoln, Davey Crockett, a Mexican girl from Miss Josephine's low second, dressed as a China Poblana. She was called in and sang "Adiós Mi Chaparrita." From where he stood Guálinto could see the space at the end of the room where the others performed their pieces, and every time Miss Huff walked into that space paper in hand to call another name his heart beat faster. But it was always somebody else, and the cold weight in his stomach came back again. The China Poblana had finished her act and came out into the hall.

"And now," said Miss Huff, "last but not least, we will hear from the low first grade. Little Guálinto Gómez will tell us about George Washington, the father of our country, when he was a little boy himself." She motioned to Guálinto. It took him two tries before he could make his legs move. He entered without looking at anyone.

"Ho, young fellow," said a jovial voice behind him. "You can't be seen from the floor." It was Mr. Baggley, who had been standing just inside the door. He took a big, solid chair, placed it facing the audience and put Guálinto on top of it. Now Guálinto had to look at the crowd. There were more people than he had ever seen at one time except in church. They sat on folding chairs facing him, and many others were standing at the back of the room and along the sides. They were nothing but faces to him, he recognized no one. There was a smattering of applause when he was lifted on the chair and then silence.

He started to smile as he had been told to, then remembering the missing tooth he sucked in his lips nervously. At last he began, very slowly and as distinctly as he could. He gestured as Miss Huff had taught him. When he finished he bowed, and there was a loud burst of applause. He smiled broadly, forgetting the tooth entirely. "Fine, fine," said Mr. Baggley as he lifted him down from the chair. Miss Huff smiled and said, "Thank you all for being with us."

Everybody rose and people began to talk with each other. Some of the ladies came and patted Guálinto on the head and said, "How cute!" and "*Qué lindo!*" Then an arm went around his shoulders, squeezing the breath out of him. It was his mother, who had been among the women in the back of the room. She hugged him close to her for a moment, then held him at arm's length and smiled proudly. "Well, well," she said, "this is the orator." Guálinto smiled without parting his lips.

"You were doing all right," his mother continued, "until you saw me. Then you began to twist and clown about." "I did not," Guálinto protested. "I didn't even see you." "You did too," his mother answered. "I know the exact moment you saw me. You started to twist around and you raised your arms."

"No, Mama," he said impatiently. "That was when I was saying that George Washington cut a tree with an axe. I had to do it with my hands also."

"Oh," said María, a bit disappointed and only half convinced. "Anyway, it was very good."

Miss Huff reappeared with Miss Cornelia in tow. "*Buenas días*," said Miss Huff, taking María's hand. "Miss Cornelia, please tell Mrs. Gómez how proud we are of her son. He did extremely well, far above his grade level."

"*La señorita* Huff," translated Miss Cornelia, "says your son did well." Then in a didactic tone, "I'm sure you don't know what he said, but he recited a piece about George Washington. Washington was the founder of this country and a very great man."

María smiled at Miss Cornelia's condescension. "Yes, I know," she answered. "That is my son's name too. We call him Guálinto but his real name is Washington, George Washington Gómez."

Miss Cornelia giggled like a little girl, putting her fist up against her chin and lower lip. "Goodness alive!" She giggled again. "George, did you say? George *Washington* Gómez?" She pursed her lips to keep from laughing outright. María got very red and she stared stonily at Miss Cornelia.

Miss Huff had understood little of the conversation except for the name of Washington. "Is anything wrong?" she asked when she saw María's face.

"Oh, no," said Miss Cornelia, suppressed laughter thickening her voice. "Nothing, except that this woman says she named her son Washington. George Washington Gómez. *Did* you ever?"

Miss Huff glanced from Miss Cornelia to María and then to Guálinto. Her face was expressionless. "There's nothing wrong with that,"
she said.

"It's a good name. *Bueno,*" she told María as she stroked Guálinto's
hair. "*Bueno, mu-y bueno.*"

María gave Miss Huff a grateful smile as she reached for her son's
hand. She turned and looked at Miss Cornelia with bitter contempt.
"*Con permiso,*" she said as she stalked out of the room in a rustle of her
black skirts.

7

For the rest of the month Miss Cornelia made it a point to call Guálinto "Mr. George Washington Gómez" whenever she spoke to him in
class, emphasizing every syllable. She would start when she called the
roll in the morning and keep it up throughout the rest of the day. Except for Miss Huff, she was the only one in school who had heard that
it was Guálinto's name, and she doubted it very much. But she made a
private joke of it, which had meaning only for herself and the boy. The
rest of the class thought the old Guajolota was complimenting Guálinto
on his performance at the PTA meeting, and they were surprised that
she was being so nice to him. They began calling him George Washington outside of class, as a new and flattering nickname. But he knew
Miss Cornelia was taunting him, and he came to hate his name, as well
as the real George Washington who was supposed to be the father of
his country. At times he even hated his dead father for having given
him that Gringo name. And he was grateful to his uncle, who had told
him to say Guálinto was an Indian name. Finally Miss Cornelia tired of
her private joke and stopped calling him George Washington. She was
pretty sure, anyway, that the boy's mother had been lying. After all, his
uncle had told Miss Cornelia during registration that Guálinto was an
Indian name.

Guálinto did not forget Miss Cornelia's harassment, but he put the
memory away in a far corner of his mind. He had other things to occupy
his thoughts. And these things revolved around the person of María
Elena Osuna, known to everyone as La Nena Osuna. La Nena and
Miguel Osuna were the children of Don Onofre Osuna, who lived in a
large brick house downtown, close to the business district. Onofre Os-

una was well-to-do, rich by standards in Jonesville-on-the-Grande, but he had old-fashioned ways and refused to move to newer parts of town, preferring to live in the house built by his grandfather in the 1880s. Don Onofre was a practical man, having taken after his grandfather. When the "cattle barons" came down like a plague on the Mexican ranchers of south Texas, Grandfather Osuna had not opposed them. He joined them. And he prospered. A government commission passing through Texas in 1880 noted that in the Osuna corrals great numbers of un-branded calves could be found at nightfall and that cows bearing all sorts of brands came to bawl outside. Meanwhile the *rinches* were killing Grandfather Osuna's Mexican neighbors for suspected cattle rustling.

Grandfather Osuna himself was no longer a Mexican. He was now a Spaniard. And as a Spaniard the grandfather amassed a great fortune, part of which his son had squandered. The grandson, Don Onofre, ded-icated himself to rebuilding his grandfather's estate. He had inherited vast ranchlands populated by lean longhorn cattle and blocks of houses in the Mexican districts of Jonesville, smalltown tenements that were rented out by the room. *Los cuartos de Don Onofre*, Mexican people called them.

The houses he never repaired. He knew he could rent them anyway, at fifty cents a month per room, each room occupied by one family, who shared an outside faucet and a privy with several other families. He gave his attention to his cattle ranches, to improving the breed of his herds, which were worked by Mexican *vaqueros* who did not ask for much. With these two sources of income the Osunas lived a life of ease, while Don Onofre spent his time building up more capital. The princi-pal drain on his resources was his wife. She loved fine dresses, jewelry, and expensive perfumes, and she was given to tempestuous scenes when he denied her anything. Don Onofre usually gave in, but on one thing he was adamant. He would not leave his ancestral home for a house in a more fashionable part of town, and he insisted that his children go to the public schools instead of to the private schools run by the Church.

That was why La Nena Osuna was in the same school as Guálinto, though she was in high rather than low first. Guálinto had been fervidly in love with La Nena ever since they had almost bumped into each other the first day of school. His love was love from a distance, the love of fools as the Mexican proverb had it. He enjoyed talking to his friends on the playground about La Nena, hinting she was his girl. They would make fun of him. "You ought to tell her she's your girl so she'll know about it," they would say. And they would chant over and over the old saying, *"Amor de lejos, amor de pendejos. Amor de lejos, amor de pendejos."* He didn't mind the ribbing as long as they were talking about her.

When some of the older girls heard about Guálinto's attachment for

La Nena they exploited it. "Guálinto," one of them would say, "give me three sheets of paper and I'll tell you what La Nena said about you." He would part with the paper in a hurry. "She said she loved you," the girl would say. At other times he was done out of a pencil or some other of his possessions for confidential reports about La Nena. Some of the girls had him running errands for them. So began his first love, at second hand.

He was sure La Nena loved him, he had heard it often enough. And she always smiled at him when they met in the hall, even after his fight with Miguel. Once, just after his George Washington speech, she stopped him in the hall and told him, "That was a very good talk. You are very smart." But she was gone into her room before he could even say, "Thank you."

She was always in his daydreams now. His mother, accustomed to his moods, was puzzled by his strange behavior. He would sit quietly by the kitchen door, too quietly for him, his head pushed forward. Then he would straighten up and begin swinging his body gently to and fro. Suddenly he would jump up, give a low whoop and prance toward the banana grove. María watched him, mystified, not suspecting the malady that possessed him. Meanwhile he would be sitting on his favorite grassy patch in the banana grove, staring at the sky and thinking up beautiful adventures in which he saved La Nena from all kinds of perils.

It was the bigger boys who thought of the letter. One day Guálinto was walking home with El Colorado, Orestes, and La Flaica. He brought up the subject of La Nena again, and La Flaica said, "How do we know she's your girl? We never see you with her."

"She sure is," said Guálinto. "I betcha anything."

La Flaica cleared his throat and spat out a gob of yellow mucus. "She's not," he said and turned the corner toward his house.

After he was gone El Colorado said, "La Flaica's right. If she's your girl you've got to go around with her, ain't that right, Orestes?"

Orestes nodded.

"How—how do you mean?"

"Walk her home," said El Colorado. "Take her to the movies and pigeon her. That's what my cousin Tiburcio does to girls."

"Pigeon her? What's that?"

"You put your arm around her and you kiss her, and you play with her bubbies."

Guálinto reddened. He didn't want to do those things to La Nena but he was afraid to say so.

"Your cousin Tiburcio is almost twenty and he has a job," Orestes told El Colorado. "None of us can do what he does with girls. Least of all Guálinto."

"He could speak her at least."

"I have talked to her a couple of times," Guálinto said quickly.

"That's not what El Colorado means. When you speak a girl you talk to her and tell her you like her and that you want her to be your girl."

"But I would never get the chance. Her mother brings her in their car and takes her back. All I get to say to her in the hall is a couple of words."

"You can also speak a girl by writing her a letter," El Colorado said. "You could do that better than any of us."

Guálinto decided he would "speak" La Nena by letter. It had to be soon because tomorrow was the next-to-last day of school before the Christmas holidays. That night he sat down at the kitchen table, saying he had some homework to do. He selected the best sheet of paper in his Red Indian pencil tablet. This was not easy because all the pages had tiny slivers of wood embedded in the paper. He finally spotted a sheet that had no slivers in the bottom half. That was all he needed. With one of his mother's kitchen knives he cut off the bottom half and wrote, "NENA TE KIERO. PALABRA DIOMBRE POR DIOS." He read it over and was satisfied. Folding the paper very carefully he hid it between the pages of his reader.

Next morning he waited for her where the short hall leading to the front door met the main hall. She smiled at him and would have gone by but he said, a bit louder than he intended, "Nena, this is for you." She looked surprised but she took the paper, unfolded and read it as she walked toward her classroom. Just before she reached the door she let the paper fall from her fingers. He rushed to retrieve it but Alicia was there before him. She had been watching from the door of Miss Cornelia's room. Alicia picked up the paper and ran into Miss Cornelia's room while Guálinto gave up his chase just outside the door.

"What?" Miss Cornelia was saying as he reached the door. She turned around, the paper in her hand, and saw him there. "What?" she repeated, seeming to grow taller as she straightened her back and raised her shoulders, chin, and eyebrows. "Alicia, you go to your seat." Alicia went. "And *you* come here." Miss Cornelia grabbed him by the ear and pulled him inside. "Now stand in that corner until I'm ready to straighten you out. Face the wall, face the wall." Guálinto could hear the rest of Miss Cornelia's pupils coming in and filling up the room, but they were quieter than usual. No loud talking or scraping of feet.

Finally Miss Cornelia grabbed him by the shoulder and pulled him around to face the class. He raised his head and looked at the top of the rear wall. Miss Cornelia rummaged in her desk and took out a thin, heavy rope which she doubled up in her hand. "And now," she said, "you will see what happens to boys who write love letters in this school." She held the paper in front of Guálinto's face with her other hand. "Read it!" she commanded. He kept looking at the wall. The rope bit into his buttocks like a whip. Guálinto winced and gnawed at his lips. "Now read it!" Guálinto shook his head, and the rope came down three more times.

"I see, I see," said Miss Cornelia sarcastically. "You know how to write but you can't read. I'll read it for you: 'Nena, I love you. By the word of a man and by God.'" She paused like a comedian waiting for laughs, but nobody made a sound. The rope went back to work again. With painful regularity, whip-swish-whip against his buttocks until he could take no more. He began to sob softly, crossing his legs defensively and wrapping his head in his arms. Miss Cornelia gave him a few more licks and finally stopped.

"That's enough for now," she said. "But I'm not through with you. We're going for a nice walk, my little friend. Alicia, sit at the desk and take names." She jerked him by the arm, down the hall and into another room. By this time his head was bowed, his tear-blinded eyes on the floor.

"Children," said Miss Cornelia, "I have something very interesting to show you. I am going to read you a letter this young man wrote to a girl in this school. Then I'm going to show you what happens to boys who go around with love affairs in school." She read Guálinto's letter again. Silence. Guálinto raised his head and saw that everybody, including the teacher, was staring at Miss Cornelia. Then he saw La Nena. She was sitting on the row directly in front of him. Her eyes seemed bigger than usual and her face was very pale. Guálinto was so intent looking at her that Miss Cornelia's rope caught him unawares, and he gave a short grunt when it hit. She struck again and again. Guálinto bit his lips and ground his fist into the palm of his other hand. Before he cried out loud Miss Cornelia stopped and jerked him out of the room. Vaguely he heard La Nena sobbing and dimly saw Miss Rathers moving toward her. Guálinto was pulled down the hall into Miss Josephine's room.

8

Every once in a while a shudder ran down Guálinto's spine, shaking him from head to foot. Now and then too, one of the many sobs he had held back that morning escaped him, as short as a hiccup. Hidden in the banana grove he had made up with interest all the crying he had held back when Miss Cornelia whipped him. He lay on his belly in his favorite grassy patch, one eye toward the house, barely visible through the green leaves and trunks, and another toward a little path leading to a thicket of reeds beyond their yard, his avenue of retreat. It was almost noon and he felt weak.

He wondered whether his mother would beat him too for the terrible thing he had done, or whether she would think up new punishments for him. His recollection of the morning's pilgrimage from room to room was somewhat hazy. His feet had moved, his arm was pulled or his shoulder pushed. And then he was flogged again and again. His buttocks were numb now and hurt only when he moved. Except for La Nena he didn't remember seeing anybody clearly. But he knew he had been taken to Miss Rathers' and Miss Josephine's room. The last one had been Miss Huff's. And at every blow that Miss Cornelia gave him, there had gone through his head El Colorado's words the day he had fought with Miguel Osuna: "Sometimes I feel like knocking her down." "Knocking her down." "Knocking her down."

It was in Miss Huff's room, he was sure. All of a sudden he could take no more. He turned around and grabbed the rope that was tormenting him. Then he butted Miss Cornelia in her little pot belly, hitting low and up like an enraged little bull. Miss Cornelia had made a most undignified sound and sat down hard on the floor. Half blind with tears, he rushed past her, out the door and out of the school building. He ran all the way home, coming in through the reeds in the back, over the fence and into the banana grove.

So had ended his first half-year in school. No punishment he could imagine could be adequate for what he had done. Some time later he had seen Maruca come home, way before noon. She had an envelope in her hand. Probably a letter saying he was expelled from school for the rest of his life. A short while later his uncle had arrived on his buggy. Carmen was with him. They were talking it over right now, thought Guálinto, trying to decide whether to send him to correctional school or just to whip him a few more times and keep him on bread and water for the rest of his life. He could imagine Maruca thinking up ways to punish him. Maruca liked to think up ways to hurt people, though she never did those things she talked about. Now was her chance.

The banana leaves parted suddenly, without the warning of a footfall. Guálinto started violently and tried to crawl backwards. A tall form came forward quickly and became his Uncle Feliciano. Guálinto recognized him but could not control his trembling.

"Come," said Feliciano softly. He picked Guálinto up very gently and made his way out of the grove almost as noiselessly as he had entered. As he reached the kitchen door, Feliciano bent down to look at Guálinto. There was a lock of hair over the boy's eyes and he brushed it back. He stooped slightly to enter the kitchen, and Guálinto looked fearfully around in search of his mother. She was standing close by, leaning with one hand on the kitchen table. Her face was very white and stiff and her eyes were red. She looked at Guálinto, but he could not tell whether she was angry or not, her look was so strange.

"In there," she told his uncle. Guálinto was carried into his mother's bedroom. "Maruca," she snapped, "bring hot water and some towels." Feliciano laid Guálinto face down on the bed, and immediately his mother began to undress him, feeling the bones and flesh of his arms and legs as she did so. Guálinto protested feebly when she started to take off his underpants. After all, he was almost eight years old.

"Be quiet!" his mother said, a tinge of hysteria in her voice. "Be quiet or I'll slap your rump for you! You've caused enough trouble already."

"Easy, easy, María," his uncle said. "You'll get yourself all worked up again." Guálinto subsided, and he was deprived of his underpants.

"Oh!" said María. She got up and raised the window shade all the way. "Oh!" she repeated when she returned to the bed. "Beast! Beast! Savage!" She passed her fingers lightly over Guálinto's buttocks. He flinched at her touch and turned his head. Tears were rolling down her cheeks.

"I brought the towels," Maruca said, coming into the bedroom. "Carmen is heating the water." Then she saw Guálinto's naked bottom. "Little mother of my life!" she exclaimed. "Just look! Such welts! Did you ever see welts like that?"

"Mama," said Guálinto, "make Maruca quit looking at me."

María almost smiled, but she said to Maruca, "Put the towels on the dresser and go back to the kitchen. But wait, before you go find me that bottle of Volcanic Oil."

"Wait," said Feliciano. "Don't do anything to him yet."

"Why? Why shouldn't I?"

"Santiago is home, I saw his car parked out front. I'm going next door to fetch him as a witness. I want him to see those welts before you doctor them."

Don Santiago López-Anguera came immediately, in his customary dark suit and carrying pen and notebook and a magnifying glass. After the briefest of formalities he verified the date and time of day with Feliciano. Then he inspected the welts on Guálinto's buttocks and took notes on his pad. "Terrible," he said to María. Then to himself as he wrote, "Buttocks covered with numerous welts. Black, blue, red. Ap-

proximately half-inch wide and idem high. Evidence of some bleeding."
He shut his notebook. "That is all the information I need, Doña María.
It is all right to tend to him now. With your permission. Your brother
and I must pursue this matter in town."

As they left López-Anguera was telling Feliciano, "We'll call him
from my office. How I wish they would install telephone lines into this
part of town. Then we can eat something and the three of us can talk
before we go. There's plenty of time between now and four o'clock."

Maruca came back with a bottle of Dr. McClean's Volcanic Oil, and
Carmen brought a pan of hot water and set it on the floor beside the
bed. As her mother bent over to dip a towel into the water, Maruca
took a bold, exaggerated ogle at Guálinto's bare rump, standing by his
head so he could see her do it. Then she wrinkled her nose disdainfully
and flounced out. Guálinto raised his head and scowled at her.

"There," said his mother when he raised his head. "I'm not going
to hurt you." She pressed hot, damp towels on his backside for some
time and then doctored the welts with the Volcanic Oil. At last she had
smeared him with *volcánico* to her satisfaction. She rose with a sigh,
wiped her hands with a wet towel and threw a clean sheet lightly over
him. She sat by the bed and stroked his hair and kissed him. Then she
asked, "Are you hungry?"

"Yes, Mama," he answered, "a little bit."

"I'll get you something. Be a good boy and don't move around too
much." She picked up the pan of water and rustled off to the kitchen.

Guálinto was left alone in his mother's bed. He could hear Carmen
and Maruca in the kitchen. They were talking softly. Once Maruca
giggled and María spoke to her sharply. After that there was silence
except for the sounds of food being prepared and served. The smells
from the kitchen whetted his appetite, and he was quite hungry when
his mother came in with a plate of meat stewed with tender squash and
sweet corn. She spooned the stew into his mouth while he munched
on a rolled-up flour tortilla he held in one hand. When he finished his
mother wiped his mouth and picked up the tortilla crumbs from the bed.
Then he fell asleep.

He woke at twilight to the sound of Feliciano's heavy footsteps in the
kitchen and wondered sleepily how his uncle could walk so softly when
he wanted to. "You sure took a long time," his mother said. "Come sit
down and have your supper."

There were the usual sounds in the kitchen as Feliciano sat down,
sounds of chairs scraping, of plates and cutlery. Then his uncle said,
"Well, we sure put her in her place."

"Huh!" said his mother savagely. "I hope you did it good and proper."

"We sure did."

"What happened?"

"First we went to Santiago's office and I called the Judge, Don Roberto. He had told me a number of times in the past that if I ever needed legal help I could use his personal lawyer. He's a Gringo but he speaks very good Spanish. The Judge said yes, so his lawyer, Santiago and I had dinner about one o'clock at the Texas Cafe. We got to the school just as the children were being let out, and I saw a red-headed boy that Guálinto knows. We stopped and talked to him and some other boys, and what they told us was hard to believe. They said this bitchy old hag has been making life miserable for your son from his first day at school. Yelling at him, slapping his face, whipping him with a ruler, and calling him names."

"But how could all this be happening and nobody know about it?"

"Everybody in school knew about it, Mama," Maruca said disgustedly. "Even the teachers."

"*You* knew about it," his mother said fiercely, "and you never told me? Me?"

"But Mama," said Carmen, pleading, "you told us from the very beginning that if one of us was punished at school and you knew about it you would punish us too."

"He was having it hard enough with Miss Cornelia. Carmen and I agreed not to tell you because of that."

"He was not being bad, really," said Carmen. "The old Guajolota just had it in for him."

"But why?"

"Perhaps because she knew he was smarter than she was," said Maruca. Guálinto was pleasantly surprised. He had never known Maruca thought he was smart.

There was a long silence. Then María said in a tired, resigned voice, "Well, tell us what happened, Feliciano."

"The letter said I was to be at the principal's office at 4:15. They were waiting for me there. Bageyly, the old Turkey Hen, and Onofre Osuna of all people. But they weren't expecting me to walk in with two lawyers at my side. That set them back on their heels. Bageyly and the old Turkey Hen. Osuna was there only because he had been asked to come. Shanahan, the Judge's lawyer, immediately demanded that the other three teachers be present. From the rooms where the Old Hag had whipped Guálinto. They were called in. Miss Josephine and two young and pretty *gringuitas*. They didn't have any kind words for Miss Cornelia, especially the blonde one named Miss Hoff."

"Oh, that's Miss Huff," said Carmen. "She's very nice."

"There wasn't very much to it after that," continued Feliciano. "We had agreed that I wouldn't say anything unless they asked me questions, so I kept my mouth shut most of the time. Santiago read his notes on Guálinto's injuries in a legal sort of way. Then Shanahan said he might have a doctor examine Guálinto tomorrow, and if he did he thought he might bring suit against the school because of the way they treated little Mexican children. That toned them down. They started calling me Mister after that." There was silence for a while except for the clink of knife and fork as Feliciano ate.

Finally María said, "But how did things end up?"

"We had to meet them halfway," Feliciano answered, his mouth still full of food. "Because Guálinto butted the old Turkey Hen when he ran away, she could sue us for assualt if we sued them for what she did to Guálinto."

"Assault? How could my poor little baby assault that monster?"

"Lawyers have their ways, and the school has some good ones from the Red party. Shanahan was telling me later how sorry he was that Guálinto had not just run away. Shanahan could have made a big case of it, which would have helped the Blues come next election."

"And what good would that have done us?"

"None. That's why I'm glad he did butt her in the belly. They tell me she let go with a great big fart before she landed on her butt. That was more manly than just running away. And at least he got some satisfaction for all those beatings. So as I said we had to meet them halfway. Everything is going to be all right. We keep quiet about the beating and Guálinto goes back to school after Christmas as if nothing had happened. By the way, Osuna talked to me after the meeting. He said he was sorry about what had happened to my nephew. That to him it was nothing to get excited about, a little boy writing a love letter to his little girl. He thought it was funny, but his wife thought different. The little Osuna girl won't come back in January. She'll be going to the Catholic school until she's ready for high school."

"I don't care about the Osuna brat!" María said. "How can you say everything is going to be all right when next month my son will again be in the claws of that old buzzard?"

"He won't," said Feliciano, "as I was trying to tell you. He's being moved to Miss Josephine to finish low first. And next year he'll be in high second with Miss Hoff."

"That's nice," said Carmen. "Miss Huff is so good. She coached Guálinto when he gave the George Washington speech, you know. And she likes him, too. She asked me once if he was my brother."

"Well," said Feliciano, "the Gringa will treat him better than Miss Cornelia, even if she is a Gringa. And she's very pretty, so he may fall in love with her, now that the Osuna girl will be gone. Har! Har! Har! Har!"

"Hush," said María, trying to sound stern. "You probably woke him up with those guffaws of yours."

9

So, at eight years of age, after having finished low first with Miss Josephine, Guálinto passed to high second with Miss Huff, and in so doing entered American school at last. Under Miss Huff's guidance he began to acquire an Angloamerican self, and as the years passed, under Miss Huff and other teachers like her, he developed simultaneously in two widely divergent paths. In the schoolroom he was an American; at home and on the playground he was a Mexican. Throughout his early childhood these two selves grew within him without much conflict, each an exponent of a different tongue and a different way of living. The boy nurtured these two selves within him, each radically different and antagonistic to the other, without realizing their separate existences.

It would be several years before he fully realized that there was not one single Guálinto Gómez. That in fact there were many Guálinto Gómezes, each of them double like the images reflected on two glass surfaces of a show window. The eternal conflict between two clashing forces within him produced a divided personality, made up of tight little cells independent and almost entirely ignorant of each other, spread out all over his consciousness, mixed with one another like squares on a checkerboard.

Consciously he considered himself a Mexican. He was ashamed of the name his dead father had given him, George Washington Gómez. He was grateful to his Uncle Feliciano for having registered him in school as "Guálinto" and having said that it was an Indian name. He spoke Spanish, literally as his mother tongue; it was the only language his mother would allow him to use when he spoke to her. The Mexican flag made him feel sentimental, and a rousing Mexican song would make him feel like yelling. The Mexican national hymn brought tears to his eyes, and when he said "we" he meant the Mexican people. "La Capital" did not mean Washington, D.C., for him but Mexico City. Of such matter were made the basic cells in the honeycomb that made up his personality.

But there was also George Washington Gómez, the American. He was secretly proud of the name his more conscious twin, Guálinto, was ashamed to avow publicly. George Washington Gómez secretly desired to be a full-fledged, complete American without the shameful encumberment of his Mexican race. He was the product of his Anglo teachers and the books he read in school, which were all in English. He felt a pleasant warmth when he heard "The Star-Spangled Banner." It was he it was who fought the British with George Washington and Francis Marion the Swamp Fox, discovered pirate treasure with Long John Silver, and got lost in a cave with Tom Sawyer and Becky Thatcher. Books had made him so. He read everything he could lay his hands on. But he also heard from the lips of his elders songs and stories that were the history of his people, the Mexican people. And he also fought the Spaniards with Hidalgo, the French with Juárez and Zaragosa, and the Gringos with Blas María de la Garza Falcón and Juan Nepomuceno Cortina in his childish fancies.

In school Guálinto/George Washington was gently prodded toward complete Americanization. But the Mexican side of his being rebelled. Immigrants from Europe can become Americanized in one generation. Guálinto, as a Mexicotexan, could not. Because, in the first place, he was not an immigrant come to a foreign land. Like other Mexicotexans, he considered himself part of the land on which his ancestors had lived before the Anglotexans had come. And because, almost a hundred years before, there had been a war between the United States and Mexico, and in Texas the peace had not yet been signed. So in assembly, while others were singing, "We're proud of our forefathers who fought at the Alamo," Guálinto and his friends would mutter, "We're proud of our forefathers who killed Gringos at the Alamo."

In all this he was no different from other Mexicotexan school children in Jonesville. They came to school and were placed in "low" first and second grades. This, said the Gringo school board, is a pedagogical necessity. The little Latins must learn the English language before they can associate with the little Anglosaxons. But wouldn't they learn English quicker if they were in the same classes with English-speaking children? No, that is a pedagogical fallacy. So the Society for the Advancement of Latin American Voters makes an issue of it in the next elections and succeeds in electing their candidate precinct chairman. *Ya estaría*, as Mexicans say.

Meanwhile, the little Latin, if he is lucky, has struggled through the highs and the lows of first and second grade and has fallen into the hands of one of those earnest young women from up north, too religious to join the CPA and too inhibited to become a vocal social reformer, but still entertaining some ideas about equality and justice. She gets a Bachelor's in Education and comes down to the Delta to teach little Latins at fifty dollars a month. Within a week she will declare she loves the little things and that their wide-eyed admiration touches her heart. She becomes the mother of the Mexicotexan's American self. She nurses that self along, shielding it from damaging influences as one would a sickly plant. She is gentle and understanding. She is patient with the struggling limitations of a new language and the barriers raised by different customs and beliefs. She sets out optimistically to undo the damage done by poverty and prejudice. She teaches him that we are all created equal. And before he knows it the little Latin is thinking in English, and he can feel infinitely dirty if he forgets to brush his teeth in the morning.

This is also the time when the little Latins come in direct contact with the little Anglosaxons. On the playground Gringo and Greaser have played in separate groups. But now they are in the same classes and they must mix because they are seated alphabetically. Out of this proximity, classroom friendships sometimes develop. But the Mexican soon learns that such friendships do not extend beyond the classroom door. He will see a classroom friend on the playground, surrounded by several other Anglos. When the dark-skinned boy approaches, the American boys stop talking, and not all of them return his greeting. They will resume their conversation, but guardedly now, without including him in it. The Mexicotexan learns to stay away; he makes them uncomfortable. And one day he learns at least one of the reasons why. He will be walking past a group of Anglo boys playing marbles, let us say.

"You're fudging!" one of them shouts.

"I'm not."

"You were!"

"I wasn't!"

They stand up and face each other, their red faces almost purple with rage, their hands balled up into fists. The Mexican stops; he has never seen a fight between two Americans. But the two just stand there, until one of them says, "You—German!"

The other answers, "You—Mexican!"

They see the Mexican standing close by. They smile, embarrassed, and go back to their game. The Mexicotexan walks away, thinking, "Gringos *sanavabiches*."

No, the Mexicotexan is not as ignorant as Calvin Coolidge, who once said, "The Alamo? What's the Alamo?" The Mexicotexan knows about the Alamo, he is reminded of it often enough. Texas history is a cross that he must bear. In the written tests, if he expects to pass the course, he must put down in writing what he violently misbelieves. And often certain passages in the history textbook become subjects of discussion.

"Isn't it horrible what the Mexicans did at the Alamo and Goliad? Why are they so treacherous and bloody? And cowards too."

"That's a lie! That's a lie! Treacherous? That's you all over!"

"It's in our textbook. Can't you read?"

"Children, children. Let's get back on the subject."

"But he's saying things about us!"

"It's the book that says them."

The teacher smiles. "That was long ago," she says. "We are all Americans now."

"But the book, the book! It talks about us today! Today! It says we are all dirty and live under trees."

The teacher cannot criticize a textbook on Texas history. She would be called a Communist and lose her job. Her only recourse is to change the subject, telling a joke, something to make her students laugh. If she succeeds the tension is over, for the moment at least. Despite the textbooks, she does her best and that is often good enough. In her classes at least, democracy exists. There, often enough, the Mexicotexan is first instead of last. If the teacher is young and pretty he will fall in love with her, in such an obvious way that it embarrasses her. But if in some instances she represents for him Beauty itself, in many more she is for him Justice, Equality, Democracy. The embodiment of all that is supposed to be good in the American people.

It was in this kind of schoolroom environment that Guálinto Gómez approached puberty. Hating the Gringo one moment with an unreasoning hatred, admiring his literature, his music, his material goods the next. Loving the Mexican with a blind fierceness, then almost despising him for his slow progress in the world.

10

Guálinto walked briskly down Fourteenth Street, enjoying the breeze that had followed the early afternoon rain. In a short while the August sun would make the rest of the day hot and steamy. It was hurricane season, when high winds and heavy rains were common. This afternoon's thunderstorm had caught him at his Uncle Feliciano's grocery store, where he had been visiting. As soon as the rain was over, his uncle sent him home to see if the wind had done any damage around the house. He went down Fourteenth until he reached the gravel street that passed in front of his home. When he was very young it had been known as the Old Fort Jones road. Now its official name was Pershing Avenue. It still was the only surfaced street in that part of town. Usually he cut across through the hackberries and came in through the back. But not today. The banana grove, where he had played so often in years past, would be a sea of mud, as it always was after a heavy rain. He didn't play there anymore; he was too old for that sort of thing.

He was feeling happy, and as he walked he hummed a song that went, "I'm sitting on top of the world, just rolling along, just rolling along." It had been a pleasant summer. There had been plenty of time to hang around with El Colorado, Orestes Sierra, and others of his friends. He had enjoyed visiting his uncle's store, where there were so many good things to eat. But best of all were the days he had spent on the farm. His uncle and Don José Alcaraz were working eighty acres of riverfront land downriver from Jonesville. That is, Don José worked the land with occasional hired help. Uncle Feliciano paid the rent on the land and they shared the profits. Guálinto really loved the country. He swam in the river with boys from neighboring farms and rode the farm horses when they were not being worked. He liked to watch the growing vegetables in their neatly ordered rows. More than that he loved to sit around an open fire at night listening to the men sing songs and tell stories. In the daytime he would take an old short-barrelled .22 rifle and walk through the leafy trails in the nearby woods. Not intending to shoot at anything, just carrying the rifle as an excuse to be alone in the woods with his own thoughts. At times he thought he would like to be a farmer, and once he had mentioned it to his Uncle Feliciano. His uncle looked angry. "Farming is not for you," he said sternly. "School. That is where you belong."

And in truth, Guálinto loved school and was looking forward to it. He always did well, as did Carmen. And this would be a special year. Last May he had finished fifth grade at the old grammar school, and this September he would enter sixth in junior high, in one of the new buildings many blocks to the north of the grammar school. Orestes Sierra and Antonio Prieto would go with him, as would El Colorado, Arty Cord, and La Víbora, who had fallen behind one more grade in grammar school. Many of the others in El Colorado's gang had already dropped out of school altogether. He would be in school once again with Francisco Four-Eyes, who would be in seventh. Next year, Francisco had told them, his father would send him to preparatory school in Monterrey. Old Four-Eyes had boasted all last year about how tough junior high was. Now he was talking about how much better schools in Monterrey were than in Texas.

Guálinto wasn't the only one excited about the coming school year, he knew. So was Carmen. She had passed to eighth and would be a freshman in high school. Graduating from high school was one of Carmen's dreams, and now her dream was coming true. It would be no problem for her. She was very smart and worked harder than Guálinto. She loved to study, to read and to know. Poor Maruca was a different matter. She had fallen behind Carmen and would have to repeat seventh grade this fall. Guálinto might very well catch up with her next year, if she stayed in school. His mother had been talking about taking her out. At sixteen, her mother said, Maruca no longer was a school child.

He had been walking in the street to stay out of the mud, and now that he came opposite his house he crossed the grassy ditch on the wooden footbridge to his front gate. As he reached the door he heard a thud in the back of the house, followed by screams from his sisters, and then his mother's heavy groaning. He rushed through the house and found Maruca and Carmen bending over his mother, who was lying on her side on the wooden walkway connecting the house with the back room.

"I told her! I told her!" Maruca cried when she saw Guálinto. "But she just had to go see if the wind had hurt her rosebushes."

"Help us get her up," Carmen said. "Gently. As gently as we can."

They took off her muddy shoes and raised her to her feet. María cried out when she put her weight on her left foot, so they carried her to the edge of the bed. "She may have broken something," Carmen told Guálinto. "We must get Uncle Feliciano."

While the girls helped María into bed, he ran next door to the López-Angueras, who had just recently got a telephone. Doña Socorrito answered his knock. "My mother," he said. "She fell and her leg hurts very much. Can I call my uncle, please?"

Doña Socorrito was a broad, pleasant lady with glasses. "Come in, child," she said. "We must call the doctor first. Let me do it for you." She got Dr. Zapata on the telephone and explained the situation. "He's coming right away," she told Guálinto brightly. "Do you want me to call your uncle for you? We have the number of the store."

"I would be very grateful," answered Guálinto. "I am not very good at using the telephone."

"I'll do so immediately. Is there anything I can do to help?"

"No, thank you. My sisters have already put her to bed and are taking care of her."

"Why don't you go back then, and help them. I'll call your uncle."

When he got back Maruca and Carmen had helped their mother wash the mud off herself, undressed her, and helped her put on a nightgown. She was lying on her right side, very pale and moaning softly. Dr. Zapata's Ford and Feliciano's buggy arrived one after the other. The doctor came briskly into the bedroom, a small man with a big mustache and a military bearing. Before the Revolution he had been a surgeon in

Porfirio Díaz's army.

"Let's see the leg," he said and lifted María's nightgown. She grabbed at his hand.

"Don't you dare!" she said.

"I am a doctor! I have to know where you are hurt or I can't heal you!" Then, "Oh, well, we can begin another way." He pressed roughly on her leg over the gown, from hip to knee, drawing a yelp from María when he was halfway between hip and knee. Then he put his hands under the gown and pressed again.

María cried out, "You're hurting me!"

"No, *señora*," the doctor replied. "You hurt yourself. I'm trying to make you well. Señor García, why don't you and the boy step into the other room. The girls can help me." Feliciano and Guálinto went into the living room. The doctor took out a big needle from his bag, lifted María's gown and stuck the needle into her buttock. Then he began to prepare a brown, smelly mixture. "You are lucky, Señora Gómez."

"Lucky?" cried María. "I fall and break my leg and you say I'm lucky?"

"Hush, now, don't move. Your thigh bone is broken, but it is a clean break, no splintering, and it did not move from its place. You are lucky because of that. You are lucky it was not your hip, or you might have been lame for the rest of your life. You are also lucky that you are still young. You will heal faster than if you were fifty or sixty." He talked as he smeared the mixture on her thigh and wrapped it into a cast.

He finished and covered María with a sheet. "Señor García," he called, "you can come in now." Guálinto followed his uncle into the bedroom. "It will be at least two months before she can put her weight on that leg," the doctor told Feliciano. "Even more before she can walk around and do any kind of housework. It is necessary that she lie still and rest. You must get someone to do the housework and someone to nurse her. Remember, if the fracture moves before it heals the bone will not mend properly."

"But I feel better already," María protested. "I don't feel pain anymore."

"That's because of the injection I gave you. But the effect will soon wear off, and you will hurt again. I am sending you some capsules. Take one only when the pain is so severe you cannot stand it. But don't take them too often. They are dangerous."

Feliciano walked the doctor to the door and paid him for the visit. He came back, his mind on his neglect in not having put a railing around the walkway, and steps with handholds. "I'll get a carpenter tomorrow," he said as he entered the bedroom. "I should have done it years ago."

"Why worry about the walkway now," María said peevishly. "How will the housework get done?"

"Doña Teodora sometimes takes in washing," Feliciano replied. "We can pay her to do that for a few months. But we cannot afford a servant and a nurse. I think it's time Maruca stopped going to school. She can do the housework and take care of you."

"It's all right with me," Maruca said carelessly. "I'm tired of school anyway."

"Maruca can do the housework," María said, "But I don't want her taking care of me. She's too hasty and rough."

"You'll need a nurse then," said Feliciano.

"A nurse all day and night?" said María. "How much do you think that will cost? You are not a rich man."

"I'll take care of you, Mama," Carmen said in a small voice.

There was a short silence, and then Feliciano said, "She could do it, with Maruca's help when she needs it. She's gentle and careful."

"But she would have to leave school," said María. "She wants to graduate from high school."

"She already has more education than any woman needs," Feliciano said.

"I don't mind, Mama," Carmen said softly. "Really I don't," she added and went into the kitchen.

Guálinto followed her. "Carmen," he said, lowering his voice. "Carmen, I'm sorry." She turned from the stove to look at him and her eyes were moist. "Remember when I was little," he continued, "and you used to read to me from your schoolbooks and sometimes you asked Uncle Feliciano for money to buy me books you thought I should read? I'll get books for you now. And when I'm in the eighth grade I'll lend you all my schoolbooks. We'll study them together."

Carmen looked as if she was going to cry. But she just swallowed hard and nodded. Suddenly she planted a kiss on Guálinto's forehead and turned toward the stove.

11

As Guálinto advanced in school, so did his uncle's fortunes, spurred by a dead man's dream. If his life had followed the path marked out for him by alien hands, Feliciano García would have been a cowboy as long as there were cattle in south Texas. Or he could have become a field hand, or at most a sharecropper such as his neighbor José Alcaraz. His sister, born like him in a one-room shack with a dirt floor and one packing-case door as only opening, would have been content with little.

But Gumersindo Gómez, the redheaded dreamer who had been María's husband, had given his only son a great man's name. The name of a Gringo but a great man, nevertheless. And Gumersindo had confidently declared that his son would be a great man. And he had put on Feliciano a burden of guilt and responsibility, to see that the son would fulfill his destiny. Gumersindo's words, spoken once playfully and again as he lay dying, took an almost religious significance for Feliciano and María, a momentousness that grew with the years, as time made the memory of Gumersindo Gómez more nebulous and therefore more heroic. Feliciano, driven by remorse, had worked hard to make Gumersindo's dream come true. To give the boy the advantages he would need to reach the goal his father had foreseen. And when the boy went to school and did very well in his classes, the fact aroused in his family not so much surprise and admiration as self-confident pride. They had known all along he would be like that.

Feliciano endeavored to make as much money as he could, by all means possible, in order to realize Gumersindo's dream because he knew that dreams are more likely to come true if one has money. There were many factors in Feliciano's increasing prosperity—hard work, luck, Judge Norris and the Blue Party, Santos de la Vega. That and his mother's fierce determination to regain for her children something of what had been lost to her grandparents when the Gringos came. Her parents had only dim memories of their own as to what life was like before the Delta became part of Texas, but they passed their parents' memories down to her generation. That was why her children had learned to read, write and figure at the *escuelita* in San Pedrito and why she had saved what little money she could throughout her life, a nickel or a quarter at a time.

She must have died in the most wretched despair, thought Feliciano, embittered by the failure of all her efforts. Her two remaining sons fugitives from Gringo law, her only daughter a widow. If she could only see them now, living in circumstances that even her grandparents could not have been able to enjoy. She would have marveled at the house, added to and improved with Feliciano's money but originally bought with his mother's life savings. Feliciano felt he could justly be proud of the house his family lived in. It was not a brick mansion like those downtown, but except for the López-Anguera house it was the best in the whole Dos Veintidós area. Now it was a house with several rooms. It had glass windows and linoleum-covered floors. Even more, it had running water and electric lights and a water toilet inside the house. There was also space for a shower stall, but they still took their baths in a washtub because they had no hot running water. But soon, perhaps. As he sat on the porch in his rocking chair one Sunday afternoon, Feliciano dwelt on the good things his work had brought, and his heart was full of contentment. Once he had lived in what in retrospect seemed unbelievable poverty. Now he felt well-to-do, if not rich. He had read by the light of a candle, whenever he was not too tired to read at all. His nephew had his own little room with a study table and an electric light.

Feliciano was waiting for Guálinto to come home that Sunday afternoon. Rumors were about that business would soon get bad, and he wanted his nephew's help in checking some figures about his inventory and the money he had in the bank. He drew out his pocket watch. It was almost five. Guálinto should be coming home from the picture show by now. Finally he saw him coming down the street. The short, chunky body made him look much like Gumersindo, Feliciano thought. Except for the cinnamon-colored hair, not red like his father's. Guálinto was walking fast and reached the gate just as a big black automobile came up the street from the opposite direction. He hesitated, stopped and then hurried forward past the gate. When he came abreast of the slow-moving car he waved. The girl driving the car waved back. They passed each other and Guálinto walked all the way around the block before he came back and opened the gate.

"Hello," Feliciano said, "are you playing some kind of a game?"

Guálinto did not answer. He sat down on the porch swing, screened from the street by the honeysuckle vines. He pushed the swing back as far as he could so that only his legs were visible from the street.

"What is the matter?" persisted Feliciano. "Were you thinking so deeply about something that you forgot you were home?"

Guálinto looked at his feet. "Let me see the figures," he said.

Maruca came out and stood outside the parlor door, her taffy-colored hair falling in two pleats over her shoulders and down to her breasts.

"Come over here," Feliciano told Guálinto. "Sit in this chair close to me and we'll go over the figures together."

Guálinto hesitated, unwilling to leave the screen of the honeysuckle vines. Finally he rose, stealing a look up the street.

"What's the matter?" Feliciano repeated. "Are you hiding from some one?"

"Sure he is," Maruca said archly. "Can't you see he doesn't want to be seen?" Guálinto stopped on his way to the chair beside his uncle's and glared at Maruca.

"He doesn't want to be seen?" echoed Feliciano.

Guálinto gave Maruca a spiteful look and bolted into the house through the other front door, into his mother's bedroom.

"Sure," Maruca told her uncle. "That was his girl that just passed by there, in that big car, and he was afraid she would find out he lived here. At least, he thinks she's his girl."

Her uncle frowned. "You are crazy. Why wouldn't he want her to know where he lives?"

"He's ashamed of the house," said Maruca, snapping some gum she tongued from her cheek. "I bet he's in the toilet right now with a book. He's ashamed of this house. It's no palace, really."

"Hush your mouth and go inside," Feliciano said.

Maruca went inside, making a grimace which Feliciano did not see. She went into her mother's bedroom and asked, "Where's Guálinto, Mama?"

"He went past," her mother replied. She was sitting on the bed cutting some cloth according to a paper pattern. "He picked up the newspaper and went right into the kitchen without even saying 'I'm home.'"

"I bet he's in the toilet right now, reading."

Guálinto was sitting on the toilet bowl with the newspaper spread out on his knees, but the type blurred and danced before his eyes, and tears dropped now and then on the paper and spread into big damp spots.

On the porch Feliciano sat for a long time in his rocker, thinking. He inspected his large, bony hands as if he had never seen them before. Then he looked around him, studying his surroundings. After that he sat in the rocker for a long while, unmoving, his eyes fixed in the distance. Finally he put on his hat and went out for a walk.

12

April. It was a beautiful month this year. Mornings were still cool, and light rains fell often, so that there still were many wild flowers on the road from Jonesville to Uncle Feliciano's farm. But Guálinto had no time now for visits to the farm. Next month his junior year would end, and next fall he would be a senior, with graduation only nine months away. After that there would be college. He had expected a car during his senior year, a car he could drive to college the year after that. But now his uncle wasn't sure about that. The first year, at least, he would not cost his uncle too much money because he was sure of a scholarship.

He felt a strange mixture of emotions on mornings like these. Elation at what the future promised. And at the same time feelings of sadness and loneliness. Perhaps it was the weather. Perhaps it was the thought that so few of his friends remained in school with him. El Colorado, Arty Cord, and La Víbora had made it through junior high with him, but they dropped out after seventh grade and went to work. El Colorado was doing well as assistant to the bookkeeper at Acme Produce, Inc. He had always been good at figures. Francisco Four-Eyes was in preparatory school in Monterrey. Only Orestes Sierra and Antonio Prieto remained of his old friends from grammar school days. And Antonio was hanging on by the skin of his teeth, it was plain to see. He still had that haggard, undernourished look, and he still came to school with shaggy hair and mended clothes. Guálinto often wondered what his parents were like, but he had never been inside Antonio's house.

And then there was that gnawing feeling of doubt, of insecurity. Guálinto had learned a lot in school. He could speak, read, and write English very well. He knew a great deal about history, literature, and other subjects. But he did not know what he wanted to study in college, or what he wanted to be once he really was an educated man. And how he was supposed to help his people, as his mother and his uncle expected him to do.

The cool spring air came through the open windows of Miss Barton's history class this morning. Miss Barton was homeroom teacher for the junior class, and next year she would be the class sponsor for the seniors. She also taught United States history, and that was what she was doing at this particular hour in the morning. The topic of discussion was the Civil War. While the United States was divided against itself, she was saying, Mexico was fighting the French, who had invaded the country in defiance of the Monroe Doctrine.

"We have an oral report on the Franco-Mexican war today," she said, nodding toward Guálinto.

Guálinto turned and smiled at the girl on his left as he rose. The girl looked at him admiringly and smiled. She was María Elena Osuna. He strode up to the front of the room somewhat ostentatiously, with the self-confidence of the superior student. His was by far the highest grade average in the junior class, and it was a foregone conclusion that he would be the valedictorian next year. He took this as a matter of course; all his life he had been taught at home that he was better than most people. That the class was composed largely of Anglos did not hurt his chances in the least. Mildred Barton's class was a true democracy. The stupid-looking boy sitting third from the back was Odysseus Patch, son of the owner of the Patch Lumber Company, "Builders Come and

Builders Go/ But Patch Stays." His father was one of the rich and influential men in Jonesville-on-the-Grande, but in the classroom Odysseus Patch looked up to Guálinto Gómez. Elton Carlton, thin, sensitive son of the cashier at the Jonesville National Bank, was not stupid and he didn't look up to Guálinto. He felt a keen resentment toward the Mexican boy, which the class atmosphere did not allow him to express. Elton was the certain choice for salutatorian next year, but he did not think of it as an honor. It irked him, and his banker father as well, that he should play second fiddle in next year's graduation ceremonies to a Mexican.

Guálinto walked in quick short steps. He was beginning to develop a barrel chest and he stuck it out like a little game-cock. There was about him an air of bustle and garrulousness even before he said a word. Watching him, Miss Barton thought, "He tries so hard to appear self-assured. If he would only loosen up a little."

Guálinto cleared his throat and said, "I'm going to tell you about Mexico's war against the Frenchies." He recounted the landing of the French army at Veracruz and its defeat at Puebla by the Mexican army. The class heard about the battle of El Cinco de Mayo and why it was celebrated by Mexicans. The Mexicans won there, he emphasized, pride making his voice ring. Then came the days of guerrilla fighting by the Mexicans and atrocities by the French. Finally the French realized they could not win so they left, and Maximilian was executed.

"Our history book," he concluded scornfully. "Our story book says it was the United States that made the French get out. That is not true." He paused to let his statement sink in. "It was the Germans, who were getting ready to whack the tar out of the French. So Napoleon III pulled out his troops and left Maximilian holding the bag." He stuck out his lower lip and gave a self-satisfied nod. "That's all folks," he said and walked off briskly to his seat.

"Very good," said Miss Barton, "very, very nice, Guálinto. But I wish you would not use all that slang. You can use very good language in your written themes. Surely you can speak the way you write."

Guálinto smiled and focused his attention on the process of sitting down. Once in his seat he looked across the aisle at María Elena and she smiled at him. The graded papers from last week's test were being passed back along the aisles. Guálinto took the sheaf of papers from the boy in front, got his paper and passed the rest to the rear. He looked quickly at the page where his grade was written and frowned. Only a 99, he had expected a 100. He looked for the point he had missed. A matter of a date. He had got the numbers mixed up and put 1876 instead of 1867. He raised his hand to contest the point but was interrupted.

"Miss Barton?" It was Ed Garloc, round Ed. He was not fat and he was almost as tall as Guálinto's friend, El Colorado. But all of Ed

Garloc was round. The seat of his pants when he started to sit down was perfectly round. His tanned, dirty-milk face was round, with round brown eyes, round cheeks and an almost round nose. "Miss Barton," Ed said in his soft voice, "do you think all he said was true?"

"There are two sides to every question, Ed," answered Miss Barton before Guálinto could speak up.

"But there can be only one side that is right, can it? I think that's our side. We have always been juster and more truthful than any other country."

Guálinto laughed a raucous horse laugh. "Look who's talking! Why don't you read something besides your school books?"

"If you don't like it here," said Ed defensively, "why don't you go— some place else?"

"Where, for example?" asked Guálinto, challenging him to say "Mexico."

"To Germany, for example."

"Why not?"

"You go to Germany and see what happens to you."

"The Germans are good people," said Guálinto hotly. "I hope they come across the sea some day and teach this country a lesson!"

Ed Garloc stared at him incredulously. "You don't know what you're saying!" he exclaimed.

"I think he's a Bolshevik," a girl piped out from the back of the room.

"Students, students," said Miss Barton, "let's discuss things calmly."

"Aren't the Germans good people?" Guálinto asked Miss Barton.

"No people are bad at heart," she answered. "But bad leaders can make a people bad. The Germans were accused of many crimes in Belgium during the World War."

"They couldn't have been as bad as the crimes the Texas Rangers committed in Texas fifteen years ago," retorted Guálinto.

"They were killing bandits," said Ed.

"Bandits, my eye. All Mexicans were bandits to them."

"Well," answered Ed gravely, "you'll have to admit that Mexicans like to break the law, most of them."

"Why you, you—!" half-screamed a girl named Elodia, who sat in front of Ed Garloc. She turned around with a lashing of her loose black hair. Her dark face worked angrily. "Look at this *pendejo*," she exclaimed.

"Elodia," said Miss Barton. "Don't use words like that."

"It isn't a bad word."

"Anyway, speak in English."

"Then make him stop."

"But it's true," Ed said slowly. "Look in the court records, or in the newspapers even. Who gets arrested all the time? Mexicans."

"It's not true! It's not true!" shouted Guálinto, raising his voice because he knew it was true but could think of no argument to refute it.

"Do you know how he gets that way?" said Elodia. "His father's a *rinche*."

"My father's a deputy sheriff," intoned Ed theatrically, "and I'm proud of it."

"He's a murderer then, " retorted Guálinto. "A killer-diller."

"You take that back!"

"I won't."

Ed and Guálinto glared at each other across the aisle. Miss Barton banged on her desk with a ruler. "Either you talk things over politely," she said, "or we won't have any more discussions in this room. You two apologize to each other."

Ed looked at Guálinto steadily for a moment, then smiled. "I apologize," he said.

"Me too," said Guálinto but he did not smile.

"I didn't mean you at all," continued Ed, his voice back to its customary softness. "After all, you're not Mexican, you're Spanish."

"I'm not Spanish," said Guálinto stiffly. "I'm a Mexican."

"Back in Rio Grande City," said Elodia, "we run the town. The sheriff is Mexican, the mayor is Mexican. We have Boy Scouts and church picnics and school dances. Here in this dirty Delta the Gringos think they're a big heap of dirt."

"Elodia, Elodia," said Miss Barton. "No more of that. We're going too much into personalities. And that isn't the topic of today's class, anyway. Let's return to the lesson. The United States protested to France concerning the invasion of Mexico, basing itself on the Monroe Doctrine."

"And what business was it of the United States?" said Guálinto.

"We were acting as a big brother to a weaker nation," Miss Barton explained.

"Yeah," said Guálinto sarcastically. "A big brother with a big stick."

Miss Barton smiled. "The big stick was intended for meddling powers. Look now, Guálinto, suppose that next door to you lives a little fellow. He's about to eat a piece of candy when suddenly a big boy your size comes into the little boy's yard and tries to take his candy away from him. What would you do? You would jump over the fence and drive the bully away, wouldn't you?"

"Sure," said Guálinto acridly. "And after I drive the big bully away I take the candy from the little fellow and eat it myself."

The class giggled, then laughed heartily, and Miss Barton laughed too. "Very good, Guálinto," she said gaily. "You are a good debater. It's nice to discuss things if we do it nicely. We can see different sides to any question and understand each other better."

The buzzer sounded and the class lost its interest in Maximilian, Mexico, and the U.S. Civil War. They all made for the door. Ed Garloc sought Guálinto out in the hall and Guálinto stiffened, expecting a fight. But Ed put out his hand. "I'm sorry for what I said in there," he said. "Let's be friends."

Guálinto shook Ed's hand. "I'm sorry too," he said.

Mildred Barton sat down at her desk, facing the empty seats, the tired look in her eyes more pronounced than usual. Then the first student in the next class came in. "Good morning, Miss Barton," she said.

"Good morning," said Miss Barton, smiling brightly.

Out in the hall Guálinto caught up with María Elena Osuna. She turned and looked at him reproachfully. "What's the matter, Nena?" he asked nervously. "Are you mad at me?"

She thrust a paper at him, her test paper. He looked at the paper stupidly and said, "Eighty-five."

"Yes," La Nena said. "Eighty-five. I saw it, I can read. What did *you* get?"

"Ninety-nine," he said uncomfortably.

María Elena's red sensuous lips pouted. "I missed three whole questions," she said. "I could have failed."

Guálinto twisted the paper in his hands. "Gee, Nena. I'm terribly sorry. But it—it's still a good grade, isn't it? It's a B."

"Do you think it's right?" she said. "Do you think it's right that your girl should get eighty-five while you get a ninety-nine? Maybe you gave me the wrong answers on purpose. How did you get all of them right?"

"Gee, Nena," said Guálinto, twisting the paper round and round, "maybe you didn't read my signals right. You know how she was looking at us all the time. I wouldn't do it on purpose, Nena."

"Don't call me Nena," she said crossly. "And give me back that paper. Why would you want to crumple it like that?" She took the paper and started down the hall.

He followed her. "Will I see you at four?"

"I don't know," she answered.

They walked down the hall in silence. Their next class was in different rooms across the hall from each other. When they reached the door of her room she looked at him and smiled. Her oval face was very beautiful when she smiled. The big dark eyes softened and the large red mouth opened to show her perfect teeth. It made Guálinto think of biting her mouth.

"All right," she said, "I'll see you at four."

13

By the fall of Guálinto's senior year the Delta economy was feeling the impact of the stock market crash. It affected the school district's budget and was directly felt by the senior class in the Jonesville high school. There would be no yearbook next spring. Also cancelled was the picnic on the beach for the seniors, which came at the end of the spring semester. The well-to-do would have their unofficial graduation party as usual, a kind of private senior prom for their own children. For the majority of the seniors there would be nothing special, aside from the graduation ceremonies. This did not sit well with Miss Mildred Barton, sponsor of the senior class that year.

Perhaps, she told the senior class, they could have a party for all the class if they were willing to get together and earn some money for it. The school Halloween carnival would be a good opportunity to make some money if the seniors were willing to run a booth and sell candy, cookies and other things they made themselves or were given to them by friends and relatives. The carnival booth was a big success, especially because of Antonio Prieto, who sang and played the guitar. Some of the girls thought of disguising him as a blind beggar, complete with dark glasses and tin cup, and having him sing in front of the senior booth. Antonio went along without complaint. Everybody said it had been a wonderful idea. Almost half of what they made at the carnival came from Antonio's cup.

The seniors voted to make it a Christmas party rather than wait for spring. It would be just before the Christmas holidays at some restaurant where there was music and dancing. As Elton Carlton put it, "You can dance if you want to. If not you can eat, watch, and enjoy the music." He was helping Miss Barton keep track of the money and looking for a suitable place for the party. Two weeks before the fall semester ended Elton announced he and Miss Barton had found the ideal place for them, La Casa Mexicana at nearby Harlanburg. But they were short on money for all expenses including tips. If everyone contributed fifty cents from their own pockets, they would have the right amount. They all brought their fifty cents, including Antonio Prieto who could least afford it.

Antonio was one of the five Mexicans in the class of thirty, if one included María Elena Osuna. The others were Guálinto, Orestes Sierra,
and Elodia, the girl from Rio Grande City. Antonio was a tall, thin,
coffee-colored boy with large ears. He was small-boned and flat-chested.
Only his wrist bones were big and prominent, and his hands were large,
with long fingers. He rarely spoke and when he did it was in a soft voice,
though he could sing in a strong, rich voice when he wanted to. He always needed a haircut. His clothes were usually frayed and patched, and
twice, when they were in grammar school together, Guálinto had seen
him go up to the blackboard with the seat of his pants torn and his underwear showing. Antonio had little to do with the other boys at school.
He did not play ball on the playground and he walked alone to and from
school. His spare time at school he spent studying and reading. Though
he was not among the first in school as far as grades were concerned,
his English teachers often complimented him on his beautiful themes,
which they sometimes read to his class, to his intense embarrassment.
He also wrote poetry that he showed only to a few people.

During this last year, the class had found out that Antonio Prieto
could also play the guitar. When Antonio discovered that people were
pleased to hear him sing and play, he started bringing his small guitar
to school. He would hide it in his locker, and during rest periods he
would take it out and retreat to some little-used doorway. Other students would seek him out and sit around while he played and sang softly
to himself. They would ask him to play this rumba and that bolero and
that foxtrot, but Antonio gave no indication that he heard them. He just
sat there, caressing the neck of the guitar as one might caress a woman,
and then he would play another of his soft, lonely little songs. There
were times when even Mr. Darwin, the high school principal would
come and stand against the doorway, listening to Antonio. Once Mr.
Darwin said, as if to himself, "I used to have a Mexican friend who told
me about 'La Zandunga' and about a poet who said in one of his poems,
'When I die, play "La Zandunga" over my body. If I do not stir, then I
am truly dead.'"

Antonio's face brightened. He played and sang the song, softly and
gravely, and a great sadness seemed to pour out of him with the sadness
of the song. The notes of the guitar followed the tune, escorting it in
a painfully sweet procession. The song ended and there was a silence.
Then Mr. Darwin said quietly, "Thank you, Antonio" and went back
into the building. Antonio rose and put the guitar away.

The prospect of the Christmas party made somber-faced Antonio
look almost gay, and he brought his fifty cents too—a shiny half-dollar
that he rubbed about on the palm of his hand before depositing it in the
box. After he dropped the coin he smiled. The party would be a big

day, a day they would all remember for many years.

At last the day arrived. Guálinto dressed in his blue serge suit that had cost fourteen dollars and hurried out to catch a *camión* that would take him to the school grounds, where those people with cars would pick up those without them. On Fourteenth Street he hailed a *camión* and climbed in, his throat throbbing with excitement. Tonight he would dance with María Elena. He would hold her close in his arms and look into her eyes. He would have her to himself the whole night, and the thought made his stomach fluttery.

The little *camión* ran along the empty street, its motor patiently chugging along and one of its rear steps rattling over every bump in the asphalt. Guálinto perched on one of the two benchlike seats that ran lengthwise on each side of the vehicle. The *camiones* that traveled the streets of Jonesville-on-the-Grande were something like a taxi, a bus, and nothing anyone in Texas had ever seen before. They seemed to be the product of someone's hasty inventiveness turned into custom. A *camión* resembled a panel truck with its sides and rear cut out for ventilation. Benches were built along each side, consisting of two wide boards, one to sit on and one as a backrest. Two steps were provided at the back for passengers to climb aboard. The *camiones* ran on more or less prescribed routes, though they would take passengers anywhere in town for a higher fee than the usual ten cents. For a quarter, let us say. They were Jonesville's only public transportation facility except for the taxis at the stand in front of the railroad station, and a few rickety horse-drawn carriages driven by very old men. The *camiones* hauled children to school and whores to the dance halls outside the city limits with equal efficiency. They also carried merchants, ladies with bulky packages, and the general population whenever they wanted to get to the center of town and back.

This particular *camión* was empty except for Guálinto and an old lady who was sitting on the opposite bench, closer to the driver. She was stout and dressed in the usual black. When she was young she must have been handsome. She was grayhaired now, and her chalk-white face was serried by wrinkles. The driver, a slight sallow-faced young man in dirty shirt sleeves, had a square jaw that contrasted curiously with his pained, shifty eyes. He leaned back on his seat as he drove, his head turned around to the old lady, scarcely watching where his vehicle was going.

"I have set my heart to it," he told the old lady, apparently resuming a conversation interrupted by Guálinto's entrance, "and you should see me now."

"That is good, very good," said the old lady in a detached motherly way.

"Every night I go straight home. And she gets it all, every single nickel. Me, I can't save. But she knows what to do with it. She figures it all out, bills, rent, and everything. What's left she gives me back."

"She's a lucky girl."

"It's because I want to do the right thing," said the driver, his eyes becoming more pained and querulous. "It's because I love her so much." He looked quickly forward, juggling the steering wheel to miss a dog crossing the street. "I promised her if she'd marry me I'd act different. No more sprees, no more women. Work and save and raise a family." The old lady murmured something pleasant.

Guálinto wondered how long the fellow had been married. Not very long, he surmised; he was still nest-crazy like a setting hen. But he would get over it soon and go back to his sprees and his women. Men of his type were like that. Guálinto, of course, was not that type of man. He wondered how he would feel married to María Elena. The thought gave him a sexy, cozy feeling. In the movies people acted like the *camión* driver and it didn't look funny. But in real life ... well, maybe *he* looked silly to other people when he talked about María Elena. And yet, it had all started so matter-of-factly. After he had sent her a love letter when he was in the first grade, he had not seen her again for many years. She had been sent to the convent school until she was ready for high school.

In the years that followed, things had gone surprisingly well for her father, Don Onofre Osuna. Oil had been discovered on his extensive cattle lands, and he became extremely rich. A millionaire many times over, people said. His new riches made Don Onofre look at life with somewhat different eyes. He sold the rundown shacks he owned in Jonesville's *barrios* to other speculators in cheap,unlivable housing for Mexican people and opened a real estate office, from which he began to dabble in building and selling elegant houses in Jonesville's new subdivisions. He got rid of his lean longhorn cattle and replaced them with better breeds. He began to raise fine horses and bought himself a long black automobile. But one thing he refused to do, no matter how much his wife nagged him about it. He refused to move out of the house his grandfather had built so many years ago. All this had Guálinto known during the years that he went from grammar school through junior high and into high school. It was common knowledge in Jonesville-on-the-Grande, along with the affairs of many other people. But he had never given much thought to Don Onofre Osuna and his family and what they did or didn't do.

It was at the start of his junior year that Guálinto met María Elena Osuna again. During registration Miss Barton asked him to drive her downtown in Principal Darwin's Model A. She had to buy some things for the school and needed help in carrying them. Guálinto drove the car from the back of the school to the front entrance and parked it beneath a palm tree. Soon Miss Barton appeared, accompanied by a girl.

"Guálinto," Miss Barton said, "this is Mary Helen Osuna. She will be in our junior class this year."

María Elena smiled impishly. "Hello there," she said in a throaty voice. "I hadn't seen you for a long, long time." She was dressed in a white silk dress, as white as her skin, and bound at the waist with a slender red belt. The curls were gone, giving place to wavy, shoulder-length hair, as black as ever, and glossier. The face was no longer chubby, but it had not lost its dimples. And it was no longer innocently guileless. It now had a half-critical, half-taunting look that made her at once slightly irritating and quite desirable.

They both laughed when Miss Barton said, "Oh, so you have met before." He asked about her curls, and she inquired if he still wrote letters to girls. No, he answered, one of them sure taught him a lesson. He drove to town, María Elena sitting between him and Miss Barton. When he shifted gears his hand would brush against her silk-covered knee, and she would look at him with a smile in her eyes. It followed naturally that he should see her often since they were in the same classes most of the time.

Coming from the indulgent tutelage of the convent sisters, she found the public schools too difficult for her, and she was in danger of passing from the good student she had been to a marginal one. They sat next to each other and he helped her as much as he could with her classes, as much as the teachers' vigilant eyes would allow. In study hall they would sit at the same table, occupying the two sides of a corner next to the wall. They would sit very close to each other, and every time their arms or their hands brushed against each other he would feel something like an electric shock run through his arm. They would study together, he telling her what she should know and she admiring him.

"Oh, how bright you are!" she would say. "I wish I was as bright as you."

It followed that as they sat in study hall day after day, his feet sought one of hers beneath the table and imprisoned it. He looked at her and they both smiled. They sat closer together after that, one on either side of the angle formed by the table corner, and soon their knees pressed against each other under the table, and they looked at each other and she blushed. They drew closer and the hardness of his knee found its way to her thigh and pressed against its resilient softness beneath the cover of the table. Their breath quickened and they talked quickly and jerkily about the studies before them, keeping their eyes on their books and not looking at each other. During the days that followed Guálinto's head was in the clouds. María Elena, meanwhile, grew to depend more and more on Guálinto to meet the requirements of her courses. He wrote her themes, and they devised a code for communicating with each other during exams. María Elena's grades improved dramatically.

One day they were sitting close to each other, his knee against her thigh, their bare forearms touching, their eyes averted. He was explaining a math problem to her and they had an open notebook between them. His irritated glands were close to bursting, and as he explained his voice became hoarse and his breath heavy. He stopped and his pencil trembled as he held it above the paper. Then he wrote on a blank space, "I love you" and looked up at her.

Her face was pink and strained. She looked up at him with a flash of her great dark eyes and looked down again, all in one movement. He remained staring at her face, feasting his eyes upon it. After a moment she took the pencil from his shaking fingers and wrote, "Thank you." At the same time she moved her leg away, and that was the last time she allowed their bodies to touch beneath the table.

Guálinto was frantic for the rest of the day. But after that he resigned himself to the happiness of being near her, and to the occasional brushing against her hand or arm while they continued to study together. That and her smile, which became sweeter and more inviting now that she had put some distance between them. He had almost no opportunity to see her after school. Her father's office was but four blocks from school, and in good weather she walked to the office so her father could drive her home. But she was always with other girls. It was only in class and in study hall that he had any intimacy with her. Anywhere else she was a little distant, emerging in his company from a classroom to mingle immediately with other students.

One day he told her he wanted to see her after school. She consented after much urging. But when four o'clock came she surrounded herself with girls and he couldn't get near her. He went home, cursing himself and her. But he tried again the next day, and this time she allowed him to walk a couple of blocks with her.

As soon as they were alone he blurted out, "Nena, will you be my girl?"

"What did you say?" she asked, cupping a hand over her ear.

He had to say it again, and when he did she laughed. "They don't do those things anymore," she said.

"Be serious, please!"

"All right. If you want to go by the old Mexican customs you'll have to wait fifteen days for my answer. If I answer in eight days it will be 'No.' If I answer in fifteen it means 'Yes'."

He pleaded with her and finally she said, "All right, I'll be your girl, but you mustn't tell anybody."

"Why?"

"Because of my father. He will be very angry if he knows I have a sweetheart at my age. If you want it like that, O.K."

"O.K.," he said breathlessly. He tried to take her hand but she snatched it away. "Don't do that on the street in broad daylight. We're very close to my father's office. People will see us." So he had to be content with walking along beside her.

The school year passed and their relationship remained very much the same, except that they were together more often outside the school building. In the mornings he would look for her and they would sit on the school steps together and listen to Antonio Prieto play the guitar. After school he would walk with her for three blocks. There she had to turn a corner and come in full view of her father's office. At that corner they would stop, sheltered from her possibly wrathful parent by somebody's garage.

The garage became in Guálinto's love life what babbling brooks and moonlit nights were to other lovers. Against its white-painted wall he and María Elena would draw out their farewell, he with ardent looks and importuning words, she with evasive answers and beautiful smiles. He rarely thought now of the days when he had sat with her in study hall, touching her thigh with his knee.

Saturdays and Sundays he lived in torment, praying for Monday when he would see her again, imagining what she would be doing, where she might be, because he could not see her except at school. The summer between their junior and senior years was one long stretch of loneliness and melancholy for him. She told him her family was going away for the summer, and he believed it was so, although a couple of times he had seen her in her father's car, riding beside him along Jonesville's main street. She did not see him, or perhaps she pretended not to because of her father. But the fall semester made up for all that. And tonight he would dance with her, hold her close to him. The tall slender palms that fringed the grounds of the high school finally came into view. The driver braked abruptly, jostling both of his passengers. Guálinto relayed two nickels to the driver by way of the old lady. He alighted and the *camión* turned left toward Fourteenth Street with a groaning of gears. Guálinto lingered for a moment, trying to picture the driver giving those two nickels to his wife that night. Then he hurried down the street toward the school's main entrance, where in the gathering dusk the members of the senior class were assembling.

They were in little groups, according to friendship or affinity. Antonio Prieto was there, his hair slicked down at the nape of his neck and wearing a jacket that matched his trousers. "Hello, Tony," Guálinto said. "Did you bring your guitar?"

"He sure did," said Orestes Sierra. "I stopped for him and made him bring it along. It's in the car." Orestes was snappily dressed in gray, down to his shoes. His father was an automobile salesman now. He also owned a big garage where he repaired and sold used cars. Orestes could always borrow good cars from his father when he needed them.

"Do you have room for us?" asked Guálinto.

"What do you mean by us?" said Orestes with a wink. Guálinto punched him playfully and Orestes added, "Sure, sure."

Guálinto walked past them, looking for María Elena. He found her among a group of American girls sitting on the school steps with Jimmy and Bob Shigemara. The Shigemaras were the sons of a prosperous Japanese truck farmer who lived between Jonesville and Harlanburg. They were fat, well-fed boys who talked a glib, smooth English and were much liked by all their schoolmates. As Guálinto approached, Jimmy Shigemara was saying, "Of course we're not the same race as the Chinese. We're much more civilized."

Guálinto sat down beside María Elena and squeezed her elbow in greeting. She gave him a seductive smile and leaned against him. The group talked a little longer about the relative merits of the Chinese and the Japanese, and Guálinto, mellowed by María Elena's affectionate mood, agreed enthusiastically with Jimmy and Bob Shigemara that the Japanese were a very wonderful people. Then Mildren Barton arrived and the group broke up.

María Elena walked to the cars beside Guálinto, swinging her arm so it would bump against his. "Darling," she said, "Miss Wilson says next week's quiz will count a lot in the final grades for the fall semester."

"She did?" said Guálinto, looking at the full moon, which was rising before it was completely dark.

"Have you studied?"

"Yes. Look at the moon. Isn't it pretty?"

"It is pretty. Do you think you'll pass it?"

"Come on, you two," called Orestes. "Let's get going."

Guálinto took María Elena's arm but she held back. "Let's go with the Shigemaras," she said.

"But I already asked Orestes," said Guálinto. "Can't we go with him?"

"My friends are going with the Shigemaras." She stopped and bit her lip thoughtfully. "Oh, all right. Let's go with him."

"If you don't want to we won't," said Guálinto contritely.

"Oh, no," she answered, smiling sweetly. "It's the same to me."

"I think we'd better go with the Shigemaras," said Guálinto.

"Just as you like," she said and they turned back and went toward the Japanese boys' car. Their shiny red sedan was almost full of girls.

"Where are we going to sit," María Elena said gaily as they came up to the car.

"You'll have to sit on his lap," said Jimmy.

Warm lust seeped through Guálinto. Blindly he groped for a place in one corner of the rear seat, wedged between the armrest and Jane Williams' sharp hipbone. María Elena sat on his knees, then slid down into his lap and he trembled. The car roared away from the curb.

Jimmy pressed his foot hard on the throttle for it was a good thirty-five miles to Harlanburg and La Casa Mexicana. La Casa Mexicana was the region's finest nightclub. Whatever the predominantly white citizens of Harlanburg might think of Mexicans as a race, they recognized their potentialities as a source of local color. Time was when tourists were told in Harlanburg filling stations, "Don't go any further south. There's nothing between here and the river but Jonesville, and it's just a dirty little Mexican town."

But the tourists still went through Harlanburg to Jonesville. So Harlanburg's answer was nightclubs like La Casa Mexicana, which was a fancy stucco building made to resemble a Mexican *jacal*. Inside, Guálinto had heard, the walls were plastered with paintings of Mexican Indian scenes imitating the murals of Diego Rivera. You reached the dining room through a curio shop filled with pottery, stone heads, sarapes, steer horns, and other such stuff. Beyond, people said, there was a small jazz orchestra dressed in silver-studded *charro* suits, and all the women patrons thought the orchestra leader was too cute for words in his black *charro* suit and his shining-pink bald head. He couldn't stand the heavy sombrero more than fifteen minutes at a time. The waiters at La Casa Mexicana were all dressed in white cotton drawers like Mexican peons. All in all, La Casa Mexicana was as Mexican as it could be without having any Mexicans around. Or so people said.

Night fell quickly as the car sped north along the white ribbon of the highway. María Elena felt soft and wonderful in Guálinto's lap. After a few mintues she leaned back and rested her shoulder against his chest. He put his arm around her and guided her head to his shoulder. It was dark in the car now, except for the brief flashes of headlights going the opposite way. The other girls in the car were singing, "You're driving me crazy; what shall I do, what shall I do ... " Guálinto put his hand under María Elena's chin and tilted her face upward. They passed a roadhouse and the weird light of its neon sign fell momentarily on her face. Her eyes were closed with an air of patience, something like that of a man in a barber's chair. He waited until her face was again in darkness before he kissed her. Her full lips came alive at the touch of his own and quivered against his mouth like a hot secret animal. When he drew away his own lips were burning.

"Guálinto," she said very softly in his ear.

"Yes."

She spoke in Spanish so the rest would not understand. "Do you think we could work out a new code, one she wouldn't get wise to?"

"Who? What?" said Guálinto, as if waking from a dream.

"Miss Wilson. For that exam next week."

"Oh," he said. The car drew up before La Casa Mexicana.

A burly tough in a Mexican bandit's costume stood just inside the door. He wore an enormous hat and had a machete slung around his fat middle. The girls passed through the door, chattering merrily, while Guálinto and María Elena followed a few steps behind. But when the two Japanese boys came through the door they were stopped by the doorman.

"Just a minute," he said, peering into their faces. "What's your name?"

"Shigemara," answered Jimmy.

"Japanese?"

"Yes."

The occupants of Orestes' car arrived meanwhile, Orestes, Elodia, Antonio Prieto, and Ed Garloc. Ed Garloc passed unchallenged, but the doorman turned from the Shigemaras in time to see Orestes going past.

"Hey, you," he said, "what's your name?"

Orestes' face became expressionless. "Sierra," he said.

"You can't go in," the doorman said. "That goes for those other two." He pointed at Elodia and Antonio.

"Now listen here," said Orestes.

"What do you mean!" Guálinto chimed in. He and María Elena had stopped to wait for the Shigemaras when they were questioned by the doorman. The doorman signaled and another bandit-costumed tough joined him.

"What's the matter?" said the bouncer.

"These three Mexicans," said the doorman. "They want to crash the party."

"What about these two?" said the bouncer.

"They're O.K." the doorman answered. "They're Japs. Go ahead, you two." The Shigemaras went ahead.

"Listen here," Guálinto repeated angrily. María Elena pulled at his arm, and he put his other hand over hers. "You can't do this to us. We're part of this party."

The doorman looked at him briefly. "Nobody's holding you, shorty," he said. "You can go on in."

"I won't go in unless they go in too," said Guálinto.

Ed Garloc came back looking for the rest of his group. "What's the matter?" he asked.

"Trouble," Orestes answered. "Go get Miss Barton." Ed hurried back into the dining room.

The bouncer was looking at Guálinto with interest. "Are you Mexican?" he asked.

"I am," Guálinto answered.

"He's not," María Elena said, tugging at his arm. "He's a Spaniard. Can't you see he's white?"

"I'm a Mexican," Guálinto said. María Elena released his arm.

The bouncer smiled sardonically. "Come on," he said. "Make up your mind."

Mildred Barton came up, her face as pink as her evening dress. "What's the trouble?" she inquired.

"They won't let us in," Orestes said.

"Because we're Mexicans," added Guálinto.

Elodia glared at the doorman and Antonio studied his hands. Miss Barton looked shocked. "There must be some mistake," she said.

"Sorry, lady," the doorman said. "No mistake. Orders is no Mexicans."

Miss Barton blinked rapidly and twisted her handkerchief in her hands. "But you can't do this," she said. "They're my students. They're part of my class."

"Sorry, lady."

"I'll talk to the manager," said Miss Barton, her voice half-choked.

"Over there to the left," the bouncer said. "Second door."

Miss Barton hurried away, her heels tapping angrily on the tile floor.

"What's the matter with her?" the doorman said.

"Dunno," the bouncer said. "Yankee maybe."

As Miss Barton entered the manager's office María Elena said to Guálinto, "Aren't you coming?"

"No," he said. María Elena turned away from him and went into the dining area by herself. The two guardians smiled. Guálinto went and stood with the other three. They stood there in uneasy silence. The bouncer went away. Only the doorman remained. He crossed his hands over his chest and hummed. The orchestra was playing "Allá En El Rancho Grande."

After a long time Miss Barton returned. She was crying. "Go wait in the car," she said. "I'll call the rest and we'll all go home." She put her handkerchief to her mouth. Elodia began to cry too. Miss Barton reached out and put her arm around Elodia, and Elodia put both her arms around Miss Barton. The doorman looked embarrassed.

"You can't do that, Miss Barton," Orestes said. "It wouldn't be fair to the rest. Let them enjoy themselves. Isn't that right, Guálinto?"

Guálinto was looking toward the far end of the dance floor, where María Elena was dancing with an older man, not one of the senior party. He thought of the time he had spent practicing dance steps at home with Carmen for the past three weeks, and he felt weak and tired. "Uh-huh," he said to Orestes.

"Well, come on then," Orestes said. He took Elodia's arm and separated her from Miss Barton. "Good night."

"Just a moment, please," Guálinto said. "I think Antonio should get his fifty cents back. He contributed his half-dollar just like the rest of us."

"All four of you should get your money back," Miss Barton said tearfully. She dug into her purse and gave Guálinto two dollar bills.

"Thank you. We'll get some change elsewhere."

The four got into Orestes' car and drove off. Miss Barton came out and stood looking after them, her handkerchief to her mouth. Then she blew her nose and went inside.

They drove slowly and in silence. Finally Antonio, who had not uttered a sound during all the argument, reached to the floor of the car and picked up his guitar. He and Guálinto were in the back seat, Elodia in front with Orestes. Elodia, her face buried in her hands, was still crying softly. Antonio Prieto's fingers passed over the guitar exploringly, making a few tentative sounds. Then he began to strum a savage, martial rhythm and sang in a hoarse, intense voice, "*En la cantina de Bekar, se agarraron a balazos!*"

Guálinto let out with a *grito*, a wild sound that began with a low, measured whoop, became a yell and ended in a series of short screams. Elodia raised her head and sat up straight. After the echoes of Guálinto's yell died out there was silence inside the car, except for the throbbing of the motor and Antonio's groping chords. Then Orestes Sierra said, "When I was in fifth grade I wrote a theme once, in geography class. About the population of Texas. And I said, 'Texas is a very big state with very little people.' The teacher took off five points for that. She said it was bad diction."

Everybody laughed. They laughed and laughed until Elodia said, "*Mamacita mía*, I can't laugh anymore. My ribs hurt."

Antonio Prieto began to play again, faster and faster, and the chords swirled into the bouncy, garrulous rhythm of a *huapango*. When they reached Jonesville-on-the-Grande they were all singing, laughing, and yelling. They stopped at the drive-in on the corner where the highway ended and main street began. Guálinto ordered ice-cream sodas for all four. They were served by a blonde carhop, whom Guálinto ostentatiously tipped.

"Hey," said Orestes, "what a big spender!"

"I brought it to spend at that fake Mexican whorehouse, and I don't want to take it back home with me. This is a much better place to spend it, with my friends."

"We're having our own party," Elodia said.

"That reminds me," Guálinto said. He reached into his jacket pocket and took out the two dollars Miss Barton had given him. "Here, Antonio, this belongs to you."

"But I only gave fifty cents," Antonio said.

"You gave a lot more than that," Orestes said.

"They're eating and dancing back there on the money you made for them, playing the blind beggar at the carnival," said Elodia.

"You know," said Orestes, "it just dawned on me. Elton Carlton chose that place. Do you suppose he knew they wouldn't let us in?"

"Of course he did," said Elodia, "the dirty *sanavabiche*."

Antonio finally accepted the two dollar bills, and Orestes drove them home. Guálinto went straight to bed and tossed restlessly for most of the night. Toward morning he fell asleep and into a nightmare in which he was running, running through the chaparral, bleeding and with his clothes torn to tatters. Finally he emerged into a moonlit plain and kept running, running, pursued by a mob of people, all of them slavering like mad dogs and howling, "Alamo! Alamo! Alamo!" He woke to a gray December dawn, the howls still ringing in his ears.

Part IV

"LA CHILLA"

1

The Monday after the Christmas party there was a subdued air among the senior class, perhaps because everyone was studying and worrying about the midyear exams. But no one talked about La Casa Mexicana, at least not openly where the Mexican members of the class could hear them. There was now a marked division between the Anglo majority and the four Mexican members of the senior class. María Elena was no longer considered one of them. For what was left of the semester Guálinto, Elodia, Orestes, and Antonio Prieto stayed together and rarely spoke to anyone else outside of class. In the classroom they sat together, emphasizing their identity as (in Elodia's words) *los cuatro mexicanos*. Guálinto, usually talkative in class, spoke little and only in answer to a teacher's question. Antonio did not bring his guitar to school anymore. Guálinto met María Elena in the hall that first Monday morning and was about to speak to her when she turned away. He did not try to speak to her again.

The midyear exam in math came the following week. The "four Mexicans" arrived as a group, with Elodia in the lead. María Elena was standing inside the door as though undecided where to sit. Elodia told Guálinto, "You sit here," pointing to a desk surrounded by other empty seats. She sat on his right and Antonio on his left, with Orestes in front of him. María Elena pouted and sat a couple of rows in front of them. The test lasted for a full hour and it was not a difficult one for Guálinto, but his mind kept straying from the questions. Fifteen minutes into the

177

period, María Elena left her seat, turned in her paper, and walked out fighting back her tears.

"Serves her right," Guálinto thought. He tried to feel happy about it but he couldn't. The "four Mexicans" did well in math that semester, all four got B's. For Guálinto, however, that was not good enough. It was the first B he had made since he entered sixth grade. But he found that it did not bother him as much as he thought it should. It was a relief, though, when the semester was over and the Christmas holidays began. Now he could think of other things besides school and María Elena. The Saturday noon after the last day of school he went to meet El Colorado downtown and talk about old times.

He walked to the corner of Pershing and Fourteenth and was waiting for a *camión* when a car going west toward town honked at him and stopped a few yards from the corner. It was Orestes, driving a 1929 Chevrolet coupé with a rumble seat. "Hop in," Orestes said. "Where to?"

"Downtown, to meet El Colorado at the WOW Club. Want to come along?"

"I sure wish I could, haven't seen him for some time. But my father just called me. He wants me down at the agency right away. Say hello to El Colorado for me."

"Sure. This is a nice little car."

"I drive a lot of them," Orestes said, "but I don't own one. They're all for sale. By the way, you know how many Mexicans a horse is worth?"

"How many Mexicans—what kind of trick are you setting me up for?"

"No trick. I was just reading the paper, and I figured it out."

"Well go ahead. Tell it."

"I was reading the paper a little while ago. Two men were sentenced in court yesterday here in Jonesville. A Mexican for stealing old man Osuna's prize Arabian stud and a Negro for killing a Mexican in a fight over the price of a bottle of tequila."

"So?"

"The Mexican got ten years, the Negro two."

"Hmmm."

"So you would think that before the law in this town a horse is worth five Mexicans."

"It figures."

"But wait. The stolen horse was recovered safe and sound from the Mexican who stole him. Not a scratch on his hide even. While the Mexican the *parna* killed is stone-cold dead. No way of getting him back to life. What if the Mexican who stole the horse had killed it? He would have got at least twenty years. So you can figure then that a horse is worth ten Mexicans."

Guálinto grinned. "You always were good at arithmetic," he said.

"But that's not all. You know that in murder cases Mexicans and Negroes get double the sentence a white man would get. So what if the Mexican had been killed by a Gringo? The Gringo would have got off with a year. One divided into twenty: a Mexican then is worth one-twentieth the value of a horse. But that isn't all of it," Orestes said as he stopped the car below the WOW Club. "Chances are that the Gringo's sentence would be suspended. Then how much would a Mexican be worth? What's one-twentieth of zero? Ask El Colorado, he's studying bookkeeping, he ought to know. And shake his hand for me."

Guálinto got off the car laughing. "I'll try it on El Colorado first chance I get. Thanks and I'll see you."

There was a narrow flight of stairs wedged in between a couple of two-story brick buildings. One of the buildings housed a shoe repair shop on the ground floor, the other building was a dry-goods store. Guálinto climbed the steps and entered the WOW Social Club, which was above the shoe repair shop, and stood at the door looking for El Colorado. The smoke from dozens of cigarets fogged the room, for it was Saturday and the pool hall was full. Click-click-click went the ivory balls with a hard sure sound. Chuc-chuc-chuc went the markers. The tables were all occupied, and the walls were lined with bench-sitting men, some waiting for a chance to play, others just looking on. Unshaven men in leather jackets and big hats, sleek men with the look of gamblers, little men, tall men, bright-looking boys in sports jackets. White faces, red faces, olive faces, and many deep-brown faces. Clothing of all colors, styles, and degree of wear. All types of Mexicans frequented the pool hall.

The players cursed once in a while at an especially good or bad shot. Then they resumed their playing and their smoking. The watchers sat and smoked. Once in a while they commented on the playing. After that they just sat and smoked. So the hours passed. Against the back wall sat an old man whose face seemed to be made of the same stuff as his wrinkled leather jacket. His black hat was rammed over his equally black hair. Around his head stray locks stuck out in all directions, stiff and straight like the thatching at the eaves of a *jacal*. The old man was a permanent fixture at the poolroom. Day in, day out, he sat and smoked and watched. He smoked a pipe, unusual for a Mexican of his type. Players came and players went, but the old man just sat. At times he seemed to be thinking deeply. Thinking of things unknown or of things long ago, perhaps. But no. His eyes seemed to stare angrily at someone or something at the other end of the room. Yet again, no. He was watching the game. Intently, very intently. His black eyes glinted with the hard glint of polished stone. But he looked so bored, so detached. He could not be interested in that smooth game those four experts were playing in front of him.

Nobody knew what the old man did when he was not in the pool hall. Who clothed him, who fed him. Nobody asked. And nobody asked what he thought, if anything, as he sat there silently, pulling at his twisted brown pipe with his twisted brown lips. Nobody asked what he saw as he stared from beneath his bushy eyebrows, staring at something no one else could see. Nobody was curious where he had eaten that egg that had spotted his grimy, striped shirt, or where he had got those brand-new oxfords, whose shiny blackness stood out against his faded blue denim trousers. The players stamped, the players laughed and cursed. They left and others came. Men rose from his side to play. Men came and sat by his side. Others reached over his head for a coat, a cue. The old man did not move. He sat there, speaking to no one, spoken to by none, probably thinking, probably watching, probably doing nothing at all.

Near the old man, leaning against the wall, one foot on the edge of the bench, was a slender boy in blue trousers and brown buttonless vest. His face was the color of unbaked dough, and his tired, red eyes were baggy like a pair of trousers worn for too long. He must have been about fourteen. One knew he would speak through his nose before hearing him talk. He was the boy who set the balls at the tables. He stood, or rather slumped, in a sort of stupid alertness, looking here and there, spitting often and copiously. He wiped a fleck of saliva from his vest with the palm of his hand, turned and spat out the window, leaning out to watch the sputum go somersaulting down to splatter on the alley below.

The poolroom was on the rear of the second floor, and the only entrance and exit was by the rickety stairway. Some time ago the poolroom craze had struck Jonesville-on-the-Grande. Pool halls blossomed all over town. The click of ivory against ivory could be heard from Main Street to the outskirts of town. Radios blared and bottles of bootleg liquor passed from hand to hand. Then all of a sudden the tables were dragged into dusty cellars and storerooms. The pool halls remained vacant or were occupied by other businesses. Jonesville-on-the-Grande's leading ladies had undergone a tremor of social reform, and poolrooms were denounced as dens of all kinds of vice. Which perhaps they were.

But soon, in backrooms like this one, pool began to be played again under the auspices of various clubs and organizations. On the wall of this poolroom, to one side of the eight-day clock and directly over an unframed picture of a smiling girl, was a big piece of cardboard that said in bold red letters: "WOW SOCIAL CLUB - MEMBERS ONLY.

No alcoholic drinks allowed Please do not use obscene language. No minors." But nobody believed in signs.

The freshly shaved man in the corduroy jacket and brown hat sitting close to the ballboy was Don Pancho the woodcutter. He still lived in the Dos Veintidós with his brother Don José, next to Guálinto's house. One could see Don Pancho often on the streets of the Dos Veintidós, going out to the woods, standing spraddle-legged on his rattling wagon, his mules at a brisk trot over the bumpy street. Or coming back after a day or two out in the chaparral, sitting atop a mountain of crooked mesquite timbers, his little mules arching their scrubby backs as they pulled the wagon along at a slow pace. Yes, Don Pancho the woodcutter was a hard worker. But today was Saturday. You rested, you had a good time. You came downtown and bought popcorn and apples and chewing gum. Then you got yourself a big cone with two heaping dippersful of icecream on it. And you came out to the edge of the sidewalk, leaned against the fender of a parked car and saw the sights while you licked away. Or you could go down the corner to the picture show, and for fifteen cents you went in and watched the cowboys. They had sound now. These Gringos! They could do anything. Yes, they had sound now, and you could hear the shots and the smacks when the cowboy hit the badman. It was nice going to the picture show. And when you came out you walked the aisle to the door with a cowboyish swagger you couldn't control, though you felt ashamed and tried to break your step. But Don Pancho was a family man, he couldn't spend money on such things. So he went to the poolroom and watched. This was also very nice, especially since it didn't cost anything. There you could sit and watch everybody and his brother, and his uncle and his cousin too. You watched and you talked with your friends. And one of them was sure to pull out a bottle of liquid fire and give you a swig. And if you didn't think that was better than popcorn and icecream, there was something wrong with you. Next to Don Pancho, sitting close together, were two chubby-faced youths, resplendent in checkered suits. Their whole attitude shouted, "Country!" without the added evidence of yellow, snub-nosed, high buttoned shoes and plastered-down hair. Their round faces wore a permanent half-grin, while their eyes darted this way and that. They looked like a couple of field mice that had strayed too far from their burrow. The pair were cowboys, the working not the movie kind.

Guálinto entered the poolroom and nodded briefly but courteously to Don Pancho, as was fitting to a neighbor who had known him since he was a baby. He hurried across to the other end of the poolroom. Meeting Don Pancho in a place like this made him feel uncomfortable. At the far side of the room, hidden from Don Pancho by a wooden pillar, he found a seat between an unshaven drunk who intermittently dozed

off and woke with a start and a slim boy of fifteen or sixteen in blue
suspenders. The slim boy was talking to his neighbor on the other side.

"I've worked for him," he was saying. "He's an old bastard and I
don't like him."

"Yuh-huh," said his neighbor, his eyes on the nearest table.

"Sure. That's why when I needed six bits or a dollar, or a little more,
I never asked him for it. What for? He'd just blow at me and try to
preach me lessons and wouldn't give me nothing."

"Don't say," said his listener.

"Yeah. I'd just take out what I needed. Hell! He never missed it.
Then he spied on me, the dirty dog."

"The dog," echoed his friend dully.

"What's a few dollars to him? He spends much more on that woman.
He never misses that. And this was one chinchy little dollar, him with
thousands."

Guálinto rose. There was El Colorado's big-boned, gangling figure
at the door, his bright-red mane brilliant against the far brick wall. He
never kept a guy waiting long. Guálinto weaved through the players,
dodging deftly as one of them, stooped and intent, swung his cue back
swiftly then forward, like a piston. There was a sharp impact and several
balls clicked-clicked violently.

"*¡Chinng-g-g-gao!*" exclaimed the man with the cue. "You whore
ball!"

Another player laughed. "No tay-neek!" he shouted. "No tay-
neek!"

El Colorado met Guálinto and drew him to one side. "Whew!" he
said. "I'm all hot and bothered."

"What with?"

"Let me tell you. I just saw a Gringo dame walking down the street
in front of me and she was wearing a pair of light-blue slacks, very tight
and *very* thin! Beneath them she had a pair of pink silk panties with a
cute lace hem that came up to about here. *Chingao*! She might just as
well have left the slacks at home."

"How far did you follow her, you bloodhound?" Guálinto said, grinning.

"Not much, man, not much. Whew! My head is swimming and I
don't feel at all hungry."

"Hey, where are you going?"

"Take a leak."

"Well, don't stay in there too long or I'll get suspicious."

El Colorado's laugh came through the door. "*¡Qué cabrón!*" he said.
In a moment he came out, buttoning his fly. "Say," he told Guálinto, "I
almost forgot. Guess who's in town. Francisco Four-Eyes."

"Christmas holidays. He's here to see his family, I'm sure."

"He's got his same line of bull, only more of it and quite ree-fiy-ahned." They both laughed. "Met him on the street just before Blue-Slacks. He almost kissed me. Hugged me like I was his long-lost grandmother or something. Here, let's sit down."

They found space on a bench. "That's the way they do things down there, you know," Guálinto said. "But Francisco overdoes it, no doubt about that."

"Well, I don't like it," said El Colorado. "If I'd met him after Lace-Panties I wouldn't have answered for him."

Guálinto laughed. "And then?"

"He invited me to a soda. Went into the Ice Palace and sat down, him ordering the boy around. And it was, 'What will you have Colorado?' and 'Come on, don't be bashful, Colorado.' He ended having a banana split and I had a cherry coke. He ordered water at least three times. To make it short, when we finished he says, 'How much?' in that grand manner of his. The boy said fifty cents. He dug in his pocket and came out with two cents. Left the wallet home, he said."

Guálinto laughed again. "So you paid," he said.

"You're goddam right I paid," said El Colorado with feeling.

"He hasn't changed much."

"Not at all. Hungry?"

"A little. What was the idea, anyway?"

"Today's my birthday," said El Colorado, grinning self-consciously. "Thought we'd celebrate by having lunch at some restaurant."

"If it's your birthday," Guálinto said, "I'm paying for your lunch." He felt inside his pocket for cash to back his offer.

"Nothing doing," El Colorado said. "I invited you. I pay."

"Listen," Guálinto said, "it's about time I treated you to something. Now's the best time to do it."

El Colorado patted Guálinto's shoulder with his big freckled paw. "No," he said. "If you got extra money, spend it on books. Save it for that college you're going to next fall. You can't spare it. Me, I'm working and earning money and don't have much to spend it on but myself and my friends."

"But it isn't fair."

"Look," El Colorado said, "there's Francisco now."

Francisco stopped at the door and searched the room with his myopic eyes, tilting his head to see better through his glasses. The light from the opposite window struck the lenses, making them look like miniature automobile headlights. He was wearing a double-breasted gray suit, the coat jauntily unbuttoned. His black wavy hair was combed back and his slender fingers toyed with his silk necktie.

At length he spied Guálinto and El Colorado, and his face lit up. *"Hola carí-i-ísimo,"* he exclaimed. Everyone looked up but he did not seem to notice. Arms stretched before him he hurried across the room toward Guálinto, who rose to meet him. Francisco enveloped Guálinto in his arms. "Dearest friend!" He almost smothered him with additional *abrazos*. "Most favorite of companions!" Pat-pat-slap. "Happy these poor eyes that gaze on you once more!"

Guálinto disengaged himself with as little brusqueness as he could manage. He caught Francisco's hand and shook it. "Hello, Francisco," he said. The spectators went back to their playing and watching.

"Let's play," Francisco said excitedly. "Let's play. Look. Those characters there are getting ready to leave. You're leaving the table, aren't you?"

"Yeh," grunted one of the players.

"But Francisco," Guálinto said. "We were about to go eat. Anyway, I'm sure somebody's waiting for this table."

"That's perfectly all right," Francisco said. "We'll play just one game and then all three of us eat together. Here! Boy! Set them up. French. No, there's only three of us. Make it pear."

With a resigned air El Colorado took a cue from the rack and Guálinto did likewise, while Francisco tried out a half-dozen, balancing them, squinting down their lengths, and rolling them on the green felt tabletop, much to the annoyance of the tableboy, who was arranging the balls on that same table. Finally Francisco selected a cue, grumbling that it was no good and that in Monterrey they really had good ones.

"Break it up," he told Guálinto. Guálinto broke up the triangle with the white ball and the game began.

"I see why you were so anxious to play," Guálinto said after a while. "You're really good at it."

Francisco frowned as he completed a shot, then smiled. "In Monterrey all the important men play pool. And they are very good. Man, this is nothing. You should see General Almazán play."

"You've played with him, of course," El Colorado said.

"Sure, many times. We're really good friends."

"I thought so," El Colorado said.

"Almazán is a good friend of ours. My grandfather helped him in his military career. You didn't know my grandfather was a general."

"No!" said El Colorado, his voice dripping with astonishment. A group of idlers had gathered to watch the trio, drawn as much by Francisco's affected manners as by his truly brilliant playing. Francisco drew them into his audience.

"He was a general," Francisco said, addressing the watchers. "My grandfather, General Epifanio Sidar, the father of my mother, was once governor of Nuevo León."

"I saw General Sidar once," said a man in the group of watchers. "He was riding a white horse. *¡Lindo penco!*" He shook his round, recently-shaven head, as if the remembered beauty of the general's horse were a tragic thing.

"You knew my father? Do you remember the flight toward the border in 1913?"

"No," the man said, his pouchy, heavy-lidded eyes very sad. "I was here in Texas then."

"That was an exciting experience," said Francisco conversationally, almost narratively. "It was a Tuesday afternoon, and we were in Monterrey when it became evident that the rebels would take the city, since they greatly outnumbered our troops. My grandfather, the general, ordered a train be readied, into which were put my mother, me, an aunt of mine, and some other families. And, of course, our servants. Protected by several regiments of all the arms, these constituting the best at my grandfather's command, we evacuated the city in direction of the border, my grandfather, the general, in command, aided by my two uncles, Claudio and César, who were colonels." He paused. Noting perhaps some flicker of disbelief in his chief listener's mild expression he added, "I was very young then, but I remember it clearly. It was such a strong impression."

Guálinto knocked the last ball into a corner pocket. The game being over, Francisco threw his cue on the table, dusted the talc off his hands and put them elegantly into his pockets. He took a couple of steps toward the group of watchers that had become listeners, while Guálinto paid the tableboy. Francisco had chosen as his main target the man who remembered the general's white horse, but he addressed himself to everyone at the same time. The man who remembered the general's white horse was a deep-dark, roly-poly fellow in blue shirt and overalls. His round, coffee-brown head looked odd, crowned as it was by a few day's growth of erect white hairs. He sat on the bench, hands between his legs, grasping the bench and looking up at Francisco in a parody of the humble attention that the Mexican *peón* used to give the *hacendado*. Francisco stood almost over him, as if afraid the man would stand up and go away. Both were surrounded by sitting and lolling idlers.

El Colorado and Guálinto paid the tableboy, put their cues away and wiped their hands on their handkerchiefs, and by the time they turned to Francisco he was halfway between Monterrey and Reynosa on his retreating troop train. The rebels had blown up a piece of track ahead and Francisco's grandfather, the general, had ordered a battle.

"We had with us a regiment of cavalry, the best in the north, in bright blue uniforms and sabers, and several batteries of 75s. We also had a regiment of *juchiteco* infantry. You've heard of the *juchiteco* infantry, Don Vicente?"

"No," said Vicente, the roly-poly man, and this shameful lack in his education literally crushed him. "I haven't."

"They are little Indians from Oaxaca, the best soldiers and marksmen in the world. They advance at a dog trot like this, with their rifles at their hips." Francisco demonstrated, stamping his thin legs up and down where he stood. "And they fire from the hip with their mausers with such deadly accuracy that they are the most feared infantry in the world. They can be making a charge, for example, rifle at hip, when at a word of command they fire a deadly volley without raising their rifles or breaking their pace."

"What do you think of that," said Vicente, the man who remembered the general's white horse.

Francisco went on. "My grandfather shouted, 'Bring out the cavalry!' The boxcars opened and the horses disembarked, neighing and pawing the ground. But wait." He put his hand to his temple. "No. It was the artillery. Yes. He ordered the artillery out first, so the gunners rolled out—though I do believe it was the cavalry after all."

"They're gonna be tired out before they fight," growled El Colorado, "if you keep taking them off and putting them back on that train."

Francisco ignored El Colorado. "Wait just a moment, Guálinto," he said, "and we'll all go eat together."

El Colorado and Guálinto strolled to the nearest window and leaned on it, looking idly at the paved alley below, where a dirty, ragged man was taking cardboard boxes out of a trashcan. "I'm hungry," El Colorado said. "Let's go before that *pendejo* runs out of breath."

"Let's wait for him, Colorado," Guálinto said. "I'll pay for his dinner."

"It isn't that," El Colorado said angrily. "The bastard gets on my nerves."

Guálinto laughed. "I didn't know you ever got nervous. But you're right. At times he's pretty hard to take."

"In 1913 he was a baby still soiling his diapers. Do you think those guys really believe what he's telling them?"

"They're listening," Guálinto said. "Let's go see if we can pry him away. If not we'll just leave him here."

Francisco was now talking about baseball. "He should have been in the major leagues," he was saying, "only he never came to the United States."

"Aw," said the tableboy, "that's too green. It doesn't freeze at all. Pitching a ball that drops straight down just in front of the plate!"

Francisco gave the boy a superior smile. "You don't understand what skill can do," he said.

"That's true," said Vicente, the man who remembered the general's white horse. "Skill can do wonderful things. I remember a man I knew up above in North Texas. He was very skilled with his hands. Owned a fighting cock that was the best in the region. Had never lost a fight."

"But one day he met his match." Vicente's eyes softened in reminiscence. "What fight! My friend took his rooster out before the other bird killed him, but he was an awfully battered bird. His right leg was so torn up it had to be cut off. But did my friend wring the cock's neck? No. Do you know what he did? He cut off the bad leg, very carefully, and sewed up the skin up very fine. Then came the real wonder. He took a piece of wood and whittled and whittled till he made a perfect rooster's leg, down to the spur and the toe-nails. He even painted it the same color, and would you believe it, anyone would've thought it was the real thing. He strapped it on to the bird's stump with leather thongs that went around the rooster's body. You should've seen that rooster flapping his wings and strutting around! A man like that you see once in a lifetime. Talk about patience! Skill! And what do you think? The wooden-legged rooster fought that other bird again and killed him."

"Very interesting," said Francisco. "The man must have been a true genius, a carver worthy of greater aspirations. That reminds me of the time—"

"But that's not the half of it," interrupted Vicente, the man who had known the general's white horse. "Some three months later, the wooden-legged rooster met up with another bird that almost killed him. This time he won, but not before the other bird tore his left wing all to pieces. And what do you think my friend did?"

"Made him a wing of wood," Francisco said.

"Oh, no, dear friend," Vicente answered. "He made the wing out of thin leather. He went to work and made a framework out of stiff wire and on this he fastened the leather cover, with a lot of care. He was a skillful man. He painted feathers on the leather wing and made it look a lot like a real one. He strapped this wing on the stump of the real one. And he did it so well the rooster could flap it and use it just as if it had been grown there. It was a sight to see that bird going after the hens with his leather wing stretched out over the ground." Vicente stopped and nodded slowly, as if mourning his friend's wasted talents.

"And then?" Francisco asked impatiently.

"Why," Vicente said gravely, "after that the cock never lost a fight. He'd just lead with his leather wing and knock them out with his wooden leg."

Everybody laughed, loud and long, except for Vicente, who seemed bewildered by all the merriment he had caused. And Francisco, who reddened beneath his olive skin and cleared his throat several times. "Well," Francisco said, "I think it's getting late."

"Guálinto."

Don José Alcaraz, Don's Pancho's brother, was standing beside him. "Your uncle Feliciano is looking for you," he said, looking at Guálinto gravely with his mild brown eyes. "He seemed very anxious to talk to you. I hope there hasn't been an accident."

Guálinto looked at the floor thoughtfully. "I'd better go. Where did he say he would be?"

"At your house."

Guálinto thanked Don José and told his friends, "I got to go. Something's happened at home, I think."

The other two went with him down the stairs. El Colorado laughed all the way down, shadow boxing as he went. "Wham with the wing!" he would say between bursts of laughter. "Then socko with the wooden leg!" Francisco was silent and Guálinto stuck out his lower lip in thought. At the bottom of the stairs Francisco parted from them with a few hurried but florid phrases, among which he mingled a promise to see them later. El Colorado accompanied Guálinto down the street to the corner.

"Boy, that was funny," he said. Then suddenly serious, "I hope there's nothing bad at your house."

"I don't think so," Guálinto said. "But no telling what my uncle is up to now. He gets funny ideas in his head sometimes."

"Old people always do."

"Oh, he isn't old. But come to think of it, he's not so young either. Queer how he and I will read the same book or the same story in the paper and get such different ideas as to what it means."

"Do you argue with him?" El Colorado asked.

"Respectfully, but I do. I never can convince him, but sometimes I get him so he can't answer back. Then he laughs and seems to like it."

"I never could argue with my father. He'd knock me down if I talked back to him."

"Don't you ever want to go back home?"

"I go when he's not there. I take the little old lady some money and candy and tobacco. But I don't stay there. I'm better off alone. Got a good job, making good money. It's okay."

"Don't you ever get tired poring over all those figures?"

"I don't do that all day, really. And there's a future in it. I don't expect to be an assistant bookkeeper all my life."

They reached the street where the *camiones* parked. There was a long row of them along the sidewalk in front of an old two-story building with a wrought-iron balcony.

"Got the fare with you?" El Colorado asked.

"Sure, sure," Guálinto said, a bit irritated by his friend's solicitude. "I got it."

They stopped at the corner. The *camión* that was first in line had a couple of passengers on board but the driver was still standing on the sidewalk, waiting for more.

"What college are you planning to go to in the fall?" El Colorado asked.

"Texas, I suppose. If I go."

"What do you mean if you go? Are you going to let that Osuna dame ruin your whole life? What are you going to study?"

"I haven't decided, to tell the truth."

"Hell, man. It's time you made up your mind."

Guálinto could not help feeling annoyed by the big-brother tone of El Colorado's voice. "Any damn thing will do," he answered huffily. "Anything is all right."

El Colorado started to answer but thought the better of it. "Look," he said. "The driver is getting into the *camión*."

"I'll see you," Guálinto said.

"I'll see you." They parted with a half-wave of the hand, like a desultory salute. Guálinto boarded the *camión* and El Colorado went toward town again.

The *camión* chugged patiently along until it reached Fourteenth Street, where it turned left toward the east. Street and street they crawled along. Guálinto sat at the end close to the steps, looking at the floor and oblivious of the chatter of the other passengers. When they reached his street he yelled, "Here!"

He walked the rest of the way, wondering what his uncle was up to.

2

He hurried the four blocks home, meeting no one on the way. It was noon and people were eating dinner. He had told his mother he would not be home at noon, so the house was empty. His mother and sisters were out visiting somewhere. "I should have gone to the store," he thought. "Uncle Feliciano never comes home Saturday noon." He looked into all the rooms just to make sure. The parlor was full of books, newspapers, and magazines, all in Spanish. They were his uncle's reading matter. Now that he was well off and had plenty of help at the store, his uncle read a lot. There were books on mesmerism side by side with books on politics, and telepathy next to history and general science, all in paper bindings. Most of them were in a home-made bookcase made by Feliciano himself out of an old china cabinet. Others were neatly stacked on tables. His uncle had read them all. Through each and every volume of books famous and books unknown, written by quacks and intellectuals, Feliciano had read with the grim resolution of educating himself.

His uncle had become quite well read, but he hadn't changed one bit. He still was the same old *ranchero* underneath his store-bought suits. His readings had only expanded his old viewpoints and ideas. There was something unusual about the parlor, though. It was the newspapers. They were strewn all about the floor, not at all like his uncle, who believed in neatness. He must have been here after all and left in a hurry.

If he had to wait he might as well eat. Guálinto went back to the kitchen and made himself a *taco* out of a flour tortilla and some lunch meat he found in the icebox. He was eating his *taco* when he heard the front gate creak. He pushed the rest of the tortilla into his mouth and went to the parlor window. It was his uncle. Guálinto watched him come up the walk to the porch. His conversation with El Colorado just a short while ago made him notice how old his uncle really looked. He was well over fifty, he guessed. He didn't look so tall anymore. The shoulders were stooped and the stomach, though still flat, was bent in and downward. His uncle's boots tapped on the porch, and Guálinto opened the door for him.

"*Buenos días, Tío.*"

"*Buenos,*" Feliciano said, coming inside. He took off his stetson and passed his other hand through his graying hair.

"You were looking for me?"

"Yes." Feliciano nodded toward the sofa. He threw his hat and coat on a chair and sat down beside his nephew. "How old are you?" he asked.

"Seventeen," Guálinto answered, puzzled by the question, "almost eighteen."

"Hm-mm. You're getting to be a man now. In my time, a boy was a full-grown man when he was fifteen. Do you shave?"

"Why, n-no."

"You ought to," Feliciano said. "You ought to. I must remember to buy you a shaving kit for your next birthday."

"Thank you," Guálinto said.

"Not at all," Feliciano said. "Not at all. You're a man now, and it's time we talked about things like one man to another." He stared at the ceiling for a while, his fingers laced over his stomach. Then he said, "The bank went broke yesterday."

Guálinto was stunned. "The Jonesville National?" he asked weakly.

"Yes. Don Roberto's bank."

"Will—will you get your money back?"

"I don't see how. It isn't there anymore."

"Forgive me. I kept telling you to put your money in the bank instead of hiding it the old-fashioned way. But Judge Norris! I would have thought that he—"

"You didn't talk me into anything," Feliciano interrupted, an edge to his voice. "And it wasn't Don Roberto who robbed us. In fact, he's the one who will suffer the most. And he's an old man now, with a bad heart. This could very well kill him."

"Then who?"

"It was that *cabrón* of a cashier, E.C. Carlton. He was helping himself to big sums from the bank to gamble in, what do you call it. The 'stock market', is that it?"

Guálinto nodded.

"And when the market went broke, Carlton lost our money in it."

"What's going to happen to him?"

"He'll go to the pen, I'm sure. But putting him in *la pinta* won't bring our money back."

"There's nothing about it in the paper."

"Not the Gringo one, I'm told. We were informed by letter today. But there are articles about it in the Spanish-language papers here and in San Antonio. They will have to print something about it in English here, sooner or later. The law has taken over the bank."

"But we still have the store, at least."

Feliciano shook his head. "We will not have the store. That's the hardest blow we'll have to take. Don Roberto, as owner of the bank, still is responsible for what the bank owes. They're taking away all his properties in town, except his home of course. The store building and the lot belong to him, so the law will take it over in a few days."

"But what's in the store is yours, isn't it?"

"Yes, if I can get it out before they take over the building. That's what I wanted to talk to you about. I've already sent word to Juan to bring the truck into town. We'll have to work hard and fast to take everything that is ours out of that store. What I have not bought and paid for will stay, what is mine I will take out."

"Where will we put all of it?"

"In the back room, as much as we can. The rest Juan will take to the farm. Beans, rice, flour, corn, potatoes. Those things will keep for a long time, and so will the canned goods, of course. The fresh meat we'll keep what we can eat soon and give the rest away."

"Give it away? Why not try to sell it to another grocery?"

"Who has money to buy it these days? Only Crispín Rodríguez, who doesn't believe in banks any more than I do. And he'll have the pick of what's in the warehouses right now, at whatever price he wants to pay. No, there are many people who will be glad to have the meat. Juan and the help at the farm. And some of our friends in the *barrio*. So much for the fresh meat. With the rest we can eat for a long time, perhaps until things get better."

"And what if they don't?"

"I can always peddle my vegetables."

Guálinto reddened. "Peddling vegetables?" he shouted. "My uncle peddling vegetables in the streets?"

"Yes," Feliciano answered grimly. "With a basket on each arm. Will you be ashamed of me then? The way you're ashamed of this house? Perhaps you'll cross to the other side of the street when you meet me in town."

Tears came to Guálinto's eyes. "I-I-I," he stammered.

"They have been teaching you strange things in that Gringo school. Honest work is not shameful, even peddling in the streets."

Guálinto bowed his head. "I'll leave school. I'll start looking for work next week, even if it is—peddling in the streets."

"You'll do nothing of the sort," his uncle said gently. "I'm not a beggar yet, Guálinto. And I have no intention of peddling vegetables in the streets. I'll be selling them as I have been doing, wholesale to grocery stores and the packing houses. Very cheap, of course, but it will bring some money. When times are bad people do without a lot of things, but they still have to eat. We'll also have plenty to eat. And I'll soon be working more land. My own land."

"Your own land?"

"Yes. I know you think I'm just an ignorant *ranchero* but I'm not as stupid as some people might think. Nobody ever talked me into putting all my money in the bank. I've never trusted banks, and I did not like the looks of that Carlton fellow either. I put money in the bank, plenty of it, because Don Roberto told me I had to so I could have good credit as a merchant. But I kept much more of it out, much more, in good gold coins. The backward *ranchero* way. I'll be using part of that money to buy land from the old Gringo who rents to me now."

"I thought he didn't want to sell."

"Not before, but now he's hurting for cash. We're dickering over the sale of the eighty acres I'm renting now and about eighty or a hundred more. I'm just waiting until he needs the money bad enough to come down to my price."

"That's a lot of land."

"True. And I'm not thinking of having it all cleared right now. We can raise a few cattle on it, some hogs, and a lot of chickens. That and the crops we raise will tide us over until things get back to normal. They will. I've read that these depressions have happened before and that things finally right themselves. They come in cycles, did you know that?"

Guálinto shook his head. "They haven't taught us that in school either."

"We'll come out ahead in the end. Meanwhile, we'll be doing better than many others. There won't be any car for you to take to college, and you'll have to stop spending money for some time. We'll have to do with the clothes we have for some time. No new suit for your graduation, I'm sorry to say. And nothing fancy for you to take to college."

"College?"

"Sure. I have been adding to a special cache for your college since you were a baby. You won't have to worry about essentials, even if things don't get better after you've been in college for a year or two."

"You've been saving all these years for that? What if I don't want to go to college?"

"You don't know what you're saying. Of course you want to go to college."

"I want to get a job and help out. I've been a burden to you long enough."

"Let's not talk about it right now," his uncle said. "We'll talk about it later."

"No. I want to talk about it now, Uncle. Why should you spend all that money on me when times are going to be so hard?"

"Your father—" Feliciano began.

"I know! I've heard it ten thousand times before. My father said I was going to be a great man and that I was going to help my people. But I'm a man already, Uncle! You just said it yourself, I'm a man. And I'm no different than I ever was."

"Your father was a very knowing man," Feliciano said.

"My father was just an ignorant Mexican! He got it into his head I was going to be a great man. A great man! And he saddled me with this silly, stupid name!"

Feliciano clenched his fists and half-rose. Then his hands relaxed and he sat back into the sofa. His face was pale. "Don't you ever again talk like that about your father," he said quietly.

Guálinto swallowed. "I'm sorry," he said.

"Why have you decided all of a sudden that you don't want to go to college? Is it because of what happened to you and your friends at that restaurant in Harlanburg?"

Guálinto started. "How did you know about that?" he said.

"It's no secret. People talk."

"No, it isn't that. You don't have the money."

"I told you I have the money. You're just upset because of the way things are right now. But things will get better. Promise me you will go back in January and finish high school."

"I will. I promise."

"Good. After that we'll talk again about college. Get yourself some paper now, and let's do some figuring before your mother and the girls get home."

Guálinto hurried to get paper and pencil, his mind still in a daze. His uncle was all action and purpose now. "Now put a column here," he said, "and another one here. That's it. Let's figure what we have in the store and what we owe. The big electric ice-box is all paid for, but we can't bring it home. Perhaps we can sell it somewhere for half what it cost me."

"Uncle," Guálinto said, looking up from the paper. "Maybe I can get a job afternoons."

"We'll look into that later, if it doesn't set you back in school. At least it would give you some spending money for the next few months."

"Not for spending money," Guálinto said grimly. "I'm through spending money having a good time. I want to earn enough to buy my school supplies, get my hair cut, buy my own toothbrushes and things like that."

"You have no idea how difficult it is to get a job right now."

"You can find one if you look hard enough. I will find one, I promise you."

"You are very optimistic," his uncle said. "But if you want to try it, go ahead and do so. Now, let's get back to working on these figures."

3

For some time now, the newspapers had been telling of strange things happening in the North. Men were blowing out their brains in

Chicago. In New York City they were jumping out of tall buildings and smearing themselves all over the pavement below. Businesses were going broke, and breadlines were coming into existence. But in Texas, especially its southern tip, things seemed to be normal, almost prosperous. The truck farmers and orchard owners still sold their produce, spent part of their earnings and banked the rest. For the Delta, the Great Depression still was far away. And to the Mexican laborer who tilled the American landowner's fields and orchards, such a thing as a depression was beyond his understanding. He could not imagine a state of things where he would be poorer than he already was. He heard about the people of Oklahoma, who were leaving their land, getting on their trucks and going west. To the Mexicotexan laborer, anybody who owned a truck was rich. He heard of some sharecropper families who had nothing to eat but flour and bacon. The Mexican laborer, who had subsisted on tortillas most of his life, wondered how people who could afford biscuits and bacon could be poor. He heard how people in the big cities were lining up to receive free soup and bread because of the Depression, and he would joke with his friends, "I wish what they call the Depression would come down here so we could get some of that." And in due time the Depression came.

La Chilla, Mexicans called it. The Squeal. Or perhaps a euphemism for that most useful of Mexican expressions: *La Chingada. Estamos en la gran chi-i-illa, compadre.* La Chilla. Sugar is two cents a pound and men are two cents a dozen, Mexicans half-price. Flour costs a quarter a sack, and a quarter costs all of a man's efforts and the little pride he has left. La Chilla. Long lines of men sitting in employment offices with a gloomy hope in their eyes. Long lines of women standing in the street before relief agencies, hunger and humility on their faces. Little groups of children playing in the sun, dirtier, skinnier, quieter than ever before.

Help wanted. Young white man to help with farm. That red-faced Gringo will get it. No matter. That's old man Lilly's farm and he's an anti-Mexican *sanabaviche*. Wanted. Nursemaid for children two and five years old. Must be English-speaking. No chance for the old woman there, not a chance. Wanted. White woman to keep old lady company. Wanted, dependable, hard-working white man.

The Mexicotexan has a conveniently dual personality. When he is called upon to do his duty for his country he is an American. When benefits are passed around he is a Mexican and always last in line. And he has nobody to help him because he cannot help himself. In the United States he is not the only racial group that often finds the going hard. But while there are rich Negroes and poor Negroes, rich Jews and poor Jews, rich Italians and Poles and poor Italians and Poles, there are in Texas only poor Mexicans. Spanish-speaking people in the Southwest are divided into two categories: poor Mexicans and rich Spaniards. So while rich Negroes often help poor Negroes and rich Jews help poor Jews, the Texas-Mexican has to shift for himself.

Now the Great Depression has arrived. Jobs are few and the Mexican gets few of those available. Relief rations are limited, and the Mexican gets more dirty looks than groceries at the RFC, the *ora sí*, as he calls it, the "Now's the Time." For one decent meal at least.

An applicant comes into an office in Jonesville-on-the-Grande.

—How are you, my boy. Sit down. Clerk's job doesn't pay very much but you know how times are these days. Finished high school? Fine. I believe you may—what's your name? Oh, I see, I see. Miss Greene, put down Mr. González's name on our waiting list. We'll call you in case we can use you.

La Chilla La Chilla. Did you hear McCrory's is firing all their Mexican salesgirls?

—Hell, they're firing everybody. McCrory's folding up.

—They say a department head at the airport was called down for having too many Mexicans in his section.

—They're putting the skids on a hell of a lot of *sebos* everywhere. They watch for any little slip. And out.

—*Sebos* did you say?

—Yes, *sebos*, that's us.

—I don't know about that. What with the trouble it takes to get a pound of lard these days, there's no grease left in a greaser anymore.

—The packing sheds are hiring people. Good pay. Ten cents an hour for unloading trucks. You stand around and wait for a truck to come and you unload it. A Gringo checks your time. You can easily make a quarter a day.

—Do you register for employment here?

—Yes. Give your name, references, work you've been doing.

—Eusebio Pérez. Just out of high school. Haven't done much except pick some cotton, I guess. But I can type and know some bookkeeping.

—Yusibio Pérez. Cotton picker.

—How about my schooling? Aren't you going to put that down?

—I don't think we need to mention that. Next! Name please? References? These damn greasers! They get snootier and lazier everyday. Worse than niggers. That one there was too good for picking cotton. I don't see why we waste tax money sending them to school. Taking the bread out of white people's mouths, these damn cheap politicians. Anything for a vote.

—You said a hunk of truth there, Mister. Some of these young spiks get too much schooling. Then they start gettin' ideas they're as good as white people.

—That's it exactly, mister. Exactly. Glad there's still people who think the way they should. Nowadays, with all these crooked politicians and labor racketeers, they'll treat a nigger or a greaser as good as a white man just to get another dirty vote.

La Chilla. La Chilla. Rows of vacant store buildings, their empty windows looking like eye-glasses on rows of skulls. And on the sidewalks, in the little lobbies formed by store entrances, groups of dark-skinned men, waiting, waiting. For nothing.

A shiny car stops, and a heavy sweaty man with a pistol belt around his middle lumbers down. A younger officer in a khaki uniform follows. They go directly to the group of men and single out one of them.

—You Juventino Grajales?

—*Sí señor.*

—Where were you born?

—Oaxaca.

—How long you been over on this side?

—Since 1915.

—Immigration paid?

—Immigration?

—I thought so. Get in the car.

—Get in the car? What for, *señor*? I haven't done anything. I'm a peaceful man.

—Get in the car, I said, or I'll give you a taste of this.

—All right, all right, *señor*. But don't push me.

—I'll push you and you'll like it. One more peep outa you and I'll lay your head wide open. Drive to the station, Joe, so we can mug and fingerprint this wetback.

—What were you telling the other *señor*? You must have the wrong man.

—Like hell we do. Don't you know it's illegal to enter the United States of America without paying immigration and getting your papers?

—I swear I didn't know, señor. Nobody ever told me. Mister Estrong himself, he went with a truck and got us from Morelos back in 1915 to pick his cotton in Alice, and we just stayed around. Nobody said for us to go home and nobody took us. Is that a crime?

—Sure is, and ignorance of the law is no excuse. But since this is your first time we'll just take your fingerprints and put you across the river. And don't you try coming back a second time if you know what's good for you.

—But *señor*, my wife. She's a Texan, my children were born here.

—Listen. We enforce the law. We don't mix up in your family affairs. Come on.

—What will they do?

—Come on! Do you get out of that car or do I drag you out.

Faces Three Year
Prison Term For
Visiting Family

Juventino Grajales, 42, was sentenced to three years at the FTI today on a charge of habitual violation of American immigration laws. The FTI, still another alphabetical term, is the Farm Type Institution. There is one at La Tuna built especially to take care of habitual violators of the immigration laws.

Grajales contended that he crossed the river illegally to see his wife, his children and one grandchild which he had never seen. His record shows a number of deportations, as well as three penitentiary sentences of one year, 15 months, and 18 months in Leavenworth on immigration charges. Grajales, through his counsel, had promised previously that he would not return any more, even for short visits.

The court also heard a complaint filed by Sr. Nestor Martinez, lawyer for the Mexican consultate, that Grajales had been slugged and otherwise mistreated at the hands of arresting officers. Officers contend Grajales resisted arrest. Charges brought by Sr. Martinez were dropped for lack of sufficient evidence.

La Chilla. Cotton is five cents a pound and pickers get ten cents a hundred. Greaser and Gringo, farmhands and office workers, old men and school boys, they all compete for the fluffy, desperately light handfuls in the long long rows. Whole families turn out, from parents to toddlers, so they can pick enough with their combined efforts to eat that day.

—Say, Nacho, have you noticed how old man Kelly gives the best rows to those Gringos. You try to take one and he steers you toward the bad ones.

—By God, you're right. Let's make sure. Finish up quick and we'll take the next two rows. They're heavy.

—Hey, you over there! These two rows right here.

—We're taking these two, Mr. Kelly. They're right next to the ones we finished.

—I told you to take them two rows.

—Mr. Kelly, we're working for you but we get paid for what we pick. Anybody can see you're giving those Americans the best rows.

—It's my field, ain't it? If I put white folks on them rows they'll starve to death.

—But we're just as human as they are. We can starve too.

—Those folks don't know how to pick cotton. Never puck any.

—How about Manuel's kids here?

—Don't give me none of your lip. Get to work or get out.

—We'll get out.

—Well, git then, damn you. But let me tell you one thing. None of you work for me again. None of you get a glass of water outa me.

—There he goes, Nacho, mad as hell.

—Well, aren't you going with me?

—Me? I can't. Got the wife and kids to worry about.

—You mean you're going to let him push you around like that? Don't you have any guts?

—What can you do?

—Hell, you got rights. You've got to show them.

—Listen, Nacho, you're fresh out of school and you don't know life. Why, hell, this is nothing. When I worked around Sinton, I share-cropped a farm for a Gringo. When the crop was ready he picked a fight with me and ran us off the farm. I went to the police and they ran us out of town.

—Good morning, Mr. Peeble.

—Hrrmph! Good morning, how are you, my boy.

—Is it true you have a job for me?

—True, my boy, true. When I saw your mother yesterday I told her to send you over. You're bright and early. Very good, my boy. Very good. You can start immediately. The other boys will show you what to do.

—Thank you, Mr. Peeble. It's nice of you to give me a chance at the job, with so many people looking for work.

—My boy, I prefer Latin Americans, always. More dependable, more conscientious, harder workers. That's what I tell all these prejudiced friends of mine. I'd bet on a Latin against two—ah—against two Anglos.

—Thank you, sir.

—Okay, you can go back and start working.

—Mr. Peeble.

—Yes! What is it?

—And the—the wages?

—Three dollars a week.

—Did you say three?

—Yes, yes. What's the matter with that?

—Why sir. I'm a friend of Johnny Mize's. You hired him last week at eight dollars.

—True, true. But his case is different. Entirely different. Entirely different.

—In what way?

—Look, my boy. You know that each case must be judged individually. There's no sense in making me go over it with you.

—I don't understand, Mr. Peeble.

—If you insist, I'll be frank with you, my boy. You know you can't expect to make as much as Johnny Mize. His standard of living is higher than yours. He needs more money to live on. You can do with less.

—But Mr. Peeble, why should I do with less? We'll be doing the same kind of work. Besides, he works for pocket money. I don't. How can I support my family on three dollars a week?

—Everybody knows that a Mexican family can live on two dollars a week with things as cheap as they are nowadays. Now, do you want that job or don't you?

La Chilla. It lay like a stupor over the town. No jobs anywhere. No full-time jobs, much less the after-school job Guálinto was looking for. It was hard enough for men who had experience in many kinds of work. It was even harder for Guálinto, who had never worked in his life. His mother and his uncle had never wanted him to waste his time on after-school jobs. Other boys in the Dos Veintidós shined shoes and sold papers when they were barefoot kids, but not Guálinto. His mother didn't want him to grow up the way they did, she said. Once his mother relented and allowed him to sell the Saturday morning paper on the streets of Jonesville. The other paper boys convinced him he should try the sections outside the business district. He wandered about the residential sections until noon. Several men stopped him, read the headlines, and went away without buying the paper. His total gain from the venture was a mild case of sunstroke and a tour of parts of town he had never seen before. After that experience, his mother never let him work again.

All through the Christmas holidays he looked for a job. His uncle, meanwhile, had bought the land he had wanted and was busy working on it. He drove his truck home every evening, bringing the family eggs and milk. He did not comment on Guálinto's efforts to find work, nor did he ever mention Guálinto's outburst when he had said he was going to peddle vegetables. But Guálinto remembered and it made him feel guilty and ashamed. He must find a job, any kind of a job.

The Saturday before classes would resume he headed home from the business district, tired and disheartened. At the edge of the Dos

Veintidós he came to the Rodríguez grocery store. There was Chito Rodríguez, loading groceries on their Model T in front of their store. Maybe ... He had never thought of that. He stopped on the other side of the street and looked toward the old building with its false front and roofed-over sidewalk. Old Don Crispín Rodríguez and his sons were prospering from the Depression because Don Crispín, like Feliciano, did not believe in banks. Now, when money was scarce, Don Crispín had ready cash. He could buy cheap, sell cheap, and still make a handsome profit on the volume of his sales. People in shiny cars came from the northwest part of town to shop at Rodríguez and Sons these days.

But hell, thought Guálinto, the Rodríguezes are the tightest tight-wads in town. They would hire nobody. He watched Chito, the elder of Don Crispín's two sons, loading the groceries. Guálinto crossed the street toward him, still not sure whether he should ask him for a job. As he approached, Paco, the younger son, came out and stood in the door-way. Paco was slender and good-looking; he sported a tiny mustache.

"Hello," Paco said. "You're Guálinto Gómez, aren't you?"

"Hello. Yes, I am."

"I used to see you in school years ago, before I dropped out to work at the store. Everybody says you're very intelligent."

Guálinto said nothing.

"What are you doing now?" Paco asked. "Still going to school?"

"Yes," Guálinto said quickly. "But I'm also looking for a part-time job."

Paco's face lost its open frankness. "Well," he said, "we don't have anything around the store right now. That is," he looked shamefacedly at Guálinto, "nothing but handing out circulars. We're going to give them out Fridays. But you wouldn't want to do that."

Guálinto swallowed hard and said, "Sure, it's a job, isn't it?"

Paco looked doubtful. "Well, if you want the job we'll be glad to let you have it. Let's see my brother over there."

Chito gave Guálinto a limp, clammy hand and smiled a sly little smile. "Sure, sure I remember you." He hitched up his trousers over his belly. His clothes were flappy and ill-fitting as if he were not used to wearing them. "You can have the job," he said, "if you want it. Just work Fridays, twenty-five cents for the day."

"Twenty-five cents?"

"That's right," Chito said. "That's what we're paying."

"Maybe," Paco said hesitantly. "Maybe we could pay him fifty cents."

Chito glanced swiftly at his younger brother, then back to Guálinto. "No," he said. "Twenty-five is all we can pay."

"All right," Guálinto said.

"Come in and we'll tell my father," Chito said. "Say, I know your uncle," he added, and his smile became slier and malicious.

Old Don Crispín was standing behind the counter with the money drawer half open, sifting coins around. He pushed the drawer quickly shut at the sound of steps. Don Crispín was a mild-mannered, roundish man. He always wore a straight-brimmed black hat, outdoors and indoors, set straight and tight on his head. His mustache was white and thick and curved out and down like a breaking sea wave. He didn't shake hands, just nodded amiably at Guálinto.

"Papa," Chito said, "this is the new boy who's going to hand out circulars next Friday."

Don Crispín nodded gravely. "Very good," he said softly, "very good." "He's Feliciano García's nephew," continued Chito. Guálinto noticed he put no *don* before his uncle's name, though his uncle was much older than Chito.

"Oh," said Don Crispín, and his mustache broke into a little smile like that of Chito's, though less malicious. "Feliciano García. He owned the store down four blocks. The one that went broke. I sure am sorry," he added and smiled. "I've heard of you. You must be his nephew."

Guálinto nodded.

Don Crispín stepped back and put his head into a door leading to the family's living quarters. "Concha," he called softly, "Concha." A tall, very pale woman came out. "This is Feliciano García's nephew," Don Crispín told his wife. "The Feliciano García who owned the store four blocks down the street that went broke. His nephew is going to work for us."

The pale-looking woman looked Guálinto over curiously while he fidgeted and got red. "You must be the boy they talk about," she said. Guálinto did not answer. "How's your mother?" she inquired.

"Well, thank you," murmured Guálinto. The pale-looking woman and his mother had never met each other as far as he knew.

"We hand out the circulars on Fridays," Chito said, his voice muffled as he tried to clean his teeth with his tongue and talk at the same time. "Be here by 7:30 in the morning. You'll have to miss school that day," he added solicitously.

"That's all right," answered Guálinto. "I'll be here." He thanked them and left.

4

The first month of school, Guálinto missed Friday classes. Coming to school on Fridays was very important, his teachers told him. That was the day when the week's work was gone over and homework for the week end was assigned. Why was he missing every Friday? He had to work. But surely he didn't have to work every Friday. It was more important to come to school. His grades were suffering. He would not be valedictorian if he didn't attend the full week. Guálinto, whose twenty-five cents earned each Friday bought him paper, pens, and other things he needed at school, didn't answer. He felt the nape of his neck, where his hair was getting long and shaggy and looked forward to having it cut next Friday evening. He had found an old man who barbered in a little shack at the edge of the *barrio*, he charged fifteen cents for a haircut.

He stubbornly refused to accept any money from his uncle for his personal needs, remembering his boast to his uncle after the bank crashed. Two or three times a week he would find two quarters or a half dollar on his study table when he came home. Put there by his mother, he knew, at his uncle's request. He would pick up the money and put it on his mother's dresser when she was out of her room.

He wrote his own excuses for Monday mornings. The teachers would protest. Wasn't that his writing? Yes, he would say, his mother didn't know English. They would go talk to his mother, they said. Then they got busy and forgot, and Guálinto went on as before.

Every Friday he got up early and was at the Rodríguez and Sons grocery store before 7:30 a.m. He formed one of a group of older boys and men who handed out the circulars advertising the Saturday bargain sale. Paco, about three years older than Guálinto, was in charge. He drove the Model T, loaded with bales of circulars to the different sections of town, parked at the end of the streets and sent out his workers, one on each side of the street, to place a circular at each house. Put them on the screen door, if there is one, were the orders given them by Chito before they started. Put them at the door, in spite of dogs, closed gates, or any other impediments. It was walk, walk, walk in the sun, kicking up the dust. Fold a circular neatly, open a gate with your heart in your mouth and slip in silently. Try to make it to the door before the dog scented you, and then beat the animal to the gate and slam it shut on the dog's snout. Too often the dog came out through a hole in the fence, and then you danced around and kicked at him till he got tired and went back into his yard. The farther the workers got away from the Model T, the less they went into the houses. They made paper airplanes out of the circulars and sailed them onto the front porches instead. Paco, from his seat in the Model T, would often see them sailing the circulars into the houses, but he would turn his head the other way and pretend he didn't see them. Guálinto knew this well enough because he often sat with Paco in the car while the others were working. Paco had taken a liking for Guálinto. He would let him stay in the car, making him miss one round in every three or four, so he could have someone to talk to. He asked Guálinto a lot about school.

"How is the last year of high school? Is it very hard?"

"Oh, not any harder than the rest," Guálinto answered, putting his aching feet comfortably against the windshield. "It isn't hard if you take them one at a time."

"I wanted to finish school," Paco said. "I wanted to graduate but Chito wouldn't let me. He convinced Papa he needed me more at the store."

"How far did you go?"

Paco looked down at the steering wheel. "Seventh," he said. "Just seventh. I was playing clarinet in the school band, too."

"I remember that! Once the junior high band came and played for us at the grammar school, and you were in it!"

"You remember that?"

"I sure do. It made me want to be a musician too, at least for a while."

"You're right in trying to finish as well as you can," Paco said, rubbing his little mustache with a long finger.

"I just hope I can, but I don't know whether I can finish or not. I won't if I don't find some after-school job pretty soon."

Paco looked away quickly and didn't say anything. After a while he said, "Do you like music?"

"I do, but I don't play anything. I know a boy who plays the guitar, though."

"I like to play the piano."

"Do you play lots of pieces?"

"Oh, no. I don't play anything really. I never took any lessons or anything. My sister is the one who takes lessons, and she doesn't play anything either. I like to peck away at the piano and make believe I'm a composer."

"Oh," Guálinto said.

Paco looked at him apprehensively. "You don't think I'm crazy, do you?"

"Oh, no. Why should you be? Lots of people think composers have to be crazy people, but they're not. Take Antonio Prieto, this boy I was telling you about who plays the guitar. He makes up songs too. The most beautiful songs you ever heard. As good as any you hear on the radio."

"But I don't make up songs. I don't make up songs or play the piano even. I just peck at the piano and make believe I can play it and that I'm a composer. And you don't think I'm crazy?"

"No," Guálinto said.

Paco sighed. "Some day I'm going to learn to play the piano. And I'm going to write songs as beautiful as those they play over the radio."

"Sure," Guálinto said, "why not?" The other workers came in and Guálinto went out with them on the next round.

There was someone else who didn't like Guálinto's absence from school on Fridays. That was María Elena Osuna. She had been angry at Guálinto over the Christmas holidays, but her anger disappeared when the first test of the semester was announced. In spite of the disappointment expressed by the other three members of *los cuatro mexicanos*, he began to help her again. But he no longer was making perfect grades. He had wrong answers for several questions on that first quiz and María Elena, sitting beside him, got the same questions wrong. They were called into Mr. Darwin's office on suspicion of cheating.

Guálinto took all the blame. He had been missing school so much that he had to copy from somebody and had copied from María Elena. "Red" Darwin smiled sardonically, told Guálinto never to do it again, and let them go without any kind of discipline.

María Elena was furious when they came out of Mr. Darwin's office. "It's all your fault," she said. "If you didn't miss school so much it wouldn't have happened. What's the matter with you anyway? Don't you want to succeed in life?"

"I'm working," Guálinto said sullenly.

"Working?" María Elena said. "What for?"

"What for?" He was finally stung into anger. "You ask what for? Not everybody can get anything they want like you can!"

"Your uncle has a big store. He has enough money to see you through school."

"He doesn't anymore. He lost everything when the Jonesville National went broke."

"That was stupid of him."

"What?"

"I said your uncle is a stupid old man. Anybody with any sense would have put their money in several banks. Or in government bonds and other things, like my daddy does."

Guálinto's face turned a deep red. "You can't call my uncle a stupid old man!"

"I can and I will. What's more, I don't want to speak to you again."

"You don't have to. You don't have to, now that my grades can't help you."

"You're horrid," she said.

"Go to hell," he answered. He turned away and walked swiftly down the hall to hide the tears of rage that threatened to spill out of his eyes. He went to his locker, took out his books and walked home, brooding over the fickleness of María Elena Osuna in particular and of all women in general. He walked faster and faster, trying to burn out his resentment in physical exertion.

After a few blocks he quieted down. He stopped at a filling station and drank from one of the water hoses, then splashed water over his eyes and dried himself with his handkerchief as best he could. The station attendant watched him silently, his attitude somewhere between resentment and curiosity. After drinking and washing Guálinto went on his way, calmer now. His rage had given way to a detached, lofty feeling of philosophical resignation. He thought of composing a poem, a fine masterpiece that would survive down through the ages and immortalize her perfidy. He groped around for a line as he walked, looking upwards at the cloud-mottled sky.

> "You who destroyed the flowers of my youth
> You who filled my declining years
> With remembrances and aching ... ."

The mood seized him and carried him away in a wave of hot exultation. He repeated the lines over and over. It was a wonderful beginning! They were wonderful lines! As good as any he had ever read. Even now he could see the open textbooks before the desks in English classes of the nation, on their pages his picture opposite the text; Gómez, Guálinto (George W.) born in Jonesville-on-the-Grande, Texas, 1914. Considered the major poet of the century. His intense "To María Elena" is considered one of the finest love poems in the English language. His early death has been attributed to his unhappy life."

She would see then—. A cold thought stopped him. Wouldn't she enjoy telling her grandchildren what a sucker she had made out of him! No, he wouldn't write her any poems. At least, if he did he wouldn't put her name in them and let her know he had written them for her. But he would finish that one he had just begun. They were such beautiful lines. But then another thought assaulted him. Hadn't he heard the lines somewhere? In his mind he went over the list of poets in his text for senior English. No, not Longfellow, not Poe, not Whitman. He was almost sure the lines were his.

But why write poetry? He would get drunk and forget everything, as the songs said. He didn't know exactly how getting drunk would feel because he had never had liquor before. He wasn't sure whether he would like the taste of it. He certainly didn't like the odor of it as he had smelled it on some men's breaths. And how was he going to get the liquor. The futility of any kind of revenge against María Elena weighed him down. He got home hands in pockets, head down, speaking to no one. At this time of day his uncle was still at his farm on the river. Juan Rubio lived there now, in a sturdy *jacal* made of clay and willow saplings. Juan was married now and raising a family.

Guálinto ate his supper without tasting it, though his mother had gone to some pains to make him one of his favorite dishes, pork stew with squash and tender corn. "Don Crispín Rodríguez sent somebody looking for you," his mother said as he was eating. "You ought to go see what he wants."

"Yes, Mama," he said, bending over his plate.

After supper he sat on the kitchen steps and watched the sun set. The open platform that had led from the kitchen to the outside room had been torn down the year before and had been replaced by a wide brick walk roofed over with wooden shingles. Guálinto stayed on the kitchen steps until the sun went down and the evening became a dull red. Then he dragged his feet toward Rodríguez and Sons, Groceries. It was night when he returned, his step light, his love grief drowned by a much stronger emotion. Paco Rodríguez had talked his father into hiring Guálinto on week ends and every evening after school hours. He would not have too much study time away from school, but now he would not miss school every Friday.

In the weeks that followed, he sat as far away as he could from María Elena and avoided her in the halls. She made a few half-hearted attempts to lure him back. When he looked in her direction in class, as he still often did, their eyes met and she smiled. He quickly turned away. After that she ignored him too, and then he spent his time feasting his eyes on her averted face. But when classes ended he walked quickly out of the room to avoid meeting her. His schoolwork did not improve very much, and everybody in senior class knew that he would not be an honor student this year.

After school he had no time to think or brood. He hurried home to a quick and early supper and was at the Rodríguez store by five. He started working as soon as he walked in. There were customers to wait on, errands to do for Doña Concha. But the bulk of the week's work was preparing for the week end. Saturday the farmers and ranchers from all over the county descended upon Jonesville-on-the Grande and into Rodríguez and Sons like a swarm of bees. Sunday the stream of customers continued until noon. So the Rodríguezes and their clerks prepared for Saturday by weighing and packaging unperishable goods such as beans, rice, potatoes, sugar, coffee, and the like. There was much bringing of heavy sacks from the building next to the grocery store that served as a warehouse. When he was not bringing in sacks, he spent most of his time before one of the scales, measuring from a sack into paper bags, weighing and tying the bundles. This went on until nine or nine-thirty, when he went home to do as much of his homework as he could manage before he was too sleepy to read.

Sunday was a relatively short workday, from seven until noon. But on Saturdays he started at seven in the morning and worked past midnight. He ate lunch and supper in one of the storerooms, reclined over the sacks of grain. He had to rustle his own meals from what was in the store. He watched the clock when it was close to mealtimes. At noon and at seven in the evening he would finish with the customer of the moment and make a dash for the meat refrigerator. He hastily gathered some lunch meat, cheese, French bread, and a bottle of soda pop and scurried to the storehouse. The greatest pleasure of these breaks was not the food, though he would be hungry enough by then, but the opportunity to get off his feet for a short while.

If he heard steps he would eat faster, hoping it was Paco. It usually was. Paco would come in slowly and casually, as though looking for something else. When he saw Guálinto he came and sat on a nearby sack and took out a couple of candy bars or bananas from a paper sack. He offered one to Guálinto, and they shared a brief dessert. Then they would talk for a few minutes, until Chito came in and said there were a lot of customers to be waited on.

The conversation usually was about music. One day Paco said, "Do you think anybody could compose a new song?"

"Sure," Guálinto said, biting into the chocolate bar Paco had brought him. "They make new songs every day. Take Agustín Lara, for instance. One shot of dope in his arm and zoom! You have another song."

"No," Paco said, "that's not what I mean."

"Antonio Prieto made up a new song," Guálinto said. "A very pretty one too. 'That was a wonderful dream I had,' it says. 'But it was only a dream that you loved me.' That's really new. He composed it just a few days ago."

Paco shook his head. "No, no. That's not what I mean. 'I dreamed

you loved me but you didn't. You loved me, now you don't.' All songs
are like that. I mean a really *new* song, a song like none of the other
songs that have been composed before. Do you think it could be done?"

"Hmm, I don't know," Guálinto said.

"I'm going to do it. I'm going to do it. Only," Paco added sadly,
"Papa won't let me learn to play the piano."

"Why don't you learn anyway?"

"If I only had a guitar," Paco said, "I could learn to play it. I would
hide it in my room and play it softly at night when everybody else was
in bed."

Guálinto snapped his fingers. "La Gata has a guitar. He just told
me this afternoon he's trying to sell it."

Paco rose excitedly. "I'm going to see him. I'll catch him alone and
ask him. Don't tell anybody about it, will you?"

"I won't," Guálinto said, immensely pleased.

Higinio Alvarado, called La Gata because of his dark catlike face
and light-gray eyes, was the other clerk who worked for the Rodríguezes.
He worked the whole week, from seven to nine at night, half-days Sunday, and Saturday until past midnight for four dollars a week. Guálinto,
who worked week-day evenings, Saturdays, and Sunday mornings, got
two dollars. La Gata was twenty-one years old, Guálinto had known
him in grammar school. But he quit school early and had been married
four years now. He had three children, all boys. He was short, muscular, and full of fun. He loved to creep up on Chito from behind, wind
his muscular arms around Chito's waist and lift him off the floor. He
also enjoyed poking Chito's behind at unexpected moments. Chito did
not like to have his dignity ruffled in such fashion. But La Gata's broad
smile was so disarming and his arms looked so strong that Chito was
only mildly annoyed.

Saturday nights the store closed its doors at midnight, but it took
another half-hour at least to finish waiting on the customers inside. Af-
terwards Guálinto and La Gata had to sweep the white salt-flats dust the
customers had brought in on their shoes. After the store was swept and
the money counted, the two clerks were paid and let go. La Gata sometimes invited Guálinto to a cup of coffee. They would walk all the way
into town for it, even though it was almost two in the morning when they
retraced their steps to the store and beyond it to their homes. To reach
the all-night restaurant where they drank their coffee, Guálinto and La
Gata had to pass by the house where María Elena lived. Guálinto felt
sad when they passed the sleeping Osuna home. In moments like these
he forgot that he and María Elena no longer spoke to each other. He
forgot how he had cursed her to himself at night before going to sleep.
Instead he made himself believe that she really loved him, that they were

only angry for a few days and that all would be all right. He would imagine all sorts of things, under the spell of the chilly pre-dawn blackness.

And he would tell La Gata, "Look. See that house? My girl lives there."

La Gata would grin his catlike grin. "Old man Osuna lives there. María Elena Osuna, eh? You sure go in for class."

Guálinto sighed. "I wonder if she's dreaming of me."

"She's sleeping all right," La Gata said. "Can you imagine her right now, in a lacy sleeping gown, all soft and warm and perfumy, sleeping alone in her little bed? Wouldn't you like to be in there with her, all one tangle of arms and legs?"

Guálinto shivered from the chill of the night and the coziness of his own thoughts.

"In truth," La Gata said, "life isn't fair. Here you are, all tired out and dirty, walking the street by her house, while she's in there, all nice and cozy, farting under the bedclothes"

"Cut it out," Guálinto said.

La Gata laughed. "She does that too. She's not an angel out of the sky, dope."

Guálinto didn't answer.

"Yet," La Gata said, "I bet with a classy dame like that, even her farts are perfumed."

Guálinto laughed. "You get the craziest ideas."

"Well you aren't crazy, I can see that. One can tell you've been to school."

"Why?"

"Picking a girl like that. That's using your head, boy. She must be worth thousands and thousands of dollars."

"I'm not in love with her money. I don't even think about it. I'm in love with her."

"Then you're a fool, a simple drooly-mouthed fool."

"Hell, man. Money isn't everything."

"That's what everybody says, but it is. Listen, don't fall for that romantic stuff. I'm married myself and I ought to know You marry and for the first six weeks or so you think you're in heaven. You want to be in bed with her all the time. But after that it's just plain hell."

"Not all marriages are like that."

"They aren't? Show me one that isn't. Outside of the movies."

Guálinto didn't answer.

"I know," La Gata said. "And I'm telling you. Money is everything in marriage. A wife wants money all the time. Now, with a rich girl like this one of yours, you won't have that problem."

"Skip it," Guálinto said. "You're just soured on life, that's all."

5

Year after year, depression or boom, the saintly fathers of Jonesville-on-the-Grande's Virgin of Guadalupe Church held their kermesses on the grounds of their parochial school. For men interested only in the ethereal realms of the Heavenly City, the fathers were pretty good business men. They held fiestas in September, after the cotton harvest, and in May, after the harvest of spring truck produce. Mexican history had conveniently given them two holidays for this purpose, Mexican independence day on the sixteenth of September and the Cinco de Mayo fiesta, the anniversary of the Mexican victory on May 5, 1862, over the French at Puebla.

Though they lived in a foreign country, Mexicotexans always celebrated these days, American citizens or not. But the biggest kermesse was neither in September nor May. It took place right before Lent, which on this particular year began the second week of February. Banks were closing and the Great Depression had reached the Delta. But the Church was needy, as always. The fathers believed in advertising. From the pulpit they thundered out the news of the kermesse to their flock.

And don't forget that next Sunday, Monday, and Tuesday there will be a kermesse to repair the church and to regild Our Lady's cape. I want every one of you to be there. The Church is poor, the Church needs money. Now don't sit there and say that you have no money. You have enough to buy beer and wallow in lechery. You have enough to buy powders and paints and all the artifices of wickedness for your wives and your daughters. Don't sit there and tell me you have no money for the Church, who is your mother, who is the guardian of your soul. Don't forget the kermesse, and don't forget to be generous and open-handed, for it is in a good cause. Blessed are they are who generous in the cause of God, for with them God shall be generous. Now we shall say a short prayer for the deliverance of our brothers in Spain, who are suffering the loss of their liberties and their beloved king. Let us pray that the Lord in his righteous anger shall give their just due to that anti-Christ Zamora and to Azaña, his partner in sin.

On Sunday afternoon young couples brought their children to the baptismal font. The ceremonies took place in a small room adorned by a plaster image of a Bleeding Christ and several little boxes along the

walls, each with a slot and its corresponding label. Give to the Santo
Niño de Atocha, give to the Holy Virgin, give, give, give. And the men
and women in washed, mended clothing dropped into the boxes some
of the coins they had made during the week. So they might get in God's
good graces, and then perhaps on the following week they might make
sixty cents a day instead of fifty, and then they would be able to buy a
piece of salt pork for their frijoles.

The rich had individual baptismal ceremonies, but poor people gathered in groups around the baptismal font, each group with their baby.
The priest came in and started the baptismal ritual, with crosses, salt,
water, and incantations like a male Doña Simonita la Ciega, the old
woman who cured people of Fright Sickness and the Eye. The priest
was more modern, though, as well as showier. He used mass-production
methods, working on five or six babies at a time, all in a circle around
him in their godmothers' arms. He called each baby by name and the
godparents answered for the baby. "Juan! Juan!" intoned the priest.
"*Dónde estás, no te vayas,*" said Doña Simonita la Ciega. It was much
the same.

The priest dabbed a finger in salt and rubbed the gums of each baby
in turn. Healthy baby, coughing baby, smiling baby, sniffling baby, all
at one time. It was a holy finger and carried no germs. He doused
each baby with holy water and wiped its face with a not-so-clean but
holy towel. When he finished he told the adults, "And don't forget the
kermesse tonight. You must be there." It pays to advertise.

The booths on the parochial schoolgrounds were already built and
decorated with brightly colored crepe paper. They were nothing but
little skeletons of stalls, made of two-by-fours on which paper streamers
had been wound. The lumber and the paper had been donated by some
pious members of the church, who had seen the doors of Heaven open
wide before their eyes because of their generosity. And the reverent
carpenters who here hammered and sawed, (gratis, of course), built not
humble booths but firm shining steps in the ladder that would lead them
to the Most High. Now the well-dressed ladies who were to oversee the
booths arrived with their daughters. They also had reserved seats in
Heaven, courtesy of the Virgin of Guadalupe Church of Jonesville-on-
the-Grande.

The booths took form and individuality. There was a restaurant
where you could get a couple of anemic tamales for a quarter, and
where blessed coffee cost twice as much as the unconsecrated stuff sold
in restaurants. There was also a bank where you were short-changed,
all in fun of course. A jail where you were fined by pretty girls dressed
as policemen. There were flower and confetti girls and all kinds of innocent games of chance, where you could gamble unsinfully. These en-

terprises were operated by young and pretty girls, the daughters of the heaven-bound matrons. Their duty was to seduce the young men in moral, unsuggestive, unprovocative, and thoroughly unsexual ways to part with their scant, hard-earned money. More persuasion was needed this year, because money was so scarce.

Anyway, it was a good show, and it filled quite adequately a certain empty spot in the Mexicotexan's life. The parochial school itself, in the center of the grounds, formed the pivot around which the crowd promenaded, the outer boundary being the circle formed by the booths. Thus the kermesse re-created the basic characteristics of the Mexican city plaza and the border *ranchero*'s *función*, or country festival. Rural and urban, rich and poor they came, to the satisfaction of all present and to the Glory of God.

But a kermesse was no place for somebody who was dead broke. Guálinto knew this and that was why he was standing in the shadows of some *retama* trees that grew by the sidewalk. You set foot inside the grounds and immediately you ran into a pretty girl selling confetti. Another one came along and pinned a paper flower on you and wanted a dime for it. Then still another dragged you off to jail, where you had to pay a fine or stay there till midnight. Then you met somebody you knew, and how could you refuse the girls then, pleading as they did for you to buy ice-cream, pop, or decorated canes? Asking you to play bingo or take a chance on a cake? Guálinto didn't want to meet anybody he knew. He would rather be home right now. It was only because Maruca was in there among the slowly moving crowd that Guálinto was here, skulking about like an escaped criminal. That and (to be honest) the fact that he hoped to see someone he knew and whom he was afraid of meeting.

He knew María Elena was in there. She was in the bingo booth on the other side of the school building from where he was. Her mother had that booth in her charge year after year. It was always built at the foot of the school wall between the ice-cream booth and the loud-speaker system platform, facing the restaurant on the outer ring.

His thoughts were interrupted by a dull whining sound that became a roar. A few magnified knocks and splutters and the young man who operated the sound system got his microphone in tune again. "The next number," he boomed, "will be the waltz 'María Elena,' dedicated to Miss María Elena Osuna by an admirer." A whir of the scratchy needle, then the violins and guitars followed by the singer's voice. "I want to sing to you my most beautiful song." Dedications cost a dime, two cents more than what Guálinto had in his pocket. Part of his hastily eaten supper rose hot and bitter in his throat. He swore under his breath at Maruca. Where could she be? It was ten o'clock already and she had not yet shown up here at the corner where he was to meet her to take her home. She was probably promenading with her friends and had forgotten all about the time.

He had just got off work a short while ago because the Rodríguez store had stayed open until seven this Sunday. The *rancheros* who came to the kermesse also bought groceries. Consequently, he hadn't got away until almost eight, just enough time to go home, gulp down some supper, change clothes and come for Maruca. Though he had changed his sweaty clothes, he was still wearing his work shoes, oily from lard droppings. In his pocket were a nickel and three pennies. He peered at the passing crowd, hoping to see Maruca among the other people. A couple of times he imagined he saw her, but it was some other girl. It was pretty close to ten-thirty and Guálinto was very tired. Besides, tomorrow was a school day, and he had homework to do. As he craned his neck, trying to get a glimpse of Maruca, he moved forward bit by bit without being aware of it until he was among the front row of idlers who stood outside and watched the people pass.

Somebody grabbed him by the shirt front and swung him around, and before he could protest, a smiling girl had pinned a flower on his shirt pocket. "Ten cents, please," she said, still flashing her smile at him. Guálinto dug out his nickel from among the three pennies, handed it to her and fled. The girl's voice came after him, "Why, the cheapskate!"

He must find Maruca. He must find Maruca and get out of here! He bumped squarely into some heavy, unmovable object and bounced back. "Colorado!" he said, steadying himself. "Good God! I thought I had run into a tree!"

It was El Colorado all right, and Francisco was with him. The red-head's broad, freckled face broke into a smile. His huge frame was not even moved by the shock of their encounter. "Goddamit!" he cried out, stretching a hammy paw. "So busy looking for you I almost run over you."

They shook hands and slapped each other on the back as if they hadn't seen each other for months instead of days. "Hi, there, Francisco," Guálinto turned and pumped Francisco's hand. "Here for the Easter holidays?"

"Old man, how are you," Francisco said with his smooth cordiality. "Glad to see you, old fellow."

"I was sure you'd be around," El Colorado said. "You wouldn't miss a kermesse, I was sure. But don't tell me you just got off work." Guálinto nodded. "Those damned Jews!" El Colorado said.

"They're good Christians," Guálinto replied. "They have a picture of the Virgin hanging behind the till."

"You won't be there forever," said El Colorado, bringing his hand down on Guálinto's shoulder. "You have a future ahead of you. But come on, let's give the girls a turn."

Guálinto backed down a step, shaking off El Colorado's hand. "No," he said, "I don't feel like going in right now."

"Why? What's the matter?"

"Well . . . it's my clothes."

"What's the matter with your clothes?"

"I'm not dressed up."

"Hell, man, neither am I." El Colorado was dressed in a sports shirt, since he didn't like wearing ties, but the shirt was silk, and he had on dress trousers and shoes.

"If you prefer I'll take my coat off," Francisco said. "Then we'll all be in our shirt sleeves."

"No! No!" Guálinto said. "Don't do that just for me, Francisco. Please don't."

"Don't worry, he won't," El Colorado said. "He's just a big fraud, that's all."

"But I will," Francisco protested. "Why not?"

"Don't do it, please," Guálinto insisted. Francisco pulled at his lapels and threw back his thin shoulders, preening like a ruffled rooster. They stood by the stream of people, undecided.

"How about it?" El Colorado said. Guálinto shook his head. "God-damn!" said El Colorado. He sounded more hurt than angry. "Are you ashamed to be seen with your friends?"

"It's not that, Colorado. Look," Guálinto dropped his voice, "the truth is I've got three cents in my pocket."

"Oh," El Colorado laughed. "You got more than that." He tapped his pocket. "I got money and any time I got money we both got money."

"That goes double," chimed in Francisco.

"But—"

"No buts," El Colorado said firmly. He grabbed one of Guálinto's arms and Francisco took the other. Between them they led him out for a walk around the kermesse grounds. Guálinto allowed himself to be led into the crowd, half unwillingly, half-eagerly, with mingled feelings of embarrassment and desire. They moved slowly along, and after a while he was relieved to see that people were not staring at him. He felt a bit freer and surer of himself. Yet, he was grateful that Francisco and El Colorado remained on either side of him. El Colorado and Francisco kept up a running fire of talk.

"I tell you," El Colorado said. "A man was originally intended to have four wives. A study of the hand proves it. It's nature's own law, I tell you, and those old Bible guys knew what they were doing."

"I never heard such nonsense," Francisco said.

"How come?" Guálinto said.

"Well, look at your hand," El Colorado said. Guálinto looked at his hand. "You too, Francho-Pancho."

"Oh, all right," Francisco said, looking at his hand.

"There," continued El Colorado, "it's plain as day. You have four slender fingers and one big fat thumb."

"You mean to say," Francisco demanded, "that you made me take my hand out of my pocket and stare at it just to tell me I have five fingers on it?"

"Hold your horses," El Colorado said. "Observe your hand. No two fingers are alike, the four long ones, but they all look more like each other than they look like the thumb."

"This is getting too deep for me," Francisco said.

"Notice also," El Colorado continued, unperturbed, "that any two of the four fingers don't go very well together. You can hold a cigaret in them, but that's about all you can do with them. They're no good by themselves. But look at the thumb now. It's opposite the other fingers and it makes them mean something. He puts them to work and makes them do things, and he uses them one at a time or all together for different purposes. The thumb is the male and he has four wives, each one different to give him variety."

"Do you lie awake nights thinking up things like this?" Francisco said.

"He's another Joseph Smith," Guálinto said to Francisco.

"Joseph Smith," said El Colorado. "Who was he?"

"He was something like you," Francisco answered, "only a lot of people believed in what he said."

"I bet you made that up," El Colorado said.

Francisco laughed and Guálinto joined him. El Colorado grinned. "Anyway," he said, "that was a long time ago. Nowadays it's hard enough to support one wife, from what I hear."

The sound system phonograph was playing "El Caballo Pinto":

> If your daddy wears a dagger
> I can also throw a knife.
> We will face each other squarely,
> We will throw and—ugh!
> My darling, for your love
> Some day I shall lose my life.
> Better, better to die fighting
> If you cannot be my wife.

Guálinto threw his head back and his nostrils widened to the challenge in the music. How sweet it must be to kill what you hate with all your being! But Don Onofre Osuna wore only a fountain pen.

> Once your mother loved me dearly,
> Now I do not have such luck.
> Once I had a lot of money,
> Now I do not have—a ...
> Darling for your love
> Some day I shall lose my life.

"Haw! Haw! Haw!" roared El Colorado. "Did you hear that?"

"Be quiet," hissed Francisco.

"Quiet, nothing. That's rich, that's great! Did you catch it? Guálinto, did you get it? What rhymes with luck?"

"Sure," said Guálinto quietly. "Sure I got it." Once I had a lot of money. Well, not money. But women could want other things besides money, and they went about it the same way to get what they wanted. He shook his head as if to drive those thoughts away. He was a fool, he thought, going off and skulking this way. In all fairness, maybe she didn't see him that other time. Maybe she had a right to be mad, the way he had treated her. She might have been ready to make up, but he hadn't given her the chance. All he had to do was see her—

Then he saw her. The suddenness with which he was transported from daydreaming to reality shook him up. His vision blurred and his legs felt weak and trembly. She was just where he had expected her to be, in the stall between the ice cream booth and the sound system. Nobody was playing bingo, so she and the other girls in her booth were just sitting or standing around.

"What's the matter?" El Colorado said, looking at Guálinto's pale face.

"Nothing. Nothing."

"Nothing! You're as pale as a corpse."

"Do you feel sick?" Francisco inquired.

"No, I just had a spell of weakness. But it's gone now."

El Colorado looked at Guálinto closely and figured that Guálinto hadn't had any supper that night. He decided to act with finesse. Offer Guálinto food? No, sir. Guálinto was too proud for that. "Look," El Colorado said, snapping his fingers as if he had just had a bright idea. "Let's have some ice cream."

"No, thanks, Colorado. Too full right now. Too full." Guálinto patted his stomach.

"Ah, come on," El Colorado said. "There's always a little room on top."

Guálinto looked toward the ice cream booth with its little green tables. There was only one empty table and that was next to the two-by-four that served as a fence dividing the ice cream stall from the bingo booth. María Elena was half-seated on the beam, some four feet from the empty table.

"Come on," El Colorado said, grabbing Guálinto by the arm.

Guálinto resisted. "No. Thanks a lot. Some other time."

El Colorado let go Guálinto's arm. "What's the matter with you? I'm inviting you. Is that the way to treat a friend?"

Guálinto knew it was useless to argue, so they went into the ice cream booth and toward the table close to María Elena. El Colorado shouted, "Hi, Antonio!"

Antonio Prieto waved from the crowd of onlookers at the edge of the grounds. "Hi, Colorado."

"Want some ice cream?" El Colorado yelled.

"Sure do."

"Come on over, then."

While El Colorado and Antonio were talking, Guálinto was watching María Elena. She did not turn her face away, as he had expected. She looked straight through him as if he wasn't there. Then, lowering her soft haunch from its resting place on the two-by-four, she stood up very straight, smoothed her skirt along her thighs and walked to the other end of her booth. Guálinto sat down. Francisco did likewise as El Colorado came up with Antonio.

"Hey, Guálinto," El Colorado said, "you know Antonio Prieto."

"Do I know him!" Guálinto stretched out his hand over the table. "I haven't seen you in school this semester, Antonio."

"La Chilla," Antonio said. "I had to go to work." His eyes shifted nervously, studying the ground on either side of his chair.

"Ah, that's too bad. I hope you can go back and finish when things get better."

"I intend to," Antonio said, with a decisiveness unusual for him.

"Good," El Colorado said. "Good."

Meanwhile a girl brought them each a little gob of ice cream in saucers from somebody's kitchen. Guálinto was sitting with his side toward the bingo booth. He was extremely self-conscious about his clothes and his shaggy nape. He ate his ice cream awkwardly, trying to forget that María Elena was so near. He was sure she was looking at him, and he sneaked a look at her. But no. She seemed completely oblivious of him. For a brief moment he feasted his eyes on her. She was dressed in white. She loved white with red. There was a pattern of red about the neck of her dress. As he turned away the other girls laughed a nasty, mocking laugh, and he knew he had been taken in.

El Colorado looked up at the laughter and said, "Why, there's María Elena. Say, Guálinto, aren't you—"

"Skip it!" Guálinto said.

María Elena and her friends moved nearer and began to talk in whispers. Guálinto knew they were talking about him, though he could not make out what they were saying. El Colorado realized he had put his foot into something, and now he was silent. Antonio was busy with his ice cream. Francisco, however, looked in María Elena's direction with a dreamy expression on his handsome face.

Then María Elena said loudly and clearly, "There's a peculiar odor around here, don't you think? Something smells like lard and rotten potatoes." Her satellites laughed shrilly. Guálinto flinched and closed his eyes. Behind his eyelids the world spun round and round. Miss Cornelia was slapping his face, Miss Cornelia was whipping him until he wet his pants. Out of the edge of the pin-wheeling world floated the leering face of La India. Movement no longer was concentric but shifting, restless, confused like a group of boys sitting in church. A smirking soft face was pushed up against his. It sniffed. It's lard, it said, smells of the frying pan. Then it snickered evilly.

And Guálinto realized how far he had traveled and how little he had moved since the days when he had been a child playing in the banana grove. He trembled as he fought the impulse to walk over and slap her pretty face, to smash his fist into that pouting mouth until it was a bloody mess. He heard El Colorado say, "The cheap little slut!"

Guálinto opened his eyes and reached across the table, grasping El Colorado's wrist. "Colorado," he said thickly, "you know, Colorado—." He cleared his throat, "Girls are the dirtiest *sanavabiches*."

El Colorado looked at him curiously and didn't answer. He did not remember. Guálinto laughed. The girls in the bingo booth laughed too, but their laughter sounded different this time as if they were looking the other way. Guálinto turned and saw they were looking at Maruca. She was standing to one side, along the watcher's line, made up mostly of men and boys who stared at her. Her limp, light-brown hair was done in pleats and wound around her head as she usually wore it. But there was something different about her. It was her little brown eyes, forever dancing mischievously in her face. Now they looked strangely large and deep, as if she had been crying. Buddy Goodnam passed in front of her with two other boys.

Her lips moved, probably calling his name, for he looked quickly at her and made as if to hurry by. She stepped forward and caught his arm. The other two boys with Goodnam seemed surprised and people around them stared. Buddy Goodnam shrugged, obviously annoyed, but she seemed to be pleading with him. He shook her arm off, turned and said something to the other two boys. Then he motioned to her with an angry jerk of his head and walked out toward the street. She followed him, a step or two behind, eyes lowered.

The girls in the bingo booth laughed again. María Elena said, "Did you ever?"

Another girl said, "The shameless thing!"

María Elena added, "Why doesn't she leave him alone? He's through with her!"

Guálinto left the table without a word and threw himself into the crowd in pursuit of Maruca and Buddy Goodnam. He pushed, lunged and jabbed against the dense, exasperatingly slow stream of people, heedless of little cries of protest and grumbled threats alike. Much like a clumsy, desperate swimmer he thrashed a path before him with hands, arms and elbows. At last he stumbled into the sidewalk and looked savagely around. Goodnam and Maruca were walking along the quiet street toward the Dos Veintidós. He went after them along the rows of parked cars, swiftly, noiselessly, and he overtook them in midblock. The two did not hear him approach. They were talking earnestly when he came up to them.

"And what do you want me to do?" Buddy was saying impatiently.

"Do? Do?" Maruca echoed, and her voice broke. "Oh, how can you be so heartless?"

"Come on, you!" Guálinto grabbed Maruca by the arm and jerked her back. "As for you," he turned on Buddy Goodnam, still speaking in Spanish, "*hijo de la chingada*, I ought to knock the mother out of you. Beat it!"

"Guálinto," pleaded Maruca, "don't talk to him like that, please!"

"Shut your snout," Guálinto said. "If you had the shame of the cheapest slut you wouldn't be saying a word. And you, I told you to beat it."

Goodnam took a step backward, glancing in the semidarkness from one to the other. Then, in sudden decision, he went back the way he had come. Maruca covered her face in her hands and sobbed deeply and fluently, with that feeling of overwhelming grief Mexicans call "sickness of the heart." Over and over she kept saying, "Oh, why did you run him off? Why did you run him off?"

Guálinto was embarrassed by her demonstration of grief. As far as he could remember, Maruca's tears had been few. And when she did cry, she shed tears of rage, of pain, or of resentment. Never had he heard her cry like this before. His anger subsided, and he shifted his weight from one foot to the other.

He caught faint creakings coming from the houses along the narrow street. The old ladies living along the street were cracking open their shutters and cocking their ears. "Come on," he whispered hoarsely. "You're giving a free show." Maruca muffled her sobs and began to walk obediently by his side. They walked to the next mid-block in silence, keeping their eyes averted from each other when they passed the bright light of the corner lamp. Finally Guálinto mustered enough indignation to speak.

"You ought to be ashamed," he said, "running like that after a man. And him a Gringo too. Do you know what kind of women let themselves be seen with a Gringo in this town?"

Maruca started crying again. "You don't understand," she sobbed. "This is different, this is different."

"It is not different," Guálinto said severely. "A Gringo's a Gringo and a Mexican girl is a Mexican. You were acting like a common soldier-woman."

She stopped crying and looked earnestly at him. "Please, Guálinto, please don't. Let's not talk about it any more."

He stuck his hands into his pockets and fell into a morose silence. After a while she said, cautiously, "Guálinto?"

"Uh-huh."

"You won't tell Mama? Please?"

"Okay," he grunted, "okay."

6

Sunday again, four weeks after his visit to the kermesse. Guálinto came home from Rodríguez and Sons after one in the afternoon, his hunger dulled by exhaustion. It was early in March, but the day was hot and clear, and he was grateful for the shade when he reached the porch of his home.

Carmen was curled up on the sofa, reading avidly from an ancient magazine that long ago had parted with its covers. He threw his greasy cap onto a chair and asked,"Has Uncle come home from the farm?"

"No," Carmen answered from behind the magazine. Feliciano now spent most of his time on the quarter-section of river land he had bought with gold coins from the old Gringo who lived in California. He was coming to town only on week ends and sometimes not even then. There was much to do on the land this time of year. When he came to town he slept as always in the one-room building behind the main house. Besides serving as Feliciano's bedroom, the "Room", as they called it, was a storeroom for much of the stock they had brought from El Danubio Azul. In bad weather, "El Cuarto" was spacious enough to serve also as a laundry room.

Guálinto looked idly at the worn magazine Carmen was holding before her face, then looked behind it at her eyes. They were moist and reddened as if she had been crying. "What are you reading?" he asked. "Don't tell me you've taken to reading silly sob stories. What magazine is that?"

Carmen did not answer. "Let me have it," he demanded, taking it from Carmen. "An old natural history magazine? What is there to cry about in this thing?"

Carmen tried to smile, but she remained silent.

"You just like to feel bad," he said, handing back the magazine. He went to the bathroom to wash. She was a funny one, he thought. She liked to read all kinds of things, especially novels about the strange and mysterious. She would take the Sunday edition of the San Antonio paper and devour the feature section. Then she would retell it in Spanish, almost word for word, to their mother. She would tell her about the Lost Atlantis, of the guessed-at secrets of the Pharaohs, of the latest theories about life on other planets. "Mama," she would say, "isn't it mysterious? Doesn't it make you feel all sad inside to think of such awfully great distances and so many millions of years?" Her voice would trail away, while her dark eyes gazed far off into nothingness. María would nod and stroke her daughter's hair.

Yes, Carmen was a strange one, Guálinto thought, forever thinking about depressing things, about ancient mysteries, dreaming about graves and funerals and dyings. And everything she read or thought about she would confide to her mother. When they were doing needle work or doing some chore in the kitchen together, she was always talking to her mother, telling her about the wonders and mysteries of the Universe, as interpreted by Hearst's feature writers.

And her mother, who talked little and had few friends, loved Carmen because Carmen was not only daughter but sister and friend, and through the daughter the mother glimpsed a world she knew almost nothing about, that huge complicated world where people spoke English.

Guálinto stamped into the kitchen, towel around his neck, bent forward so as not to spatter himself with water. Carmen was there, making his lunch. "Where's Mama?" he asked.

The half-smile faded from Carmen's face. "She's gone to see the doctor. She and Maruca."

"Doctor? On Sunday? Doctors close on Sundays the way storekeepers do, don't they?"

"They went to his house."

"Oh," Guálinto said. He threw the towel over a chair and sat down at the table. "Funny—say!"

"What?"

"Who's sick? Is something the matter? I—I hadn't thought—"

"No," Carmen said, "nobody's sick." Guálinto stared at her, a bare speck of worry in his mind. He flicked it off with a shrug and bent his head over his plate. Carmen went and stood at the window, looking out toward the street. He was not interested in what she was doing, not being in a mood for conversation. He was finishing his meal when a *camión* stopped out in the street.

Carmen turned from the window. Her face was pale. "Here they come!" she breathed. "Here they come!"

Not until then did Guálinto think that perhaps something was wrong. He rushed to a front window and was immensely relieved to see his mother, straight and slim, beside the *camión* driver, paying the fare. She looked entirely her usual self in the long-skirted black silk outfit she wore when she went out, her head wrapped in a black lace shawl.

Maruca got out of the *camión* and Guálinto could see right away that it was Maruca who was sick. Her face was very red, and she looked like she was walking in her sleep. The *camión* rasped and roared away as María took Maruca by the arm and led her up the porch steps. Maruca hung her head and walked with groping, unsteady steps. María opened the door and for a moment her face was framed in it, pale, worn, strained. Then she reached back and jerked Maruca inside, so roughly that the girl was sent stumbling halfway across the room. Maruca steadied herself. She looked frightened, very frightened.

Rage transformed her mother's handsome face into a mass of wrinkles. "Go to the Room!" she snarled through clenched teeth. Maruca slunk out obediently and María followed close behind, trembling visibly. Just inside the kitchen door there was a sturdy barrel stave as wide as a man's hand. María picked it up and hefted it as though it were a baseball bat. Carmen gave a low moan and covered her face. Guálinto followed them, fascinated, to the Room. There Maruca was waiting, crouching in a corner like an animal. Her mother came in and the girl stared dully at the barrel stave. María paused, as if undecided how to begin. She stared at her daughter for one terrible silence. Then she whispered gustily, "*Pu—! Pu—!*" Suddenly she screamed, "*Puta, puta, puta!* You whore! You whore!"

She lifted the stave in both hands and brought it down on Maruca's back. Maruca dropped to her knees from the blow. María kept screaming and striking. "You bitch! You filthy—dirty—bitch!" She punctuated each curse with a thudding blow on head, shoulders, back. There were several sacks of beans and corn in the room. Maruca sought a measure of shelter by crawling along on her haunches from one sack to another. She had endured the first blows in strangled whispers. Now she started moaning, "Don't hit me, Mama; don't hit me, Mama." Then in a frenzied scream, "Mama! You'll hurt it! You'll hurt—"

"I'll kill it!" María screamed back. "I'll kill you both, you unspeakable slut. You harlot! You *sanavabiche!*"

The stave struck reedily, then split. María kept beating her daughter with the splinters, also kicking at her sides. Maruca crouched close to the floor, seeking to protect her belly. And the blows went on, the horrible thudding and cracking, and the two women cursing, panting, grunting, pleading. Guálinto stood at the doorway, holding on to both sides of the jamb to steady himself. The blows stunned him as if they were pounding on his flesh. The animal sounds coming from his sister filled him with a crushing sense of shame. But it was his mother who sickened him most. He had never heard her curse before. Nor had he ever thought whether or not she knew about such words. If he had done so, he would have stopped thinking about it immediately, with a sense of impropriety and defilement. Now these words were pouring out of her mouth like a stream of filth.

He wanted to rush in and put his hands over his mother's twisted, spitting mouth, to rub desperately at her lips, to make them soft and gentle again, to shout at her, "Mama, Mama, you are cursing yourself away. You're not my mother anymore." He must crawl away somewhere and hide. He must find some way to cease to exist until this was over. María kept cursing and beating until Maruca no longer moved about but sank to the floor with each blow, growing smaller and smaller it seemed. Then the blows and the curses stopped. Silence except for the hoarse breathing from two throats.

María made a low bestial sound deep inside her throat and turned toward the door. Her silk dress was disarranged and spattered, her hair was hanging in shapeless gobs over her ears and forehead. Guálinto stepped aside to let her pass. At the kitchen door she shot out a nervous claw and seized Carmen, who was standing there. She held her by the hair with one hand and slapped her face with the other. Carmen neither resisted nor made a sound. She just turned her face away and endured the blows. María shook her back and forth by the hair and slammed her against the wall. "You knew!" María said hoarsely. "You knew!" She broke off hysterically and dashed into the house. Carmen sat down on the kitchen step, rubbing at her face. From the front came the creak of bedsprings as María crashed down upon her bed. Then silence.

Guálinto summoned enough courage to look into the storeroom.

Maruca was lying face-down on the floor, her hands on the sides of her stomach. One leg was doubled up under her and her skirt was rumpled up to her thighs. Her dress was torn at the back. Her long hair was loose and thrown into a confused circle around the back of her head. There was a trickle of very dark blood running down through it. Guálinto took his head out of the doorway. His stomach tried to vomit but his throat would not let it. He put his hand on the wall to steady himself and looked up drunkenly as Carmen came up with a cloth over her shoulder, a tin bucket in one hand, and a square bottle of alcohol in the other. She handed him the bucket and asked shakily, "Will you fill it with water?"

He nodded and tried to say "Yes" but his throat rebelled again and merely croaked an answer. He stumbled to the faucet and turned it on.

The afternoon dragged by like a stifling dream. Everything looked unreal and somehow bigger than usual. The bird that hopped about on the mulberry bush by the side of the house looked like no other bird Guálinto had ever seen. Its feathers were sickly yellow, angry orange, dull black. Each color stood out, separate from the others as if it were part of a different object. Or as if it were a drawing made by a small child. The bird's beak was pink with funny little ridges around the edges. He had never noticed how birds' beaks were made.

The world seemed all disjointed and fallen into parts. Ordinarily, things blended into each other to form just one picture. But now everything stood out, by itself, and clashed visibly with its surroundings. In the hot dry distance some insect chirped monotonously, the heavy, sticky odor of the sun-cooked jazmines in the garden choked the lungs like the smell of flowers around a coffin. The afternoon dragged itself along, smearing itself on the ground in shimmering waves of torpid heat. The world had stopped.

Finally a miracle occurred and it was evening. Guálinto still sat on the kitchen door step, his chin in his cupped hands, looking toward the gloomy doorway of the storeroom. Once Carmen came to the door with the empty bucket and asked him to fill it again for her. She took the water at the doorway, whispering, "You can't come in. She's ashamed." Then, with that professional air some women wear when cooking or healing, "She's better now, much better. Conscious and resting. I laid out Uncle Feliciano's cot and helped her into it. I think she'll go to sleep in a minute." Guálinto sat down on the kitchen doorstep again.

Now Carmen came out of the storeroom and went silently into the kitchen. Guálinto edged to one side to let her past and remained sitting where he was. In the kitchen Carmen turned on a light and went about making supper with as little noise as possible. After a succession of gray smells from the stove, she came and said softly in his ear, "Supper's ready." Then she went reluctantly into the front bedroom. Her voice murmured humbly, María's brittle voice answered.

Carmen stole back into the kitchen. "She doesn't want to eat," she whispered. "She says she's going to die."

Guálinto didn't answer. He chewed at the food in his mouth without tasting it. He managed to force several swallows down his throat, then he gave up and went to sit at the doorstep again. Carmen washed the dishes and went out to the storeroom with a plate and a cup. Again Guálinto moved aside to let her pass and remained where he was. A light went on in the storeroom.

A cricket chirped lazily. The moon rose, yellow and round like an egg yolk. The evening turned cool, chilling his ankles. From the storeroom the sound of whispers and murmured groans came and went. Guálinto sneezed. He rubbed his chilled ankles and wrapped his trousers legs tightly around them.

"Guálinto!" cried his mother from her bed. Under the veneer of anger her voice had a trace of embarrassment. It was the first time she had noticed his existence since she had arrived that afternoon. "Guálinto!" she repeated. "Don't you hear me? Go to bed." Guálinto went to bed.

Late that night his uncle came in from the country. Guálinto awoke from a light, troubled sleep to hear him pounding on the door. It creaked open and Feliciano said, "Where is she?"

María murmured something and Feliciano strode through the house and into the storeroom. María went to bed again. Guálinto strained his ears. He heard his uncle's knock and Carmen's anxious, "Who?" Then silence. After a long while Feliciano's booted footsteps returned. He went into María's bedroom. He whispered fiercely at María, who whispered back tearfully. Once her voice rose and she cried, "I will not!" Feliciano hissed again at her.

"I am not sorry," she said loudly, "and I will not have her in my house." Feliciano stopped whispering, and there followed several frightening crashes.

Guálinto sat up in bed. Oh, God! His uncle was beating his mother! He threw back the sheet and put one foot down on the floor. Then he heard his uncle say, "This is their bed, and they can sleep on it! If you don't want them in the house I'll set it up in the Room and put my cot in their bedroom!"

Guálinto sank back on his pillow, weak and trembling. A moment later Feliciano struggled through the kitchen, close by Guálinto's door, with part of the girls' bed, the foot under one arm and the head under the other. Guálinto could see him clearly in the light coming from the kitchen. His uncle shot a worried glance at the blackness of Guálinto's room, and Guálinto cowered among the covers, ashamed to let his uncle know he was awake.

Next morning they couldn't look each other in the face. Feliciano and María had said many things to each other the night before, they who had never spoken in real anger to each other. Feliciano had a quiet affection for his baby sister, and María's attitude toward the eldest of the family had always been one of respect. Now they did not speak to each other or look directly at anyone. And neither of them looked at Guálinto, as though his presence made them more ashamed of themselves. Guálinto sensed it and it made him even more embarrassed and uncomfortable. Maruca stayed in the Room, hidden from everyone else except Carmen, who seemed less affected by the tense atmosphere than the others. She acted as liaison between the different members of the family, who stood apart from each other, each of them marooned on his own island, separated by desolate feelings of cheapness and degradation.

It was Carmen who, silently and with lowered eyes, prepared breakfast and called the others when it was ready. Feliciano, María, and Guálinto sat down at the table and ate without looking up while Carmen took a plate out to Maruca. When Guálinto finished he got up without a word and left for school. No one spoke to him when he left either. Stepping into the street, he felt that a great weight had been lifted from his shoulders. But it was only lifted, not taken away. It hovered just above him, casting a shadow on his thoughts.

The next day María and Feliciano had a quiet talk in her bedroom. Then, with Guálinto's help, Feliciano brought the girls' bed back into their bedroom. He also bought a spring cot for Carmen to sleep in so Maruca could have the bed to herself. But María remained a stranger to them all. She walked around with an expressionless look on her face and would talk to no one unless she had to. Feliciano was also sparing of his words, but those he did utter were kinder than María's. He had now spent several days in town, keeping in touch with the work on the farm through Juan Rubio, who made daily trips to town in Feliciano's truck.

Carmen had got a job Saturday's at Woolworth's, a lucky break since jobs were scarce. She left her job after a short exchange of words between María and Feliciano. María said that both girls had the instincts of whores and that Carmen should not be walking the streets every Saturday evening. Guálinto winced at her words. He could not get used to hearing such words coming out of his mother's mouth. Carmen gave up her job willingly, as she had given up high school some years before. She stayed home, did most of the housework, and took care of Maruca as she had taken care of her mother when she broke her leg.

María was seized with frequent sick spells, and Carmen tended both her mother and Maruca as best she could. She seemed to take it all in stride, the only change in her being that she became even quieter than usual. As for Maruca, those times that Guálinto caught a glimpse of her, her face was white and haggard, and her eyes were red from crying. She stayed in her room most of the time and came to the kitchen table only after everyone else had eaten.

7

The morning after Maruca and Carmen returned to their bedroom, Feliciano told Guálinto at the breakfast table, "Don't go to school today. I need you." Guálinto finished his breakfast in a hurry. As soon as they were through, Feliciano put on his black suit and his best hat. Guálinto wiped his mouth hastily and followed him outside. They walked swiftly down the street, Feliciano's long legs taking enormous strides. Guálinto was hard put to keep up with him. He would have liked to ask where they were going, but his uncle's face was so grim, and he looked straight ahead so intently that Guálinto thought it better not to do so. They caught a *camión* that took them to the edge of the northwestern part of town. They walked again, along a wide, quiet street past rows of solidly built brick houses with spacious porches, wide lawns, and double garages. They squatted on their lawns, these houses, like fat, contented Rotarians sitting on the grass at a picnic, substantial, self-assured, inelegant.

His uncle stopped at last before a one-story house of grayish-yellow brick with white stone trim stained black by the rains of many years. The lawn and the garden were protected from outsiders by an ornate wrought-iron fence set in a low ridge of brick. The iron gate had cut into it in letters a foot high the initials M.I.G., and the cement walk at the gateway had "Goodnam" carved into it. Feliciano hit the gate with the flat of his hand to push it open. A walk of hexagonal concrete slabs led up to the brick steps. The lawn was well trimmed and dotted with round garden plots where grew rainbow-colored phlox, blue larkspur, deep-scarlet bougainvillea. On the south corner of the house a vine of night-blooming jessamine had crawled up the brick wall and hung like a green drapery. Guálinto thought it was a beautiful house and wondered how it would feel to live in a place like that.

Feliciano marched up the steps and rapped loudly on the door. Silence. Somewhere in the depths of the house a door slammed. Feliciano rapped again, harder. The door opened suddenly and a fat-faced man stuck his head out. He drew it quickly back, then opened the door wider.

"My name is Feliciano García," Feliciano said. "Perhaps you remember me."

"Of course," Mr. Goodnam said, in Spanish also, his red face dissolving into a smile. "Of course. We've known each other for a long time, haven't we."

"I believe so," Feliciano said drily.

Martin Goodnam chuckled. "I know every Mexican in town." Then with a confidential wink, "You have to know everybody to be in politics."

"You should remember me a little better than that. If you remember Pete Severski."

"How could I forget," cried Mr. Goodnam. He threw the door wide open. "But do come in. Come into your house." He gestured toward a sofa with a sweep of his hand.

Martin I. Goodnam was a fat man in his fifties. His bulk made him look short, though he was of average height. His sparse sandy hair began at the top of his head, giving him the forehead nature had denied him. Martin's grandfather, James, came down with General Taylor. He concluded that even if you do beat them, you can profit by joining them. Accordingly, he stayed on the border, learned Spanish, was baptized into the Catholic church, acquired the confidence of the Mexican population, and became rich. Martin's father, Frank, called Pancho, grew up in an atmosphere of side arms and the Spanish language. He had been a good friend of Robert Norris, and together they entrenched the Blue party in the city at the turn of the century. Pancho Goodnam was only forty when he died of a stray bullet during a heated election.

Don Pancho had an ability for duping Mexicans and making them like it. This gift, along with cattle ranches and money in the bank, was Martin Ignatius Goodnam's inheritance. M.I. Goodnam was an important cog in the city's political machine, a respected, upright citizen of Jonesville-on-the-Grande, and what was more *muy gente* among the Mexican voters. Don Martín, as he was called by everyone, the accent on the second syllable in the Spanish manner, Don Martín did not take to the Catholic faith as he had done to the Spanish language. He was a devout Baptist and loved to quote from the Bible. His wife, it was said, had been a Christian Scientist. She tried to pray her way through the flu epidemic of 1918, whereupon she died. She left in her husband's care a big tomboy of a daughter named Sarita and a frail, smartly handsome, Mexican-minded son, he whom Maruca loved.

Mr. Goodnam and his guests sat down. "And what," he said in easy amiability, "may I do for you?"

"This is my nephew," said Feliciano. "Guálinto Gómez."

"I've heard of you, my boy," Mr. Goodnam said. "You will go far."

"I have brought the boy with me," continued Feliciano, "because it was his sister whom your son deceived."

Goodnam started, then smiled. "You certainly don't waste words, Feliciano. But this is not a matter to be arranged in a hurry. Let's talk the thing over slowly. Grain by grain the chicken fills her crop, you know." He laughed.

Feliciano crossed his arms. "All right, go ahead."

Goodnam spread his hands out, palms down, fingers curved upward like a pair of wings. "Let's begin at the beginning. You have a grievance, I believe, and you have come to me for redress."

"Let's leave the frills aside, Martín. Let's get to the point. This is a serious matter and something must be done about it. Soon."

"Of course." Martin Goodnam smoothed the air placatingly with his open hands. "Of course something must be done about it and something will be done. I am ready to cooperate with you to the fullest, Feliciano, to straighten out this painful matter, painful to me as much as to you, I assure you."

Feliciano looked at him and said nothing.

"Let's start at the beginning," Goodnam repeated. "Now, let's see, how many months has the girl been this way?"

"About four months, according to the doctor. People will soon be talking."

Goodnam leaned back in his chair, hands folded on his round belly, his face gazing at the ceiling. "Hm-mm" he said. "And what doctor have you been consulting?"

"Doctor Zapata. It was several days ago, but we had some trouble getting her to tell us who the father was for sure."

"Naturally. She wouldn't want to implicate her sweetheart. You can tell the doctor to send the bill to me at my office."

"Very well."

Martín waved his hand airily. "Yes," he said. "I want to do the right thing. Ah ... as you say, time passes, and we must not waste it. So..ah ... " He drummed on the chair arm with his fingers. "What do you consider a sufficient amount to cover the whole incident?"

Feliciano stiffened, his fingers digging into the sofa's fine mohair. "Just what do you mean?" he said coldly.

"Well," Mr. Goodnam laughed a little and chucked his hands up in the air. "I mean that money is necessary. We need it to live, you know. Even Jesus admitted money was necessary. Remember he once said, 'Give unto Caesar what is Caesar's.' " He fidgeted under Feliciano's stare and drummed again on the chair with his fingers. "I had in mind to—. Well, we could arrange it this way. I'll pay all your niece's doctor's bills until the child is born. It may be too late for an—ah—abortion, I believe. And you probably would not want that anyway. I'll pass her a weekly amount, any reasonable amount, you name it. If she wants to have the child in some other place, I'll pay all the bills. San Antonio, Monterrey. It will be a nice, diverting trip for her. And after the child is born, as far as his education is concerned—"

"*¡Basta!*" Feliciano snarled. "You have said enough."

Martin Goodnam blinked. "*¿Cómo? ¿Cómo?*"

Feliciano thrust his head forward. "I came here to talk of only one thing, and it's not money, *¡cabrón!* If you mention money to me once more, I'll grab your tongue and jerk it out. Like this!" He ground one fist against the other and jerked them suddenly apart.

Goodnam paled and swallowed several times before he could summon up some indignation. "Sir!" he said, half-rising from his chair, "I'll have to ask you to leave my house!"

Feliciano remained seated. Guálinto did likewise, he was too frightened to move. "You will have to ask me again," Feliciano said, "and many times more, but I won't leave till we settle what I came here for. Then you can have your filthy house."

Martin Goodnam regarded him intently and then sat down. "All right," he said. "No offense meant, no offense meant at all." He passed his hand over his scanty hair and smiled. "But tell me, just how do you wish to arrange this matter?"

"What way can such a matter be arranged, except by marriage?"

"But my dear sir!" exclaimed Goodnam. "My dear sir! We can't do that! We just can't do that!"

"Why? Is your son married?"

"No, but some day he will be and it must be to the right girl. Not that your niece is anything but a nice girl. It's just that she isn't Buddy's type. She just wouldn't do."

"She wouldn't do," mimicked Feliciano nastily. "Well, she already did, and there's no way around it now. What you mean is that you don't want your son to marry a Mexican. You lying, two-bit politician! You whore-monging pillar of virtue! The friend of the worker! The Mexican's loyal helper! You low-down *sanavabiche!*" He stopped, still staring at Goodnam while Guálinto stared at him.

Goodnam took Feliciano's insults calmly, leaning back on his arm chair. "The Bible says," he intoned, " 'Thou shalt not let thy cattle gender with a diverse kind. Thou shalt not sow thy field with mingled seed.' " He shrugged. "That has always been God's law."

"God's law be damned! My niece is not a cow. You must get this into your head, Martín. I'm here for action not talk. Your son marries my niece or something unpleasant is going to happen."

Goodnam sat up like a nervous rabbit. "Is that a threat?" he said. "Is that a threat?"

"Is it a threat?" Feliciano repeated disdainfully. "So you want to sic the law on me? I'm willing. I'll raise such a stink that come next election you'll see who has more to lose."

"Calm yourself, man," Goodnam said quickly. "We mustn't lose our tempers."

Feliciano rubbed down his bristling mustache with his palm and glared silently.

"I would give my consent readily," Goodnam said, "but for several important details. Now, don't get excited again, but there are certain things I must know, as the boy's father. The first is how can we be sure about the girl's virtue before she met my boy? Now don't get angry again. We have to be frank to get anywhere. Second, how can we know for certain my boy is the father of this girl's child?"

"As for the girl's virtue," Feliciano said, his voice trembling with rage, "anyone of dozens of people who know her can tell you what sort of a girl she was before she met your son. She's not an adventuress, Martín. As for your second question, why don't you call your son and ask him?"

"He's not here right now," said Martin.

"Father." Buddy Goodnam was standing at the door leading to the dining room. He was dressed in slippers and striped pajamas. His hair was rumpled and his longish, sad face was pale. He avoided Guálinto's truculent stare. "Father," he began again.

"Buddy!" exclaimed Martin Goodnam. "You're sick, my boy. You should be in bed."

"I didn't know these people were here," said Buddy.

"Go to bed, my boy! Go to bed!"

Buddy smiled a patient little smile. "I feel all right, father." Then to Feliciano, "Father has been keeping me shut up in the house these days. He thinks you might kill me. He's afraid you haven't heard the one about 'Vengeance is mine, saith the Lord.'"

Feliciano looked at him, undecided what attitude to take. Guálinto glared. Then Feliciano told Martin, "Well, here he is. Ask him."

"All right," Martin said, shrugging. "You win. There will be a wedding, a quiet wedding."

"A wedding, that is all we want," Feliciano said. "You can make it as quiet as you like."

Feliciano walked with a brisk, light step on their way home, and he looked almost happy. Guálinto, as always, had a hard time keeping up with his uncle's long stride, breathing audibly from the effort. Feliciano laughed and walked more slowly. Seeing his uncle in such good humor, Guálinto ventured the question that had been itching inside him since they were in the Goodnam house.

"Uncle," he said, "Where did you meet Don Martín before?"

Feliciano laughed again, stuck his hands up to the thumbs in his coat pockets and said, "It's a long story. About the year 1917 I saved his life, more or less."

"You never told me about that before."

"You never asked, so we're even. Anyway, the *rinches* and some deputies were trying to kill Pete Severski in the saloon. So I went out—"

"Wait, Uncle, wait! You're leaving most of it out. Who was Pete Severski? What saloon? Why did the *rinches* want to kill him?"

"*¡Vamos!*" his uncle said. "If I start telling you about somebody you want to know how he was like down to the color of his shoes."

"But, Uncle, I wasn't there and you were. You think I can guess who everybody was."

"All right, all right. Now listen. After they killed Joe Dashielle—"

"Who was he?"

"The chief of police. He was a Mexican, see?"

"With a name like that?"

"Yes. The police were almost all Mexicans. But they belonged to the Red party, and we ... and the Blues had won the new elections. But the police didn't want to hand in their badges. So old man Poole, he was Keene's man, brought down *rinches* and sheriff's deputies to force them out."

"There must have been some big gun battles," Guálinto said.

"Gun battles? It wasn't a picture show. You'd better get it out of your head, all that trash about standing in the middle of the street and shooting it out. I've seen a lot of men shot, and if any of them were killed in what you might call a gun battle, it was because somebody's plans didn't work out right. That happened in Pete Severski's case, but it was rare. I've seen more men shot in the back than died with their guns in their hands.

"Joe Dashielle was killed while walking up to the bar for a drink. A *rinche* named McAllen did it. He was hiding his gun under his hat when Joe walked in."

"What about the rest of the police?"

"They crossed over to Morelos until things calmed down."

"Were you one of the deputies?"

"No, I wasn't involved in any of that. I was working for Judge Norris at the Danubio Azul. The saloon. But I was telling you about Pete Severski. Pedro was his name but they called him Pete. He was a good friend of mine, even though he was a Red. About the same time Joe was killed, Sheriff Boyer of Costilla county tried to shoot Pete from behind in the Blue Danube saloon. Pete saw him in the mirror and shot first. In haste and pretty low. He hit Boyer in his private parts. Boyer must have been quite a sight running down the street with both hands on his fly! That's what he got for meddling in the affairs of Palo Alto county. And that's why I laugh now when the papers carry stories about how brave Boyer was in the old days."

"But what about Severski?"

"Oh, Pete. Well, the *rinches* and a number of deputies were just outside, backing Boyer up. When the shooting started, everybody in the saloon ran out except for Martín Goodnam. He was too scared to run. I was in the backroom, changing clothes and getting ready to leave. When I heard the commotion I came out in my undershirt. I wasn't wearing a gun, and to tell the truth I didn't know just what I was going to do. There must have been at least fifteen *rinches* and deputies surrounding the place from the outside, pointing their guns through the windows. Pete was backed up between the piano and a beer cask, and he was holding Martín Goodnam in front of him. Martín was really scared, and he kept telling the *rinches*, 'Don't shoot! Don't shoot!' The *rinches* at the windows were weaving their rifles back and forth, looking for a clear shot, and Pete pushed Martín this way and that in front of him, holding his pistol to Martín's head. Martín kept yelling at the *rinches* not to shoot and they were cursing Pete and Martín both.

"I thought I might get Severski out of there alive if I was lucky, so I walked into the saloon from the back, very slowly. They didn't shoot at me, perhaps because they knew I worked there and was a Blue. And anyway, I was in my undershirt and they could see I wasn't wearing a gun. I went over and took Martín by the arm and told him, 'Come on, Martín, I'll get you out of here.' Pete looked at me and I looked at him, and he whispered to Goodnam, 'If they start shooting you're dead.'"

"Martín kept shouting at the *rinches* not to shoot. They didn't because Pete managed to keep behind me and Goodnam until we reached the back door. Then he ran into the dark and over the backyard fence. The *rinches* wanted to kill me then, but the deputies took my side, saying I was just saving the life of another Blue, and Charlie Burns put his arms around me so they couldn't shoot without hitting him, and they got me out of there. Martín Goodnam didn't even say thanks, he was too scared to talk. He looked as if he was going to faint."

Guálinto said, "That was a real fix you got into."

"Yes," Feliciano said pleasantly. "But it looks like it was worth it now. Besides saving Pete Severski's life."

They walked in silence for a while. Then Guálinto said, "What was Don Martín doing at El Danubio Azul anyway? I thought that when it was a *cantina* the only Gringos that went there were soldiers from Fort Jones."

"He was rubbing shoulders with his Mexican friends," Feliciano said. "He has always loved us very, very much."

8

For a few days there was something approximating well-being in the house. Graduation day was approaching, and Guálinto gave as much time as he could on weekday nights and Sunday afternoons to studying for finals. He would not be an honor student, let alone the valedictorian. His grades this last semester precluded that. But the relaxed atmosphere at home more than made up for it. One Friday morning he noticed that María Elena was not in class. Later in the day he heard that she had married the night before and left for California with her husband, not waiting for the last weeks before graduation. She had been failing anyway, but the story was that she had not had time to wait until the end of school. She was in what was known as "an interesting condition." The girls sniggered and the boys smiled knowing smiles at each other. And Guálinto, crushed by the finality of his loss of María Elena, was also embarrassed by the rumors that she had married in haste because she was pregnant. He reddened when somebody mentioned it in his hearing, thinking about Maruca. She should hurry and get married soon, he thought.

Friday night, Saturday, and Sunday morning he was too busy at Rodríguez and Sons to brood about María Elena. He came home Sunday afternoon too tired to feel very much about anything.

His uncle was waiting for him in the kitchen. "Hurry up and eat," he said. "Our neighbor Don Santiago is coming over to talk with us."

"What about?" Guálinto asked as he ate.

"He comes with word from Martín Goodnam, and it is about time. Don Santiago will be here at two o'clock."

Guálinto ate hurriedly and changed clothes. At two sharp Santiago López-Anguera knocked at the door. Feliciano and Guálinto were waiting for him in the living room. After the usual greetings López-Anguera said, "Would you wish to discuss this somewhere else? It is a confidential matter."

"It is a family matter," Feliciano replied. "I would rather talk about it here in my nephew's presence."

"Very well," Santiago said and took a deep breath. "Feliciano, I am your friend and I come to you as your friend, though Martín Goodnam sent me over to see you in my capacity as a lawyer."

"Understood, Santiago," Feliciano said cheerfully. "What arrangements has he made for the marriage?"

Santiago took another, deeper breath. "There will be no marriage," he said.

Feliciano stared at the wall beyond López-Anguera. "No marriage," he said softly, as if talking to himself.

"Feliciano," López-Anguera said, "I hate to be the bearer of such painful news. But perhaps it is just as well that I do it and not some total stranger."

"You are right," Feliciano said calmly, "so please be so good as to tell me."

"Goodnam's son was married Thursday by a justice of the peace. To Onofre Osuna's daughter. Only Goodnam and the girl's parents were present."

"A quiet wedding. That's what that *cabrón* of a Martín said it would be. A quiet wedding."

"The Osuna's were not very happy, but it seems that their daughter was—ah—also ... "

"A stud. A real stud he was. Who would have thought it of that pasty-faced *sanavabiche*."

López-Anguera looked embarrassed.

"And Martín sent you to offer me money."

"Yes."

"And you are advising me to take it."

"No." Santiago looked directly at Feliciano. "I know you better than that."

"Thank you."

"But I would like to give you some advice of my own, if you will allow me."

"Go ahead."

"One has three options in a case like this. The first is making the boy marry the girl. Martín has blocked any move on your part in that direction by having his son marry the Osuna girl."

Feliciano nodded.

"Second, you could take Goodnam to court, which is what most Americans would do. All you would get out of that is money, which Goodnam is willing to give you without going to court and which you do not want. And the scandal of a lawsuit would hurt you and your family more than it would hurt Goodnam politically. He could claim that he would like nothing better than having his son marry a nice Mexican girl like your niece, but unfortunately his son is already married.

Again Feliciano nodded.

"Third would be for you to resort to violence. The boy and his bride have left town and the state. They are somewhere in California, I understand. And Martín wants you to know he has hired two *pistoleros* from outside the county as his bodyguards. They have orders to shoot you if you come anywhere near him." Feliciano made as if to speak, and Santiago raised his hand to stop him. "I know from—ah—a mutual friend that once you were very fast and accurate with a pistol. It is possible that you could kill Martín Goodnam. But you would be killed immediately afterward. What good will that do your family?"

"Thank you," Feliciano said. "Thank you."

López-Anguera rose to leave. They shook hands. "Please consider, Feliciano," López-Anguera said.

"Thank you," Feliciano said. "Thank you."

There followed a nightmarish afternoon, during which Feliciano sat in the kitchen, his hat on his head, a revolver and a bottle on the table beside him. He sat there staring at the pistol and passing his hand over his face. Every once in a while he poured some liquor into a glass and tossed it down his throat. Then he stared at the pistol again. Guálinto and Carmen watched him from outside the door. Behind them, at the door to her bedroom, Maruca wrung her hands and whimpered softly.

Finally their mother came out of her bedroom and into the kitchen, closing the door behind her. She talked softly to Feliciano. He grunted back at her. She kept talking, very fast, her voice low and earnest. At last María opened the door. She was carrying the gun, holding it as she might have held a rattlesnake. She hurried with it into her bedroom, closing the door behind her.

Feliciano remained sitting at the table, filling and emptying his glass and filling it again from the bottle. He shook his head savagely, muttering undistinguishable oaths, and his hat rolled off his head. He leaned down and clawed at the air under the table, failed to locate it and straightened up again, leaving the hat under the table. His gray hair was wet with sweat and plastered to his head. Guálinto came quickly into the kitchen, picked up the hat and put it on his uncle's head. Then he got out of the kitchen as fast as he could. Feliciano took another drink, from the bottle this time. He rose unsteadily, looking very tired, and as pathetic as a drunken old man can look. He put the bottle in his coat pocket and lurched out of the house. A moment later they heard his truck roar as he started it with the throttle wide open. He eased the throttle down and drove away to the farm, where he stayed for a week before coming back to town.

His uncle's behavior depressed Guálinto more than any other thing that had happened to him and his family. It seemed as if everybody was determined to act strangely and shamefully. First Maruca, then his mother, now his uncle. He felt ill at ease even in Carmen's presence. Next day's papers carried a story about the marriage of Buddy Goodnam and María Elena Osuna, and that was another twist of the dagger in his flesh. Gossip took care to spread the circumstances of their hasty marriage. And Maruca's condition could no longer be kept a secret, if it ever was to neighbors like the Gracias across the street, who took care to investigate everything and let the rest of the *barrio* know. The family now bore the full burden of its shame.

At this time a change came over his mother. She seemed to resign herself to the situation and no longer abused Maruca. Soon she was taking care of her with a mother's solicitude. But she did not go out, even to the backyard or her garden. Carmen hung out the clothes to dry and watered the rosebushes. Carmen ran the errands, while Guálinto walked to and from school alone, then went to work and back. At work, no one said anything, but the knowing looks between Chito and Don Crispín enraged him. He no longer went for coffee with La Gata after work on Saturday nights or talked with Paco about music.

At school, Orestes and Elodia made no reference to Maruca, or even mentioned his house or family whenever they talked to him. But he knew that they knew and began to avoid them also. He stayed away from El Colorado and Antonio Prieto and felt extremely lucky that Francisco had gone back to school in Monterrey. If Francisco had been in town he would have come to Guálinto's house some Sunday afternoon on the pretext of visiting his uncle and aunt next door. And the last thing Guálinto wanted was Francisco's sympathy.

A couple of times he woke up in the morning and thought, "It was all a bad dream. I'll get up and everything will be as it has always been." But then he became fully awake and remembered that the nightmare was real. Normalcy in his home had run down like an unwound clock, and life just stumbled along in hazy numbness. He was grateful, even, for the unremitting labor at the Rodríguezes. It kept him from thinking about anything else. And when he came home, mercifully exhausted, he was able to sleep. It was less than six weeks before his graduation from high school.

9

Four blocks from Guálinto's house, on Fourteenth Street, there was a tomblike structure made of concrete with a platform in front. Here an old man in a blue uniform sold ice from the Central plant on the northwest side of town. The hangers-on of the *barrio* liked to gather about the icehouse, which stood on a corner. They sat on the concrete platform and made remarks at the girls when they passed by, and sometimes they drank out of a bottle.

That Sunday evening Guálinto came to buy a piece of ice. In the dusk he did not see the boys on the platform until he was crossing the street. There were three of them, in starched striped shirts with wide cuffs unbuttoned and folded back so the sleeves flapped about between elbow and wrist, in trousers tight around the hips and belled at the bottoms, wide black belts with great buckles. They were rolling a pair of dice on the smooth concrete of the platform, while the man who sold the ice stood watching them indulgently, almost respectfully.

One of the boys was Chucho Vázquez. There were all kinds of stories told about Chucho. He was supposed to keep a list of all the boys and men he had cut up or beaten. He had never been in jail, though. The code of the *barrio*, Guálinto thought, to stand people like Chucho rather than complain to the police. Chucho was rubbing the dice between his hands when Guálinto reached the icehouse. He looked up, a loose-lipped smile on his yellowish face.

"Hello there, boy," he said.

Guálinto looked at Chucho briefly and turned to the iceman. "Five cents worth of ice, please," he said.

Chucho stared for a moment before throwing the dice. The iceman looked tired and sleepy. He took Guálinto's nickel and went into the little office to get a pair of tongs.

When the iceman was gone Chucho again turned to Guálinto and said, "Hey Gómez, have a drink? It's good stuff." He reached under his shirt and took out a small flat bottle of mezcal.

"No," Guálinto said. "I don't want any of your mezcal."

Chucho looked at him in mock surprise. "Okay," he said. "If that's the way you want it, okay."

"Come on, Chucho," said one of the other two. "Throw those dice."

Chucho threw them. "Five," he said. "I'll make it, you sons of seven fathers." He picked up the dice again and rubbed them against his palm. He threw and said, "*Chin*—! I wish I had a car like Buddy Goodnam's."

The other two did not look at the dice. They looked at Guálinto and grinned. Guálinto's neck grew hot but he pretended not to hear. The iceman came out of the office with his tongs, swung open the heavy door into the iceroom and went in, closing the door behind him. Chucho looked at Guálinto and grinned, showing his long, tobacco-stained teeth.

"Yeh," he said, "I sure wish I had a car like Buddy Goodnam's. It has the most wonderful cushions in the world. The girls just cry for them. Oh, boy! Ugh!" And he gave a short, libidinous grunt.

"You—! You—!" Guálinto lunged at him.

Chucho scrambled to his feet on the platform and kicked down at Guálinto, hitting him on the shoulder. Guálinto rushed back to the foot of the platform as Chucho drew a large clasp knife from beneath his shirt. Its shiny handle was as long as his hand. He touched a spring and the blade sprang open. "Step back," he said, "or I'll see what you had for supper."

"Drop that knife!" Guálinto said. "Drop that knife and I'll kill you."

Chucho looked down on him and laughed. "Listen," he said. "Just listen to the kid. I don't want to fight you, boy."

"I'll—I'll break your neck!"

"Listen to the student. Just listen to him. I don't want to fight kids like you, schoolboy. I don't want to, see? Go home to your mama and your big-bellied sister."

Guálinto began to cry, and the three of them laughed.

"He doesn't like it," Chucho said. "He doesn't like to hear about his sister and Buddy Goodnam."

"I'll get you! I'll get you!"

"His sister's too good for guys like us," Chucho said. "She's strictly highsassiety."

The other two guffawed.

"Come down and fight!" Guálinto bellowed.

"Does she dye her hair?" Chucho asked. "Or is it the same color between her legs too. You tell us, Gómez. You ought to know."

The iceman came out with the ice and stared stupidly at Guálinto. Guálinto snatched the ice from him. "I'm going home for a knife," he told Chucho, "and you're going to need yours when I come back!"

"Run along now," Chucho said.

"I'm coming back!"

"Okay, okay. I'll be waiting for you. Run along."

Guálinto hurried home. He could hear their laughter behind him, and he was glad it was growing dark because if he met someone on the street they would not be able to see his face. He thought he would go crazy if he did not hit something and destroy it, so he banged a fist against the ice he was carrying tied to a piece of thin rope. He hit the ice until his knuckles throbbed numbly. It gave him a measure of relief and he was able to reach home without crying openly in the street.

The kitchen was dark as it often was these days. He carried the ice around the back and put it in the icebox as silently as he could. Then he felt about in a drawer until he found a sharp, pointed knife his mother used to quarter chickens. He took it into his room and wrapped a piece of cardboard around the blade, securing it with some rubber bands. He stuck the knife in his belt and put on his leather jacket to hide it. Then he went out again.

The pain and the rage, and a cold lump of fear beneath them, alternately drove him forward, then held him back, then drove him on again, until he was once more in front of the icehouse, standing there in a dull sort of amazement, as if suddenly aware of where he was and what he intended to do. The place was dark. There was no one there. The fear underneath surfaced in joyous little jumps. Chucho had not waited! He had run away.

He thought of his study table, of the study lamp bright and warm upon his forehead. Then he looked at the bare concrete platform and again saw Chucho's slack-faced smile, his long yellow teeth. He was not going back home! Instead he plunged into the black streets beyond the icehouse, seeking Chucho in his own haunts—through the alleys, around the dark corners, into places where he had never been, until so much walking burned the last of his anger out.

"Damn coward!" he said under his breath. I waited half the night for him, he would say. I walked up and down those streets looking for him, and the coward never showed up. His imaginary audience was vague and faceless at first, but as he let his fancy go he began to see among his listeners people he knew: his mother, his sisters, his uncle—. That jerked him back to where he really was. What had he been about to do, he asked himself? He shuddered and started quickly home. He walked fast for a block before he realized he wasn't sure just where he was in this part of the *barrio*. He looked at the stars but they told him nothing. Then he saw a brightness in the sky above a dark rooftop. The moon. He turned and walked in the opposite direction, down a street he had not traveled before, and that was how he ran into the *baile*.

Down a side street he heard the music, and he stopped. Guálinto had never been to a *baile* because neither his uncle nor his mother approved of them. He had always wanted to see what one was like. Not that he thought he would like it, but he would just take a look and go away. He squared his shoulders under his leather jacket and plunged into the side street.

The dance was at somebody's house. All the doors and windows were wide open, and there was a bright gasoline lantern hanging from the ceiling of the large, unpainted room, empty except for the row of chairs along the walls. Here the girls sat, all dressed up in their pink, yellow, and light-blue organdies. The music had stopped as Guálinto came up, and the men had come outside to drink and start arguments over who was dancing with whom. One of them was not in an arguing mood. He leaned against the fence and vomited. The sight turned Guálinto sick with disgust. He was about to pass on but decided he might as well look, so he stopped near the gate.

In a corner, beneath the shelf that served as an altar for the Virgin of Guadalupe, were the musicians, a guitar player and an accordionist. They sat on stiff-backed chairs, a bottle on the floor between them. Suddenly the accordionist picked up his instrument and began to play. The guitar player started after him, but the accordionist was already half through one chorus before the guitarist could get into position. The music was a fast, shrieking polka, played so fast that the tune was barely recognizable. The men streamed in and took the girls out on the floor, where they danced furiously in a hop-step-skip fashion. The little house trembled on its slender foundations to the scraping and stamping.

Guálinto was left alone on the sidewalk with the man who had become sick, and who now was peacefully asleep in his own vomit. He lay full length on the dirt sidewalk, snoring. Guálinto was about to leave when another man came out of the dark from the alley behind the house. He was a middle-aged man and he was half-drunk.

"Hello there," the man said. "Why don't you go inside and dance?"

"Oh, I'm not invited," Guálinto said.

The man put his arm about Guálinto's shoulders. There was a strong unwashed smell about him, a pungent garlicky smell. "You don't have to be invited," the man said. "Know who I am? I'm the man of the house. That's my daughter over there, dancing in the blue dress. Pretty, isn't she?"

"Yes," Guálinto said, "she sure is pretty."

"Fifteen years old today," the man said, blowing his liquor-rotten breath in Guálinto's face. "My youngest, and the best daughter I ever had. Such a little housewife you never saw. She can cook better than her old lady." He looked meaningfully at Guálinto and sighed. "Oh, well, it won't be long before she gets married. If she don't start living with some man. These girls of today." He shook his head sadly. "Why don't you go in and dance?"

"I—I can't dance," Guálinto said, shrugging off the man's arm. "I'd rather just look."

"Well go ahead and look, son," the man said. "Look all you want to. It's my daughter's birthday and you can look all you want to." He staggered through the gate and around the house.

Guálinto looked in at the daughter, who had stopped dancing now and stood spread-legged in the middle of the floor, talking to her partner, a wasted-looking fellow whose coat didn't match his trousers. She wore her hair in a pompadour and she was pretty. Very dark but very pretty, in a way quite different from María Elena's white-skinned beauty. As she talked she jerked her head now to one side, now to the other, and the glittering silver pendants on her earrings trembled and flashed against her cheeks.

Pretty, but not for him, he thought. He thrust his hands in his pockets and walked away. And at the mouth of the alley he met Chucho Vázquez.

Chucho was dressed for a party, suit and all. He stopped and Guálinto stopped too, his heart pounding. With a quick movement Chucho unbuttoned his double-breasted coat and took it off. Then he stepped cautiously backward, peering through the half-light coming from the lantern at the dance, peering at Guálinto and wrapping his coat over his left arm.

Guálinto took off his leather jacket and wrapped it around his left arm too, feeling for the knife under his belt. Chucho sprang open his knife with a loud click. Guálinto heard it distinctly above the sound of his own breathing.

Chucho looked at him, a strange half-smirk on his face. Guálinto stared back, twisting his jacket about his left forearm with the hand that held the knife, in imitation of Chucho. A few yards away the accordion began another polka with a sudden, ear-piercing shriek. Guálinto started violently and Chucho sprang back.

Almost in the same movement Chucho leaped forward and slashed at Guálinto's neck. Guálinto raised his arm and felt the knife strike his leather jacket. He ripped at Chucho's shirt front as Chucho sprang back again, but he did not follow him. Chucho watched him cannily, waiting, but Guálinto did not attack. He didn't know how.

Chucho began to feint and circle, using his long legs and reach to advantage, making short, false rushes that threw Guálinto off balance. Guálinto had to content himself with wheeling about to keep Chucho in front of him, raising his jacket-covered arm again and again against the dull-gleaming blade that was ever before his face, and slashing back where Chucho had been but no longer was.

After a while he no longer struck out when Chucho feinted. His arm was tiring. He had discovered that Chucho would come near, then leap backward without striking, to make Guálinto attack. Chucho feinted again and Guálinto half-raised his aching arm. Then Chucho moved in. One of his long legs came up, and Guálinto grunted as Chucho's foot slammed into his belly, hurling him against the board fence behind him. His hands went down to his stomach, and at the same instant he saw Chucho's knife coming at his throat. He jerked up his arm. It hit Chucho's hand and threw it upwards. He felt the knife tearing the skin along his jaw up to his temple.

He pushed at Chucho with his knee in panic-striken fury, and Chucho stumbled backward, falling on his back on the hard-packed ground. His knife clattered out of his hand as Guálinto, half-blinded by his own blood, threw himself upon him. Chucho tried to get up. Guálinto beat him back. He struck out with his knife, sinking it deep into the coat wrapped about Chucho's arm. For the moment Guálinto did not realize that it was nothing but cloth he had pierced, and he fell on top of Chucho, snarling savage, triumphant curses as he gouged the knife round and round in the cloth. Then they rolled over and Chucho sprang away.

Guálinto got to his knees to find Chucho standing over him, looking wildly about. He bunched his legs under him, one hand on the ground, the other holding the knife rigid in front of him. Then he lunged upward at Chucho's middle, his knife held like a sword, his whole body in the thrust. The knife hit Chucho's belly with a thud. Chucho screamed and hugged himself. He turned and ran down the alley, dropping his coat as he ran. The other end of the alley opened into a clump of brush, and Guálinto stopped when he heard the breaking of branches as Chucho crashed his way through, cursing and moaning. He unwrapped his jacket from his arm and returned to the street.

The street was full of people. It seemed that everyone but the musicians had left the *baile* and gathered, men and women, around Guálinto as he came out of the alley.

"Did you see that Chucho?" someone said.

"And did I!"

"I stood right here and saw it all."

" ... and this kid—"

"—wearing a new suit."

"It's in the way you hold the knife as you—"

"No, no! It's in the thrust."

"—nothing like it."

"Serves the bastard right."

"—and then he hit—"

"Ha! Did you see him run?"

They crowded about him, laughing, whooping and chattering all at once. He had never seen so many happy, friendly people. They patted him on the back. They dusted his clothes for him. One of them took the knife, cleaned it, and returned it to him. Another helped him with his jacket.

Out of the warm smother of talk came a woman's voice like a breath of cold. "Is he dead?"

"I—I don't know," Guálinto said.

"Let somebody else worry about that," said the man who had invited Guálinto to dance. "Mercedes!" he bawled. "His face is cut!"

The pretty girl in blue organdie came up to Guálinto. "He *is* hurt," she said. "The poor thing." She held his head against her with one hand and pressed her handkerchief to his face with the other. Her breasts were firm against his cheek, and heavily scented.

"It isn't bad," Guálinto said. "Just a scratch, not bad at all." She was pressing him very close to her. He turned his eyes this way and that as she stroked his face, afraid someone might notice how close they were to each other. Nobody seemed to notice or to care. Everyone was laughing at a man who had just said that now the *baile* was a success, because no *baile* was a success without at least one cutting.

Mercedes' father came up with a bottle and said, "Have a drink of this. It's good for lockjaw." He laughed loudly at his own joke.

Guálinto hesitated, and Mercedes let him go and said, "Go ahead. Don't be bashful."

He drank a bit of the mezcal, struggling hard not to choke. It tasted like something that had begun to rot and then had caught fire. But once down it did not feel bad at all. It made his stomach feel warm and cozy and exceedingly in its right place. And he liked these people, their gaiety and noise, the friendly way they treated him.

"Let's go back to the house," said someone in the crowd. "Let's go before the law comes poking its nose around here."

"The law?" said Guálinto, suddenly alarmed.

"Don't you worry," Mercedes' father said. "No canaries in this crowd."

"He's not afraid we'll sing, Papa," Mercedes said, moving close to Guálinto again. "Are you, dear?"

Her perfume was heavy and sweet, too sweet. But underneath it, when his face had been against her breasts. Had he imagined it? She leaned against him now, and there it was again, rising through the blanket of scent, a naked female smell that set his blood pounding. Then it seemed to drain away from him, leaving him weak and spent.

"Here!" someone said. "Give him another drink. The poor fellow's tired."

He took the proffered bottle and drank. He drank again. It didn't taste so bad, really, not at all bad. The feeling of warm coziness returned.

They drifted back toward the house, walking slowly to enjoy the cool of the night. The breeze was pleasant on Guálinto's hot face. He felt snug and light-headed, walking along beside Mercedes, their arms brushing against each other as they walked. She seized his hand and squeezed it in hers, a firm cool hand. An almost uncontrollable surge of desire took hold of him.

"I must go home now," he said.

"Home?" Mercedes' father said. "Don't you like us?"

"Of course I like you," he said, smiling at Mercedes.

"You've got to come in and dance," she coaxed.

"But I can't dance."

"I'll teach you how," Mercedes said, slipping her arm around him.

He fancied he could smell her again beneath her perfume, and it was like having her naked beside him. "The way I am?" he said, slipping away from her arm and standing before her to show her the way he was.

"I'll wash your face," she said. "And the jacket is all right. Come in party clothes some other time."

"I really must go," he said.

"He's got a girl, Mercedes," one of the crowd said loudly.

They had reached the gate to the house, and she stopped with her hand upon it. She smiled at him, her dark face confident beneath its cocky pompadour.

"No, it's not a girl," he said.

She smiled at him.

"It's—. It's—oh, well. The law knows about me. I've been in trouble before. If they come snooping around and find me here ... "

"Then he'd better go, Mercedes," her father said, almost soberly. "But come back again, ah ... What is your grace?"

"Guálinto."

"Guálinto?" the old man said. "Never heard the name before."

"It's an Indian name."

"Aztec," said a man in spectacles. "Like Guatémoc. Am I right?"

"Yes," Guálinto said eagerly, "you're right."

"Well, come back, Guálinto. You are always welcome here. My house is your house."

In the old man's mouth the old saying had a noble sound. He seemed to grow, and the outlines of his body quivered as if he were an image in water. Guálinto put a hand on the fence to steady himself. "I must go," he said, "but I will come back."

Mercedes pressed his other hand. "I'll be waiting for you," she said.

"I'll come back," he repeated.

He would go back, and then he could be alone with her. He told himself that as he walked slowly down the middle of the dark street, breathing deep of the cool night air. He would. The air was heavy with the scent of flowers. He stopped abruptly. It was not flowers but the scent of her perfume, clinging to his clothes and face. And underneath the perfume he smelled, or remembered perhaps, the thin, strong sexual smell of her. Her acrid, naked smell. He felt desire rise in him again. His blood pounded in his ears as sensual images rose like vapors before him. Strange pictures filling the empty spaces of his loneliness. He would go back.

When he got home everybody was asleep. He let himself in through the back door and went directly to the bathroom to wash his face. The cut on his cheek had been but a scratch. He put some iodine on it and covered it with a piece of plaster tape. With things like they were at the house, no one would ask about the tape tomorrow, and if they did he just wouldn't answer. There were some nicks on his leather jacket and two small tears. The few spots of blood on his shirt collar would look like brown stains from the sap of a banana bush by tomorrow. All in all, things had come out pretty well for him.

He sneaked into bed, triumphant, but found it hard to go to sleep. Yes, he would go back to her. These were his people, the real people he belonged with. His place was among them, not the "Spaniards" like the Osunas. He would marry Mercedes and live on the farm. He would go back. Tomorrow night he would go back. He never did.

10

Guálinto lived a few anxious days. Every time there was a knock on the door of his house he started. When he met a man that looked like a policeman or a deputy sheriff on the street he crossed to the other side, and if he saw the man when he was working behind the counter at Rodríguez and Sons, he would duck under the counter as if he was getting something there, or he would scurry to the storeroom under any other excuse. He was aware that the Rodríguezes knew about Maruca, but they had the decency not to talk about it in front of him. Nobody had talked at the store about a boy being knifed to death, so after a few days Guálinto took heart. He knew that if Chucho had died, the

Rodríguezes would have known about it soon after.

Rodríguez and Sons was the clearing house for all types of gossip about what went on in Jonesville-on-the-Grande. Old Don Crispín was the best informed man in the *barrio*. He got into conversation with every *ranchero* that came in from the country, every housewife that passed by and bought a bar of soap. He even quizzed the children that came to buy candy, asking them personal questions about their families and what went on in their houses. So when no news of Chucho Vázquez's death came to Rodríguez and Sons, Guálinto was pretty sure Chucho was alive.

Finally the news arrived. An old woman that came to buy at the Rodríguezes all the way from the Diamante *barrio* told how a boy named Chucho had been wounded in a knife fight a few days before. "These boys!" she said. "They don't mind if they kill each other." No, she said to Don Crispín's question, it was not serious. He had been wounded in the belly but it had just been a gash. The big belt buckle he wore had made the knife glance away, or he would have been disemboweled.

"Who did it?" Chito asked. He was as keen on gossip as his father was.

"They say it was a boy named Gómez," the old woman said.

Chito turned to Guálinto, who was weighing out a pound of rice beside him. "It wasn't you, Guálinto, was it?" he said playfully.

Guálinto reddened and looked fixedly at the scales, and Chito and Don Crispín laughed. The side of Guálinto's face where Chucho's knife-point had torn his skin was away from the old woman, and he hoped Chito would not bring it into the conversation. It still was painted over with iodine but it was scabbed over. He had told them at the store that he had scratched his face with a sharp loose wire on his mother's clothes-lines, and the Rodríguezes had laughed at his awkwardness. Chito said, "I'm sure it couldn't have been this Gómez here. He's not a brawler."

"Well, I'm sure glad you're not mixed in it, sonny," the old woman said. "That Chucho is very mad, and he says he's going to kill the boy next time he sees him. He says the boy cut him when he wasn't looking. Oh, these young people." She turned to Don Crispín. "They're not afraid of death or prison."

After that Guálinto got into the habit of carrying the knife in his belt underneath his shirt at all times, even when he went to school. He made the knife a leather scabbard and tipped it with a pop bottle cap beaten flat and shaped around the tip with a pair of pliers. He did this after he almost stuck himself in the groin when he bent over to pick up a sack of grain in the store. And he took to wearing it under his hip pocket. With the knife in its metal-tipped scabbard he felt safer, but he always walked the streets on the alert. At home he secretly honed the knife to a razor sharpness. On Sunday afternoons he would go into the banana grove, his childhood refuge, and practice thrusts with the knife and defensive footwork. El Colorado found him there when Guálinto was practicing a straight-arm thrust on a banana stalk.

"Hey," El Colorado said, "leave the poor thing alone."

Guálinto reddened and tried to hide the knife behind his back. "Hello," he said shamefacedly.

"What are you doing? Studying to be a second Gaona?"

"Practicing, just practicing. Just had this knife and decided to practice using it. Might come in handy some day."

El Colorado regarded Guálinto intently. "I hear you was the one who knifed Chucho Vázquez."

Guálinto took out his handkerchief and wiped absently at the blade. "Yeah," he said, "it was me."

"And now you're practicing. What for? Are you going to hunt him down and finish the job?"

"From what I've heard he's the one who's looking for me."

"Him? Where did you hear that damn foolishness?"

"An old lady who came by the Rodríguez store."

"That's old women's gossip. Everyone in the *barrio* knows that Chucho's scared to death of you. If he met you on the street now he would go hide some place."

"Perhaps. But there might be others."

"Others?" echoed El Colorado. "Look man, don't fight. Don't get mad if they start hinting about it. It won't do any good." Then, when Guálinto feigned ignorance. "Ah, what's the use of not talking about it? It's not your fault. And don't get mad. They'll just pour it on you."

Guálinto wiped silently at the knife blade.

"What's the use of killing a guy and getting sent to the pen?" El Colorado said. "It won't help your family at all. And the next time it might be you who gets a knife in the guts."

Guálinto still didn't answer. It was the first time El Colorado had come by the house since Maruca's condition had become known. Now that he showed up so unexpectedly, Guálinto did not know what to say. He continued to wipe stupidly at the blade.

"Say, that stuff stains, don't it?" El Colorado said.

Guálinto hastily took the handkerchief away from the blade, rolled it up into a ball and put it into his pocket. "Sure does," he muttered. "I'm a damn fool."

They walked away from the banana grove into the hackberry trees behind the Gómez yard and sat down on a fallen tree trunk. "What are you going to do when you finish school?" El Colorado asked. "Will you keep working at the Rodríguez store until you get enough money to go to college?"

"Save money working for old Don Crispín? Don't make me laugh. I'm making two dollars a week now. If I work fulltime on weekdays I'll get four."

"So what are you going to do?"

"Don't know. Don't give a damn, really. Quit the grocery store and go live on my uncle's farm, I guess."

"What's the good of that? You oughta look for a better job, one that pays enough for you to help your family out and still save something for college later on. Maybe I can get you something where I work. Driving a truck isn't your kind of work, but it's a beginning."

"There's something you don't know, Colorado. I didn't know it either until last Christmas, when the bank went broke. My uncle has been saving for my college education since before I could walk. He has plenty to send me to college if I want to go. And he bought a good piece of land last January and is doing pretty well. Not much cash yet, but we have plenty to eat."

"He didn't have it in the Gringo bank," El Colorado said.

"No."

"So you don't need the money but you're still killing yourself working for those slave drivers and letting your grades go to hell. You must like to hurt yourself just for the hell of it. Why did you start working at that grocery for, anyway?"

Guálinto couldn't bring himself to talk about his guilty feelings toward his uncle, so he answered with a question. "Why do you want for me to go to college so much, anyway?"

"Because we will need you here in Jonesville. Men like you and Orestes and me and Antonio Prieto. Our people will need us here. It's time we quit being driven like sheep by the Gringos. And you are the one who can be our point man."

"What about Orestes? He's going to college."

"That's true, but you're the man we'll need most. Remember how you used to argue with the teachers in school?"

"Just getting rid of some of the anger inside me."

"That's just it. You're full of anger inside. All of us are, but you can speak out about it. You have that gift. You can get people to listen."

Guálinto did not answer.

"Don't throw it all away," El Colorado insisted.

"I don't want to go to school anymore. I don't want to go downtown even. I just don't want to see people."

"Look. Just because your family's having some trouble the world's not going to end, and you don't have to crawl into a hole and die. My family's had its troubles too, and look at me. You don't see me hiding nowhere. Why, my old man used to get drunk and beat my old lady almost every Saturday night. That's trouble. Hell, you don't know what trouble is."

He stopped and looked sideways at Guálinto. "Did you know," he said, "that one of my sisters dances at La Calandria?"

Guálinto raised his head and looked his unbelief.

"Sure," El Colorado said, very gravely and sadly, "she does. She had her trouble so the old lady calls her a whore and runs her out of the house. So what does she do? She becomes a whore, that's what. Pretty soon the old woman is sorry and wants her back. But what does the wench say? Hell no! She likes it fine, living that kind of life. See? That's what comes from making a big fuss about things like that. But does that get me down? Do I leave town?"

"Dammit, Colorado. You don't understand. In our case it's different."

"How?"

"Well, such a thing can happen to you and it doesn't mean much to you. But to me it means a lot, don't you see? Oh, I don't mean we're better than you or anything like that. But you're tough, not sensitive like me. You don't feel things the same way."

El Colorado's mouth twitched. He nodded his head in a slight rocking motion. "I don't feel things," he said. "I don't feel things. Do you think that when I was a kid and my old man beat me half to death because I saw him with a whore it didn't hurt? Do you think that when us kids had nothing to eat, I wasn't hungry? And when I used to fight with tough kids twice my size for the nickels they threw in front of the church at christenings so I could buy a loaf of bread maybe for me and my mama and the smaller kids. What do you think came out of my nose when they socked it? Strawberry soda? It was blood, just like yours!"

"I'm sorry, Colorado. I didn't mean it that way."

"Listen," El Colorado said, "I've crouched in a corner and watched my father beat my mother and my mother try to beat back till the police came and dragged the old man away. It made me just as ashamed to have it happen as it could have made you. When I was ten, my father beat me with a buggy whip because I saw him enter a saloon with a whore. And when I was seven my mother gave me the whipping of my life because I spilled a half-cup of rice that was all we had to eat that day. When I was six my eldest sister, who was then eight years old, would stir a little sugar in a cup and give it to us four smaller kids for our supper. And all five of us would climb into the only bed we had, and we'd shiver and hug each other and try to sleep until midnight when our mama would come home from the Gringo's house where she worked.

We'd hope she'd bring home some leavings from the supper table. The trouble with you is that you've had it too easy.

"You went to school because your mother and your uncle sent you. I went to school because I wanted to do something for my mother when I got older. When the going got tough I didn't run away. I kept going to school. My face was dirty and my hair was full of lice the first time I was in Miss Cornelia's class. She gave me hell and sent me home. Sometimes my pants were so old they broke open all of a sudden and I'd go around with my ass half-bare till four o'clock. Do you think I didn't feel that?

"So I learned to wash and delouse myself. I sewed the seat of my own pants and I went to school without breakfast if I had to. But I stuck to it. I failed again and again till I almost grew up to be a man and I still was in school. Evenings I worked, just like you're doing now. Meanwhile I saw one of my sisters become a whore, while the other two slaved in Gringo houses like my mother did. My younger brother was sent to the reformatory for stealing a bike. He had always wanted a bike, and my old man couldn't get him one. My father is now a doddery old fool from too much cheap mezcal and my mother was taking in washing to make up for what little he used to bring home after spending all of his wages on women and drink. That's when I quit school, so she wouldn't have to do that.

"What do you think all that makes me feel like? Laughing? Oh, I'm always joking and acting dumber than I really am, but I'm not laughing inside. And after going through all that for the sake of going to school I barely reach junior high and then I have to drop out. And what have I been doing since then? Crying? I'm working and I'm gonna study nights. Sometimes I get to thinking and I say to myself, 'Who the hell am I? Just a poor damn Mexican that's worth less than a dog in this cursed country. I won't ever get nowhere, I don't have a chance, I was born behind the eight-ball, that's all there is to it.' And it makes me feel very sad. But by God, it isn't very many times I feel that way. I'm gonna get my high school by studying nights. And then I'll go to the Jonesville business college and become a real accountant, not just an assistant bookkeeper. How I wish I had half a chance to go to the University. Even if I had to scrub every damn floor and sweep every sidewalk and polish every stinking spittoon in Austin.

"What if my father don't know how to read? I know how, don't I? What if my mother don't even know what an accountant is? I know what an accountant is, and I want to be one. And I'm going to be one, whatever it costs me. I'll show these bastards!"

He stopped, exhausted and hoarse from the longest speech he had ever made to anyone in his life, and he looked at Guálinto with a timid expression on his big, freckle-splotched face as if the baring of these inner thoughts of his had somehow made him vulnerable. Guálinto looked at him admiringly The red-head was a better man than himself. "He could really have done something great," he thought. "He's the kind of guy I should have been." He tried to say it but the words stuck in his throat. Instead he said, "You're a fighter, I'm a coward."

"No," El Colorado said, softly now, "you're not a coward. You just need to learn how to fight back."

"I don't think I'll ever learn. I hurt too easily."

"All of us hurt. But the first rule you must learn is not to let the other guy know you're hurt when he gets a good lick. If you do, he'll keep hitting you in the same spot."

They lapsed into a strained, self-conscious silence, ashamed of having bared their feelings to each other. For a long while they sat until they felt the silence soften up and mellow again.

Finally El Colorado said, "I'm going to look for Chucho Vázquez and beat the hell out of him. He won't pull no knife on me."

"Don't do that," Guálinto said quietly.

El Colorado smiled. "Okay. But don't go hunting for him. There's no use in looking for *that* kind of a fight."

"I won't. I'll just carry this knife for a few more days just in case. There's a certain person I'd much rather use it on. I'd like to stick it into her pretty white throat and then saw her windpipe and break it backwards like they do to a *cabrito*."

"Why don't you just forget her? I bet she has more to do with you not wanting to go to college than anything else."

"I'll never forget her as long as I live. How can I ever love another after having loved her?"

El Colorado smiled faintly. "You will, in time. Time is the best of friends."

"I can't understand how she could have changed so much in so short a time."

"She didn't change. She was just stringing you along. I was sure of that from the very beginning."

"If you were so sure, why didn't you ever tell me?"

"You wouldn't have believed me," El Colorado said, his eyes on the ground between his outstretched legs. Again they were talking with their faces averted. "You would've got mad and maybe we wouldn't have been friends anymore."

"But I wouldn't have got mad at you, Colorado, just for telling me what you think. I've always trusted you. You always tell me when you think I'm doing something wrong."

"Yeh, but this time it was different. People do funny things when they're all sexed up." Guálinto flushed and thought of telling El Colorado he hadn't been all sexed up, that the love he had felt for María Elena was of a different kind. But he knew the red-head wouldn't believe him. "You've seen a dog go after a bitch," El Colorado continued. "He's ready to bite his master if he's bothered. There's things where friendship don't count."

Guálinto wished El Colorado would change the subject, but El Colorado went on. "I knew right from the start that she was out to use you for her grades. She was out for what you knew, not for what you were. A woman is always out for something when she goes after a man. Most of the time it's money, but it can also be something money will buy or something that'll get her money or will show her up pretty nice. That's why a dame wants money, really. It's not because she cares to be rich of itself but because she wants to show off. The Osuna girl also wanted to show off. How smart she was. And that's why she needed you. She wouldn't have given you a second look if you hadn't been first in the class."

Guálinto winced. "She's not really that bad. If I hadn't talked to her the way I did—"

"Don't kid yourself, Guálinto. She's a rich dame, and good looking. She could get any man she wanted. You, you're all right, but you're just a guy, know what I mean? You're bright in school and a regular guy too. But that don't count with women. All the time, she was going around with that Goodnam bastard behind your back."

"That son-of-a-bitch!" Guálinto cried. "I'd like to blast his mother! I'd like to cut him into little pieces."

"What can you expect from a Gringo?"

"I'd like to kill them all, all of them!"

"I feel the same way," El Colorado said, "even if my grandfather was one of them."

"Your grandfather?"

"Where do you think I got this red hair? He was an Irishman, though, and they're not real Gringos. Good Catholics, all of them. But he went away before my father was born. Never married my grandmother. She didn't even know how to pronounce his name. My father took his mother's name, Alvarado. And my mother named me Juan José, so that's my full name, Juan José Alvarado."

They didn't speak for some time, each of them sunk in his own gloomy thoughts. Finally Guálinto said, "Don't you believe in love at all, Colorado?"

"Nah. There's no such thing as love. That's what my mother says, and I think she's right. She's been married twenty-five years and she ought to know."

"Haven't you ever fallen for a girl, ever?"

"Have you ever seen me with one?"

"No. That's why I ask."

"I've never wanted a girl except for one thing, and girls won't give it to me. They want marriage, that's what they want. But hell, I don't need girls for that. That's what the district is for over on the other side of the river."

"Oh."

"Have you been with a woman yet?"

Guálinto shook his head and looked down. "No," he said.

"That's what's the matter with you, then," El Colorado said. "Man, it isn't healthy to stay away from women all your life. How old are you? Eighteen? Hell, I started going over there when I was sixteen. Going too often is bad, too, but not going at all is worse. It's just as necessary as moving your bowels. You've got all those poisons inside all this time, burning you up. You've got to get rid of them from time to time or you'll get sick. What do you say we go across tonight?"

"Not tonight. I can't make it tonight."

El Colorado put his hand in his pocket. "After I got paid last night I got into a crap game and won. I'm flush."

"It isn't the money, Colorado. I got to study. Final exams are coming soon, and I have little enough time to study. If I don't pass them I won't graduate."

"All right. Then we'll make it some other Sunday night, but don't worry about the money. I'll save this wad I won."

"Listen. I've let you pay my way for a lot of things. But I'll be damned if I let you treat me to that."

"Why not? You buy it, just like anything else."

"Anyway, I'd rather not."

"All right. Have it your way."

El Colorado left and Guálinto went inside to study. It was getting closer and closer to the end of the school year, and he still wasn't sure whether he would get his diploma or not. Already his mind was on many other things. María Elena, the red-light district in Morelos. He would not study much that night.

11

The following Monday Guálinto told the Rodríguezes he could work only until eight that night because he needed more time to study. In a rare fit of generosity they let him go at seven. He had supper, washed and changed, and went to a late show instead. When he came out of the movie it was almost midnight, and the light mist of earlier in the evening had become a drizzle. Sunshine in February, winter in April, summer and winter on the same day. That morning it had been oppressively hot, now it was almost cold. So much for the Golden Delta, where it's always sunny and the gentle breezes blow. Tomorrow it would be clear again, the wind would stop blowing, and it would be hot again. At least, he hoped so. He hugged his raincoat closer to his body.

A heavy rain would be disastrous for the vegetables that were maturing on his uncle's farm by the river. Especially the tomatoes. They got bloated with too much rain and lost their taste. Oh, God, he thought, don't let those vegetables be ruined by too much rain, and let there be a good market for them. He grinned. In times like these there should be a God. If the crops were good perhaps he could persuade his uncle to let him become a farmer. He didn't want to go to college, and he was tired of being a slave at Rodríguez and Sons, Groceries. Except for Paco, he had no use for the Rodríguezes. Chito he could not stand at all. If only Chito would die all of a sudden, then it might not be so bad working for the Rodríguezes.

But at four dollars a week? That was what La Gata was paid for about 130 hours. Something like three cents an hour. Even the most anti-Mexican Gringo paid better than that. When there was work. But it was not good to wish for a person's death, even if it was somebody like Chito. Anyway, it would be much nicer working on the farm with Juan Rubio and Don José. Since he was in grammar school Guálinto loved to come to his uncle's farm. He liked to squat at the end of a plowed furrow and look down its straight, beautiful length. He would scoop up a handful of the rich, black earth and let it run between his fingers. His Uncle Feliciano did not own the land then. He rented it from an Anglo who now lived in California. Once he had told his uncle, "I wish it were our land."

His uncle had answered with a roughness that surprised him. "I don't care whose land it is," he said. Then, more gently, "As long as I can farm it, it doesn't matter."

Now his uncle owned that land and more, much more. But he did not want Guálinto to be a farmer. Finish school and go to college, be somebody so you can help your people. That was all he ever heard. Guálinto shivered under his raincoat. It was the sort of night to be sitting in front of a wood fire in the kitchen of his uncle's farm. Or even better yet, to be buried in soft bedclothes warmed by naked female flesh. It was on nights like these that he longed for a woman. As a matter of course, his thoughts went to the actress he had just seen in the movies. He remembered the shape of her buttocks as she turned and walked away with her back to the camera. God, what beautiful women there were in the movies! He made up his mind to go with El Colorado to the whores in Morelos next Sunday. That other kind of women, he wondered how they were like and the thought made him more lascivious still. El Colorado went to them whenever he felt his body required it and thought nothing about it. They weren't much, he said. But then, El Colorado did not believe in love.

His thoughts went back to the movie he had just seen. Good thing it had not been a musical comedy; he didn't like those very much. He wondered why Anglos thought so much of them. Must be something wrong with them. Childish songs and unfunny jokes. And those nightmares of legs and thighs and torsos they put on the screen, he never could understand or like them. Looking at one woman was much better than watching a couple of dozen. All those sexual fireworks churning around made him dizzy and disgusted. Perhaps it was part of their religion, he thought. Looking at one half-naked woman was immoral, but watching twenty or thirty of them was not. Anglos had funny ideas like that. Anyway, he was not particularly excited watching all those women with their frozen smiles cavorting around on the screen. He smiled. If he told El Colorado, the redhead would think he was a pansy or something.

Before he knew it he had reached the corner where he turned into the Dos Veintidós. He stayed on the right-hand sidewalk, stooping under the low-hanging branches of the willows that grew in some of the front yards. The street was chill and lonely in the rain, not even the dogs came out to bark. Ahead of him he thought he saw a shadow huddled against somebody's fence. He looked again and the shadow moved. It came toward him, pretty close to the ground, in a sort of crouch. A pistol barrel gleamed in the half light. Chucho! Chucho was waiting for him! He leaped back and pawed futilely at his raincoat, panic clutching at his throat. He had forgotten to carry his knife that night.

He retreated, walking backwards, slipped on the wet grass and fell on one knee. The shadow was upon him now. "Give me your coat," the

shadow said in a quavering whisper. "Hurry it up, and don't make any
noise." Guálinto's right hand was resting on the grass beside his knee.
As he moved to comply, his hand hit a compact, heavy object. In one
quick movement he clutched the brick and hurled it where the shadow's
head ought to be. The brick landed with a thud, the gun went off with a
stunning boom, and he felt a sharp jerk at his raincoat. A moment later
he was on his feet, running, stumbling, slipping; then he stopped when
he heard the voices of neighbors awakened by the shot.

He turned and looked at the man with the gun. He was lying very
still. Lights began to go on in the houses along the sidewalk. Guálinto
went up cautiously to the man, who was lying on his back, his head
twisted sideways. The gun was a few inches from his half-open hand.
Guálinto pushed the gun gingerly with his foot, farther away from the
man's hand, just as people started coming out of the houses nearby. A
man with a leather jacket over his undershirt was holding a lantern at
arm's length. "*¿Qué fue?*" he asked. "What was it?"

"A—a man," stammered Guálinto.

Leather Jacket turned the light on the fallen figure, and Guálinto
moved closer to look at his face. It was not Chucho Vázquez, he already
knew that. It was an older man, an old man in truth, but with a shrunken
childish face and a very small body. He was dressed in trousers and a
thin white shirt which was soaked and sticking to his thin ribs. Though
unconscious, he was shivering and shuddering. His head was bloody
and beginning to swell where the brick had hit him.

"Are you hurt?" the man with the lantern asked. Guálinto became
aware of the smell of gunpowder and of a hole in his raincoat. He put
his hand inside and it felt damp. He leaned against the fence; then the
world became a kind of black merry-go-around.

He came to with a burning taste in his throat. Mezcal. He was
helped to his feet as the police were arriving. If they noticed the smell
of the liquor they said nothing about it. An ambulance drove up and
took the unconscious man away, along with a police guard. Guálinto
was taken to the police station over the market place, where a doctor
bandaged the bullet graze on his ribs and kidded him for fainting. The
police asked a lot of questions and then Mac, the chief, told him, "You
may get a reward, boy. That's Arnulfo Miranda that we've been looking for, several days now. If it hadn't been for you he'd be in Mexico by
now. But you took a big chance. He's a mean one, stabbed a guard and
took away his gun." Guálinto hoped he wasn't kidding, like the doctor.

He had coffee with the chief of police in Jonesville's all-night restaurant, which was on the first floor of the market place, just below the police station. There were only a couple of night owls in the place when
Guálinto sat down with the chief. He wished it would have been day-

time, during the restaurant's rush hour, so there would have been a lot of people to see him drinking coffee with the chief of police. Then he remembered the little old man in shirt sleeves lying in the mud, his shirt soaked, his head bloody, and he didn't feel so good.

Guálinto's Uncle Feliciano had come in from the country that night, and he was drinking coffee before going out in search of his nephew when Guálinto got home in the chief's car. The night was beginning to lighten into dawn. María came to answer the knock, a black shawl over her head as if she were in mourning. When she saw her son together with the lawman, she let out a wail and threw her arms around him. MacHenry tried to tell her everything was all right, but she wouldn't listen to his halting Spanish. The girls had awakened at their mother's crying and were peeking through the curtains covering the living-room doorway. Then Feliciano came in from the kitchen and invited the policeman in. They sat down and the chief explained things.

María would not listen. She went into her room, sat on a rocker with her black shawl over her face and wept as though there were a corpse in the house. Maruca and Carmen brought her a bottle of spirits that was kept in the house for medicine and tried to make her swallow some, but she would have none of it.

Feliciano listened proudly while MacHenry told him about Guálinto's capture of a dangerous prisoner. His shoulders straightened and his face brightened as he sat there. The glow of the lamp on the table gave his features a soft but triumphant look. For the moment he was no longer an old tired man bowed down by work and trouble. Finally MacHenry left and Guálinto went to bed after drinking a cup of hot tea Carmen made for him. When he was in bed Feliciano came in and stood looking down at him, the strange triumphant look still on his face. "And this Gringo you captured," Feliciano asked, "was he much bigger than you?"

"Oh, no," said Guálinto. "He was Mexican. And he was just a little runt of a man, looked like a dwarf. He had a little puckered-up face, I remember."

Feliciano's face changed. "A little runt of a man," he repeated. "A puckered-up face. Did they say what his name was?"

"Miranda," Guálinto replied. "They said his name was Arnulfo Miranda."

"I must be going," said Feliciano and walked out.

The Jonesville-on-the-Grande Chronicle had it all over the front page next morning, under the second-biggest headline. The big eight-column banner was taken by an article about the former cashier of the Jonesville National Bank, now closed, who had been indicted. But Guálinto was a hero, no doubt of that. He could have stayed home all day, but he slept only a few hours and got up so he could be at school a good while before classes began. It was a long time since he had received so much attention. Even the teachers took up a few minutes of class time talking about his exploit. Hazel Brown's father was a doctor who worked at the hospital, and Hazel said her father said the man might not live.

"Gee!" said a fellow behind Guálinto. "You'll be a killer then." The teacher changed the subject by talking about the coming exams. After classes, Guálinto hung around until the last of the students and teachers had left. Then he discussed the matter with the janitors who were sweeping the halls, finally leaving for home when it was nearly dark. He had completely forgotten about his job at Rodríguez and Sons, Groceries, and now that he remembered he didn't care. He would live on the money he would get from the reward, and later he would look for another job. Much later. He went home and told his mother about it, and she agreed. He looked sort of peaked, she said; there was no need for him to work anyway. And maybe he could go to college with the reward money so he wouldn't have to depend on his uncle so much.

Some time after supper, Feliciano came home. He said he had eaten already and went and sat down in the parlor. Guálinto and his mother came in after him. "Guálinto wants to quit that store," said María. "Those Mexican Jews work him too hard, and now that he's going to get that reward money he doesn't think he needs to work there anymore."

Feliciano looked tireder than usual. "If he don't want to work there he don't have to," he said. "It was his idea."

"Well, I wanted to help," Guálinto said. "But now, with that money, I can help that way."

"I don't think we should take that money," Feliciano said. "Don't think we ought to at all."

"Why not?" said María sharply. "What kind of funny ideas are you getting?"

"It's blood money. The man's dead."

"Oh," María and her son said in unison. Guálinto felt a queer sinking feeling in his stomach, and he looked at his hand, which had killed a man.

"It doesn't matter," said María, somewhat unsteadily. "We can use the money and we'll take it. Five hundred dollars is——"

"It isn't five hundred, it's two hundred fifty. The police are keeping half for arresting him. And you didn't kill him, Guálinto; he died of pneumonia. Doctor says he was already dying of consumption anyway."

"Well, whatever they give us is good enough, and we're keeping it, no matter what."

"No matter what, María?"

"No matter what."

Feliciano rose and moved close to where María was standing. "Well, I hope you change your mind," he said softly. "That man was Lupe."

María stared at Feliciano as if she had not understood. "Lupe?" she whispered. "Lupe?" Then she sobbed and began to fall. Feliciano caught her before she reached the floor and carried her to her bedroom. The girls had been standing in the doorway, and when they saw their mother fall they came running forward. Feliciano laid María across the bed. A silent hysteria possessed her; her body was contorted by convulsions so that Feliciano had to hold her arms to keep her from hurting herself. Maruca and Carmen stood on either side of the bed and wailed.

"Shut up!" yelled Feliciano, and they throttled down their grief to whimpers. He left María in their care and returned to the parlor, where Guálinto sat dazed, uncomprehending. Feliciano eased himself into a rocker opposite Guálinto's chair without saying a word. He reached into his pocket for tobacco and a leaf of cornhusk and made himself a cigaret while Guálinto watched. From the bedroom came the sound of sobbing and whimpering and the heavy rasping breath of the unconscious woman as she thrashed about in bed. Finally Feliciano raised his head.

"Lupe García was your uncle," he said, "your mother's brother."

Guálinto stared at him as María had stared. Then he put his hand over his chin and crouched in his chair. "It wasn't your fault," Feliciano went on, "it just happened that way. And you did *not* kill him."

Guálinto's eyes filled with tears; he bowed his head trying to hide them. "It's my fault," said Feliciano. "I should have told you. There's lots of things I should have told you a long time ago."

Guálinto looked up, his eyes brimming. "Is he really dead?"

"Yes. I went and saw him at the funeral home."

Guálinto shuddered. "I thought it was Chucho."

"Who's Chucho?"

"A boy."

"Oh."

"What was he doing in jail?"

"He killed a man, an old *rinche*."

"Oh."

"He was the best rifle shot in the state of Texas, Lupe was. He could shoot a deer straight through the heart while holding his rifle in the crook of his arm."

Guálinto looked interested for an instant and then began to weep. "Oh, why did I ever go to that show last night!"

Feliciano waited till Guálinto finished crying before he said, "One can't keep things from happening the way they're going to happen. It was Lupe's time to die, and you are not to blame."

They were silent for a while, and then Guálinto asked, "Why did he kill the *rinche*?"

"It's a long story. It's a story I should have told you a long time ago, but I didn't because your father told me not to, just before I—he made me promise that if anything happened to him you should not be told about it."

"My father?"

"Yes. You see, Lupe was our brother, María's and mine. He was younger than me and older than María. Sort of in-between, you know." Guálinto nodded and waited. "Well," Feliciano said at last, "Lupe was always a wild sort. He was always getting into shooting scrapes and the law was always looking for him. Then he got into the De la Peña business."

"*¿Los sediciosos?*"

"Yes. He led a band during the fighting. I—he had to leave for the other side of the river after it was all over, and he changed his name to Arnulfo Miranda. Nice name, wasn't it?"

"Yes. It has a nice sound to it."

"Lupe liked pretty things. He had an ear for music and an eye for pretty pictures. He liked pretty girls too, but they didn't like him. Even as a boy he looked like a little old man. 'El Muñequito' they used to call him, but not to his face. He shot a man once who laughed at him. That was when he first had to go into the chaparral and hide. But he loved pretty things. He could carve on wood, really hard wood like the heart of the ebony. He'd carve roses on ebony wood, each petal like the real thing. Mama used to have an ebony Virgin of Guadalupe (we buried it with her) that he carved for her. He used to come and visit Mama before the De la Peña affair. At night and he'd stay just for a little while. He carved that Virgin in the woods where he was and brought it in one night. Mama cried."

Feliciano shifted laboriously in his rocking chair and spat into a brass spittoon he kept under the lamp table. "When Lupe became Arnulfo Miranda not even your mother knew his name. Only I did. I went over to Morelos every once in a while and saw him over there. Then, not too long ago, he came over to this side and killed this *rinche*, an old man by then. He was called MacDougal, I think I remember."

"But why?" asked Guálinto. "Why did he cross over to this side just to kill the *rinche* when he was safe over on the Mexican side?"

"This MacDougal," Feliciano said cautiously, "he was the *rinche* that killed your father." Guálinto clutched the sides of his chair. "I should have told you this long ago, but I promised. Your father did not want you to hate. When you were little you used to ask about him, and we would tell you stories. The girls, they were a bit older when it happened, and they sort of remembered for a little while but they forgot before they grew up. I wish I had told it to you before."

"Go on!" Guálinto said savagely. "Tell me all there is to it! Don't beat around the bush!"

Feliciano shut his eyes for a moment as though he was in pain, but when he spoke again his voice was calm as before. "Your father was killed one day while the *rinches* were taking him from San Pedrito to Jonesville. They said he tried to run away. They killed him because he was Lupe's brother-in-law. They wanted to know where Lupe was and your father couldn't tell them. He wouldn't have told them even if he had known. There were four *rinches* but the only one whose name we heard about was MacDougal, who was their leader. I knew MacDougal. He had been a *rinche* for a long time."

"And where were you? Where were you when my father was killed?"

Feliciano looked away. "I—I was in Monterrey then."

Guálinto looked at his uncle. His uncle, who sat there, an old good-for-nothing without courage, without pride. Who had run away to Monterrey when his father was killed, who had not been man enough to demand an accounting of Martin Goodnam for Maruca's shame. How he hated him! Why wasn't he raised by a man like his Uncle Lupe, a man who really was a man. He would have been proud of such an uncle, just as he had once been proud of the man now sitting in front of him, when he was a little kid and didn't know any better.

Feliciano read the hatred in his nephew's face, and it made him sad. He was too tired to be resentful. Nowadays he was tired most of the time, so tired he often thought how restful it would be to die. And that was unhealthy for a man not yet sixty and with family responsibilities. But they had been hard, those years. Except for his "trip to Monterrey," he had worked and worked as long as he could remember. And the kind of work Feliciano and his fellow Mexicans did made old men out of boys in their teens. But he had weathered all those years because for some reason he had been born big and strong. Big for a Mexican at least, almost six feet tall, lean and large-boned. His parents' oldest and biggest child out of the sixteen his mother had brought forth. Only two others had survived—María, small and slender, and Lupe, a dwarf. Bigger than most, he thought, but perhaps for him life had been harder than for most.

He looked at the boy sitting in front of him, staring at him with such open contempt. His only son. How often, when the boy was a baby, had he lain in his cot in the storeroom and longed for a wife and family of his own. And at times the desire was so strong that it almost overwhelmed his sense of guilt. But he had known better than to bring another woman under the same roof with María. Once he had brought up the subject and María had been furious. She began to cry, saying he could marry when he wanted to, that she would leave immediately and take the children with her. Finally he calmed her, telling her it was all a joke. After that María became jealous of him when other women were about. Well, he thought, he couldn't really blame her. He was the only one she could depend on.

So Feliciano had become a kind of eldest child to his younger sister, a middle-aged *muchacho de familia*. When he came home late, María would want to know where he had been, and she would sulk if his breath smelled of mezcal. Feliciano sighed softly. Somewhere in North Texas there was a girl who was his daughter. He had never seen her and he often wondered what she looked like, whether she was dark or light, pretty or homely. Her mother had been dark and pretty. He had lain with her in secret during the nights of one summer. Though she was a loose woman, she had wanted him to marry her when she got pregnant. When he refused she left Jonesville and went north. Every once in a while he sent her money. The girl must be fifteen now. She wrote to Feliciano once in a while in care of Don José, and her letters began, "Dear Papa". She had a very pretty hand. But she never sent him photographs.

Sometimes Feliciano thought of telling Guálinto all of this, but there are things too personal to be told to a boy. And as for his having ridden with Lupe, he would end up in prison if anybody knew. And then who would take care of the family. Gumersindo had given him a job to do. The boy was too young to understand. Let somebody else tell him after Feliciano was dead.

He was jolted out of his thoughts by Guálinto's sob. "I would like to *kill* somebody," Guálinto blubbered.

"People always want to kill people," Feliciano said. "That's where all kinds of trouble start."

"Why isn't it 1916 right now?" sobbed Guálinto. "Then I could get a rifle and go into the woods and kill and kill and kill."

Feliciano looked at him sadly. "You weren't made for killing people."

"I seem to be pretty good at it."

"Stop that! It was an accident, and it wasn't the rock that did it. But I'm glad you've changed your mind and want to finish school. If this rain lets up I can harvest quite a bit of beans next week. That's for expenses at home. Your college money remains untouched. We'll forget about that reward money, of course. But you don't have to work for those Mexican Jews anymore. I should have known you were killing yourself just to be stubborn."

"I don't want to go to school anymore. What's the use of going to school?"

"You must remember that your father—" began Feliciano.

"Don't mention my father again to me!" shouted Guálinto. "I don't want to hear about him again, especially from you. I've heard it hundreds of times: help my people, help my people, be a great man and help my people. I'm not going to be a great man. I'll just be another Mexican with the seat of his pants torn and patched up. That's all I'll ever be. And I don't want to help my people. Help my people? What for? Let them help themselves, the whole lot of ragged, dirty *pelados* . I can't even help myself and you want me to help a lot of people I don't even know." He got up and walked out into the steady drizzle.

Feliciano started to call after him to put something on or he'd catch cold, but he checked himself. He sat in the rocker for a few moments, then rose and went into María's bedroom. Maruca's big-bellied form was dimly visible in the gloom by the side of the bed. Feliciano winced; she was due very soon. "How is your mother?" he whispered.

"She's better now," Maruca said softly. "She's stopped twitching and gone to sleep."

Feliciano went out by the kitchen door into the damp of the storeroom. He rummaged behind some sacks and took out a square bottle that glinted in the dim light. He sat down on a sack and gulped at the fiery *aguardiente*. He coughed a little and his eyes watered. He sat for a long time on the sack, holding the bottle between his knees. Then he wiped his mouth and took another drink.

12

The last days of May were a period full of crises for many people in Jonesville-on-the-Grande, crises that resolved and unresolved themselves again. For Guálinto, the days following his Uncle Lupe's death were a time of conflicting emotions. He felt guilty and ashamed about the disrespectful way he had talked to his Uncle Feliciano the night he learned how his father died. He had walked out his anger and his grief under the drizzling sky that night. But a sense of betrayal remained, akin to what he felt toward María Elena. His Uncle Feliciano had been for Guálinto not only his substitute father but a being of heroic proportions. How could he forgive him now, after finding out that his uncle had run away during the De la Peña uprising, when Guálinto's father was murdered? How could he reconcile himself to the fact that his Uncle Feliciano was a coward?

He returned very late that night, wet and uncomfortable, and had gone to bed as soon as he changed into dry underwear. Next morning his uncle was gone before Guálinto got up. The sun was shining. Guálinto was glad of that, and of the fact that he did not have to face his uncle at the breakfast table. Dependable Carmen prepared breakfast for him and he left early for school. His mother was still asleep. It was no minor fault to break the code of *respeto* toward one's elders. And this was the second time Guálinto had done it. Last January he had committed the same offense, though not so blatantly as last night. In January he had attempted to punish himself by doing hard labor at the Rodríguez grocery, neglecting his classes and not really caring whether he finished high school or not. Now his atonement took a diametrically opposite form. He did not return to the grocery store, even to say he was quitting. He resolved to work as hard as he could the remaining days of the semester and graduate with the best record he could achieve. Then he would work on the farm or get a job in town. He was adamant about not going to college, solely because he knew he could hurt his uncle that way without being openly disrespectful. He would be polite and obedient, but he could not forgive his uncle for running off to Monterrey when his father was killed.

His grades improved immediately and he did very well on the finals. But not well enough to be an honor student, much less valedictorian as everyone had once expected him to be. The valedictorian would be Elton Carlton, and the salutatorian was Minnie Markoss, a shy little Jewish girl who had stayed in the background during class discussions but whose grade average, to the surprise of many, was just a little below that of Elton's.

Guálinto, however, was not the only person in the school system who had problems. Elton Carlton was the son of E.C. Carlton, former cashier of the defunct Jonesville National Bank, who was now under indictment for misappropriation of funds. Elton had worked hard and hoped to be first in his class, but he had always been overshadowed by Guálinto. Then, in their final semester of school, Guálinto's grades suddenly went down, and Elton knew the valedictorian's spot was his. But his joy did not last long. His father was indicted and faced a well-publicized trial and an almost certain prison sentence. Elton told the principal he would not go on stage and deliver the valedictory during commencement. He had decided, it seemed, that he could not face a crowd of people and give the valedictory, with its usual moral and optimistic platitudes, when half of Jonesville were already calling his father a crook. He threatened not to attend the ceremonies at all if he was pressured into doing so. Minnie, on the other hand, did not want to give the salutatory if Elton did not present the valedictory.

School officials were in a real predicament. Merely doing away with the salutatory and the valedictory talks from the program would only accentuate the embarrassing situation the Carlton family was going through. Mr. Baggley, the superintendent, suggested a solution: recognize Elton and Minnie on the printed program as valedictorian and salutatorian but have some distinguished figure from the academic or literary world present a lecture instead. His suggestion was hailed as a great idea by the school board. But when they thought it over they discoverd there was a hitch. Money. And time. Time and money.

It would be difficult to find a really distinguished person who would agree to come down to Jonesville on such short notice. And then there was the honorarium. On top of that the expenses, which probably would be a bigger sum than the speaker's fee. And the school district's cupboard was bare. They sat around their conference table and thought of ways to raise money until Mr. Baggley shouted, "Harvey!"

The rest of the board perked up. "He certainly fills the bill," said Mr. Rutledge, the manager of Woolworth's. "We couldn't get a more distinguished person than Hank Harvey."

O.D. Patch, owner of the Patch Lumber Company, said, "He's a friend of yours, isn't he, Baggley? But he's somewhere deep down in Mexico. How could we get hold of him in a hurry?"

"And how much would he want?" said Mr. Aziz of Aziz's Jewelry Store.

Mr. Baggley could scarcely contain his glee. "He's on his way back! I'm picking him up at the Morelos railroad station the day before commencement. And he plans to rest for a couple of days at my house before taking the train back to Austin!"

"Then we wouldn't have to worry about travel expenses," Mr. Patch said.

"He wouldn't have to prepare a speech, you know," Mr. Rutledge said. "He can talk off the cuff about almost anything. And he's always entertaining."

"Since he's your friend, Baggley, he may be reasonable about his fee," Mr. Aziz added.

They adjourned in a happy mood.

At his farm along the river Feliciano was not happy but he did feel something approaching contentment. He was sitting on the porch of the little unpainted house he and José Alcaraz lived in when they were not in town. From where he sat he had a good view of his fields, and he liked what he saw. The early corn was tall, and the green beans and tomatoes would soon be ready for picking. The crops would be good, and some hard cash would be coming in at last. There was still Maruca to worry about. But Guálinto had quit the grocery store and was studying hard for graduation. He was again accepting money for his personal needs, not directly from his uncle but through his mother. That included what was necessary to rent a cap and gown for the graduation. He did not want a ring. The boy still acted distant toward Feliciano, polite but cold. The story about Monterrey had not sat well with him. Feliciano was certain he was a coward in his nephew's eyes. Ah, well. Perhaps he would get over it after some time. If not, then Feliciano would just have to live with the situation.

He saw Juan Rubio emerge from his *jacal* with an empty basket. To pick some tender corn for roasting, he was sure. Juan's dwelling was made of clay and *zacahuistle* thatch, thick-walled and sturdy. Stronger and more weather-proof than his wooden cottage, Feliciano knew. But a wooden house had some prestige attached to it. That was the way things were. As owner of the land, he could not live in a *jacal* as he had lived most of his life. Juan began filling his basket with roasting ears as Feliciano heard the motor of his truck coming up the dirt road from the paved highway that went from Jonesville to the coast. The truck stopped at the side of the house and José Alcaraz came around to the porch. "I have a letter for you," he said.

Feliciano recognized the purple ink and the clear, pretty handwriting. His daughter. He had not heard from her for some time. Eagerly he tore open the envelope as José went into the house. The first words puzzled him: "Don Feliciano García, *presente*." Then the salutation: "*Muy estimado Don Feliciano*." Was she joking? Was she angry with him for some reason? He read hurriedly on.

> It is very hard for me to write this letter. When you receive it you will think it is from your daughter Eduviges, your dear little Vica as you called her in your letters. Little Vica does not exist. She never did. Gloria had an abortion soon after she left Jonesville. I went with her because we were very close friends. I'm sure you remember me, Tina la Alazana. Gloria got money out of you by writing to you about your daughter. Then five years ago she got very sick. Cancer the doctor said. She needed all the money she could get so she talked me into writing those letters to you as if they came from a daughter of yours. My conscience bothered me but Gloria was my best friend and I thought I would only have to write two or three letters since the doctor said she would not last the year. She lived five years more and I kept writing you

those Dear Papa letters because she wanted me to. Gloria died two weeks ago so now I can tell you the truth. I pray you to forgive me.

Your humble servant,
Tina

Feliciano stared out over the fields. Juan Rubio had filled his basket with tender ears of corn and was bringing it over to the house. Feliciano chuckled. Then he began to laugh. Soon he was roaring with laughter. José Alcaraz came out to the porch as Juan came hurrying up with his basket of roasting ears.

"Is there something the matter?" Juan asked.

José Alcaraz smiled. "There must have been something very funny in that letter," he said. "Is it good news?"

Feliciano stopped laughing with some effort. "Very good news," he said. "Very, very funny news. There's been a death in the family."

Juan and José stared at him, not knowing what to say. They knew about Maruca's condition, as did everybody else, and they were also aware of Guálinto's strange behavior in recent months. Also, there were rumors in Morelos that Feliciano and Arnulfo Miranda had been related. Besides, Feliciano had been drinking lately, something he had rarely done before.

"Are you feeling all right, Feliciano?" José Alcaraz asked.

"I haven't been drinking, if that's what you mean," Feliciano answered. "Here. Let me read you this letter you just brought me." He read the letter to them in a clear, even voice, folded it and put it in his shirt pocket.

"I am sorry," José said. "I am very sorry."

"No need to. That's life. In less than a week, a daughter I thought I had is vanished like smoke in the wind. And a nephew who once looked up to me now despises me. Life is made up of things like that. The crops will be good this spring, though."

José Alcaraz was embarrassed. "I'm sorry," he repeated.

"Speaking of smoke," Feliciano said to José, "did you notice whether there still is fire in the stove?"

"There is. I just stoked it to heat some coffee."

"I'll add this letter to the bundle I have in my chest. They should make some very pretty smoke."

"I'll go see about the coffee," José said and went into the house.

Juan Rubio put his basket down on the porch, almost at Feliciano's feet, and stood silently until Feliciano looked at him. "I thought you might want to take some of these to your family," he said softly.

"Yes," Feliciano said, "thank you."

"It was your brother Lupe's death, wasn't it?" Juan's voice was softer still. "You didn't tell him all the truth, did you?"

"I told him I was in Monterrey. He thinks I'm a coward."

"Why didn't you tell him? Doña María knows. So does that lawyer, your neighbor. And there are others on the Morelos side of the river who know."

"Perhaps I should have done so. Some time ago. Now I'd rather just leave it as it is."

"I'm taking the bay horse," Juan said, more loudly. "I think I should ride all around the fences. We don't want the stock to break into the fields, and I think there are weak spots in some places.

"Good."

13

Long ago there were some blind men in Hindustan who were exceedingly wise. They liked to find out things about things, especially things close to them. On one occasion they decided to discover all there was to know about the nature of the elephant. So they carefully examined an elephant, each one of them doing a detailed examination of one particular portion of the beast. They then put their findings together and came up with the picture of an incredible monstrosity.

That was long ago, of course, before science, journalism, and the modern world. Today they would have relied on someone interested in researching elephants. This individual would have gone around the world interviewing elephants, perhaps even learning a few words of their language. He would have compiled his findings in several books and published them for everybody's edification. The result could have been somewhat grotesque, perhaps, but much more convincing since it was done by an experienced and self-assured specialist. And everybody would then know everything there was to know about elephants. In other words, our man would have become an authority on elephants.

K. Hank Harvey was not an expert on elephants, but he was considered the foremost of authorities on the Mexicans of Texas. Hank Harvey had been born in New York City some sixty years before. He had gone to grade school there and then worked in a delicatessen to make some money so he could come down to his dreamland, Texas. In Texas he arrived, at the age of twenty-one, his soul on fire with the wonders and beauties of this most wonderful and beautiful of states.

At sixty K. Hank Harvey was what newspapermen call a colorful figure. He had a Santa Claus physique and a kindly, slightly vacant face that anyone would swear had first seen light of day in some southern mansion and not close to the sidewalks of New York. He wore a large, widebrimmed Stetson under which his flowing white locks dropped to his shoulders in a very patrician way. The cuffs of his finely tailored trousers were neatly tucked into the tops of his ornate cowboy boots, which he wore on all occasions, whether he was talking to a Texas cowboy or entertaining the crowned heads of Europe with his pithy anecdotes. His coat never met in front.

Hank Harvey was a self-made man. After he had come to Texas, with only a few years of schooling, he resolved to become an authority on Texas history and folklore. In a few years he had read every book there was on the early history of Texas, it was said, and his fellow Texans accepted him as the Historical Oracle of the State. There was a slight hitch, it is true. Most early Texas history books were written in Spanish, and K. Hank didn't know the language. However, nobody mentioned this, and it didn't detract from Harvey's glory.

The turning point in his career came when, as a cowboy on a West Texas ranch, he spent five years of his spare time in research to settle the controversy then raging in the Lone Star State as to what the Mexicans at the Battle of San Jacinto had said as they were cut down by Sam Houston and his buddies. Hank Harvey took no active part in the argument. He quietly went about his research, and after five years he exploded a bombshell in the midst of the debate with his book *San Jacinto Guncotton*. In it he definitely established that the Mexicans had said, "Me no Alamo! Me no Goliad!" before receiving the quietus. A grateful populace acclaimed him, and the University conferred on him an honorary doctor's degree and invited him to teach there.

From that day on, K. Hank Harvey was a made man. He learned a few words of Spanish, which he introduced into all his later writings, somewhat indiscriminately, and which made him sound something like the barkeep in William Saroyan's story, whose favorite expression was, "Nice day, aren't you?" Harvey's fame grew too big even for vast Texas, and soon he was a national and then an international figure. For K. Hank Harvey filled a very urgent need; men like him were badly in demand in Texas. They were needed to point out the local color, and in the process make the general public see that starving Mexicans were not an ugly, pitiful sight but something very picturesque and quaint, something tourists from the North would pay money to come and see. By this same process bloody murders became charming adventure stories, and men one would have considered uncouth and ignorant became true originals.

This made everybody feel fine, so K. Hank became quite a celebrity. He went all over the United States telling his Mexican anecdotes and historical vignettes. And a sizable school grew up around him, a following of newly made "Texians" who mashed a little Spanish into their conversation for the same reason Mexicans mash *chile piquín* into their frijoles, for spice and aroma, and who mispronounced out of preference the same English words early Texans had mispronounced out of ignorance.

The spring that Guálinto Gómez graduated from high school, K. Hank Harvey had been sent to Mexico as a goodwill ambassador. When graduation day came around, Harvey found himself in Jonesville-on-the-Grande on his way back from his mission. He was a bit disillusioned about Mexico. The Mexicans he had met knew little or no English, and he had quite a time making himself understood. Mexicans didn't seem to appreciate his homespun humor, or his homespun manners either, and Hank Harvey's kindly old soul was sad at the chill reception given to one of his favorite jokes. It was a pet one of his about Santa Anna and Sam Houston. He had uncovered the joke during his research about what Mexicans had said at San Jacinto. Well, he thought, perhaps it lost its original flavor in translation, or perhaps the young fellow who had translated it for him hadn't done it the justice it deserved.

So K. Hank Harvey's spirits were a bit low when he got to the border. But when he alighted from the train at Morelos, a delegation from the Jonesville High School was there to meet him. The delegation escorted him across the border and invited him to address the graduating classes that night. Hank Harvey accepted with pleasure.

The Jonesville-on-the-Grande Public School Auditorium was packed tight with sweating bodies that graduation night. The weather had changed definitely toward summer, and it was oppressively hot. As usual, two different classes graduated simultaneously that night, the junior and the senior high school graduates. The junior high class was large, almost a hundred pupils of which some eighty percent were Mexican. The high school seniors were less than twenty and there were only four Mexicans among them, one of them being Guálinto Gómez.

The audience, however, was predominantly Mexican. It was an important event for a Mexican family to see a child of theirs graduate from junior high. Mexicans came in large numbers. They brought their near relatives with them, and their distant relatives, their aged and infirm and their tiny children. There were so many of them that some had to stand at the back of the auditorium. The scent of many sweating bodies filled the air, as did the varied sounds that went with the bodies: the wailing of babies, the buzz of conversation as people called to each other while still others read aloud the ads written on the asbestos curtain of the stage. When the curtain finally went up Mr. Baggley, the superintendent, came up to speak. Then it was necessary to translate what he said for the benefit of those who did not understand English, so the buzz of talk was continuous. The Anglos bore it all with unwonted stoicism because this was one of those days when it was necessary to show that we do live in a democratic society.

Fat, egg-faced Mr. Baggley came up to the front of the stage, said a few words and cracked a joke. The assembly laughed, whether they understood or not. Guálinto did not laugh. Feeling strange and uncomfortable in his gray cap and gown, he stared at Baggley with contempt. He hadn't even heard what the man said. His mind was on other, bitter things.

They were the cause of all evil, he thought. All the tales of hate and violence from his childhood came back to him from the half-consciousness in which they had been submerged. They came, they took away everything we had, they made us foreigners in our own land. He thought how there had always been an Anglo blocking his path to happiness, to success, even to plain dignity. An Anglo had taken away his girl, the same Anglo had ruined his sister. Because of the Anglos he would never find decent work. And even when his uncle had made a few dollars, an American banker had stolen most of them. Because of the Gringos he had killed his other uncle. He looked again at his hands, as he had done hundreds of times since that night. They were the same hands as always, but he wondered if they would ever stop looking strange to him. And he had to keep this secret to himself, he could not tell anyone about it and unburden part of his grief. He almost wished he still believed in the church. Then he could tell the priest and maybe that would do him some good. As it was, nobody knew but his mother and his Uncle Feliciano, and they were not much help. His mother cried all the time, and his uncle drank more and more every day. At least, they had not embarrassed him by coming tonight.

He was startled when Mr. Baggley called his name. Baggley was motioning for him to stand up. He had to try twice before his legs obeyed. "And this boy," Mr. Baggley was saying, "unmindful of personal danger captured a dangerous criminal so that justice would be done. Ladies and gentlemen, we have before us a genuine hero!" Everybody applauded and Guálinto hung his head till the flat part of his graduation cap covered his face. Mr. Baggley came down from the stage and put into his hand a medal with a ribbon, which he said had been awarded to him for heroism in capturing Arnulfo Miranda. Guálinto hid the hand that held the medal under his robe and sat down.

And now it was time for K. Hank Harvey to give his talk. "Ladies and gentlemen," he said, "I am here before you by accident, as the rabbit said when he met up with the coyote. I was just coming up the trail and they snagged me. Once the coyote saw a rabbit coming up the trail, and the coyote says, the coyote says—"

Even the Anglos had heard the story about the coyote who tried to catch the rabbit by playing dead, not once but many times. But everyone listened patiently while Mr. Harvey told it. Then he told a ghost story of the range, in an English interspersed with random *carambas* and *ojalás*. After that he got down to the business of the night.

"Ladies and gentlemen," he said, "we are foregathered here to honor this here bunch of young mavericks that will be branded tonight. It's my dutiful pleasure to give each of them a rolled-up piece of paper, signifying their achievements. Now, a piece of paper can be a powerful thing. At times, it can even be a dangerous thing. I remember a Mexican hand I used to have who decided to quit me for no reason at all. And he had the gall to come and ask me for a 'letter of commendation', as he called it. So I ask him, 'Who you gonna work for?' And he says, 'Mister Dale.' Now, I knew Johnny Dale. He was an ornery cuss but always ready for a good joke. So I wrote this here letter for Pedro and I tole him to take it to Dale. I followed him some distance away to watch the fun.

"He tuck it up to John Dale and Johnny opened it and read it. And he says, 'Come here.' And he tuck the Mexican behind the barn and pulled out his six-shooter. And the Mexican says, 'What you going to do Mister Dale?' And Dale, that ornery cuss, he says, 'I'm going to do what it says in this letter. It says to take you behind the barn and shoot you.' And he starts shooting at his feet. Boy, did that Mexican dance the fan-dang-o!" Harvey grinned and allowed himself a little chuckle. His audience tittered politely.

"But seriously," continued Hank Harvey, "we're here to honor this bunch of fine young people, citizens of this great and glorious state of Texas, who are going out into the world. May they never forget the names of Sam Houston, James Bowie, and Davey Crockett. May they remember the Alamo wherever they go." The audience shifted nervously in their seats. But K. Hank Harvey was oblivious to all external influences. "When our forefathers rose on their hindlegs and demanded independence," he continued, "when they arose with a mighty shout and forever erased Mexican cruelty and tyranny from this fair land, when they defeated bloody Santy Anna and his murderous cohorts at the heroic battle of San Jacinto, they set an example which younger, weaker generations would do well to follow. Girls and boys, I give you the world; it is at your feet as young Americans and as Texans. For was there ever a thing a Texan could not do?" He spoke on and on for another hour or so, his voice becoming softer, his speech slower, until he ran down like an old alarm clock. His audience waited until he sat down before applauding politely.

The gentlemen of the school board gave up their privilege of handing out the diplomas in favor of the visiting luminary. Hank gave the rolled papers to the pupils as they filed past him, and he gave each of them a squeeze of the hand, a shy smile, and a wink. When he winked at Guálinto, Guálinto glared at him. He walked down the aisle toward the exit at the back of the auditorium, looking straight ahead at the cap and gown before him. People in the audience were staring at him as he passed, he knew.

Halfway down the aisle Guálinto turned and saw Mike Darwin, the high school principal. Darwin smiled and Guálinto looked away. Once out in the hall he quickly took off his cap and gown and put them under his arm. El Colorado came through the crowd and shook his hand with his hammy paw covered with copper-colored hair. They moved toward the door. Somebody called Guálinto's name. El Colorado looked back and said, "Mike Darwin's been looking for you. He wants to talk to you about going to the University."

"Let him call, the sonofabitch," said Guálinto. "Let him call." And he led the way out of the building. "I never want to see him or any of them again."

14

Parallel to Feliciano's farmhouse, a bit lower on the high ground that led to the fields, was his tool shed. On the Monday morning after Guálinto received his diploma, Feliciano and Juan Rubio were working just outside the open double doors of the shed in the light of the sun, which was not yet hot enough to be uncomfortable. Feliciano was mending some harness, while Juan sharpened a posthole digger with a small grindstone. José Alcaraz was out looking after the stock. They heard the creak of the gate that led to the *llano* and looked up. It was Guálinto. He came in slowly, obviously tired from much walking, and took off a brand-new field-hand's straw hat he was wearing. He was dressed in the rough clothes he had worn when he worked for the Rodríguezes.

"Good morning, Uncle," he said with exaggerated formality. "Good morning, Juan."

Juan returned the greeting and went back to his work. He was finishing the edge of the digger with a file. Feliciano said, "Did you walk all the way from town?"

"No sir. A couple of Gringos in a pickup gave me a ride on the highway. I just walked down from the highway to here."

"It isn't a very long walk, and you probably enjoyed it. The sunshine and fresh air is good for you, after so many hours sitting at a study table."

"Yes sir."

"How did the graduation ceremonies go?"

"Well." Guálinto thought it best not to mention K. Hank Harvey or the medal he had been given and which was now gone with the garbage. "I have my diploma, at least."

"I congratulate you."

"I came by to see if you could find something for me to do at the farm."

"There's always something to do on a farm."

Juan said without looking up from his work. "He could help me set up the new posts and put up the wire at those weak spots in the fence."

Feliciano looked pleased. "Good. Then I can stay and finish with these harnesses." He got up and took down a pair of heavy canvas gloves that were wedged between the roof and the rafters at the rear of the shed. "Take these with you. You'll need them to handle the barbed wire."

Juan got the old bay horse and hitched him to a two-wheeled cart they used to transport things on the farm. There already was a roll of barbed wire in the cart. Juan added two posthole diggers, a wire cutter, a wire stretcher, a box of large staples and a hammer.

"Where are the posts?" Guálinto asked.

"They already are at the spots where we will need them. I went around looking for weak spots a couple of days ago, and then I left the posts to mark the places where we will set them up."

He's more intelligent than I had imagined, Guálinto thought as they started down the gentle slope to the road along the edge of the fields. Even a simple job like this requires thinking and planning. Feliciano watched them go, Juan leading the horse and Guálinto walking on the other side of the cart. He's stubborn, Feliciano thought. I wouldn't be surprised if he works until he drops. We'll see.

Guálinto quickly found out that digging an acceptable posthole was not as simple as he had thought it was. It also was hard work, harder than picking up sacks of grain at the grocery store. Stretching and nailing the barbed wire from one post to another required a good deal of effort too. And skill, also, if you were to avoid getting your hands and arms torn to shreds by the sharp barbs. By noon he was exhausted. His hands were red when he took his gloves off. Blisters were beginning to form on his palms. His forearms were scratched by the barbed wire. He had never felt so tired and sore in all his life. But he did not say anything. He would stick it out, no matter what.

They sat down on some fence posts in the shade of a large willow and drank from a jug of water Juan had brought in the cart while they waited for Juan's young son to bring them their lunch. Soon the boy appeared, carrying a basket covered with a towel. Two glass bottles full of hot coffee, bowls of beans with *chile* sauce, and a pile of freshly made tortillas. He and Juan had talked very little while they worked, only when Juan told Guálinto what to do and how to do it. Now, when the boy was gone, Juan said, "Your uncle finally told you how your father died."

Guálinto nodded and kept his eyes on the tortilla he was about to dip into his bowl of beans. He did not want to start a conversation about anything, least of all about his father.

"My father was killed by the *rinches* too," Juan said.

Guálinto raised his head. "I didn't know that," he said.

"About the same time your father was killed. My father and my three brothers too."

"Did—did you see them do it?"

"I wouldn't be here if I had. They shot my younger brother who was only fourteen, two years younger than me."

"What about your mother?"

"She was dead already. She died of consumption four years before the *rinches* came."

"You found the bodies."

"No. Some other people did, and they wouldn't let me see them. I went to the funeral, but they were in wooden boxes by then."

"What did you do after that?"

"Friends took me in for a while. Then I got a job with a Gringo, a *varillero*. A very kind old man. I was sure he would protect me if we met *rinches* on the road when we went around selling things."

"And he protected you?"

"For some time. Until we met some *sediciosos*. They tied us up and killed the old Gringo. They would have killed me too, except that your uncle saved my life."

"Uncle Lupe saved your life!"

Juan laughed softly. "It was your uncle Lupe who wanted to kill me. Your uncle Feliciano would not let him do it."

"Uncle Feliciano!"

"Only a few people know he wasn't in Monterrey during that time. If the Gringos had known he would have been dead long ago, or in prison. And no telling what would have become of you and the rest of your family."

"That was a brave thing to do."

"Yes. Your uncle Feliciano is a brave man. And very kind and generous too. Your uncle Lupe, if you will permit my saying it, was a wicked man. There is much you should know, and since Don Feliciano will not tell you I will."

Juan talked for a long time, longer than he had talked to anyone in years. When he finished he sighed and said, "I have been wanting to tell you all this for months now. I'm glad I did."

"I am glad too," Guálinto said.

"But come," Juan said. "Our food is cold already, and we must finish eating. We still haven't finished with the fence."

They ate hurriedly. Guálinto was surprised to find he was hungry, even though the coffee was cold and the beans and tortillas were barely warm. As they picked up their tools again Guálinto said, "Juan."

"Yes?"

"From what you tell me, Uncle Lupe was a hard-hearted kind of man."

"You do not believe me?"

"I do. But one thing bothers me."

"What?"

"If he was that heartless, why did he cross the river to kill the *rinche* who killed my father?"

"Consumption," Juan said.

"Consumption?"

"He was dying. Have you ever seen anybody die of that disease?"

"No."

"My mother died from it. I remember it well. She also got pneumonia towards the last, just as Lupe did. You choke to death, slowly, very slowly. It's a death I wouldn't wish on anyone, not even your uncle Lupe."

"But he knew he would be hanged for killing the *rinche*."

"No, he didn't expect that. He thought he would be shot to death. He was trying to reload when they came after him, but he was too weak and slow. So they took him alive."

"Oh."

"Also, trying to be fair. Don Feliciano told me Lupe was very fond of his sister, your mother. And that he and the old *rinche* were enemies from far back. Perhaps Lupe hoped to get some revenge for your family and die a quick death at the same time."

"Oh."

"I hear he never came to after you hit him with the brick. He died in his sleep, you might say. He never knew it when the phlegm choked him to death. In a way you did him a favor, don't you think?"

Guálinto did not answer.

"Let's get to work," Juan said. "There are just a couple of places left. We'll finish by midafternoon."

They got to work.

It was not long after noon that Feliciano saw them returning with the cart. He had finished his work on the harness before eating his noon meal and was now sitting on the edge of the porch, smoking one of his corn-husk cigarets. Even from a distance Feliciano could see a difference in the way Guálinto was walking. He was holding his head higher, shoulders squared and arms swinging at his sides. The way he usually had walked until lately. And much like the way Gumersindo had walked. It must be the build of the body, Feliciano thought.

Well, Lupe had avenged Gumersindo's death at last. Feliciano had once thought of doing something very much the same with Martín Goodnam. Shoot him and then die in a gunfight with the police. But then, there was María and her children. Always, there was María and her children.

Juan stopped the cart at the shed and began to unhitch the bay, but Guálinto came striding to the porch where Feliciano sat. The boy was smiling. "I wonder," he said. "Will the truck be going to town later this evening?"

"Do you want to go back tonight?"

"Yes sir, if it is possible. I would like to see Mr. Darwin tomorrow morning."

"Mr. Darwin?"

"He's the principal of the high school."

"Yes. Now I remember."

"When I—when my grades were not so good this spring, he told me I could still go to college if I wanted to."

"How could he promise you that?"

"My grades are still good over the four-year period. And he knows some important people at the University. He'll write a letter in my favor. He will also talk to them on the telephone."

"He must think well of you."

"He does. Better than I—better than I deserve."

"I'm sure you must deserve it. Is it not too late for you to get in?"

"There are a few more days left when one can apply. And I am sure Mr. Darwin will help me make the application if I see him soon."

"He must be a good man, this Mr. Darwin."

"He is. Also, I took some classes with him and he liked my work. He likes students who don't always agree with the textbooks."

"I see."

"He says he will try to get me a job over there to help me pay my way."

"Do not get a job. I have the money. Better said, you have the money."

"Yes sir."

"Go clean up and have a cup of coffee with some *pan dulce*," Feliciano said. "I was thinking of spending tonight in Jonesville. You can go with me."

"Thank you, Uncle," Guálinto said and went into the house.

Feliciano took a few thoughtful puffs on his cigaret. So Juan had told him everything. But he's made of good stuff, he thought. I was afraid he would get emotional and weep and ask to be forgiven. He handled himself well.

Feliciano took a final draw on his cigaret and went to help Juan Rubio unload the cart.

PART V

"LEADER OF HIS PEOPLE"

1

He is lying on his stomach at the summit of a hill, watching through a spy glass. The battle of San Jacinto has just ended with the rout of Santa Anna's forces and the capture of the dictator in his underwear. The wild horde of land pirates that form Sam Houston's command have satisfied their blood lust on the Mexican wounded and are now gathered in triumph. The time has come. He gives the command.

There is a barrage of mortar fire from behind the hill, and out of the woods come wave after wave of *rancheros*, superbly mounted and carrying sabers and revolvers. They are followed by ranks of Mexican soldiers dressed in simple brown uniforms but carrying revolving rifles and hand grenades. He already knows what is to follow. Carnage. Houston is easily captured. Santa Anna is joyous at what he thinks is his deliverance. But his joy does not last long. He is immediately hanged. The Yucatecan traitor, Lorenzo de Zavala, will meet the same fate soon after. Texas and the Southwest will remain forever Mexican.

He woke with a start, stared at the unfamiliar ceiling of the bedroom and cursed softly to himself. Again, the same mother-loving dream. The third time this past week. Goddam ridiculous, having the daydreams of his boyhood come back to him in his sleep. They had helped relieve his bitterness and frustration when he was a boy, those daydreams. He had never mentioned them to anyone, not even to the best friend of his early days in Jonesville-on-the-Grande, Juan José Alvarado, alias El Colorado. "Playing with his little wooden soldiers," he had called those daydreams, looking back on them when he reached maturity.

He would imagine he was living in his great-grandfather's time, when the Americans first began to encroach on the northern provinces of the new Republic of Mexico. Reacting against the central government's inefficiency and corruption, he would organize *rancheros* into a fighting militia and train them by using them to exterminate the Comanches. Then, with the aid of generals like Urrea, he would extend his influence to the Mexican army. He would discover the revolver before Samuel Colt, as well as the hand grenade and a modern style of portable mortar. In his daydreams he built a modern arms factory at Laredo, doing it all in great detail, until he had an enormous, well-trained army that included Irishmen and escaped American Negro slaves. Finally, he would defeat not only the army of the United States but its navy as well. He would reconquer all the territory west of the Mississippi River and recover Florida as well.

At that point he would end up with a feeling of emptiness, of futility. Somehow, he was not comfortable with the way things ended. There was something missing that made any kind of ending fail to satisfy. And he would stop there, to begin from the beginning a few days later. But he had outgrown those childish daydreams long ago. Lately, however, now that he was a grown man, married and with a successful career before him, scenes from the silly imaginings of his youth kept popping up when he was asleep. He always woke with a feeling of irritation. Why? he would ask himself. Why do I keep doing this? Why do I keep on fighting battles that were won and lost a long time ago? Lost by me and won by me too? They have no meaning now.

He turned on his side, toward his wife. Ellen was still asleep, her back to him. A ray of the spring sun filtered through the blinds and struck her yellow hair. She had it done into tight little curls just before they left Washington, and in the sunlight it looked like a mass of gold coins. He loved her hair, it was one of the first things that had attracted him to her. She was rather plain, and some of her lower teeth were crooked, but she had beautiful hair. And a wonderful disposition too. She turned over on her back and opened her eyes. Leaning on one elbow he kissed her, passing his other hand lightly over her rounded belly.

"Good morning, sweetheart," he said. "How are the both of you?"

She smiled. "Fine, honey. Is it time to get up?"

"I'm afraid so. We have a busy day ahead of us."

"Let me use the bathroom first," she said, getting up hastily.

He lay back, hands behind his head. He (it would be a he) would be blond and blue-eyed like his mother. The thought pleased him very much. It should also please his father-in-law, the old curmudgeon. When he first met Ellen Dell she was an out-of-state student from Colorado getting a Master's in sociology. She was very different from the first love of his life, María Elena Osuna. María Elena was beautiful, with wavy black hair and a heart full of laughter. But she did not have much in the way of brains. Ellen's blond hair was naturally straight and lank, and she had a long Anglo-Saxon face. A horse's face, his mother once said when, on one of his infrequent visits home, he had shown his mother Ellen's picture.

Ellen was not pretty, but she was serious, gentle, and kind. She was intelligent and, above all, she listened to him talk. She got to know almost everything there was to know about him: his problems, his aspirations. When he finally talked himself out, he thought of asking her about herself and was surprised to learn she had been born in Texas.

"Where?" he asked.

"The same place where you were born. San Pedrito." Her family had moved to Boulder when she was ten, but she had returned to Texas on a graduate scholarship to study Mexican migrant labor in central Texas. It was then that he knew they were meant for each other.

After they fell in love she told him he should go to Boulder to meet her family during Easter vacation. She took the train a day before him, to prepare her family for his arrival. At the station, just before she left, she told him, "Since we are going to get married, there is something I must tell you about myself. I should have told you about it long ago, but I was afraid you would stop loving me if I did."

"What?" he asked, expecting the worst.

"When my family lived in San Pedrito, about the time I was born, my father was a Texas Ranger."

He laughed, relieved. "Then we're just about the same age."

"He was a special Ranger, but just for a short while, and then he quit. He never killed any—anybody. But he used to tell us after we moved away about the terrible things some of the others did. She squeezed his hand.

"That is not a very serious sin to confess," he said, squeezing back.

Yet, on their wedding night he was somewhat surprised to discover she was a virgin. Getting the Mexican out of himself was not an easy job, he thought.

He got up and started making coffee and toast.

She had met him at the station and they had driven, not without some trepidation, to her parents' house. Her mother was small, with dark hair and a round face that must have been pretty once. But there was Ellen's gentleness and equanimity about her, though she was obviously nervous. She received him kindly and tried to make him feel at home. Ellen's father was another matter.

"So you're Ellen's Meskin," he said, without getting up from his easy chair. He was the one with the long face and blue eyes. And his hair must have been yellow once, though it was now gray, like the stubble on his unshaven face.

"Very pleased to meet you, sir," George said.

"George Washington Go-maize," Ellen's father said. "They sure screwed you up, didn't they, boy?"

"Frank," his wife said gently. "Don't use such language, please."

"You look white but you're a goddam Meskin. And what does your mother do but give you a nigger name. George Washington Go-maize."

"Now Daddy," Ellen said, as if chiding a naughty child. "There's nothing wrong with his name. It was George's father who gave it to him, because he admired the father of our country."

"Anyway," the old man said, "it don't sound right."

It was then that he decided to legally change his name to George G. Gómez, the middle G for García, his mother's maiden name.

"If my daughter wants to marry you," Frank Dell went on, "I guess it's all right with me. She oughta know what she wants to do. And anyway, she's always managed to do what she wants to do instead of what I tell her. But there will be children, won't there?" He sounded as if he wanted to be told there wouldn't be any.

"Of course there will be children," Ellen replied.

The old man frowned. "What if they come out with a touch of the tar brush?"

"Oh, come on, Frank," Mrs. Dell said. "You can see he's white."

"Daddy's right," Ellen said. "I'm sure they'll be brown, every one of them. The color of black coffee."

The old man grinned. "That's my baby," he said to George, "always taking advantgae of her old man." Then to Ellen, "You told me you was going back to Texas to study Meskins. I never thought you'd want to study them this close." He grinned again, and for the rest of George's visit he was civil enough though not very communicative.

Back in Texas again, George promised Ellen he would take her down to Jonesville to meet his family, but he never got around to it. Much of his time was spent getting his degree and being admitted to the bar. He made sporadic, overnight trips home but he went alone. He did take some photos of Ellen for his mother and Carmen to see, and he brought back pictures of his family. And then, when he finished he got this incredible opportunity in Washington. They were married in a private ceremony at Ellen's home, and he did not think it necessary to let his family know about it until after the wedding.

Ellen came out of the bathroom, looking pale. "Feel better now?" he inquired.

"Yes, it wasn't a bad spell. But I don't think I'll have anything except a cup of coffee. And some toast, perhaps."

"Coffee's ready. I made it while you were in the bathroom."

"I'm sure I'll be all right by the time we're ready to go."

As he shaved, he cursed the bureaucratic ineptitude of the people in Washington. He had been trained for almost three years for an assignment in southern California. And what did they do but send him down to the one place he should have stayed away from.

2

After shaving and showering he had a couple of soft-boiled eggs and toast, which he prepared himself. He would have preferred fried eggs and bacon, but the smell of frying food might upset Ellen's stomach. Besides, he still had trouble cracking eggs over a skillet. Ellen sat opposite him, sipping her coffee and eating a piece of dry toast. It was their first breakfast together in Jonesville, and he hoped there would not be too many of them. A few weeks and no more, once they knew his visit had received so much advance publicity.

They had arrived by plane the night before, but news of their coming had preceded them. His mother had asked Aquiles to give the news to the man who handled the Spanish edition of the local newspaper, and the English-language paper had picked it up. As often was the case, both had distorted the matter. "Prominent lawyer returns from Washington to practice in his home town." The return of the home-town boy who made good sort of thing. Damn those fools in Washington. Or perhaps they were trying to test him.

At Jonesville's tiny airport terminal, Aquiles was waiting for them. "Ellen," George said, "this is Aquiles Sierra, my brother-in-law. Carmen's husband." Aquiles was dark, much darker than his younger brother Orestes. George had never really noticed how very dark Aquiles was until he saw him standing beside Ellen. Of course he hadn't seen his brother-in-law for more than three years, but he couldn't have got any darker sitting at the manager's desk of the Sierra Auto Agency. No wonder Carmen's kids looked like little Indians.

"It's so nice to meet you," Ellen was saying. "I've seen pictures of you with Carmen and the children. And George's mother, of course. How are they all?"

"All very well," Aquiles said, beaming with pleasure at Ellen's cordiality. "Everybody is waiting to meet you."

"I'm looking forward to that."

"Not tonight," George said. "We're very tired. Tell Mother we'll be there first thing in the morning. And I'll call her when we get to our apartment. If the phone is working."

"It's working. Somebody from the outside came and got everything ready for you. Down to leasing this car from us that you can use till yours and all the rest of your things get here by rail. You must have had a lot of pull with the company you used to work for."

"I'm still working for them, that's why. But it was a long, tiring trip. Especially for Ellen, who is expecting."

"Oh, I'm sorry, Guálinto," Aquiles said. "Let's load your bags in the car and get going. I'll drive you there and the man your agent has at the apartment can drive me home."

"George," Ellen said as the three of them got into the front seat. "Let's stop just for a minute and say hello to your mother. She'll be expecting it."

"Tomorrow morning will be time enough, sweetheart. I don't want you to get overtired."

Ellen did not pursue the point. She was sitting in the middle, and as they drove off Aquiles leaned forward to speak to George. "Guálinto, do you think you can get away tomorrow just before noon for some *tacos* and beer with the old gang?"

"Tomorrow?"

"Sorry to rush things, but we were expecting you last Wednesday. That's what the paper said. So we scheduled it for tomorrow, which is a Sunday and all of us can be there. It's an important meeting, and we all hope you can make it."

"Politics?"

"Well, sort of. But a lot of your old friends just want to see you again. It's at Antonio Prieto's place, and you're the guest of honor."

"What time?"

"About ten in the morning. Antonio and Elodia don't open on Sundays until one so we can have the place to ourselves for three hours."

"What place?"

"Oh, I guess you didn't know. You did know that Antonio and Elodia got married, didn't you?"

"Yes, but what about their place?"

"They borrowed from me and José Alvarado. El Colorado, you remember him. And they have a restaurant-bar just outside of town on the road to the beach. All decorated Mexican style. Antonio put together a Mexican orchestra, dressed up in *charro* suits, and they have dances every Saturday night. Weekday nights and Sundays Antonio and a couple of others sing and play for the people who come to eat. The tourists just love it. Elodia supervises the cooking and takes care of the cash register. They're just raking the money in."

"I'm glad to hear they're doing well."

"And what do you think they named the place? La Casita Mexicana!" Aquiles laughed.

"It must have been Elodia's idea," George said. "She has her sense of humor." He did not explain to Ellen why the name of Antonio and Elodia's place was funny, and she did not ask.

"That place in Harlanburg has lost more than half of their business to La Casita," Aquiles said. "It's a much better place, and it's the real thing too. I sure hope you can make it." He looked at Ellen. "If it's all right with your Mrs., of course."

"Oh, by all means," Ellen said. "You should go, George. We'll see your mother and Carmen the first thing in the morning, and I'll stay there while you go see your friends."

"I won't stay too long, though," he said. "I want to visit my uncle at his farm in the afternoon." Might as well get it all over with in one day, he thought.

"Wonderful!" Aquiles said. "When you come back from your uncle's you can have supper with us. Please invite your uncle too." By now they were in town and moving toward the far northwestern side. "You'll be in an apartment house called the Golden Delta Apartments. It's a new subdivision built since you last were here, Guálinto. Called Las Anacuas. Very high tone."

"How many stories is it?"

"Four. But you're on the ground floor as you wanted. Your wife won't have to climb any stairs. And anyway, they have an elevator. How about that."

"*Muy jatón*," George said. "That's the way we say it in Spanish, Ellen. At least around here."

The apartment house turned out to be a substantial brick building surrounded by what passed for mansions in Jonesville-on-the-Grande. Las Anacuas. He wondered who had thought up that name. Some guy who had never seen an *anacua* bush, he was sure. The apartment was on the ground floor, as Aquiles had said.

A young man came out to meet them. He was wearing white coveralls such as those worn by airport service personnel, and his hair was cut very short. He carried their bags inside and proceeded to show them around the apartment as if he were a bellboy: the sitting room, the bedroom closets, the bathroom, the kitchen. He turned on the gas jets on the stove to show they were working and opened the refrigerator to display its contents—milk, fruit, bacon, eggs, butter. He identified them all. And the pantry with its bread, coffee, sugar. Tea in case the lady preferred it. Dishes, towels, toilet paper. As he showed them around he kept calling George "sir". Finally the young man was satisfied he had done his job.

"Is there anything else that you wish, sir?"

"Not tonight," George said. "Everything looks fine."

"Thank you, sir. If you should need anything else, please call. You have the number, sir?"

"Yes. Yes. Of course."

"Then, if you will excuse me, sir, I'll see that the Ford is put in the garage and then I'll take your brother-in-law home."

He finally left, taking Aquiles with him.

"That was a very polite young man," Ellen said.

"Too polite. The damn fool did everything but salute."

So the next morning they were driving to Aquiles and Carmen's house. "I'm sorry to be putting you through all of this, sweetheart," he said. "Especially leaving you alone for most of the day."

"Why, honey, I won't be alone. I'll be with your family."

"They'll probably bore you to death. And then they'll want to come visit you."

"I won't mind. I'll appreciate having company while you're at work."

"You're always so understanding. Anyway, it shouldn't be for long. I'm sure we'll move to San Diego pretty soon. After all, I was trained to work with our people in Baja."

"I wish you hadn't forgot to call your mother last night," she said.

"It's all right. We'll be seeing her in a couple of minutes."

George knew the area well. It was what had been one of the middle-class Anglo sections of town when he was growing up. Quiet, broad streets, tree-lined. Substantial wooden houses with porches supported by brick pillars. The neighborhood was just south of the high school building. He found the house easily enough, a two-story structure, white with green trim and surrounded by a white picket fence. Aquiles is doing quite well, he thought, as he stopped the Ford by the front gate.

He got out of the car and went around to help Ellen out onto the sidewalk as an ear-piercing wail came from the house. Just as he had feared. His mother came running out, sobbing wildly, her arms out-stretched, crying, "My baby! My little boy!"

He hurried to the gate before she could reach it, so she wouldn't run screaming out into the street. She hung to his neck, kissing him and sobbing.

"Now Mama," he said, "quit it! Quit it, please! Mama, calm down. Nobody is dead. Calm down. People are watching."

Ellen got out of the car by herself and came up to the gate. María stopped wailing and said, calmly enough, "So this is your *gringa*."

"What did she say?" Ellen asked, smiling.

María's face registered mock surprise, all traces of her fit of weeping gone. "Did she understand what I said? She speaks Spanish?"

"You know she doesn't, except for a few words," he said. "But anybody knows what *gringa* means." María embraced and kissed Ellen, and he hurried them inside.

"You must have coffee and *pan dulce*," María said.

"Mama, we just had breakfast."

But he could not get out of it. They sat down to coffee and *pan dulce* once Ellen had met Carmen and her children. Ellen, Carmen, and María sat on one side of the table, with Carmen in the middle so she could serve as interpeter. Aquiles and George were on the other side, George opposite his mother at her insistence. The conversation became two instead of one. María talked to her son in Spanish, with Aquiles adding brief remarks now and then, while Carmen and Ellen conversed in English.

"You must forgive our mother," Carmen said to Ellen. "She hasn't seen Gual—George for three years, and she gets emotional sometimes."

"I understand," Ellen answered, biting into a piece of *semita*.

"If she doesn't cry she feels she hasn't done her duty in welcoming her son."

"I did some work with ... Latins in San Antonio while I was in college," Ellen said. "It's a general custom. And among other peoples too."

They began to talk about the customs of people in different parts of the world, while at the other end of the table his mother was bringing George up to date on what had been going on in Jonesville since his last visit three years before. Most of it he already knew from Carmen's letters. Aquiles' brother, Orestes, had got his pharmacy degree out-of-state and was now a registered pharmacist working for the Jonesville Drug Store. But he hoped to start his own pharmacy soon. José Alvarado was doing well as bookkeeper for Acme Produce, Inc. and was also a public accountant on the side. Francisco López-Lebré had got a degree in dentistry from some college in Monterrey nobody had ever heard of, according to María. He had trouble getting certified to practice in Texas but had finally made it. Don José Alcaraz, Aquiles said, was no longer farming for Don Feliciano. He had a job in town with the City and had married a country girl much younger than he was.

"I thought he would finally talk you into marrying him, Mama," George said.

María made a face. "Why would he want to marry a wrinkled old woman like me," she said. She must be in her mid-forties, he thought, but she looked much older. Mexican women did age early. "Anyway," his mother added, "I never did encourage him." He thought there was a note of regret in her voice. Oh, well. It was her fault, after all.

After that she was silent, and George asked Carmen in English about Maruca. Soon after she had borne Buddy Goodnam's baby Maruca had got a job as elevator girl in Jonesville's new hotel, which at eight stories was the tallest building in town. A middle-aged Anglo widower, in Jonesville on business, had married her, adopted the baby, and taken them to California. That was years before.

"Oh, she's doing very well," Carmen answered, also in English. "She has another baby now, her third one. Her husband keeps on making money."

He insisted that Ellen be shown pictures of Maruca and her children, and he remarked more than once on their blue eyes and light-colored hair.

"They *are* very cute," Carmen said.

"So are yours," Ellen said. "I just love those big brown eyes of theirs."

His mother leaned over and asked Carmen, "What are you two talking about?"

"About Maruca's babies."

"Guálinto was a darling little boy. But always getting into trouble. I'm sure Elena would like me to tell her about him."

"Carmen, please," he said in English. "Ellen isn't interested in hearing about such things."

"What things?" Ellen asked.

"About George when he was a little boy."

"But I am interested," Ellen said, looking at George mischievously.

Carmen hesitated and then asked Ellen to tell the family something about herself. Ellen told them about her parents and her brothers. She was the only girl and the youngest in the family. She talked about the state of Colorado and how beautiful it was. She did not mention the fact that her family had once lived in Texas and that she had been born in San Pedrito.

All this took time, since Carmen had to translate back and forth from English to Spanish and back to English again. For the moment George was relieved, but he knew that as soon as he and Aquiles left his mother would begin telling Ellen about the time he was cured of *susto* by Doña Simonita la Ciega. He kept looking at his wrist watch. Finally it said 9:20.

"Mama," he said, "we must go now."

"So soon?" María protested. "You just got here. I haven't had a chance to get acquainted with your wife."

"She's staying. Aquiles and I have to go to a meeting, but we'll be back for supper. And we'll be here in Jonesville for some time."

"I hope it will be forever," his mother said.

3

He followed Aquiles' car when they left the house, all the way across town and beyond the southeast city limits. Here Riverside Drive became the highway leading to the beach. As they pulled into the parking lot, he recognized the place. It had been the site of an ice cream parlor during his high school days. This was La Casita Mexicana, rival establishment to Harlanburg's La Casa Mexicana. He uttered a scornful grunt. It was a ridiculous parody of the restaurant-nightclub in Harlanburg. But tourists seemed to like it, from what Aquiles had said. You never knew what tourists would like.

They were all there, waiting for him: Elodia and Antonio Prieto, El Colorado, Arty Cord, La Gata, and many others, including a man named Leytón whom he was sure he had met before but could not place. They were gathered at the bar in the otherwise vacant place, eating *tacos* prepared by a man in the kitchen and drinking bottled beer served by Elodia from behind the counter.

He was received with raucous enthusiasm. Here he is! The man we've been waiting for! *Abrazo* followed *abrazo*, including a tremendous bear hug from El Colorado. Then beer and reminiscence. For the better part of an hour he forgot who he was now and where he was, in a surge of affection and nostalgia. Finally Elodia shouted above the din, "Last call for beer and tacos! You can bring your plates and bottles with you!"

A row of square dining tables had been set end to end on the dance floor to resemble a long conference table. They sat around it, a score of them. Some were mature men, such as Leytón. But those in the majority were George's age mates such as Orestes and El Colorado, men in their mid or late twenties. Elodia, the only woman present, took her place at the head of the table and tapped her knife against an empty glass.

"The meeting will now come to order!" she announced. Part of the meeting did. The rest divided their attention between her and their *tacos* and beer. He had the feeling he was watching a comic skit or children at play. He was sitting at Elodia's right and he smiled at her to keep from laughing. She smiled back happily.

Elodia raised her voice again. "Members of the executive committee of Latins for Osuna. We are gathered here today to welcome home one of our own, a man who has been a strong defender of the Mexicotexan's rights since he was a schoolboy. And it is fitting that it should be at this place that we make him welcome. For it was at a place like this, La Casa Mexicana in Harlanburg, *once* a favorite tourist spot— [Several committee members chuckled.]—that Guálinto Gómez first publicly showed how he could stand up for the rights of our people. Three of us ... [She was interrupted by applause and shouts of *viva!*] Three of us here present were witness to those events of nine years ago. At that time he was only a senior in high school. Today he returns to us, a famous lawyer from Washington, D.C. I propose a toast for the man who will give us the benefit of his leadership and experience."

The members picked up their beer bottles and drained them in tremendous gulps.

"Leandro!" Aquiles shouted to the man in the kitchen. "Bring us another round!"

"Thank you. Thank you," George said. "My heart is full of gratitude for this welcome. But I have no idea what this is all about."

"We're going to break O'Brien's hold on city politics, that's what," Elodia said. "Mike Osuna is our candidate for mayor and we have two other Mexicans on the ticket, Orestes and Enrique Leytón. For the first time Mexicans will have a say in city government."

"Mike Osuna? Oh, Miguelito. Well, he has enough money to play around with. But why isn't he here with us?"

"He's on the other side of town meeting with some influential Gringos who are tired of having O'Brien run the show. With their support we can win, if we can just get out the Mexican vote. After all, we're more than eighty percent of the population in this town."

"How many of those have their poll taxes paid?"

"We mounted a poll tax drive this time," Orestes said, "and I think we did pretty well."

"You didn't buy their poll taxes, did you?"

"How could we," Leytón said, "when there's nothing but O'Brien people in the court house?"

"So you just gave them a couple of dollars each and hoped they wouldn't spend the money on beer."

"You sure have a lot of confidence in your own people," Elodia said.

"All right, suppose they did pay their poll taxes. You still have to get them out of the beer joints and into the polling places come election day."

"That's where we're counting on you," Orestes said. "You always have been a good speaker, in Spanish as well as in English. And people are looking up to you after what the paper said about you last week. With you speaking at our rallies we can get the people really fired up."

"I can't do that," he said. "I'm down here on assignment for the company I work for. They won't like it if I engage in local politics."

"Your company," Elodia said. "What company?"

"You don't have a chance anyway," he said. "You won't be able to get many Mexicans to vote for you. Oh, they'll come and eat your *carne asada* and drink your beer. And they'll yell themselves hoarse shouting *vivas* for Miguel Osuna. But in the end it will be the same old story. Most of the Mexicans who actually vote will be those on the City payroll, they and their relatives. They're the ones with their poll taxes paid, one hundred percent. Their hearts will be with you, but their bellies won't. They'll vote for Willie O'Brien."

"Your company," Elodia persisted. "What company is that?"

"I can't tell you."

"Where's your office going to be?"

Orestes answered for him. "They've already rented an office for him. In that building on the corner of Riverside and Main."

"Across from the main gate to Fort Jones!" Elodia cried.

"All right!" he said, exasperated. "I'm a lawyer for a big company based in Washington. They buy and sell large tracts of land. They have confidential information that Fort Jones and other military posts along the border will soon be closed. The troops will be needed elsewhere. There's a war going on in Europe, as you know. My company is interested in buying the land that will be vacated. I'm supposed to inspect the land, see what it can be used for, and so forth. I'll be dealing with some army officers about it, here and farther upriver."

"You want us to believe that?" Elodia said.

"I don't care whether you believe it or not. It's the truth, and I've told you more than I should. I could get fired for it."

There was a moment of silence except for the purr of the refrigerating machine. Then Elodia said quietly, "Tell us. Are you with the FBI?"

"No," he said. "I am not."

"Would you swear by your mother's life that you are not?"

"That's a foolish thing to ask me, Elodia," he said. "We're not children anymore. I give you my word that I am not working for the FBI."

"Then why all the secrecy?"

"Business, Elodia. There will be other companies trying to buy the land once they hear about it." He rose. "Thanks a lot for the party, but

I must go now. I'd like to see my uncle today, before I get too busy."

"You're welcome, Guálinto," Orestes said, almost in a whisper.

"In any case, I'll probably be gone before November. And even if I stayed and my company allowed me to dabble in politics, I wouldn't work for Miguel Osuna. Big things are coming your way if you have the kind of city government that can take advantage of the right opportunities. Osuna is a political innocent. Willie O'Brien has connections at the state and national level. He can develop this town into a real city during the next few years, war or no war. That will bring jobs to Jonesville."

"The same old story," Leytón said dully, as if talking to himself. "Good jobs for a herd of Gringos coming down from the north. And for our people? Clearing more brush. Digging more ditches."

"If that's all they can do."

They remained sitting around the table as he walked away, past El Colorado's broad back. The redhead had not joined in the argument, and now he did not turn as his old friend went by.

It wasn't until he reached the door that Elodia found her voice.

"Ge-or-ge," she called in an exaggerated Gringo accent. He looked back. Tears were runnning down her rigid, expressionless face.

"*Cabrón!*" she said. "*Vendido sanavabiche!*"

He opened the door and stepped out into the bright sunlight.

4

He was driving down the narrow highway leading to the beach, well on his way to his uncle's farm, when he finally remembered where he had seen Leytón before. It was more than three years before, when he had last visited Jonesville. He had finished law school and was getting ready to move to Washington. He needed a haircut, so he went to the old barber shop in front of the market square, the one he used to visit before he left Jonesville. It was Saturday and the shop was full, but mostly with people who were sitting around talking. He quickly gained possession of one of the two chairs in the shop, the one with the younger barber.

He had always enjoyed getting a haircut. The precise, unhurried sound of the barber's shears. The ever-exploring comb, the almost imperceptible tug of the busy scissors. They caused a gentle, pleasant tingle to the scalp. A caress. He liked the barber's massaging, the comb's teeth through his hair, and the light scraping of metal against the back of his neck. It relaxed him, and he felt at peace with the world. Often he had wondered if dogs felt like this when they had their ears scratched. But dogs did not have to put up with barber shop conversation.

"What are all the flags for?' asked the man in the other chair. He spoke through a blanket of shaving soap around his mouth.

"Columbus Day," the younger barber said. "The day of the Discovery of the New World."

"Ah, that's right," said a gray-haired man with a paunch and a big mustache. "Tomorrow is the day of Columbus."

The younger barber shot a glance at the leaf calendar on the wall above the row of chairs, which said October 12. "Yes, Don Manuel," he said. "Today is Columbus Day."

"October the twelfth," added the older barber with authority. "That's today."

Manuel pulled at his great mustache. "How long ago was that?" he asked.

"In the year one thousand and—what was it, *Licenciado*?"

"Four hundred and ninety-two," George answered.

"Four hundred and ninety-two years ago!" exclaimed the man in the other chair. "*Car ... acoles!* Quite a few years!"

"*Cualquier bicoca*," Manuel said facetiously. "Four hundred and ninety-two years. Why that isn't even five hundred."

A pasty-faced, clean-shaven man came in. "*Hola!*" he said cheerfully to everybody. Then, "*Ese* Leytón!"

The man in the other chair turned his head, braving a cut from the razor. His dark face crinkled into a grin. "Hello, González, how are you."

"All right. But I'm still laughing," González said as he took a chair.

"Go on," Leytón said. "Tell us about it, man."

"I was down at the poolroom. And you know José Carmona's wife and Willie O'Brien. Well, José was there too, with a bunch of us and old Rocha, drunk and half-asleep on a bench."

"That old man is a real joker," the older barber said.

"Well, gentlemen, we got to talking about the birth of Christ. Some said he really was the Son of God and others that he was the son of San José. The argument got pretty hot. Then Leal bangs on the table. 'I tell you,' he says, 'He's the son of José!'

"Then old Rocha sits up and rubs his eyes. 'Son of José *una chingada!*' he says. 'He's the son of Willie O'Brien.' "

When the laughter died down, the conversation drifted back to Columbus Day. "Yes," González said airily. He still felt good about creating such a sensation with his story. "I saw the flags. Long time since it happened, eh?"

"Five hundred and ninety-two years," Leytón said as he was raised to a sitting position.

"Bah! It's been longer since the Deluge," Manuel said.

"Now, that was something," González said.

"Huh. What's a war, eh?" Manuel said. "Think of the Deluge, hah. That was something serious. Water, water, water. In a war many are left alive, but in the Deluge everybody died. Except for Noah and his family."

"Our Good Lord said, 'Here it goes, you ungrateful.' And he drowned the whole world," murmured González.

"Not all of it," Leytón said. "The Chinese escaped the whole thing."

"They must have been very good people," González said.

"Perhaps they were then, but not now," Manuel said. "They're killing each other over there as pretty as you please. Civil wars. Invasions. *Caciques* fighting each other."

"But they can't help it. There have been interventions by all the other nations of the world. Like France and the United States with Mexico."

"All the same, they're fighting and killing," Manuel said with finality.

"The trouble with the world," González said, "is that there's too many of us. Some of us have to be killed off."

"Yes," Leytón said. "And there's no doubt we'll be in the middle of another great war in the next few years. Bigger than the last one. The world is going to end like in the Deluge."

"It's better, it's better," Manuel said. "Let us have new civilizations. This old one's no good. As for me, I would rather see a war than a Deluge. At least, some of us will be left alive."

"The ire of God," González said. "It shall fall on the world for sure."

"Take cities like New York, for instance," Manuel said. "Dens of perdition and vice. Where people live on top of the houses and underneath the ground. They say there are whole neighborhoods living in tunnels."

"Like rats," González said. "What a barbarity."

"Ten or twelve million people all piled up together. It must be the biggest city in the world."

"No," Leytón said. "Chicago is the biggest."

"What about Mexico City?" said Manuel.

"New York is bigger."

"Mexico City is pretty big anyway," Manuel persisted. "Millions and millions of people."

"There is no doubt that there are too many people in the United States," Leytón said. "They're going to have to expand pretty soon and grab more territory."

Manuel scowled. "They'll probably try to expand to the south again, damn their souls."

The younger barber stopped dusting off George's neck. "Nah," he said. "There's lots of space left in the United States."

"Where?" Leytón demanded.

"You just have to go from Alice to Falfurrias. You can find more land than you would need to fill a whole state. And in the Midwest there's lots of land."

Leytón waited while George paid the barber. "Yes," he said, "but all that land is no good. I've been in the Nebraskas and the Oklahoomas myself. And in places there is nobody because in summer it is a hell and in winter it freezes every day."

"That is true," González said. "We are fortunate to live near the sea and have a gentle climate. That's because of the sea breezes."

"If we are to believe the newspapers and the salesmen, we have a wonderful climate," Manuel said indignantly. "But it's hot enough in this town. It was cooler twenty years ago, but now? Whew!"

"Maybe it's because of the pavements and all the new buildings," González suggested.

"Pavements nothing!" Manuel said. "It's the lack of air, that's what. Twenty years ago there were no automobiles to speak of, and there was a lot of air. Now all the air is stored in these gasoline stations so they can fill the tires of all these automobiles. We don't have enough air left to breathe cool."

Driving down the highway toward his uncle's farm, George Gómez smiled, remembering old Manuel's joke that day in the barber shop. Or had it really been a joke? Manuel was stupid enough to believe what he had said about the lack of air. They were all a bunch of dum-dums. And here was Leytón himself, a member of Elodia's "executive committee"! What a laugh!

5

He almost missed the turn-off from the highway to the road that led to his uncle's farm. It looked somehow different. Yes, it was still dirt but it had been graded. His uncle and other farmers along the river must have talked the County into doing the job. The usual way: votes and contributions to the right candidates. It still must be difficult to travel in wet weather, but it would no longer become a swamp after every good rain. It was dry weather now, however, and the fine alkali dust swirled around his rented car. A few yards beyond the gate to the farm the ground rose, where alluvial soil from thousands of floods had created a rich delta land. Now he could see the house. It was a new one or the old one had been renovated, he could not tell. But it had glass and screens on the windows, and it was painted white. As he drove up to the gate he could see his uncle sitting on the porch in a rocking chair.

Feliciano had been watching the distant cloud of dust approach until it became an automobile. He was pretty sure who his visitor was. He watched from his rocker as his nephew got down to open and shut the gate and suppressed a smile when Guálinto dusted off his shoes with his handkerchief before climbing back into the car and driving up to the house. Feliciano rose and they shook hands formally. Then he sat down again and motioned his nephew to a wicker arm chair on the porch. He surveyed Guálinto from foot to head. The shiny reddish-brown shoes, the brown suit. Brown tie and tiny brown hat pushed to the back of his head.

Finally he said, "It was about time you came back home. I'm sure your mother was glad to see you."

"I suppose she was. She cried and carried on as if I was back from the dead."

Feliciano looked at his nephew shrewdly. "That's the way women are."

"Mexican women," his nephew said.

"You're right. Gringo women are different."

His nephew fidgeted. "I'm sorry I have been away so long," he said. "It doesn't seem like three years. But I've been kept quite busy in Washington. And I'm sorry, but I'm not coming home to stay. The paper had it wrong. I'll be here for a short time and then I'll have to go away again."

"Where will you go this time? China? It seems like every time you come home for a visit you go farther and farther away from where you were born."

His nephew looked embarrassed. "I really don't know where my company will send me when I leave here," he said.

"Your company?"

"I'm a lawyer for a company that is building new plants in different parts of the United States, and perhaps Mexico," his nephew said. "There is a possibility that Fort Jones will be reduced in size once the war in Europe is over, so I am here looking at their land. I will also be making trips across the border for the same reasons." He shifted in his chair and crossed his legs. "When I finish here I will be assigned to another job."

Feliciano said, "You look uncomfortable in that suit. Why don't you take your coat off."

"No, thank you," his nephew said. "I feel all right." He reached under his coat and took out a pack of cigarets, lit one and offered Feliciano the pack.

"You offer me a cigaret?" Feliciano said sharply. "Have you forgotten that I am your uncle?"

With the flustered look of a child caught misbehaving, his nephew dropped his cigaret and ground it out with the toe of his shoe. "I'm sorry," he said.

"All you have told me," Feliciano said in a more conversational tone. "I don't believe a word of it."

His nephew pocketed the pack of cigarets and said nothing.

"When did you become a soldier?" Feliciano asked. "And why aren't you dressed like one?"

His nephew was startled. "What makes you think I'm a soldier?"

"Just a guess. You walk like one now. You talk like one. I can tell; I've seen plenty of them in my time."

His nephew's face hardened. "Yes, I know. Some of them over the sights of your rifle."

"You've known that for many years now."

"All right, I'll tell you the truth. I am in the Army. I'm a first lieutenant in counter-intelligence."

"What does that mean? You are a spy?"

"My job is border security. That's why I must wear civilian clothes and keep my work a secret."

"Whatever face you put on it, you're still a spy."

"There's a war in Europe," his nephew said, somewhat impatiently. "The United States will soon be in it. The truth is that we already are in it in all but in name."

"You don't expect another insurrection, do you?"

"No. But we have to watch for sabotage. And infiltration by German or Japanese agents."

"I hope you're smart enough not to mistake a slant-eyed Indian from southern Mexico for a Japanese agent. That has been done before, you know."

"I doubt there will be any foreign agents at this end of the border. If any spying or sabotage takes place it will be by some of our own people."

Feliciano smiled. "That political organization headed by Antonio Prieto's wife," he said. "Perhaps you should have them watched."

"They are being watched, you can be sure of that. Though I doubt they are dangerous. Prieto's wife might be. She's crazy enough."

"Are you serious?"

"Of course I am."

"The leader of his people," Feliciano said.

"What do you mean?"

"That was what you were going to be, have you forgotten? The Prietos will be disappointed when they hear you have changed your mind."

His nephew snorted disdainfully. "I had a meeting with them before I came out here. They're a bunch of clowns playing at politics. And they're trying to organize yokels who don't know anything but getting drunk and yelling and fighting."

"Then you see no future for us."

"I'm afraid not. Mexicans will always be Mexicans. A few of them, like some of those would-be politicos, could make something of themselves if they would just do like I did. Get out of this filthy Delta, as far away as they can, and get rid of their Mexican Greaser attitudes."

"Do like you did," Feliciano said.

"Oh, I know I didn't do it alone. I am grateful for your help. I couldn't have done it otherwise."

Feliciano had been looking out toward the river, where he could see Juan Rubio outside his house. "There's Juan out there," he said. "Perhaps if we send him to Minnesota or Alaska his skin will turn white and he can get rid of his Mexican Greaser attitudes."

His nephew shrugged impatiently.

"Why don't you go down and say hello to him?" Feliciano said. "He knows you're here, I'm sure."

His nephew did not turn around to look. "If he knows I'm here, why doesn't he come up and say hello to me?"

"You owe him thanks, you know that. He was the one who talked you into 'doing like you did.'"

"I know, I know. Please give him my regards, but I can't go all the way down there. I really must hurry back to town."

"It's early," Feliciano said. "You haven't told me about your wife."

"She stayed at Carmen's with her and Mama."

"Carmen has been good to her mother. Your mother would have been left alone, except for me, if Carmen and Aquiles had not asked her to come live with them. She helps. Takes care of the children. And they talk about all the things Carmen reads, as they always have."

"That is very good of Carmen and Aquiles."

"Of course I give something to your mother every month, as always. And take them vegetables and eggs and other things. Just as I did when we all lived in the old blue house. You know that José Alcaraz lives there now."

"I was told about it."

"That made it easier for you, didn't it?"

"In what way?"

"You didn't have to take your wife there to meet María. I remember how ashamed you were of that house, even when you were in high school."

His nephew did not answer.

"Does your wife know Spanish?" Feliciano asked.

"No. Just a few words. But Carmen is translating for Mama and her. I'm sure they're getting along all right."

"Is she learning Spanish?"

"No. There's no reason for her to. We won't be here that long."

"What about children. Do you plan to have any?"

"There's one on the way. And I suppose we'll have others. But if you mean whether they will learn Spanish, no. There's no reason for them to do so. They will grow up far away from here."

It was Feliciano's turn to be silent.

"You have a beautiful farm here," his nephew said.

"I have improved it and added more acreage. But I'm sixty-five, and I'm beginning to feel very tired. I'm thinking of making a will so there won't be any arguments when I die."

"I don't want any of the land," his nephew said. "I'm not a farmer and I won't be coming down here often. I have a good income besides."

"Do I have your word on that?"

"Yes."

"That simplifies matters. I want to leave half to your mother, and that half will pass on to Carmen after your mother dies. Maruca doesn't need anything from me. Like you she is well off and doesn't come down here. The other half will go to Juan, who has been like a son to me these past few years. With the understanding that he will continue to work both parts of the farm. Or buy Carmen's part if she so wishes."

"That sounds all right to me." His nephew looked at his watch. "I will have to leave now if I'm going to get to Carmen's for supper. By the way, Carmen says you're invited to. If you can come."

"I don't think I'll be able to. Give my regards to your wife."

"I'm sorry you cannot come."

"But don't look so relieved when you say it. A spy should learn to conceal his feelings."

His nephew got up and looked at his watch again. "I don't know what you mean," he said.

"Perhaps it's just that I know you too well," Feliciano said.

"You will keep my secret, even from Mama. Just as I have kept yours. It would ruin my career if it became known at this time."

"Have no fear about that. And you can turn me in if you want to, if it helps keep you in the good graces of your masters."

"I have no 'masters'. I am doing what I do in the service of my country."

"And your career, of course."

"What is wrong with that? Would you rather see me carrying a rifle in the infantry?"

"Does 'your country' include the Mexicans living in it?"

"I'd rather not go into that again. I must leave." He extended his hand. His uncle took it without getting up from his rocking chair.

"I'll tell you," his uncle said. "This is one of those times when I wish I believed in another life, in a life after death."

"It is?"

"Yes. Then I could look forward to seeing your father in purgatory or limbo or wherever it is that Mexican yokels go. We could sit down and have a good long talk about you."

George smiled. "I didn't know you had a sense of humor," he said.

"I don't," his uncle said.